Instructor's Manual to Accompany
Levin / Rubin / Stinson / Gardner, Jr.

Quantitative
Approaches
to Management

Eighth Edition

JOEL P. STINSON

School of Management
Syracuse University

McGraw-Hill, Inc.
New York St. Louis San Francisco Auckland Bogotá Caracas
Lisbon London Madrid Mexico Milan
Montreal New Delhi Paris San Juan
Singapore Sydney Tokyo Toronto

Instructor's Manual to Accompany
Levin/Rubin/Stinson/Gardner, Jr.:
QUANTITATIVE APPROACHES TO MANAGEMENT
Eighth Edition

0-07-037558-5

1 2 3 4 5 6 7 8 9 0 W H T W H T 9 0 9 8 7 6 5 4 3 2

NOTES TO INSTRUCTOR

The major changes in the eighth edition of Quantitative Approaches to Management are:

(1) The addition of a second diskette. Along with the QAM diskette which was provided with the previous seventh edition, another diskette which provides LOTUS templates may be used by your students to solve many of the end-of-chapter exercises.

(2) Case studies are included which incorporate use of the new program diskettes. Solutions to the case studies are included in this manual.

(3) New exercises have been added to most chapters, and except for about the last ten exercises in each chapter, all others have been grouped together in the order the material is presented in the book.

(4) New material is presented on the formulation of integer programming problems.

SUGGESTED SCHEDULES

		Number of meetings one-semester course	Number of meetings one-quarter course
1.	Introduction	1	1/2
2.	A Review of Probability Concepts	3	2
3.	Forecasting	2	1
4.	Decision Making Using Probabilities I	2	2
5.	Decision Making Using Probabilities II	3	2
6.	Inventory I	3	2
7.	Inventory II	3	2
8.	Linear Programming I: Solution Methods	1	1
9.	Linear Programming II: The Simplex Method	4	3
10.	Linear Programming III: Building LP Models and Interpreting Solutions	3	2
11.	Specially Structured Linear Programs	3	2
12.	Networks	3	2
13.	Extensions of Linear Programming	4	2
14.	Waiting Lines	2	2
15.	Simulation	3	2
16.	Markov Analysis	2	1
17.	MS/OR: Past, Present and Future	1	1/2
18.	Exams	2	1
		45	30

CONTENTS

INSTRUCTIONS FOR USING

THE QAM PROGRAMS

The QAM programs are designed to accompany the text
Quantitative Approaches to Management, 8th Edition, by
Levin, Rubin, Stinson, and Gardner. To use the QAM
package, you will need an IBM PC/XT/AT or compatible with a
minimum of 277K of available memory (290K recommended), at
least one double-sided disk drive (5-1/4 inch diskette),
and DOS version 2.1 or higher. A printer is also
recommended so that you can produce a hard copy of your
results.

STARTING THE QAM PROGRAMS

The disk enclosed with the text can be used as is, copied
to another disk formatted with the DOS system, or loaded
onto a hard disk if one is available. The QAM diskette
comes with three files: QAM.EXE, DEFAULT.TXT, and
MSHERC.COM. The QAM.EXE file contains the program routines
and is always required. DEFAULT.TXT is not required for
program execution, but contains the defaults for the data
drive and screen colors. The MSHERC.COM file is required
only if you want to display graphic output on a monochrome
screen with a Hercules graphics adapter.

To run the programs, simply enter QAM at the DOS prompt.
In a few moments the title page shown in Figure 1 will
appear on the screen.

The prompt asks you to enter the drive on which you wish to
store the data files for this session. The default will be
Drive A. The letters C and D can be used for data input
from hard disks. Subdirectory designations may also be
used.

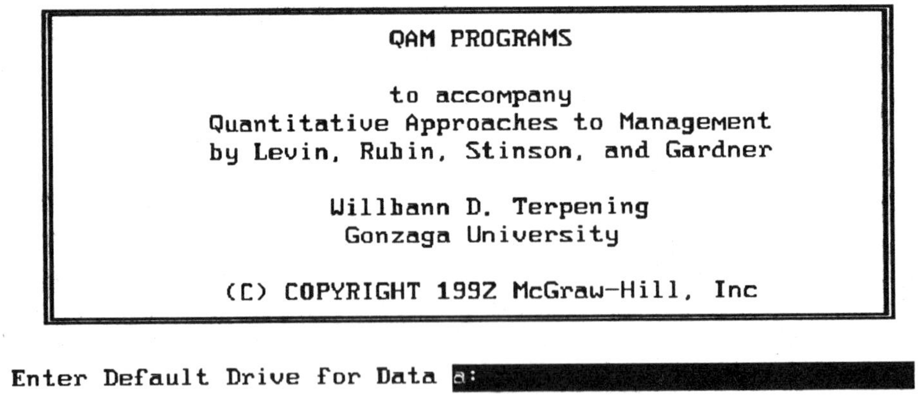

```
┌─────────────────────────────────────────────────┐
│                  QAM PROGRAMS                     │
│                                                   │
│                  to accompany                     │
│      Quantitative Approaches to Management        │
│        by Levin, Rubin, Stinson, and Gardner      │
│                                                   │
│               Willbann D. Terpening               │
│                 Gonzaga University                │
│                                                   │
│          (C) COPYRIGHT 1992 McGraw-Hill, Inc      │
└─────────────────────────────────────────────────┘
```

Enter Default Drive for Data `a:`

Figure 1: Opening screen of QAM programs

INITIAL PROGRAM MENU

After you have entered the default drive, the screen will
clear and the menu and data display box in Figure 2 will
appear.

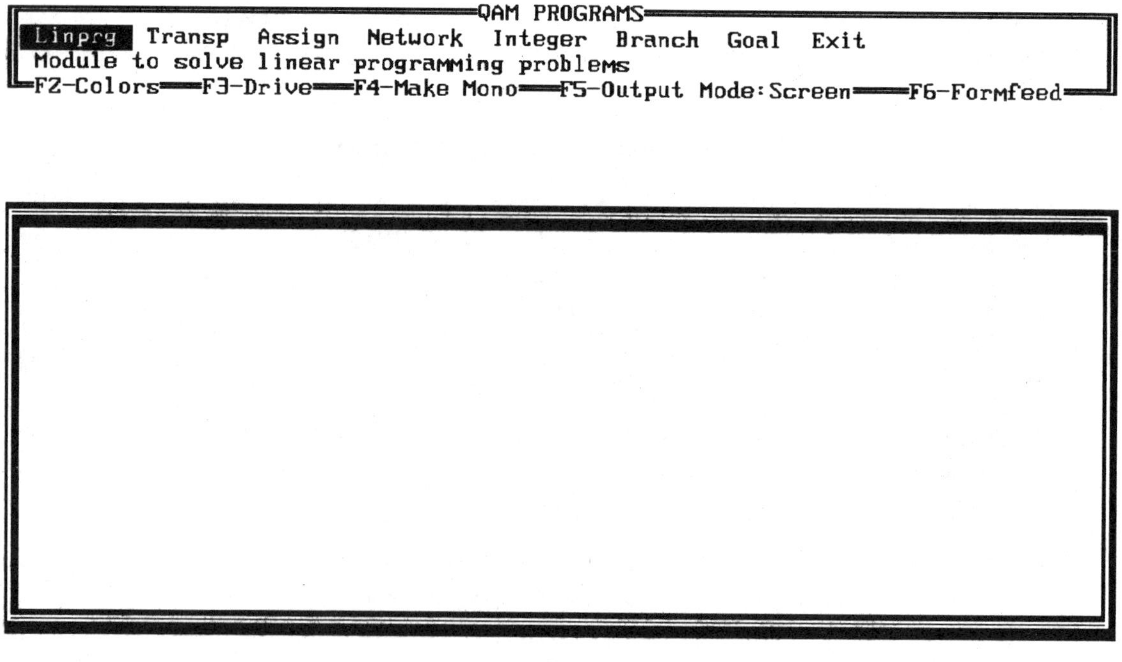

```
═══════════════════════════QAM PROGRAMS═══════════════════════════
│ Linprg  Transp  Assign  Network  Integer  Branch  Goal  Exit    │
│ Module to solve linear programming problems                     │
└─F2-Colors──F3-Drive──F4-Make Mono──F5-Output Mode:Screen──F6-Formfeed─┘
```

```
┌─────────────────────────────────────────────────┐
│ ┌─────────────────────────────────────────────┐ │
│ │                                             │ │
│ │                                             │ │
│ │                                             │ │
│ │                                             │ │
│ │                                             │ │
│ │                                             │ │
│ │                                             │ │
│ │                                             │ │
│ └─────────────────────────────────────────────┘ │
└─────────────────────────────────────────────────┘
```

Figure 2: Initial program menu

Initially the first menu entry will be highlighted. To
select an option from the menu either enter the first
letter of the option which is capitalized, use the arrow
keys to highlight the desired option and hit the enter key,
or if you have a mouse installed move the mouse cursor

above the item and press the left mouse button. As a short cut for long menus, the **home key** will go to the first option in the menu and the **end key** will go to the last option in the menu. A prompt describing the highlighted option appears below the menu items.

The function keys F2 through F6 can be used to perform certain tasks when the programs are in the menu mode. The **F2** key can be used to change the default foreground, background, and border colors. The **F3** key allows you to change the default disk drive for data input and output. The **F4** key forces the screen to monochrome mode. Some monitors, such as those used on laptop computers, may appear as color monitors to the QAM programs, but are actually monochrome monitors. The resulting screens will then be difficult to read. This option forces the use of monochrome output to make the display more readable. The **F5** key is used to direct program output to the appropriate device. Output can be directed to the computer screen (the default), to a printer, or to a disk file. The programs assume that printed output is to be sent to the current default disk drive. The **F6** key will send a formfeed to the printer if one is attached. The QAM programs do not automatically send a form feed to the printer after printing output to conserve paper. If you want to eject a page after printing press the **F6** key.

The following is a brief description of the program options and program limitations.

Linprg: This module solves linear programming problems with up to 20 constraints and 30 decision variables. Constraints can be less than or equal to (designated <), greater than or equal to (>), or equality (=). Either minimization or maximization problems can be solved. Output includes the optimal solution, shadow prices, RHS change vectors, and sensitivity analysis for the objective function coefficients and the right-hand-sides. Alternative optimal solutions can be computed if they exist. If the problem has two decision variables, you may also produce a graph of the solution space with the optimal solution indicated on the graph.

Transp: This module implements the standard stepping stone method to solve transportation problems with up to 30 origins and 30 destinations. The supplies and demands need not be balanced; the program will automatically add a dummy destination or origin, whichever is appropriate. The objective function can be either minimized or maximized.

Assign: This module solves the standard assignment problem with up to 30 rows and 30 columns. The rows and columns need not be equal; the program will add dummy rows or columns as appropriate. The objective function can be either minimized or maximized.

Network: This module solves the network problems described in the text. The choice of this option also leads to a submenu describing the available model options. In all cases, the program allows for up to 40 arcs and 60 nodes in the network.

Integer Programming: This module allows you to solve linear programming problems where the decision variables are required to be integer. The input to this module is identical to that for linear programming. As with linear programming, a graphical solution may be produced for two variable problems.

Branch: This module uses the branch and bound approach to solve assignment type problems as described in the text. The input to this module is identical to that for the assignment problem.

Goal: This module allows you to solve goal programming problems. The model can contain up to 20 constraints, 30 decision variables, and 10 priority levels. Constraints can be of four different types depending on the deviations allowed from the right-hand-side of the constraint: only negative deviations allowed (designated by an L), only positive deviations allowed (G), no deviations allowed (E), or both positive and negative deviations allowed (B).

COMMON OPTIONS

When a program has been selected, an options menu will appear on the screen. Although the programs differ in many respects, the menu options are common to all modules in QAM and are illustrated in Figure 3.

The **Data** option is used to enter a new problem from the keyboard or to edit the existing data. To input a problem from a file use the **File** option. The **File** option allows you to manipulate disk files. Using this option you may input data from a file, save data to a file, delete a file, view the contents of a file, or change the name of a disk file. The **Solve** option allows you to solve the current problem using the appropriate solution method. The **View** option allows you to direct all or part of the solution output to the current output device (screen, printer, or a file). You may also display or print out the current problem data using this option. The **Title** option allows you to enter or modify a title which appears at the top of all problem output. The last option is always the **Return** option which will return you to the main program menu. This can also be accomplished by pressing the **Esc** key.

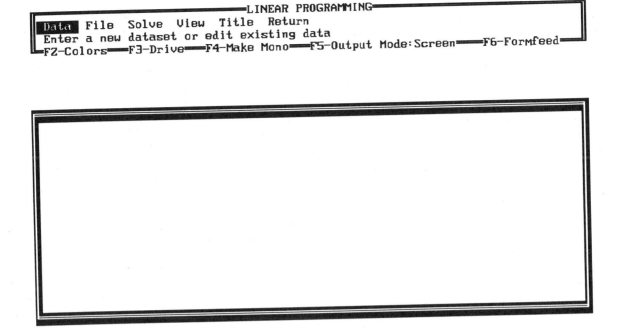

Figure 3: Options available for all programs

ENTERING AND EDITING DATA

Data entry and editing in the QAM program utilizes a
spreadsheet format. Figure 4 illustrates the data entry
screen for the linear programming module.

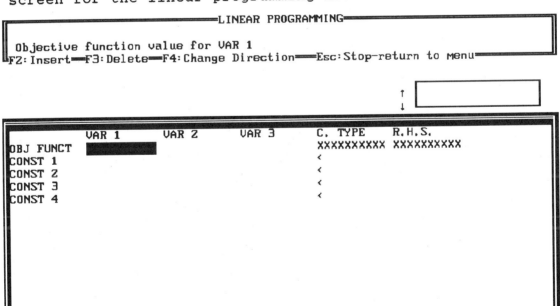

═LINEAR PROGRAMMING═
 Objective function value for VAR 1
F2:Insert═══F3:Delete═══F4:Change Direction═══Esc:Stop-return to menu═

	VAR 1	VAR 2	VAR 3	C. TYPE	R.H.S.
OBJ FUNCT				XXXXXXXXX	XXXXXXXXX
CONST 1				<	
CONST 2				<	
CONST 3				<	
CONST 4				<	

Figure 4: Data entry screen

The top row and the first column always contain text information which identifies that row or column. Many of these items can be changed to provide descriptive information specific to the current problem. The current cell of the worksheet is highlighted. The cursor can be moved using the arrow keys. For large problems the page up and page down keys can be used. Cells for which no entry is allowed are marked with a string of X's. Up to 10 characters may be entered in a cell. The program will automatically check to make sure that the entry is the appropriate type. For example, if a cell requires a numerical entry, trying to enter text information will result in the display of an appropriate message.

Certain special keys are available for your use during data entry and editing. The F2 function key can be used to insert a new row or a new column. To utilize this option the cursor must be located in the text row or the text column, i.e., the first row for column insertion or the first column for row insertion. The F3 key is used to delete a row or a column. As with insertion, the cursor must be located in the text row or the text column. The F4 key can be used to change the direction arrows which determine the direction of movement when the enter key is pressed. The direction is indicated by the two arrows beside the data entry box. The escape key (Esc) is used to stop data entry and return to the options menu.

USING DISK FILES

The QAM programs allow you to save data to a disk file and then recall that data at a later time. You may also want to save program output to a disk file to use later with a word processor. Names for disk files must follow the DOS naming conventions. Extensions may be used, but are not required. Whenever you choose one of the File options, the program will list all of the files on the disk currently in the default drive. You may then enter the name of the file, move the cursor to the file name with the arrow keys and press enter, or select the file by double clicking with the left mouse button. If you are saving data and you choose the name of an existing file, you will be warned that the file exists and asked if you want to replace that file. If you elect to replace the file, the information saved previously to that file will be lost. Therefore, do not use the name of an existing file unless you want to replace the contents of that file with the current information.

THE ESCAPE KEY

The escape key (Esc) serves an important function in the
QAM programs. As described earlier, the escape key is used
to indicate the end of data entry. However, as its name
implies, it can also be used to escape from what you are
currently doing. There likely will be times when you will
want to stop the execution of a program. This can occur,
for example, if you realize that you have entered the wrong
option, or if the program has been executing for some time
without results and you suspect that there may be a problem
with the data. At any time that a program is asking you to
input information, or when the program is executing, you
can halt execution by hitting the escape key. This will
stop what the program is doing and return you to the
program menu. The escape key can also be used to return to
a previous menu from a submenu.

USING A MOUSE

A mouse can be used for certain operations in the QAM
program. The mouse can be used to select menu options,
function key options, and when choosing from lists of
options. In most cases, a single click of the left mouse
button selects an option. There are three exceptions to
this rule. The exceptions are when selecting a file name
under the **File** option, selecting screen colors, and
selecting the beginning and ending nodes for the Shortest
Route Module. In these cases a single click of the left
mouse button highlights the selected item. To choose an
item rapidly double click the left button.

A NOTE ON TEACHING

WITH SPREADSHEETS

The eighth edition contains a total of 29 new spreadsheet models for use with Lotus 1-2-3 and compatible software. The spreadsheets can be used at two levels. Beginners can use the models simply as computational tools. Students with more background in spreadsheets can study the cell formulas to gain insight into the model-building process.

Given computer projection equipment, the spreadsheets can be used in a variety of ways in the classroom. We recommend the following approach: First, do a brief chalkboard review of the key formulas for a model. Don't do any actual computation on the chalkboard. Instead, follow up immediately with a demonstration of these formulas in action in a spreadsheet. Arrange the room so the students can see the chalkboard and the projection screen at the same time. Find the key formulas in the spreadsheets and point out the correspondence between them and the chalkboard formulas. The computer demonstration should always include tests of the sensitivity of the spreadsheet models to alternative input data. Ask the class to predict what will happen if you were to change inputs, then make the changes and review the results. For example, in simple exponential smoothing, you can ask the class to predict the effects of increasing the smoothing weight. The graph attached to this spreadsheet provides a dramatic illustration of the effects.

Since it is usually impossible to have students take tests using a computer, you need to make some adjustments in homework assignments. We recommend that students be required to turn in a mix of traditional, hand-computed solutions and computer solutions. Have them do at least one hand-computed solution for a given type of problem, followed by computer work to study the behavior of the model.

Early in the course, you can expect two problems with spreadsheet novices. First, novices sometimes become confused when entering numbers in cells that display dollar signs or percentages. Even though a cell displays a dollar sign, most spreadsheet programs will not accept a dollar sign in data entry. You must enter the number without a dollar sign. When a cell displays a percent sign, you must enter the number as a fraction. For example, 20% is entered as .2.

Second, novices may also be confused by cells that display a series of asterisks (******). The asterisks indicate that the column width is too small to display the number in that cell. To fix this problem, the first step is to press the slash key (/). On the menu displayed at the top of the screen, select Worksheet Column Set-Width. At this point, the prompt at the top of the screen will say: "Enter column width (1..240):" followed by the current width of the column in characters. Type in a larger number than the one displayed and press the Enter key. This is a trial-and-error process so you may have to repeat the operation until the asterisks disappear.

CHAPTER 1

INTRODUCTION

1-1   Possibly the more traditional tools of management were adequate. There has been great growth both in size of industrial firms and in intensity of competition. Sometimes management may fear the new, the untried, the little understood. There has been considerable refinement of techniques since World War II. In addition, the introduction of the high speed digital computer has made many OR models an attractive approach to solving real world problems. Such problems were too time consuming to solve by hand in the pre-computer era.

1-2   The World War II applications were, of course, focused on military and related logistics problems. Here is seen the emergence of the team effort, probably as much due to the coordination requirements among the services and among the allied nations as to the problems themselves. The scope of the allied operation apparently was far beyond any military operation to that point in cost, size, and complexity. This focused substantial thought on methods of finding solutions to very complex problems in situations which demanded close coordination. It seems clear that the entrance into the military services of many civilian scientists had a substantial effect on the introduction of the operations research point of view to the solution of military problems.

1-3   One of the major characteristics of pre-World War II operations research was that it was carried on at a very low level of activity. Still another problem during that period was the difficulty of publishing research findings and the problems of operations researchers communicating

1

with each other and being made aware of each other's work. The work that was done in this period was on a much simpler level mathematically than later work, probably because the problem environment was "ripe" for this kind of approach and somewhat less sophistication was required to generate success. In the main, work was done individually, not by team effort.

1-4   Forecasting and planning cash flows

Relevant Variables	Input data required	Output form
Accounts payable	Current assets,	Forecasted by
Accounts receivable	current liabilities	period of cash
Liquidity of assets	and past records	flows and
Line of credit		short term
		cash needs

Determining to which customers to extend credit

Relevant Variables	Input data required	Output form
Line of credit	Past history of	Projected line
Current debt	debts and payments	of cash rec-
		ommendations

Collection systems for delinquent accounts

Relevant Variables	Input data required	Output form
Current assets	Past history of	Recommended
Account receivable	debts and payments	alternative
Age of receivables		

Allocation of investment capital

Relevant Variables	Input data required	Output form
Return on Investment	Market forecasts,	Rank ordering
Cost of capital	competition, long	of preferred
Future cash flow	range objective	investments
Risk		

Managing an investment portfolio

Relevant Variables	Input data required	Output form
Current ROI	Current prices of	Buy/Sell
Cost of capital	stocks and stock	recommendation
Cash flows	performance, rate	
Risk	of return, taxes	

2

Improving the effectiveness of cost accounting

Relevant Variables	Input data required	Output form
Standard wages and prices	Historical records of costs, accuracy and variability of prior cost projections	Recommendations to model for improved accuracy
Overhead rates		

Improving the accuracy of auditing

Relevant Variables	Input data required	Output form
Accounting standards	Accounting data	Assessment of accuracy and financial performance
Tax standards		
Statistical and sampling procedures		

Assigning auditing teams effectively

Relevant Variables	Input data required	Output form
Experience and education of staff	Size and complexity of scheduled workload	Recommendation for auditing teams

1-5 Determining the last product mix, given market demands

Relevant Variables	Input data required	Output form
Price and profit	Production capacity	Required output of the products
	Labor availability	
	Distribution systems	
	Competition	

Deciding whether a company should acquire marketing rights to a new product

Relevant Variables	Input data required	Output form
Profitability	Forecasts of demand	Recommendations and projected profitability
Risk	Competition	
Return on investment	Acquisition cost	
Future cash flows	Production capacity	

Allocation advertising among different media

Relevant Variables	Input data required	Output form
Sales performance	Consumer behavior	Recommended assignments and sales projections
Market share	Advertising exposure	

Finding the best time to introduce a new product

Relevant Variables	Input data required	Output form
Profitability	Market surveys	Projected
Return on investment	Forecasts	demand and
Future cash flows	Production capacity	returns as a
Risk		function of
		time

Assigning salespersons to territories

Relevant Variables	Input data required	Output form
Sales and revenues	Forecasts	Recommended
Market share	Demographic data	assignments
Service to customer		and sales
		projections

Locating warehouses more effectively

Relevant Variables	Input data required	Output form
Distribution costs	Cost of land and	Recommendations
Timely delivery	construction	for an inte-
Inventory costs	Rental costs	grated, low
	Overhead costs	cost distribu-
	Transportation costs	tion system

Evaluating the market strength of a competitor's marketing strategy

Relevant Variables	Input data required	Output form
Market shares	Advertising and dis-	Projections of
Prices and profits	tribution strategy	revenues and
	Forecasts	market shares
	Competition	

Comparing the marketing attractions of various packaging alternatives

Relevant Variables	Input data required	Output form
Market shares	Consumer behavior	Recommendations
Revenues	Market surveys	based on
Profits	Competition	market share
		and revenue
		performance

Planning salesperson's travel to minimize the total miles
traveled

Relevant Variables	Input data required	Output form
Customer servica- bility	Demand forecasts Transportation costs	Recommended itinerary
Travel costs	Highway distances, speed limits, etc.	for travel

1-6 The management of information system attempts to create a
merger of the human and the computer so that the relative
strengths of each are emphasized. The flexibility,
insight, and creativity of the human should be harmonized
with the speed, accuracy, and consistency of the computer.

1-7 The five major components are the (1) input devices, (2)
output devices, (3) control unit, (4) storage and (5)
arithmetic unit. The last three components taken together
are known as the central processing unit.

1-8 It is true that most managers will never have to work out
the solutions to quantitative models by hand. However, it
is vitally important for the manager to recognize the
nature of the information he uses in formulating decisions.
Hence, he must have a familiarity with the models which are
providing the information.

1-9 The what-if system has all the features of the report
generator plus something additional--the ability to respond
to what-if queries. The decision support system, in turn,
has all the features of both the other two plus its ability
to develop recommendations and output them to the decision
maker. In many cases, the people who interact with
computers place greater demands upon it after they have
become more familiar with its operation. They may start by
using only the report generator feature. Later, they may
begin to seek further benefits thus expanding the
computer's role. In many information system applications,
the role of the computer has evolved in direct response to
the growth of experience of those decision makers who
interact with it.

1-10 The managerial generalist
   A. Identifies when a problem exists.
   B. Determines the variables involved.
   C. Helps to determine which solution procedure is most
       effective based on those constraints which exist in the
       organization.
   D. Selects the preferred solution procedure to be used.
   E. Facilitates managerial acceptance of the solution.

1-11 A management information system which supports quantitative applications should make the best use of both the human and electronic elements. It should take fullest advantage of the strengths of each. The computer is fast and can store almost unlimited data. The human, on the other hand, is more flexible and possesses a broader knowledge of qualitative factors which might influence decisions.

1-12 Applications of expert systems
   A. Quality and process control
   B. Purchasing
   C. Shop floor control
   D. Transportation scheduling
   E. Vendor selection
   F. Manufacturing lot sizing
   G. Expediting
   H. Assignment of inspection activity
   I. Material selection

CHAPTER 2

A REVIEW OF PROBABILITY CONCEPTS

2-1 The total area of the Venn diagram is 1.0, so we scale 25% of the total area for A and 40% for B ensuring that the two overlap for 10% of the area.

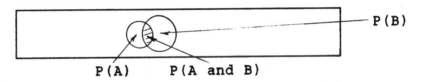

P(A)   P(A and B)

The shaded area is P(a or B), which appears to be slightly over half of the total area. From equation (2-3):

P(A or B) = P(A) + P(B) - P(A and B)
          = .25 - .40 - .10
          = .55 or 55% of the total area.

2-2 The arrival of jobs is assumed to be statistically independent.

(a) We use equation (2-4)

P(WWW) = P(W) x P(W) x P(W) = $(.2)^3$ = .008

(b) The following possibilities exist for getting two matching jobs from the next three arrivals:

P(MMW)
P(MWM)
P(WMM)

7

For any of the three the probability is:

$$(.8)(.8)(.2) = .128$$

The total of all three is:

$$.128 + .128 + .128 = .384$$

2-3   We wish to know the probability of 3 or more days of rain during the four days. From Appendix 2 at n=4, r=3, and p=.30:

Prob (3 or more days of rain out of 4) = .0837

2-4   Since we have assumed in the problem that the events male and redhead are statistically independent, we may use equation (2-4) to determine the probability that a random member of the population is both male and redheaded.

$$P(\text{male and redhead}) = P(\text{male}) \times P(\text{redhead})$$
$$= (.46)(.08) = .0368$$

The expected number of persons, N, which must be sampled in order to find 1000 redhead males is:

$$.0368N = 1000$$
$$N = 27,174 \text{ persons}$$

2-5   Based upon past experience we assess the probabilities of failure for the three parts as:

$$P(A) = \frac{18}{812 + 18} = .0217$$

$$P(B) = \frac{212}{618 + 212} = .2554$$

$$P(C) = \frac{53}{777 + 53} = .0639$$

We use equation (2-4) to obtain the probability that all three will be rejects.

$$P(ABC) = P(A) \times P(B) \times P(C)$$
$$= (.0217)(.2554)(.0639)$$
$$= .0003541$$

8

2-6   We first find that the probability that the first vial is
      type A.

          P(A) = 1/4

      Now, given that the first vial is a type A vial, the
      conditional probability that the second vial is a type B
      is:

          P(B|A) = 1/3

      From equation (2-7) we find the probability that B follows
      A:

          P(BA) = P(B|A) x P(A)
                = (1/3)(1/4) = 1/12

      Similarly, P(C|BA) = 1/2

      And,   P(CBA) = P(C|BA) x P(BA)
                         = (1/2)(1/12) = 1/24

      If the first three vials are A, B, and C, then the fourth
      one must be vial D with certainty. Therefore, the
      probability of obtaining the exact order A, B, C, and D is
      1/24.

2-7   If we denote A as the event--Dow Jones increases--and B the
      event--the stock goes up, we have:

          P(B|A) = .85
          P(A) = .70

      Since event B is dependent upon A, we use equation (2-7) to
      obtain P(BA), which is the probability that both will
      increase:

          P(BA) = P(B|A) x P(A)
                = (.85)(.70) = .595

2-8   Let us denote the event as:

          $\underline{I}$ = interest rates increase
          $\overline{I}$ = interest rates do not increase
          H = home sales increase

      From the data given, we have:

          P($\underline{I}$H) = .20
          P($\overline{I}$H) = .30
          P(I) = .40 and P($\overline{I}$) = .60

9

Home sales are dependent upon interest rates, so equation (2-7) is appropriate. We are looking for $P(H|\bar{I})$.

$$P(H|\bar{I}) = P(H\bar{I})/P(\bar{I})$$
$$= .3/.60 = .50$$

2-9 We use the notation:

$\underline{L}$ = child from low income family
$\bar{L}$ = child not from low income family
C = college graduate

The data given are:

$P(L) = .15$ and $P(\bar{L}) = .85$
$P(C|\underline{L}) = .20$
$P(C|\bar{L}) = .40$

From equation (2-7) we first find $P(CL)$ and $P(C\bar{L})$:

$P(C\underline{L}) = P(C|\underline{L}) \times P(\underline{L}) = (.20)(.15) = .03$
$P(C\bar{L}) = P(C|\bar{L}) \times P(\bar{L}) = (.40)(.85) = .34$

Now, we determine the marginal probability, $P(C)$, by summing joint probabilities as follows:

$$P(C) = P(CL) + P(C\bar{L}) = .03 + .34 = .37$$

Finally, we use equation (2-7) to find $P(L|C)$:

$$P(L|C) = \frac{P(LC)}{P(C)} = \frac{.03}{.37} = .081$$

2-10 Sales of machine B are considered by Lane to be dependent on sales of machine A. This is evident by the fact that the equation for joint probability under independence is not satisfied by Lane's estimates:

$P(AB) \ne P(A) \times P(B)$
$.15 \ne (.20)(.30)$

Therefore, we find the conditional probability of selling B, given that we have sold machine A.

$$P(B|A) = P(AB)/P(A) = .15/.20 = .75 \text{ or } 75\%$$

2-11	Existing Conditions	Job Enrichment Conditions	Total
Improved rating	$\frac{30}{200} = .150$	$\frac{40}{200} = .20$	
Same rating	$\frac{60}{200} = .300$	$\frac{55}{200} = .275$	
Lowered rating	$\frac{10}{200} = .050$	$\frac{5}{200} = .025$	
	.500	.500	= 1.00

We want to test for independence: i.e., does:

P(improved rating|job enrichment) = P(improved rating)?
and, P(lowered rating|job enrichment) = P(lowered rating)?

P(improved rating) = .150 + .200 = .350
P(improved rating|job enrichment) = .200 ÷ .500 = .400

Since, .40 ≠ .35, independence does not exist.
.400 ÷ .350 is 1 1/7 times greater with job enrichment.

P(lowered rating) = .050 + .025 = .075

P(lowered rating|job enrichment) = .025 ÷ .500 = .050

Since, .050 ≠ .075, independence does not exist.
.075 ÷ .050 is 1 1/2 times greater without job enrichment.

Since the results of the test indicate a more significant effect on reducing the incidence of lowered ratings than they do in increasing the incidence of improved ratings, the test might suggest to management that job enrichment enhances morale to a more significant degree than it does performance.

2-12 We let: P = profitable well
              B = breakeven well
              D = dry well
              C = closed structure
              O = open structure
              N = no structure

The data given are:

$$P(P) = .40$$
$$P(B) = .40$$
$$P(D) = .20$$
$$P(C \mid P) = .60$$
$$P(O \mid P) = .30$$
$$P(N \mid P) = .10$$
$$P(C \mid B) = .30$$
$$P(O \mid B) = .20$$
$$P(N \mid B) = .50$$
$$P(C \mid D) = .10$$
$$P(O \mid D) = .40$$
$$P(N \mid D) = .50$$

Since our tests have shown a closed structure:

Elementary event	Probability of Elementary event	$P(C \mid \text{elementary event})$	$P(C, \text{event})$
Profitable	.40	.60	.24
Breakeven	.40	.30	.12
Dry	.20	.10	.02
			$P(C) = .38$

Using equation (2-6), our revised probabilities are:

$$P(P \mid C) = \frac{P(P, C)}{P(C)} = \frac{.24}{.38} = .632$$

$$P(B \mid C) = \frac{P(B, C)}{P(C)} = \frac{.12}{.38} = .316$$

$$P(D \mid C) = \frac{P(D, C)}{P(C)} = \frac{.02}{.38} = .053$$

2-13 First we find the probability that the salesman sells 4
refrigerators to 10 customers given that he is a superior,
average, or inferior salesman. We refer to Appendix Table
2 with n = 10, r = 4, and r = 5.

Event	P	Prob (4 or more)	Prob (5 or more)	Prob P(exactly 4)
Superior	.40	.6177	.3669	.2508
Average	.30	.3504	.1503	.2001
Inferior	.20	.1209	.0328	.0881

Now we compute joint probabilities:

P(sell 4 and superior) = (.2508)(.20) = .05016
P(sell 4 and average) = (.2001)(.70) = .14007
P(sell 4 and inferior) = (.0881)(.10) = .00881
                              P(sell 4) = .19904

We now compute our updated probabilities:

$$P(\text{superior}|\text{sell 4}) = \frac{.05016}{.19904} = .2520$$

$$P(\text{average}|\text{sell 4}) = \frac{.14007}{.19904} = .7037$$

$$P(\text{inferior}|\text{sell 4}) = \frac{.00881}{.19904} = .0443$$

There is less than a 5% probability the salesman is inferior, and he should therefore be retained.

2-14   Assuming a binomial distribution, we find from Appendix 2 (at n=5, p=.08, and r=2), the probability that 2 or more do not repay their loans:

1 - P(2 or more not repay) = P(4 or more repay)
    P(2 or more not repay) = .0544
        P(4 or more repay) = 1 - .0544 = .9456

Alternately using equation (3-2):

$$P(\text{4 out of 5 repay}) = \frac{5!}{4!\,(5-4)!}\,(.92)^4(.08)^{5-4} = .28656$$

$$P(\text{5 out of 5 repay}) = \frac{5!}{5!\,(5-5)!}\,(.92)^5(.08)^{5-5} = .65908$$

P(4 or 5 repay) = .28656 + .65908 = .94564

2-15   We use the binomial formulas--equations (2-9). First we compute 8! = 40320.

Event	Calculations		Probability
6 out of 8	$\dfrac{40320}{(6\times5\times4\times3\times2\times1)(2\times1)}$	$(.7)^6(.3)^2$	.296475
7 out of 8	$\dfrac{40320}{(7\times6\times5\times4\times3\times2\times1)(1)}$	$(.7)^7(.3)$	.197650

(Continued)

13

8 out of 8	$\dfrac{40320}{(40320)(1)}$	$(.7)^8(.3)^0$	.057648

where $(3)^0 = 1$ $\Sigma = .551773$

The probability of 6 or more successes out of 8 trials is .551773.

In order to use the binomial tables which go up to $p = .50$, we look up the probability $q = .30$ for $n = 8$ and $r = 3$. This is because:

Prob(6 or more successes out of 8 trials) is equal to 1 - Prob(3 or more failures out of 8 trials)

From Appendix Table 2 at $p = .30$, $r = 3$, and $n = 8$: P(3 or more failures out of 8 trials) = .4482

So, Prob(6 or more successes) = 1 - .4482 = .5518 which checks with our previous result.

2-16   From Appendix Table 2, we find at $n = 8$ and $P = .3$:

Event	Prob.
0 or more failures	1.0000
1 or more failures	.9424
2 or more failures	.7447
3 or more failures	.4482
4 or more failures	.1941
5 or more failures	.0580
6 or more failures	.0113
7 or more failures	.0013
8 or more failures	.0001

Now, we determine the probability of failure for the discrete events.

Event	Probability	Event x Prob
0 failures	1.0000 - .9424 = .0576	0.0000
1 failures	.9424 - .7447 = .1977	0.1977
2 failures	.7447 - .4482 = .2965	0.5930
3 failures	.4482 - .1941 = .2541	0.7623
4 failures	.1941 - .0580 = .1361	0.5444
5 failures	.0580 - .0113 = .0467	0.2335
6 failures	.0113 - .0013 = .0100	0.0600
7 failures	.0013 - .0001 = .0012	0.0084
8 failures	.0001 - .0000 = .0001	0.0008
	Expected value =	2.4001

The expected number of successes is 8 - 2.4 = 5.6
Alternatively, $\mu = np = 8(.7) = 5.6$

2-17 Using equation 2-9 with n = 4, r = 4, and p = .4:

Probability of 4 successes in 4 trials:

$$= \frac{4!}{4!(4-4)!} \; (.4)^4 (.6)^{4-4}$$

$$= \frac{24}{(24)(1)} \; (.0256)(1) = .0256$$

In order for Philadelphia to win in exactly seven games, the first six games must be split with 3 wins going to each team and Philadelphia must then win the seventh game.

$$\text{Prob of 3 successes in 6 trials} = \frac{6!}{3!(6-3)!} \; (6)^3 (.4)^{6-3}$$

$$= .27648$$

Prob (3 successes in 6 trails and Philadelphia wins 7th):

$$= (.27648)(.60) = .165888$$

2-18 From the binomial tables, Appendix 2 at n = 9 and p = .27; and n = 10 and p = .27:

P(5 or more out of 9) = .0622
P(5 or more out of 10) = .1037

2-19 From Appendix 2 at n = 15 and p = .5, we find:

P(12 or more out of 15) = .0176
P(13 or more out of 15) = .0037
P(12 successes in 15) = .0176 - .0037 = .0139

2-20 P(late) = .07. From Appendix 2 at n = 13, p = .07, and r = 5:

P(5 or more out of 13) = .0013 or well under 1%

2-21 We assume the arrivals are distributed Poisson with:

λ = 24 arrivals/hr or 4 arrivals/10 minutes

and e^{-4} = .01832 from Appendix Table 4.

Event No. arrivals/10 minutes	Calculation Equation (3-3)	Probability (Event)
0	$\dfrac{(4)^0\,(.01832)}{0!}$	.01832
1	$\dfrac{(4)^1\,(.01832)}{1!}$	.07328
2	$\dfrac{(4)^2\,(.01832)}{2!}$	.14656
3	$\dfrac{(4)^3\,(.01832)}{3!}$	.19541
4	$\dfrac{(4)^4\,(.01832)}{4!}$	.19541

$$\text{Prob (4 or less)} = .62900$$

The probability of more than 4 arrivals is $1 - .6290 = .3710$

2-22 We use equation (2-9) where $e^{-6} = .00248$

$$P(7 \text{ arrivals}) = \frac{(6)^7\,(.00248)}{7!} = \frac{(279936)\,(.00248)}{5040}$$

$$= .1377462$$

$$P(8 \text{ arrivals}) = \frac{(6)^8\,(.00248)}{8!} = \frac{(1679616)\,(.00248)}{40320}$$

$$= .1033097$$

$$P(9 \text{ arrivals}) = \frac{(6)^9\,(.00248)}{9!} = \frac{(10077696)\,(.00248)}{362880}$$

$$= .0688731$$

$$P(7, 8, \text{ or } 9 \text{ arrivals}) = .1377642 + .1033097 + .0688731$$
$$= .309929$$

2-23 Using equation 2-10, we find $e^{-7} = .00091$

$$P(0) = \frac{(7)^0 (.00091)}{0!} = .0009$$

$$P(1) = \frac{(7)^1 (.00091)}{1!} = .0064$$

$$P(2) = \frac{(7)^2 (.00091)}{2!} = .0223$$

$$P(3) = \frac{(7)^3 (.00091)}{3!} = .0521$$

$$P(4) = \frac{(7)^4 (.00091)}{4!} = .0912$$

$$P(\text{less than } 5) = \overline{.1729}$$

7,000 chips per batch of dough will not enable her to claim 90% of the cookies contain 5 or more chocolate chips.

2-24   Using equation 2-10, where $e^{-10} = .00005$

P(0) = .0001	P(6) = .0694
P(1) = .0005	P(7) = .0992
P(2) = .0025	P(8) = .1240
P(3) = .0083	P(9) = .1378
P(4) = .0208	P(10) = .1378
P(5) = .0417	

P(read 2 chapters) = .0001 + .0005 + .0025 + .0083 + .0208
            + .0417 + .0694 + .0992 = .2425
    (less than 8 cars)

P(read 1 chapter) = .1240 + .1378 + .1378 = .3996
    (8, 9, or 10 cars)

Expected chapters per hour = (2)(.2425) + (1)(.3996)
                = .8846 chapters per hour

In an 8 hour shift he expects to read (.8846)(8) = 7.1 chapters.

2-25   We use equation (2-10):

$$\mu = 1/2 \text{ and } e^{-\mu t} = e^{(-\frac{1}{2})(4)} = e^{-2}$$

From Appendix Table 4, $e^{-2} = .13534$

$$P(T \le 4 \text{ hours}) = 1 - e^{-\mu t} = 1 - .13534 = .86466 \text{ or } 86.5\%$$

2-26 We are given:

$$P(T \leq 2 \text{ hours}) = .40$$
$$P(T \leq 4 \text{ hours}) = .60$$
$$P(T \leq 8 \text{ hours}) = .85$$

Using equation (2-10), we have:

$$P(T \leq 2 \text{ hours}) = .40 = 1 - e^{-2\mu} \quad \text{so:} \quad e^{-2\mu} = .60$$
$$P(T \leq 4 \text{ hours}) = .60 = 1 - e^{-4\mu} \quad \text{so:} \quad e^{-4\mu} = .40$$
$$P(T \leq 8 \text{ hours}) = .85 = 1 - e^{-8\mu} \quad \text{so:} \quad e^{-8\mu} = .15$$

From Appendix Table 4, we find the values of $t\mu$ to be:

Case	t	$e^{-t\mu}$	$t\mu$
1	2	.60	.5
2	4	.40	.9
3	8	.15	1.9

We now compute the $1/\mu$, the mean time in hours to be:

Case 1 $1/\mu = 2/.5 = 4$ hours

Case 2 $1/\mu = 4/.9 = 4.44$ hours

Case 3 $1/\mu = 8/1.9 = 4.21$ hours

Our estimate of the mean time is therefore about 4.2 hours, the average of the three observations.

2-27 Using equation 2-11 at $\mu = 4$ per hour and $t = .25$ hours:

$$P(T \leq .25) = 1 - e^{-(4)(.25)} = 1 - e^{-1} = 1 - .36788$$
$$= .63212 \text{ or } 63\%$$

At $\mu = 6$ per hour and $t = .25$ hours:

$$P(T \leq .25) = 1 - e^{-(6)(.25)} = 1 - e^{-1.5} = 1 - .22313$$
$$= .77687 \text{ or } 78\%$$

2-28 The total number of observations is:

$$27 + 32 + 43 + 55 + 52 + 42 + 29 + 16 = 296$$

We obtain probabilities for each level of daily sales by dividing each number of observations by the total. We use equation (2-8) to compute expected value.

Daily Sales	Probability	Daily Sales x Prob.
43	.0912	3.9216
44	.1081	4.7564
45	.1453	6.5385
46	.1858	8.5468
47	.1757	8.2579
48	.1419	6.8112
49	.0980	4.8020
50	.0541	2.7050
		Expected value = 46.3394

2-29 The mean, μ, is computed using equation (2-12):

$$\mu = (87 + 63 + 74 + 92 + 94 + 78 + 73 + 88 + 83 + 77) \div 10$$
$$= 80.9$$

Observation x_i	Mean μ	Deviation $x_i - \mu$	Deviation² $(x_i - \mu)^2$	Observation² x_i^2
87	80.9	6.1	37.31	7569
63	80.9	-17.9	320.41	3969
74	80.9	-6.9	47.61	5476
92	80.9	11.1	123.21	8464
94	80.9	13.1	171.61	8836
78	80.9	-2.9	8.41	6084
73	80.9	-7.9	62.41	5329
88	80.9	7.1	50.41	7744
83	80.9	2.1	4.41	6889
77	80.9	-3.9	15.21	5929
809			840.90	66289

From equation (2-13):

$$\sigma = \sqrt{\frac{\Sigma x_i - \mu^2}{N}} = \sqrt{\frac{840.90}{10}} = 9.17$$

From equation (2-14):

$$\sigma = \sqrt{\frac{\Sigma x_i - \mu^2}{N}} = \sqrt{\frac{66289}{10} - (80.9)^2} = 9.17$$

2-30 Since the velocity added is assumed to be normally distributed, we compute the mean and standard deviation with the equations:

$$\mu = \frac{\Sigma x_i}{N}$$

$$\sigma = \sqrt{\frac{\Sigma (x_1 - \mu)^2}{N}} \qquad \text{or} \qquad = \sqrt{\frac{\Sigma x_1{}^2}{N} - \mu^2}$$

Value	Value-mean	(Value-mean)^2	(Value)^2
6,820	12	144	46,512,400
6,790	-18	324	46,104,100
6,840	32	1024	46,785,600
6,810	2	4	46,376,100
6,830	22	484	46,648,900
6,770	-38	1444	45,832,900
6,830	22	484	46,648,900
6,790	-18	324	46,104,100
6,810	2	4	46,376,100
6,790	-18	324	46,104,100
$\Sigma x_1 = $ 68,080		4560	$\Sigma x_1{}^2 = $ 463,493,200

$$\mu = \frac{68,080}{10} = 6808 \text{ feet/sec}$$

$$\sigma = \sqrt{\frac{4560}{10}} = 21.35 \text{ feet/sec} \qquad \text{or} \qquad \sigma = \sqrt{\frac{463,493,200}{10} - (6808)^2}$$

$$= 21.35 \text{ feet/sec}$$

2-31

Absences, x_1	μ	$x_1 - \mu$	$(x_1 - \mu)^2$	$x_1{}^2$
103	96	7	49	10609
91	96	-5	25	8281
100	96	4	16	10000
87	96	-9	81	7569
65	96	-31	961	4225
104	96	8	64	10816
119	96	23	529	14161
103	96	7	49	10609
96	96	0	0	9216
84	96	-12	144	7056
98	96	2	4	9604
97	96	1	1	9409
104	96	8	64	10816
112	96	16	256	12544
88	96	-8	64	7744
96	96	0	0	9216
114	96	18	324	12996
69	96	-27	729	4761
89	96	-7	49	7921
93	96	-3	9	8649
88	96	-8	64	7744
102	96	6	36	10404
109	96	13	169	11881
93	96	-3	9	8649
2304			3696	224,880

from (2-15):

$$\sigma = \sqrt{\frac{\Sigma(x_1 - \mu)^2}{N}}$$

$$= \sqrt{\frac{3696}{24}}$$

$$= 12.41$$

from (2-16):

$$\sigma = \sqrt{\frac{\Sigma x_1^2}{N} - \mu^2}$$

$$= \sqrt{\frac{224880}{24} - (96)^2}$$

$$= 12.41$$

The probability there will be more than 100 people absent is a point $(112-96)/12.41 = 1.29$ standard deviations right of the mean.

From Appendix 1, this is a probability of .90147. Therefore, there is about a 90% probability absences will be 112 persons or less and about 10% probability they will be 112 or more.

2-32   Given: μ = 120,000 pounds
                 σ =   40,000 pounds
                 x = 185,000 pounds

From equation (2-15) we will find z, the number of standard deviations above the mean.

$$z = \frac{185,000 - 120,000}{40,000} = 1.63 \text{ standard deviations}$$

From Appendix Table 1, we find:

Prob = .94845

Since .94845 is the probability of 185,000 or less, we subtract this from 1 to find the probability of 185,000 pounds or more.

Prob (185,000 or more) = 1 - .94845 = .05155

2-33   Given: μ = 150 psi
                 σ =   25 psi

at x = 220 psi, we find from equation (2-15):

$$z = \frac{220 - 150}{25} = 2.8 \text{ standard deviations above the mean}$$

at x = 105 psi we find:

$$z = \frac{105-150}{25} = -1.8 \text{ standard deviations below the mean}$$

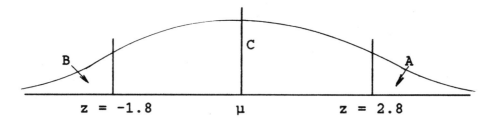

$z = -1.8$ μ $z = 2.8$

From Appendix Table 1, at z = 2.8 we find:

        P(220 psi or less) = .99744 (area B plus area C)
So, P(220 psi or more) = 1 - .99744 = .00256 (area A)

From Appendix Table 1, at z = 1.8 we find:

        P(105 psi or more) = .96407 (area A plus area C)
So, P(105 psi or less) = 1 - .96407 = .03593 (area B)

The unusable material (areas A and B) has a probability:

     P(unusable) = .00256 + .03593 = .03849

And, tons not usable = (50)(.03849) = 1.9245 tons per day.

2-34   Given: μ = 10%
               σ =   5%

From equation (2-15) at x = 16%:

$$z = \frac{16 - 10}{5} = 1.2 \text{ std. dev. above the mean}$$

From equation (2-15) at x = 22%:

$$z = \frac{22 - 10}{5} = 2.4 \text{ std. dev. above the mean}$$

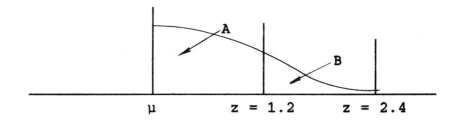

μ $z = 1.2$ $z = 2.4$

From Appendix Table 1:

at z = 1.2, Prob(16% or less) = .88493 (area A)
at z = 2.4, Prob(22% or less) = .99180
(area A plus B)

Prob(16 to 22%) = .99180 - .88493 = .10687 (area B)

This is (1300)(.10687) = 139 companies

2-35   We found from Exercise 2-30 that the mean velocity added
       was 6808 feet per second. Therefore, the acceptable range
       is:

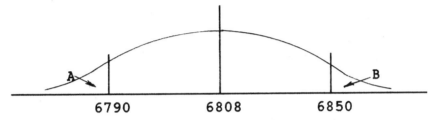

First we find area A from Appendix Table 1. Note that we
are looking for the area to the left of a point which is to
the left of the mean. The table is designed to read left
of points which are to the right of the mean. This poses
no problem, however, since we may visualize the mirror
image of the normal curve as follows:

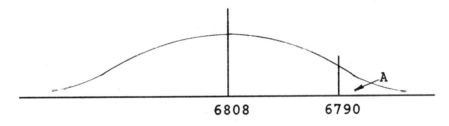

The point of 6790 is now seen to be 18 feet per second to
the right of the mean. The number of standard deviations
to the right is:

   z = 18 ÷ 21.35 = .84 std. dev. to the right of the mean

From the table we now read the area to the left of 6790
feet/second as .79955. Therefore,

       Area A = 1 - .79955 = .20045

Now we will find area B:

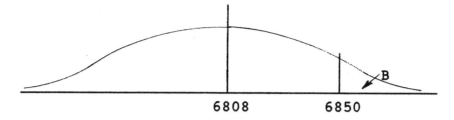

6808   6850

We find that the point 6850 feet per second is 42 feet per
second to the right of the mean. The number of standard
deviations to the right of:

   z = 42 ÷ 21.35 = 1.97 std. dev.

From the table we read the area to the left of 6850 feet
per second as .97558. Therefore:

   Area B = 1 - .97558 = .02442

The probability of mission failure is the sum of area A and
area B:

   Probability (failure due to incorrect transfer orbit)
       = 20045 + .02442 = .22487, or 22.49%

2-36 $z = \dfrac{145-100}{20}$ = 2.25 standard deviations. From Appendix 1

we read .98778 who score 145 or less.

       Percentage = 1 - .98878 = .01222 or about 1% who score
                                               145 or more.

2-37   The first step to solving this problem is to find the
       number of standard deviations to the right of the mean
       which correspond to a probability (or area under the normal
       curve) of .90. We read this figure from Appendix Table 1.
       At a probability of .90:

           z = 1.28 std dev

       Since 1 standard deviation is 30 days, then 1.28 standard
       deviations is 1.28 x 30 = 38.4 days to the right of the
       mean, or:

           Quoted completion date = 200 + 38.4, or 238.4 days.

24

2-38 Using equation 2-8, we obtain:

$$E = \Sigma x \cdot P(x) = (.20)(5)+(.33)(10)+(.36)(15)+(.11)(20)$$
$$= \$11.90$$

2-39 Let: S = short, L = long, F = fine, and C = coarse
From the problem we know the following:

$$P(S) = .52 \qquad ①$$
$$P(L \text{ or } F) = .83 \qquad ②$$
$$P(L \text{ and } C) = .28 \qquad ③$$

Since short and long are mutually exclusive:

$$P(S) + P(L) = 1.00$$
$$\text{and, } P(L) = 1.00 - .52 = .48 \qquad ④$$

The events (L and C) and (L and F) are mutually exclusive, thus:

$$P(L \text{ and } C) + P(L \text{ and } F) = P(L)$$
$$\text{so, } P(L \text{ and } F) = P(L) - P(L \text{ and } C) = .48 - .28$$
$$= .20 \qquad ⑤$$

Now we use equation (2-3) to solve for P(F):

$$P(L \text{ or } F) = P(L) + P(F) - P(L \text{ and } F)$$
$$.83 = .48 + P(F) - .20$$
$$P(F) = .55 \qquad ⑥$$

Since fine and coarse are mutually exclusive:

$$P(F) + P(C) = 1.00$$
$$\text{and, } P(C) = 1.00 - .55 = .45 \qquad ⑦$$

The events (S and F) and (L and F) are mutually exclusive, thus:

$$P(S \text{ and } F) + P(L \text{ and } F) = P(F)$$
$$P(S \text{ and } F) + .20 = .55$$
$$P(S \text{ and } F) = .35 \qquad ⑧$$

The events (S and F) and (S and C) are mutually exclusive, thus:

$$P(S \text{ and } F) + P(S \text{ and } C) = P(S)$$
$$.35 + P(S \text{ and } C) = .52$$
$$P(S \text{ and } C) = .17 \qquad ⑨$$

To summarize, the following chart shows the number of screws in each category. The results given in the chart are described by step number from the above calculations. Note to instructor: This table can be filled in as each step is done to illustrate the logical sequence of the calculations:

	Fine (F)	Coarse (C)	Totals
Short (S)	35 ⑧	17 ⑨	52 ①
Long (L)	20 ⑤	28 ③	48 ④
Totals	55 ⑥	45 ⑦	100 given

(a) To find P(S or F) we use equation (2-3) because short and fine are not mutually exclusive:

$$P(S \text{ or } F) = P(S) + P(F) - P(S \text{ and } F)$$
$$= .52 + .55 - .35$$
$$= .72$$

(b) To find P(L or C) we also use equation (2-3):

$$P(L \text{ or } C) = P(L) + P(C) - P(L \text{ and } C)$$
$$= .48 + .45 - .28$$
$$= .65$$

(c) To find P(S or C) equation (2-3) is again appropriate, because short and coarse are mutually exclusive:

$$P(S \text{ or } C) = P(S) + P(C) - P(S \text{ and } C)$$
$$= .52 + .45 - .17$$
$$= .80$$

2-40 We use the notation:

F = factual statement
$\underline{G}$ = good credit risk
$\overline{F}$ = nonfactual statement

The data given are:

$$P(F) = .9 \text{ and } P(\overline{F}) = .1$$
$$P(G|\underline{F}) = .8$$
$$P(G|\overline{F}) = .3$$

From the equation (2-7) we find P(GF) and P(G$\overline{F}$)

$$P(G\underline{F}) = P(G|\underline{F}) \times P(\underline{F}) = (.8)(.9) = .72$$
$$P(G\overline{F}) = P(G|\overline{F}) \times P(\overline{F}) = (.3)(.1) = .03$$

Now, we determine the marginal probability, P(G), by summing joint probabilities:

$$P(G) = P(GF) + P(G\overline{F}) = .72 + .03 = .75$$

We now solve for the probability that the applicant's financial statement is not factual given that he has shown himself to be a good credit risk using equation (2-7).

$$P(\overline{F}|G) = \frac{P(\overline{F}G)}{P(G)} = \frac{.03}{.75} = .04$$

2-41   Using equation 2-12 with μ = 14 units/hr = .2333 units/min and t = 6 minutes (Note: the same result is obtained if t and μ are defined in terms of hours where μ = 14 units/hour and t = 0.1 hour):

$$P(T \leq t) = 1 - e^{-\mu t} \quad \text{where } \mu t = (.2333)(6) = 1.4$$

From Appendix 4 at λ = 1.4, $e^{-\lambda}$ = .2466:

$$P(T \leq 6 \text{ minutes}) = 1 - .2466 = .7534$$

The probability T exceeds 6 minutes is .2466.

2-42   From Appendix Table 2 at n = 5, p = 50, and r = 5, we read 0.0313.

With $0.60 paid back for each $1.00 ticket, the profit per ticket is about:

$$\frac{0.60}{0.0313} = 19.169$$

2-43   From the data given, we summarize:

	Regular	Special
Increased	250/2000 = .125	350/2000 = .175
Decreased	500/2000 = .250	250/2000 = .125
Same	250/2000 = .125	400/2000 = .200
	.500	.500 = 1.00

We wish to test for independence, i.e., does:

P(increased|special) = P(increased)?
and, P(decreased|special) = P(decreased)?

P(increased) = .125 + .175 = .300

P(increased|special) = .175/.500 = .350

Since .35 ≠ .30, independence does not exist.

.350 ÷ .300 = increased usage is 1-1/6 times greater with the special campaign.

P(decreased) = .250 + .125 = .375

P(decreased|special) = .125/.500 = .250

.375 ÷ .250 = decreased usage is 1-1/2 times greater without the special campaign.

Since the results indicate a more significant effect on reducing decreased use of your products than on increasing the use, the test might <u>indicate</u> to you that the special campaign does more to increase brand loyalty than to increase sales.

2-44   Here the elementary events are that gout is present or gout is not present, where P(gout) = .15 and P(no gout) = .85. The conditional probabilities for a positive test event are:

P(positive|gout)   = .96
P(positive|no gout) = .08

Now we introduce the data and calculations in tabular form:

Elementary event	Probability of Elementary event	P(positive|event)	P(positive, event)
Gout	.15	.96	.144
No gout	.85	.08	.068

P(positive) = .212

The revised probability that the patient has gout is:

$$P(gout|positive) = \frac{P(pos,gout)}{P(positive)} = \frac{.144}{.212} = .6792 \text{ or } 67.92\%$$

2-45 Using equation 2-10 with $\lambda = 3$ and $e^{-3} = .04979$:

$$P(0) = \frac{(3)^0(.04979)}{0!} = .04979$$

$$P(1) = \frac{(3)^1(.04979)}{1!} = .14937$$

$$P(2) = \frac{(3)^2(.04979)}{2!} = .22406$$

$$P(3) = \frac{(3)^3(.04979)}{3!} = .22406$$

$$P(4) = \frac{(3)^4(.04979)}{4!} = .16804$$

$$P(5) = \frac{(3)^5(.04979)}{5!} = .10082$$

$$P(5 \text{ or less}) = .04979+.14937+.22406+.22406+.16804+.10082$$
$$= .91614$$

Therefore, the probability 6 or more arrive in an hour is $1 - .91614 = .08386$.

2-46 From Appendix 1, we find the area .96 is 1.75 standard deviations right of the mean and corresponds to 8 hours. We find the mean by the equation:

$$1.75 = \frac{8 - \mu}{\sigma} = \frac{8 - (7.5/n)}{(6.8/n)}$$

$$\frac{(1.75)(6.8)}{n} = 8 - \frac{7.5}{n}$$

$$\frac{11.9 + 7.5}{n} = 8$$

n = 2.425 crew size or 3 people.

3-1

t	Model A		Model B	
	Error	Error²	Error	Error²
13	10	100	18	324
14	8	64	2	4
15	6	36	1	1
Sum	24	200	21	329
Mean	8	66.7	7	109.7

Model B is better on the MAD criterion whereas Model A is better in terms of MSE. As the text points out, the "best" model depends on the criterion.

3-2

Year	Qtr.	X_t	F_t	e_t	$\lvert e_t \rvert$	$e_t{}^2$	$\lvert e_t/X_t \rvert \times 100$
1988	1	34	38	-4			
	2	37	40	-3			
	3	41	43	-2			
	4	45	44	1			
1989	1	46	48	-2	2	4	4.3
	2	48	48	0	0	0	0.0
	3	52	50	2	2	4	3.8
	4	53	54	-1	1	1	1.9
			Totals	-9	5	9	10.0

Forecasting sample (periods 89-1 to 89-4):
    MAD = 5/4 = 1.25
    MSE = 9/4 = 2.25
    MAPE = 10/4 = 2.5%

The forecasts appear biased, because Wanda almost consistently forecasts too high. The error terms are all negative except for two of them. Ideally, an unbiased set of forecasts would result in $\Sigma e_t = 0$.

3-3 For the naive model:

Year	Qtr.	X_t	F_t	e_t	$\lvert e_t \rvert$	$e_t{}^2$	$\lvert e_t/X_t \rvert \times 100$
1988	1	34					
	2	37	34	3			
	3	41	37	4			
	4	45	41	4			
1989	1	46	45	1	1	1	2.2%
	2	48	46	2	2	4	4.2
	3	52	48	4	4	16	7.7
	4	53	52	1	1	1	1.9

Forecasting sample (periods 89-1 to 89-4):
  MAD = 8/4 = 2
  MSE = 22/4 = 5.5
  MAPE = 16/4 = 4%

Wanda Wade's forecasts are slightly better than the naive model in terms of the MAD and MSE measures of performance.

3-4 For the naive model:

Month	X_t	F_t	e_t	$e_t{}^2$
Jan	218			
Feb	216	218	-2	
Mar	206	216	-10	
Apr	188	206	-18	
May	192	188	4	
Jun	209	192	17	
Jul	202	209	-7	49
Aug	223	202	21	441
Sep	231	223	8	64
Oct	218	231	-13	169
Nov	219	218	1	1
Dec	225	219	6	36
				760

MSE = 760/6 = 126.7

3-5

Month	X_t	F_t	e_t	$e_t{}^2$	Forecast for $t+1$
Jan	218				
Feb	216				
Mar	206				213.3
Apr	188	213.3			203.3
May	192	203.3			195.3
Jun	209	195.3			196.3
Jul	202	196.3	5.7	32.5	201.0
Aug	223	201.0	22.0	484.0	211.3

(Continued)

Month	X_t	F_t	e_t	$e_t{}^2$	Forecast for t + 1
Sep	231	211.3	19.7	388.1	218.7
Oct	218	218.7	-0.7	0.5	224.0
Nov	219	224.0	-5.0	25.0	222.7
Dec	225	222.7	2.3	5.3	220.7
				935.4	

MSE = 935.4/6 = 155.9   (not as good as the naive model)

3-6   a. This exercise demonstrates that simple smoothing cannot track a rapidly changing time series. The best we can do with the model is set alpha = 1 (equivalent to the naive model). But even then, we lag the data.

Model-fitting statistics		Alpha	MSE
Warm-up periods	= 5	0.10	1.0
MSE (warm-up)	= 0.8	0.20	1.0
First F	= 1.0	0.30	0.9
Best alpha	= 1.0	0.40	0.9
		0.50	0.9
		0.60	0.9
		0.70	0.9
		0.80	0.9
		0.90	0.8
		1.00	0.8

t	Data	Forecast	Error	Forecast for t+1
1	1.0	1.0	0.0	1.0
2	2.0	1.0	1.0	2.0
3	3.0	2.0	1.0	3.0
4	2.0	3.0	-1.0	2.0
5	1.0	2.0	-1.0	1.0
		1.0		

b. If the series is constant, it doesn't matter what the smoothing parameter is. If we have the correct starting value, the errors will be zero.

c. This exercise shows that simple smoothing is resistant to outliers provided alpha is relatively small.

Model-fitting statistics		Alpha	MSE
Warm-up periods	= 5	0.10	0.2
MSE (warm-up)	= 0.2	0.20	0.2
First F	= 1.0	0.30	0.2
Best alpha	= 0.1	0.40	0.2
		0.50	0.3
		0.60	0.3
		0.70	0.3
		0.80	0.3
		0.90	0.4
		1.00	0.4

32

t	Data	Forecast	Error	Forecast for t+1
1	1.0	1.0	0.0	1.0
2	1.0	1.0	0.0	1.0
3	2.0	1.0	1.0	1.1
4	1.0	1.1	-0.1	1.1
5	1.0	1.1	-0.1	1.1
		1.1		

d. Simple smoothing cannot keep up with a trend. We lag behind no matter what the alpha value.

Model-fitting statistics		Alpha	MSE
Warm-up periods = 5		0.10	4.8
MSE (warm-up) = 0.8		0.20	3.8
First F = 1.0		0.30	3.0
Best alpha = 1.0		0.40	2.4
		0.50	2.0
		0.60	1.6
		0.70	1.3
		0.80	1.1
		0.90	0.9
		1.00	0.8

t	Data	Forecast	Error	Forecast for t+1
1	1.0	1.0	0.0	1.0
2	2.0	1.0	1.0	2.0
3	3.0	2.0	1.0	3.0
4	4.0	3.0	1.0	4.0
5	5.0	4.0	1.0	5.0
		5.0		

e. This series has a constant mean which is what we assume when we use simple smoothing. Thus alpha is small--there is no significant difference between .10 and .20.

Model-fitting statistics		Alpha	MSE
Warm-up periods = 5		0.10	0.3742
MSE (warm-up) = 0.3706		0.20	0.3706
First F = 1.0		0.30	0.3828
Best alpha = 0.20		0.40	0.4067
		0.50	0.4406
		0.60	0.5
		0.70	0.5
		0.80	0.6
		0.90	0.7
		1.00	0.8

t	Data	Forecast	Error	Forecast for t+1
1	1.0	1.0	0.0	1.0
2	2.0	1.0	1.0	1.2
3	1.0	1.2	-0.2	1.2
4	2.0	1.2	0.8	1.3
5	1.0	1.3	-0.3	1.3
		1.3		

3-7 Using a large alpha improves the response to sudden, permanent changes in the series, such as the step change here. In theory, the forecasts never exactly catch up to the new level of the series but we get very close.

Alpha = 0.50

t	Data	Forecast	Error	Forecast for t+1
12	100	NA	NA	50.0
13	100	50.0	50.0	75.0
14	100	75.0	25.0	87.5
15	100	87.5	12.5	93.75
16	100	93.75	6.25	96.875
17	100	96.875	3.125	98.4375
18	100	98.4375	1.5625	99.21875
19	100	99.21875	0.78125	99.609375

3-8 For exponential smoothing, the weights are:

Period	Weight
t	α
t-1	$\alpha(1-\alpha)$
t-2	$\alpha(1-\alpha)^2$
t-3	$\alpha(1-\alpha)^3$
t-4	$\alpha(1-\alpha)^4$
t-5	$\alpha(1-\alpha)^5$
t-6	$\alpha(1-\alpha)^6$

The first specification states that the weight for period t must be three times the weight for period t-3.

$$\alpha = (3)(\alpha)(1-\alpha)^3$$

Solving for α, we find that $\alpha = .3$ satisfies this specification.

The second specification states that the weight for period t should be 8.5 times that of period t-6.

$$\alpha = (8.5)(\alpha)(1-\alpha)^6$$

Again, solving for α, we find $\alpha = .3$ to be the solution. Consequently, an alpha value of .3 satisfies both specifications.

3-9 a. If both alpha values are 1, the forecasts are the same as regression.

b. If α_2 is 0, the forecasts are the same as simple smoothing for any value of α_1.

c. If α_1 is 1 and α_2 is 0, the forecasts are the same as the naive model.

Note: Strictly speaking, all answers to exercise 3-9 assume that the same starting values are used in the two models being compared. But even if this is not true, the forecasts in each case will be equivalent in the limit (after a very large number of data).

3-10 Deseasonalized sales are the original sales divided by the indexes.

Year	Qtr.	Index	Sales	Des. sales = Sales/Index
1988	1	0.5	204	408.0
	2	0.9	379	421.1
	3	1.5	633	422.0
	4	1.1	430	390.9
1989	1	0.5	191	382.0
	2	0.9	342	380.0
	3	1.5	650	433.3
	4	1.1	388	352.7

3-11 We perform simple smoothing as usual with the deseasonalized data. No attempt is made to reseasonalize at this point.

Alpha = 0.10

Year	Qtr.	Des. Sales	Des. F'cst.	Des. Error	Des. F'cst. for t+1
1988	1	408.0	398.8	9.2	399.7
	2	421.1	399.7	21.4	401.8
	3	422.0	401.8	20.2	403.8
	4	390.9	403.8	-12.9	402.6
1989	1	382.0	402.6	-20.6	400.5
	2	380.0	400.5	-20.5	398.4
	3	433.3	398.4	34.9	401.9
	4	352.7	401.9	-49.2	397.0
1990	1		397.0		
	2		397.0		
	3		397.0		
	4		397.0		

Notice that the forecast for each quarter of 1990 is the same. To get the final forecasts for 1990, we multiply the deseasonalized forecasts by the indexes.

Year	Qtr.	Des. F'cst.	Index	Final F'cst.
1990	1	397.0	0.5	198.5
	2	397.0	0.9	357.3
	3	397.0	1.5	595.5
	4	397.0	1.1	436.7

3-12   Steps 1 and 2:   Centered moving averages and ratios.

Year	Qtr.	Sales X	4-Qtr. MA	Ratio:X/MA
1988	1	60		
	2	91		
	3	277	115.5000	2.3983
	4	34	126.7500	0.2682
1987	1	105	136.5000	0.7692
	2	130	197.7500	0.6574
	3	522	207.5000	2.5157
	4	73		

Steps 3 and 4:   Mean ratios and normalization factor.

1	0.7692	Factor = 4/4.1518 = 0.9634
2	0.6574	
3	2.4570	
4	0.2682	
Sum	4.1518	

Step 5:   Final seasonal indexes.

Qtr.	Mean Ratio	Factor	Final Index
1	0.7692	0.9634	0.7411
2	0.6574	0.9634	0.6334
3	2.4570	0.9634	2.3671
4	0.2682	0.9634	0.2584
Sum			4.0000

3-13   Note: The seasonal indexes in exercise 3-12 were computed
        using all the data. These indexes should be used in 3-13
        and 3-14. There aren't enough data to compute indexes
        using only the warm-up sample (periods 1-6).

a. Naive model

Year	Qtr.	Sales	Forecast	Error
1988	1	60		
	2	91	60	31
	3	277	91	186
	4	34	277	-243
1989	1	105	34	71
	2	130	105	25
	3	522	130	392
	4	73	522	-449
1990	1		73	
	2		73	
	3		73	
	4		73	

MSE for periods 1989-3 and 1989-4 = 177632.5

The MSE is quite large, indicating that we should improve accuracy by taking the seasonal pattern into account.

b. Deseasonalized sales are the original sales divided by the indexes.

Year	Qtr.	Index	Sales	Des. Sales
1988	1	0.7411	60	81.0
	2	0.6334	91	143.7
	3	2.3671	277	117.0
	4	0.2548	34	131.6
1989	1	0.7411	105	141.7
	2	0.6334	130	205.2
	3	2.3671	522	220.5
	4	0.2584	73	282.5

A strong trend shows up in the deseasonalized data. Taking the trend into account should also improve accuracy.

c. Linear regression

All calculations are with deseasonalized data.

t	X	tX	t²
1	81.0	81.0	1.0
2	143.7	287.3	4.0
3	117.0	351.1	9.0
4	131.6	526.3	16.0
5	141.7	708.4	25.0
6	205.2	1231.4	36.0

	t	X	tX	t²
Sum	21	820.2	3185.5	91.0
Mean	3.5	136.7		

$$b = \frac{3185.5 - 6(3.5)(136.7)}{91 - 6(3.5)^2} = 18.0$$

$$a = 136.7 - 18.0(3.5) = 73.7$$

$$F = 73.7 + 18.0t$$

Year	Qtr.	t	Des. Sales	Des. F'cst.	Des. Error
1988	1	1	81.0	91.7	-10.7
	2	2	143.7	109.7	34.0
	3	3	117.0	127.7	-10.7
	4	4	131.6	145.7	-14.1
1989	1	5	141.7	163.7	-22.0
	2	6	205.2	181.7	23.5
	3	7	220.5	199.7	20.8
	4	8	282.5	217.7	64.8

(Continued)

Year	Qtr.	t	Des. Sales	Des. F'cst.	Des. Error
1990	1	9		235.7	
	2	10		253.7	
	3	11		271.7	
	4	12		289.7	

d. The seasonalized forecasts for the last two quarters of 1989 are found by multiplying each index by the deseasonalized forecast.

Year	Qtr.	Index	Des. F'cst.	Final F'cst.
1989	3	2.3671	199.7	472.7
	4	0.2548	217.7	56.3

Year	Qtr.	Sales	Final F'cst.	Error
1989	3	522	472.7	49.3
	4	73	56.3	16.8

MSE for periods 1989-3 and 1989-4 = 1355.0
   (big improvement over naive model)

e.	Year	Qtr.	Index	Des. F'cst.	Final F'cst.
	1990	1	0.7411	253.7	174.7
		2	0.6334	253.7	160.7
		3	2.3671	271.7	643.1
		4	0.2584	289.7	74.9

3-14   a. Linear exponential smoothing

Model-fitting statistics
Warm-up periods =   6
MSE (warm-up)   = 599.2
Alpha 1   =   0.20
Alpha 2   =   0.10

Year	Qtr.	Des. Sales	Des. F'cst.	Des. Error	Des. Level	Des. Trend	Des. F'cst. t+1
					73.7	18.0	91.7
1988	1	81.0	91.7	-10.7	89.5	16.9	106.5
	2	143.7	106.5	37.2	113.9	20.6	134.6
	3	117.0	134.6	-17.5	131.1	18.9	149.9
	4	131.6	149.9	-18.4	146.3	17.1	163.3
1989	1	141.7	163.3	-21.6	159.0	14.9	173.9
	2	205.2	173.9	31.4	180.2	18.0	198.2
	3	220.5	198.2	22.3	202.7	20.3	222.9
	4	282.5	222.9	59.6	234.8	26.2	261.1
1990	1		261.1				
	2		287.3				
	3		313.5				
	4		339.7				

b.

Year	Qtr.	Index	Des. F'cst.	Final F'cst.
1989	3	2.3671	198.2	469.2
	4	0.2584	222.9	57.6

Year	Qtr.	Sales	Final F'cst.	Error
1989	3	522	469.2	52.8
	4	73	57.6	15.4

MSE for periods 1989-3 and 1989-4 = 1514.6
  (big improvement over naive model; worse than regression
  model)

c.

Year	Qtr.	Index	Des. F'cst.	Final F'cst.
1990	1	0.7411	261.1	193.5
	2	0.6334	287.3	182.0
	3	2.3671	313.5	742.1
	4	0.2584	339.7	87.8

d. Even though the regression model beats linear smoothing
for the last two periods of 1989, the smoothing forecasts
look more reasonable for 1990. The smoothing model appears
to pick up the change in trend and gives larger forecasts
for 1990. Again, we should keep in mind the rationale of
smoothing--giving recent data more weight should improve
accuracy on average.

This exercise illustrates how difficult it is to select a
model. This exercise also shows the tremendous gains to be
had from taking seasonality and trend into account in
forecasting.

3-15 Intercept = 30   Slope = 3.7

Year	Qtr.	Actual Demand	F'cast Demand	F'cast Error	Abs. F'cast Error	Abs. % F'cast Error
1988	1	34	33.7			
	2	37	37.4	-0.4		
	3	41	41.1	-0.1		
	4	45	44.8	0.2		
1989	1	46	48.5	-2.5	2.5	5.4%
	2	48	52.2	-4.2	4.2	8.8%
	3	52	55.9	-3.9	3.9	7.5%
	4	53	59.6	-6.6	6.6	12.5%

Forecasting sample (periods 89-1 to 89-4):
   MAD = 4.3
   MAPE = 8.53%
   MSE = 20.665

3-16   Seasonal indices (using all data)

Year	Qtr	Actual sales	Moving Average	Ratio	Sum of Ratios	Div- isor	Initial Index	Normalized Index
1988	1	30.3			1.27	2	.635	.648
	2	98.9			2.90	2	1.450	1.479
	3	58.8	57.3	1.03	3.35	3	1.117	1.139
	4	41.2	58.2	.71	1.44	2	.720	.734
1989	1	33.8	55.0	.61		Sum =	3.922	4.000
	2	86.3	58.4	1.48				
	3	72.3	59.1	1.22				
	4	43.9	60.4	.73		Factor = 4/3.922 = 1.02		
1990	1	39.1	59.0	.66				
	2	80.6	56.8	1.42				
	3	63.6	58.0	1.10				
	4	48.6						

3-17   Intercept = 53.493; Slope = 0.643

Year	Qtr	Actual Sales	Index	Des. Sales	Des. Forecast	Final Forecast
1988	1	30.3	.648	46.759	54.136	35.080
	2	98.9	1.479	66.870	54.779	81.018
	3	58.8	1.139	51.624	55.422	63.126
	4	41.2	.734	56.131	56.065	41.152
1989	1	33.8	.648	52.160	56.708	36.747
	2	86.3	1.479	58.350	57.351	84.822
	3	72.3	1.139	63.477	57.994	66.055
	4	43.9	.734	59.809	58.637	43.040
1990	1	39.1	.648	60.340	59.280	38.413
	2	80.6	1.479	54.496	59.923	88.626
	3	63.6	1.139	55.838	60.566	68.985
	4	48.6	.734	66.213	61.209	44.927
1991	1		.648		61.852	40.080
	2		1.479		62.495	92.430
	3		1.139		63.138	71.914
	4		.734		63.781	46.815

3-18   Parameters: Level = 0.30   Trend = 0.20

Year	Qtr	Actual Sales	Index	Des. Sales	Des. F'cast	Des. Error	Des. Level	Des. Trend	Final F'cast
							53.493	0.643	
1988	1	30.3	.648	46.759	54.136	-7.377	51.923	-0.832	35.080
	2	98.9	1.479	66.870	51.091	15.779	55.824	2.323	75.563
	3	58.8	1.139	51.624	58.148	-6.523	56.191	1.019	66.230
	4	41.2	.734	56.131	57.209	-1.079	56.886	0.803	41.992
1989	1	33.8	.648	52.160	57.689	-5.528	56.030	-0.303	37.382
	2	86.3	1.479	58.350	55.728	2.623	55.514	0.222	82.421
	3	72.3	1.139	63.477	56.736	6.740	58.758	1.570	64.623
	4	43.9	.734	59.809	60.328	-0.519	60.173	1.466	44.281

40

1990	1	39.1	.648	60.340	61.639	−1.299	61.249	1.206	39.942
	2	80.6	1.479	54.496	62.455	−7.959	60.068	−0.386	92.371
	3	63.6	1.139	55.838	59.682	−3.844	58.529	−1.154	67.978
	4	48.6	.734	66.213	57.375	8.838	60.026	0.613	42.113
1991	1		.648		60.639				39.294
	2		1.479		61.253				90.593
	3		1.139		61.866				70.465
	4		.734		62.479				45.860

3-19 a. $\phi = 1.2$

Using equation 3-17:

$F_{12+1} = S_{12} + (1.2)T_{12}$
$F_{13} = 100 + (1.2)(10)$
$F_{13} = 112$

$F_{12+2} = S_{12} + (1.2)(T_{12}) + (1.2)^2(T_{12})$
$F_{14} = 100 + (1.2)(10) + (1.44)(10)$
$F_{14} = 126.4$
$F_{12+3} = S_{12} + (1.2)(T_{12}) + (1.2)^2(T_{12}) + (1.2)^3(T_{12})$
$F_{15} = 100 + (1.2)(10) + (1.44)(10) + (1.728)(10)$
$F_{15} = 143.68$

$F_{12+4} = S_{12} + (1.2)(T_{12}) + (1.2)^2(T_{12}) + (1.2)^3(T_{12}) +$
$\quad\quad (1.2)^4(T_{12})$
$F_{16} = 100 + 12 + 14.4 + 17.28 + 20.736$
$F_{16} = 164.416$

b. $\phi = .8$

$F_{13} = 100 + (.8)(10)$
$F_{13} = 108$
$F_{14} = 108 + (.8)^2(10)$
$F_{14} = 114.4$
$F_{15} = 114.4 + (.8)^3(10)$
$F_{15} = 119.52$
$F_{16} = 119.52 + (.8)^4(10)$
$F_{16} = 123.616$

3-20 This exercise is a little tricky. We treat each watch as a separate "season." There are 3 watches, or 3 "seasons" per day. 3-quarter moving averages are centered on the second watch. There are n-2 moving averages.

Steps 1 and 2: Centered moving averages and ratios.

Week	Watch	Calls X	3-Qtr. MA	Ratio: X/MA
1	1	10.1		
	2	23.8	32.1000	0.7414
	3	62.4	31.5333	1.9789

(Continued)

41

Week	Watch	Calls X	3-Qtr. MA	Ratio: X/MA
2	1	8.4	32.5000	0.2585
	2	26.7	35.1667	0.7592
	3	70.4	35.4000	1.9887
3	1	9.1	33.6000	0.2708
	2	21.3	36.3000	0.5868
	3	78.5	35.8000	2.1927
4	1	7.6	38.5333	0.1972
	2	29.5	34.3333	0.8592
	3	65.9		

Steps 3 and 4: Mean ratios and normalization factor.

1	0.2422	Factor = 3/3.0323 = 0.9894
2	0.7367	
3	2.0534	
Sum	3.0323	

Step 5: Final seasonal indexes (normalize to sum to 3).

Qtr.	Mean ratio	Factor	Final Index
1	0.2422	0.9894	0.2396
2	0.7367	0.9894	0.7288
3	2.0534	0.9894	2.0316
Sum			3.0000

3-21 a. Naive model

Year	Quarter	Net Deposits	Forecast	Error
1989	1	20.0		
	2	16.5	20.0	-3.5
	3	19.9	16.5	3.4
	4	22.9	19.9	3.0
1990	1	21.4	22.9	-1.5
	2	24.6	21.4	3.2
	3	20.7	24.6	-3.9
	4	25.5	20.7	4.8
1991	1		25.5	

MSE for periods 90-3 and 90-4 is $[(-3.9)^2+(4.8)^2]/2 = 19.1$.

b. Simple smoothing model

Alpha = 0.2

Year	Quarter	Net Deposits	Forecast	Error	Forecast for t+1
1989	1	20.0	20.9	-0.9	20.7
	2	16.5	20.7	-4.2	19.9
	3	19.9	19.9	0.0	19.9
	4	22.9	19.9	3.0	20.5
1990	1	21.4	20.5	0.9	20.7
	2	24.6	20.7	3.9	21.4
	3	20.7	21.4	-0.7	21.3
	4	25.5	21.3	4.2	22.1
1991	1		22.1		

MSE for periods 90-3 and 90-4 = 9.1 (improvement over the naive model)

3-22

t	X	tX	t^2
1	20.0	20.0	1.0
2	16.5	33.0	4.0
3	19.9	59.7	9.0
4	22.9	91.6	16.0
5	21.4	107.0	25.0
6	24.6	147.6	36.0
Sums	21	125.3	458.9	91.0
Mean	3.5	20.9	76.5	

$$b = \frac{76.5 - 6(3.5)(20.9)}{91 - 6(3.5)^2} = 1.2$$

$$a = 20.9 - 1.2(3.5) = 16.8$$

$$F = 16.8 + 1.2t$$

Year	Qtr.	t	Net Deposits	Forecast	Error
1989	1	1	20.0	18.0	2.0
	2	2	16.5	19.2	-2.7
	3	3	19.9	20.4	-0.5
	4	4	22.9	21.6	1.3
1990	1	5	21.4	22.8	-1.4
	2	6	24.6	24.0	0.6
	3	7	20.7	25.2	-4.5
	4	8	25.5	26.4	-0.9
1991	1	9		27.6	

MSE for periods 90-3 and 90-4 = 10.5

It is interesting that the MSE is worse than simple smoothing. The best model at this point depends on a subjective judgment--Is there a trend in the data? There are big differences in the forecasts between no trend (simple smoothing) and a linear trend (regression).

3-23 The beginning level and trend are taken from Problem 3-22.

Alpha 1 = 0.10
Alpha 2 = 0.05

Year	Qtr.	Net Deposits	F'cast	Error	Level	Trend	F'cast for t+1
					16.8	1.2	18.0
1989	1	20.0	18.0	2.0	18.2	1.3	19.5
	2	16.5	19.5	-3.0	19.2	1.2	20.4
	3	19.9	20.4	-0.4	20.3	1.1	21.4
	4	22.9	21.4	1.5	21.6	1.2	22.8
1990	1	21.4	22.8	-1.4	22.6	1.1	23.8
	2	24.6	23.8	0.8	23.9	1.2	25.0
	3	20.7	25.0	-4.3	24.6	1.0	25.6
	4	25.5	25.6	-0.1	25.5	1.0	26.5
1991	1		26.5				

MSE for periods 90-3 and 90-4 = 9.4

Linear smoothing does worse than simple smoothing, although the difference in MSE is small. However, there are big differences for 1991-1.

3-24 Parameters: Level = 0.10   Trend = 0.05 ϕ = 1.10

Year	Qtr.	Actual Deposits	F'cast Deposits	F'cast Error	Level	Trend
					16.81	1.16
1989	1	20.00	18.09	1.91	18.28	1.37
	2	16.50	19.79	-3.29	19.46	1.34
	3	19.90	20.94	-1.04	20.83	1.43
	4	22.90	22.40	0.50	22.45	1.59
1990	1	21.40	24.21	-2.81	23.93	1.61
	2	24.60	25.70	-1.10	25.59	1.72
	3	20.70	27.48	-6.78	26.81	1.55
	4	25.50	28.51	-3.01	28.21	1.56

Forecast sample (Periods 90-3 and 90-4)
MSE = $(6.78)^2$ + $(3.01)^2$ = 55.03

3-25 It is difficult to justify a trend in this data, especially since it is a new time series. Thus we will try simple smoothing with a six-period warmup sample.

Naive model (benchmark)

Month	Sales	Forecast	Error
1	50		
2	45	50	-5
3	60	45	15
4	52	60	-8
5	69	52	17

(Continued)

Month	Sales	Forecast	Error
6	60	69	-9
7	47	60	-13
8	53	47	6
9		53	
10		53	
11		53	
12		53	

MSE for months 7 and 8 = 102.5

Simple smoothing Model-fitting statistics		Alpha	MSE
Warm-up periods = 6		0.10	67.7
MSE (warm-up) = 67.7		0.20	71.5
First F = 56.0		0.30	74.1
Best alpha = 0.10		0.40	76.5
		0.50	79.4
		0.60	83.4
		0.70	89.0
		0.80	96.6
		0.90	106.7
		1.00	120.0

Month	Sales	Forecast	Error	F'cast for t+1
1	50.0	56.0	-6.0	55.4
2	45.0	55.4	-10.4	54.4
3	60.0	54.4	5.6	54.9
4	52.0	54.9	-2.9	54.6
5	69.0	54.6	14.4	56.1
6	60.0	56.1	3.9	56.5
7	47.0	56.5	-9.5	55.5
8	53.0	55.5	-2.5	55.3
9		55.3		
10		55.3		
11		55.3		
12		55.3		

MSE for months 7 and 8 = 47.9 (beats naive model)

3-26 There is a strong trend in the data. Trends are always more obvious in time series composed of annual totals. We will start with the naive benchmark, then do a linear regression, then do linear smoothing. The warm-up sample will be the first 6 years.

Naive model

Year	Conversions	Forecast	Error
1982	9.4		
1983	10.7	9.4	1.3
1984	11.0	10.7	0.3
1985	15.1	11.0	4.1
1986	20.6	15.1	5.5

(Continued)

Year	Conversions	Forecast	Error
1987	22.1	20.6	1.5
1988	25.8	22.1	3.7
1989	23.0	25.8	-2.8
1990		23.0	
1991		23.0	
1992		23.0	

MSE for periods 1988 and 1989 = 10.8

Linear regression

t	X	tX	t²
1	9.4	9.4	1.0
2	10.7	21.4	4.0
3	11.0	33.0	9.0
4	15.1	60.4	16.0
5	20.6	103.0	25.0
6	22.1	132.6	36.0

Sum 21	88.9	359.8	91.0
Mean 3.5	14.8		

$$b = \frac{359.8 - 6(3.5)(14.8)}{91 - 6(3.5)^2} = 2.8$$

$$a = 14.8 - 2.8(3.5) = 5.1$$

$$F = 5.1 + 2.8t$$

Linear regression forecasts

Year	t	Conversions	F'cast	Error
1982	1	9.4	7.9	1.5
1983	2	10.7	10.6	0.1
1984	3	11.0	13.4	-2.4
1985	4	15.1	16.2	-1.1
1986	5	20.6	19.0	1.6
1987	6	22.1	21.8	0.3
1988	7	25.8	24.5	1.3
1989	8	23.0	27.3	-4.3
1990	9		30.1	
1991	10		32.9	
1992	11		35.7	

MSE for periods 1988 and 1989 = 10.1 (beats naive model)

Linear exponential smoothing

Model-fitting statistics	Alpha 1	Alpha 2	MSE
Warm-up periods = 6	0.10	0.01	2.3
MSE (warm-up) = 2.3	0.10	0.05	2.4
Alpha 1 = 0.10	0.10	0.10	2.7
Alpha 2 = 0.01	0.20	0.01	2.5
First F (from = 7.9	0.20	0.05	2.7
linear regression)	0.20	0.10	2.9

Year	Conversions	F'cst	Error	Level	Trend	F'cst for t+1
				5.1	2.8	7.9
1982	9.4	7.9	1.5	8.0	2.8	10.8
1983	10.7	10.8	-0.1	10.8	2.8	13.6
1984	11.0	13.6	-2.6	13.3	2.8	16.1
1985	15.1	16.1	-1.0	16.0	2.8	18.8
1986	20.6	18.8	1.8	18.9	2.8	21.7
1987	22.1	21.7	0.4	21.8	2.8	24.5
1988	25.8	24.5	1.3	24.7	2.8	27.5
1989	23.0	27.5	-4.5	27.0	2.7	29.8
1990		29.8				
1991		32.5				
1992		35.3				

MSE for periods 1988 and 1989 = 10.7

This is a case where smoothing does worse than the
regression model. However, the difference in the
forecasting sample is small. We should use the smoothing
model because of its rationale--on average it should be
more accurate since it gives more weight to the recent
data.

3-27 Seasonal indices (using all data)

Year	Qtr.	Actual sales	Moving Average	Ratio	Sum of Ratios	Div- isor	Initial Index	Normalized Index
1988	1	6.5			1.57	2	0.7868	0.7699
	2	8.2			2.18	2	1.0920	1.0686
	3	12.4	8.08	1.54	4.66	3	1.5545	1.5212
	4	5.2	8.28	0.63	1.31	2	0.6544	0.6404
1989	1	7.3	8.83	0.83		SUM =	4.0877	4.0000
	2	10.4	9.93	1.05				
	3	16.8	10.48	1.60				
	4	7.4	10.88	0.68				
1990	1	8.9	11.93	0.75				
	2	14.6	12.85	1.14				
	3	20.5	13.45	1.52				
	4	9.8						

47

3-28   Intercept = 6.34   Slope = 0.67

Year	Qtr.	Actual Sales	Index	Des. Sales	Des. F'cast	Final F'cast
1988	1	6.5	0.7699	8.4429	7.01	5.40
	2	8.2	1.0686	7.6737	7.68	8.21
	3	12.4	1.5212	8.1517	8.35	12.70
	4	5.2	0.6404	8.1202	9.02	5.78
1989	1	7.3	0.7699	9.4821	9.69	7.46
	2	10.4	1.0686	9.7325	10.36	11.07
	3	16.8	1.5212	11.0442	11.03	16.78
	4	7.4	0.6404	11.5556	11.70	7.49
1990	1	8.9	0.7699	11.5603	12.37	9.52
	2	14.6	1.0686	13.6630	13.04	13.93
	3	20.5	1.5212	13.4766	13.71	20.86
	4	9.8	0.6404	15.3034	14.38	9.21
1991	1		0.7699		15.05	11.59
	2		1.0686		15.72	16.80
	3		1.5212		16.39	24.93
	4		0.6404		17.06	10.93
1992	1		0.7699		17.73	13.65
	2		1.0686		18.40	19.66

3-29   Parameters: Level = 0.30   Trend = 0.20

Year	Qtr.	Actual Sales	Index	Des. Sales	Des. F'cast	Des. Error	Des. Level	Des. Trend	Final F'cast
							6.34	0.67	
1988	1	6.5	0.7699	8.4429	7.01	1.43	7.44	0.96	5.40
	2	8.2	1.0686	7.6737	8.40	-0.72	8.18	0.81	8.97
	3	12.4	1.5212	8.1517	8.99	-0.84	8.74	0.64	13.68
	4	5.2	0.6404	8.1202	9.38	-1.26	9.00	0.39	6.01
1989	1	7.3	0.7699	9.4821	9.40	0.09	9.42	0.41	7.23
	2	10.4	1.0686	9.7325	9.83	-0.10	9.80	0.39	10.50
	3	16.8	1.5212	11.0442	10.19	0.85	10.45	0.56	15.50
	4	7.4	0.6404	11.5556	11.01	0.55	11.17	0.67	7.05
1990	1	8.9	0.7699	11.5603	11.84	-0.28	11.76	0.61	9.12
	2	14.6	1.0686	13.6630	12.37	1.29	12.76	0.87	13.22
	3	20.5	1.5212	13.4766	13.63	-0.15	13.58	0.84	20.73
	4	9.8	0.6404	15.3034	14.43	0.88	14.69	1.02	9.24
1991	1		0.7699		15.71				12.09
	2		1.0686		16.72				17.87
	3		1.5212		17.74				26.99
	4		0.6404		18.76				12.01
1992	1		0.7699		19.77				15.22
	2		1.0686		20.79				22.22

CHAPTER 4

DECISION MAKING

USING

PROBABILITIES I

4-1 Using maximin we first list the maximum payoff for each decision as follows:

Arena	Minimum payoff
A	10,000
B	8,000
C	-1,000
D	-5,000

From this set of minimum payoff values, we select the maximum value, which is $10,000. Our decision is to select Arena A.

4-2 Using maximax we first list the maximum payoff for each decision:

Action	Maximum payoff
Buy 200	50
Buy 300	75
Buy 400	100

Now, from this set of maximum payoff values, we select the maximum value--$100. Our decision is to buy 400.

4-3 Using the minimax regret criterion we first compute the regret for each decision alternative. This is done by subtracting each entry in the payoff table from the maximum value in its respective column.

Regret values (all in 1000's of dollars)

Trend	Type of Investment			
	Blue Chip	Growth	Venture	Treasury Bills
Boom	250	125	0	(470)
Mod. growth	75	0	50	120
Mod. decline	30	80	180	0
Collapse	(330)	(430)	(530)	0

The maximum regret values for each decision are circled.
The minimum of the circled values is 330 so the decision is
to invest in blue chip stock.

4-4 The maximum and minimum payoffs (given in 1000's) for each
decision are:

Decision Alternative	Maximum payoff	Minimum payoff
Overhaul	30	-50
Expand	60	-70
Buy	50	-60
Do nothing	3	-5

Using equation (4-1) we solve for the measure of realism:

Overhaul	Meas. of realism = $(.8)(30) + (.2)(-50)$	$= 14$
Expand	$(.8)(60) + (.2)(-70)$	$= 34$
Buy	$(.8)(50) + (.2)(-60)$	$= 28$
Do nothing	$(.8)(3) + (.2)(-5)$	$=1.4$

The largest measure of realism value of $34,000 is
associated with the optimum decision--expand.

4-5 If the decision maker were indifferent between decisions A
and B, each would have the same measure of realism, where:

measure of realism $= \alpha$ (max decision A) $+ (1 - \alpha)$ (min decision A)
$\qquad\qquad\qquad = \alpha$ (max decision B) $+ (1 - \alpha)$ (min decision B)

$$\alpha(800) + (1 - \alpha)(-100) = \alpha(700) + (1 - \alpha)(200)$$
$$800\alpha - 100 + 100\alpha = 700\alpha + 200 - 200\alpha$$
$$400\alpha = 300$$
$$\alpha = .75$$

Making the same comparison between decisions B and C:

$$\alpha(700) + (1 - \alpha)(200) = \alpha(600) + (1 - \alpha)(400)$$
$$700\alpha + 200 - 200\alpha = 600\alpha + 400 - 400\alpha$$
$$300\alpha = 200$$
$$\alpha = .67$$

The decision maker's index of optimism lies between .67 and .75.

4-6 The conditional profit table is:

Possible demand	Possible stock action			
	20 units	25 units	40 units	60 units
20 units	40	30	0	-40
25	40	50	20	-20
40	40	50	80	40
60	40	50	80	120

a. The expected profit if 25 mangoes are stocked is:

$$EP|25 \text{ stocked} = (30)(.10) + (50)(.30) + (50)(.50) + (50)(.10)$$
$$= \$48 \text{ per week.}$$

b. At a stock of 60 mangoes, the expected profit is:

$$EP|60 \text{ stocked} = (-40)(.10) + (-20)(.30) + (40)(.50) + (120)(.10)$$
$$= \$22 \text{ per week.}$$

c. The other actions have the expected profits:

$$EP|20 \text{ stocked} = \$40 \text{ per week.}$$

$$EP|40 \text{ stocked} = (0)(.10) + (20)(.30) + (80)(.50) + (80)(.10)$$
$$= \$54 \text{ per week.}$$

The store should stock 40 mangoes to maximize expected profits.

d. With perfect information, the expected weekly profit would be:

$$EP|PI = (40)(.10) + (50)(.30) + (80)(.50) + (120)(.10)$$
$$= \$71 \text{ per week.}$$

The expected value of perfect information is the difference between the expected profit with perfect

information ($71) and the expected profit with the
optimal action of stocking 40 mangoes ($54):

$$EVPI = 71 - 54 = \$17 \text{ per week.}$$

4-7   a.   The first decision alternative--stock W only is
dominated by either of the other two decisions, because the
loss due to stocking W only is higher for each possible
state of nature.

b.   Using the criterion of rationality, we assign a
probability of .33 to each state of nature.   The expected
value calculations are:

$$EL|\text{stock V only} = (80)(.33) + (250)(.33) + (350)(.33)$$
$$= 224.4$$

$$EL|\text{stock W \& V} = (20)(.33) + (200)(.33) + (550)(.33)$$
$$= 254.1$$

The optimum action is to stock 1000 units of vaccine V
only.

4-8   We wish to compute a mean score for each applicant, where
the mean is a weighted average of several criteria as
follows:

Wgtd mean =
$$\frac{(4)(\text{interview}) + (3)(\text{education}) + (2)(\text{exam}) + (1)(\text{community})}{4 + 3 + 2 + 1}$$

Applicant	Weighted Mean Score
Steve	(4)(75) + (3)(84) + (2)(90) + (1)(80) ÷ 10 = 81.2
Celeste	(4)(91) + (3)(88) + (2)(83) + (1)(88) ÷ 10 = 88.2
Carole	(4)(86) + (3)(93) + (2)(90) + (1)(92) ÷ 10 = 89.5
Frank	(4)(94) + (3)(90) + (2)(88) + (1)(75) ÷ 10 = 89.7
Linda	(4)(94) + (3)(84) + (2)(86) + (1)(89) ÷ 10 = 88.9
Cam	(4)(82) + (3)(70) + (2)(94) + (1)(93) ÷ 10 = 81.9
Bill	(4)(74) + (3)(89) + (2)(85) + (1)(68) ÷ 10 = 80.1

The two highest weighted means are for Frank and Carole.

A weighted mean has a similarity to expected value which is
also a mean value with its weights being probability
figures.

4-9 The conditional profit table is:

Possible	Possible action	
weather	Go to beach	Stay home
fair	80	40
bad	10	35

The expected profits for the two actions are:

$$EP|beach = (.4)(80) + (.6)(10) = \$38$$
$$EP|home = (.4)(40) + (.6)(35) = \$37$$

The optimal action is to drive to the beach.

With perfect information, the expected profit is:

$$EP|PI = (.4)(80) + (.6)(35) = \$53$$

So, EVPI = 53 - 38 = $15, which is the most Fred would pay for a perfect forecast.

4-10 We define: G = guaranteed 1% defective supplier.
V = variable defective supplier.

At a repair cost of $2 per defective, the expected repair costs for 30,000 crystals is:

$$E \text{ repair}|G = (2)(30000)(.01) = \$600 \text{ per order}$$

$$E \text{ repair}|V = (2)(30000)[(.005)(.05) + (.02)(.55)$$
$$+ (.05)(.40)]$$
$$= \$1875 \text{ per order}$$

Since the added cost of $1,000 and the $600 repair cost for supplier G = $1,600 is less than the repair cost of supplier V, we should select the guaranteed defective supplier, G.

4-11 We define the probability of Stark competing as p. Our table of conditional profit is:

Possible	Possible actions	
Event	SPT 10	SPT 20
Stark competes	160,000	20,000
Stark does not compete	280,000	500,000

53

Now we define equations for expected value of profit for the two actions:

$$EV|SPT\ 10 = 160,000p + 280,000(1-p)$$
$$EV|SPT\ 20 = 20,000p + 500,000(1-p)$$

Our breakeven condition is met when the two expected values are equal. Setting the two equations equal and solving for p, we obtain:

$$160p + 280\ (1-p) = 20p + 500\ (1-p)$$
$$160p + 280 - 280p = 20p + 500 - 500p$$
$$360p = 220$$
$$p = .611$$

He will be indifferent when the probability of Stark's competing is about 61%.

4-12 Let us define X as the number of returns audited. The expected value of additional tax revenue per return audited is:

$$EV\ per\ return = (.1)(100,000) + (.2)(50,000)$$
$$+ (.2)(10,000) + (.50)(0)$$
$$= \$22,000\ per\ return$$

If X returns are audited, 22,000X of added revenue will be received at an audit cost of 2000X. To meet the target of $5 million, we have:

$$\$5,000,000 = 22,000X - 2,000X$$
$$X = 250\ returns\ must\ be\ audited.$$

4-13 We construct the payoff table using a total cost figure of $500 + $40, as follows:

Bidding Alternative	States of Nature	
	Win Contract	Lose Contract
Cost plus 15%	81	-40
Cost plus 20%	108	-40
Cost plus 25%	135	-40
Cost plus 30%	162	-40

The expected value of profit per lot for each of the bid policies is:

Cost plus 15%	(81)(.90) + (-40)(.10) =	$68.90
Cost plus 20%	(108)(.80) + (-40)(.20) =	$78.40
Cost plus 25%	(135)(.80) + (-40)(.60) =	$30.00
Cost plus 30%	(162)(.05) + (-40)(.95) =	-$29.90

Suburban should adopt a policy of bidding cost plus 20% and
its long-run profit will be $78.40 per lot cleared.

4-14 The payoff table for this problem is:

Decision maker's	States of nature		
Alternatives	1,000,000 sales	800,000 sales	400,000 sales
Limited	1,400,000	1,000,000	200,000
Large scale	1,500,000	900,000	-300,000

The figures in the tables are computed as follows:

Decision	State of nature	Conditional Profit	
Limited	1,000,000 sales	(1,000,000)(2)-600,000	=1,400,000
Limited	800,000 sales	(800,000)(2)-600,000	=1,000,000
Limited	400,000 sales	(400,000)(2)-600,000	= 200,000
Large scale	1,000,000 sales	(1,000,000)(3)-1,500,000	=1,500,000
Large scale	800,000 sales	(800,000)(3)-1,500,000	= 900,000
Large scale	400,000 sales	(400,000)(3)-1,500,000	= -300,000

The expected value of annual profit for each alternative
is:

Alternative	Expected annual profit (in millions)
Limited production	(1.4)(.40)+(1.0)(.45)+(.2)(.15) = $1.04
Large-scale prod.	(1.5)(.40)+(.9)(.45)+(-.3)(.15) = $0.96

The company president will choose limited production.

4-15 First we apply dominance reduction. We find that the
decisions of issuing 8000 and 9000 licenses are dominated
by the decision to issue 7000 licenses since the moose
population would be less regardless of the state of nature
encountered. The 8000 and 9000 license decisions are
therefore eliminated.

$$\text{EV pop}|5000 \text{ lic} = (38)(.20) + (35)(.30) + (28)(.40)$$
$$+ (22)(.10)$$
$$= 31.5$$
$$\text{EV pop}|6000 \text{ lic} = (36)(.20) + (33)(.30) + (30)(.40)$$
$$+ (26)(.10)$$
$$= 31.7$$
$$\text{EV pop}|7000 \text{ lic} = (34)(.20) + (33)(.30) + (32)(.40)$$
$$+ (30)(.10)$$
$$= 32.5$$

The optimum decision decision is to issue 7000 licenses,
and the expected springtime size of the moose population is
32 thousand animals.

4-16   The conditional loss table is:

Possible demand	Possible stock action			
	20	25	40	60
20	0	10	40	80
25	10	0	30	70
40	40	30	0	40
60	80	70	40	0

EL|20 stocked = (0)(.10) + (10)(.30) + (40)(.50) + (80)(.10)
      = \$31

EL|25 stocked = (10)(.10) + (0)(.30) + (30)(.50) + (70)(.10)
      = \$23

EL|40 stocked = (40).10) + (30)(.30) + (0)(.50) + (40)(.10)
      = \$17

EL|60 stocked = (80)(.10) + (70)(.30) + (40)(.50) + (0)(.10)
      = \$49

The optimum action is to stock 40 mangoes for an expected loss of \$17. The EVPI = \$17 per week.

4-17   The conditional loss table is:

Possible demand	Possible stock action				
	100	200	300	400	500
100	0	2000	4000	6000	8000
200	3500	0	2000	4000	6000
300	7000	3500	0	2000	4000
400	10500	7000	3500	0	2000
500	14000	10500	7000	3500	0

EL|100 stocked = (0)(.20) + (3500)(.30) + (7000)(.30)
      + (10500)(.15) + (14000)(.05)
      = \$5425

EL|200 stocked = (2000)(.20) + (0)(.30) + (3500)(.30)
      + (7000)(.15) + (10500)(.05)
      = \$3025

EL|300 stocked = (4000)(.20) + (2000)(.30) + (0)(.30)
      + (3500)(.15) + (7000)(.05)
      = \$2275

```
EL|400 stocked = (6000)(.20) + (4000)(.30) + (2000)(.30)
                 + (0)(.15) + (3500)(.05)
               = $3175

EL|500 stocked = (8000)(.20) + (6000)(.30) + (4000)(.30)
                 + (2000)(.15) + (0)(.05)
               = $4900
```

The optimal action is to stock 300 swimsuits for an
expected loss of $2275.
The EVPI is also $2275.

4-18   The table of conditional losses is:

Kilograms demanded	Stocking decisions (kilograms)		
	6000	8000	10000
6000	0	300	600
8000	1300	0	300
10000	2600	1300	0

```
EV loss|stock 6000  = (0)(.20) + (1300)(.60) + (2600)(.20)
                    = $1300
EV loss|stock 8000  = (300)(.20) + (0)(.60) + (1300)(.20)
                    = $320
EV loss|stock 10000 = (600)(.20)+ (300)(.60) + (0)(.20)
                    = $300
```

The optimum decision is to stock 10,000 kilograms of
sausage at an expected loss of $300. The expected value of
perfect information is $300.

4-19   MP = 16 - 9 = $7 per dose
       ML = $9 per dose

From equation (4-2) we obtain the probability:

$$P = \frac{ML}{MP+ML} = \frac{9}{9+7} = .5625$$

The optimal action is to stock 40 doses per week since the
cumulative probability of this outcome (.70) is greater
than .5625.

4-20   Using marginal analysis we find:

       ML = $4 per pound
       MP = 7.50 - 4 = $3.50 per pound

Using equation (5-2) we find:

$$p = \frac{ML}{MP+ML} = \frac{4}{3.5+4} = .5333$$

The company's optimal action is to stock 12,000 pounds (cumulative probability = .55).

The conditional payoffs for stocking 12,000 pounds are:

	Possible demand				
Action	3,000	5,000	8,000	12,000	18,000
Stock 12,000	-$25,500	-$10,500	$12,000	$42,000	$42,000

The expected profit given a stock level of 12,000 pounds is:

$$\text{EP}|12,000 \text{ pounds} = (-25.5)(.05) + (-10.5)(.20) +$$
$$(12)(.20) + (42)(.40) + (42)(.15)$$
$$= \$22,125 \text{ per week}$$

Given perfect information the conditional payoffs are:

Demand and Stock	Payoff
3000	$10,500
5000	17,500
8000	28,000
12000	42,000
18000	63,000

And,
$$\text{EP}|\text{PI} = (10.5)(.05) + (17.5)(.20) + (28)(.20) + (42)(.40)$$
$$+ (63)(.15)$$
$$= \$35,875 \text{ per week}$$

The expected value of perfect information is:

$$\text{EVPI} = 38,875 - 22,125 = \$13,750 \text{ per week.}$$

Assuming the forecasting model can provide perfect forecasts for $7,500 a week, the company would be better off using the model.

4-21

Pounds Demanded	Cumulative probability that sales will be at this level or greater
20	1.00
21	.90
22	.78
23	.65
24	.53
25	.42
26	.32
27	.23
28	.15
29	.08
30	.03

$$p = \frac{ML}{MP + ML} = \frac{.27}{.37 + .27} = .422$$

Her optimum decision is to stock 25 pounds of haddock which has a cumulative probability of .42.

4-22 For this problem, we use marginal analysis where:

$$MP = 10 - 4 = \$6 \text{ per pound}$$
$$ML = 4 - 2 = \$2 \text{ per pound}$$

The minimum probability from equation (4-2) is:

$$p = \frac{ML}{MP+ML} = \frac{2}{6+2} = .25$$

This means it is optimal to stock at a level where .75 of the area lies to the left of the normal curve. From Appendix Table 1 we find that this point is associated with $z = .67$ standard deviations to the right of the mean. Our optimum stock level is:

$$\text{Stock} = \text{mean} + .67(\text{std. dev.}) = 5000 + (.67)(425)$$
$$= 5285 \text{ pounds}$$

4-23 We approach this problem using marginal analysis.

The marginal profit (MP) for loaves sold is:

$$MP = .95 - .50 = \$.45$$

The marginal loss (ML) for loaves unsold is:

$$ML = .50 - .35 = \$.15$$

Therefore, the minimum required cumulative probability is found by the equation:

$$p = \frac{ML}{MP + ML} = \frac{.15}{.45 + .15} = .250$$

We now look in Appendix Table 1 (for 1 - .250, or .750) to find the number of standard deviations to the right of the mean corresponding to the area .750. This is Z = .67 standard deviations.

The daily production level of loaves of bread, Q, is now found to be:

$$Q = \text{mean} + .67 \text{ standard deviations}$$
$$= 6000 \text{ loaves} + (.67)(900 \text{ loaves})$$
$$= 6603 \text{ loaves}$$

4-24 The table of conditional expenses is as follows:

Possible demand	Possible actions (meals prepared)				
	8	9	10	11	12
8	24	29	34	39	44
9	30	27	32	37	42
10	36	33	30	35	40
11	42	39	36	33	38
12	48	45	42	39	36

Using the criterion of rationality, we assume that each of the possible demands is equally probable. Therefore, we assign a probability of .20 to each of the five. Now we may compute expected expenses for each action as follows:

$$EE|8 = (.2)(24) + (.2)(30) + (.2)(36) + (.2)(42) + (.2)(48)$$
$$= \$36.00$$

$$EE|9 = (.2)(29) + (.2)(27) + (.2)(33) + (.2)(39) + (.2)(45)$$
$$= \$34.60$$

Computed in a similar fashion:

$$EE|10 = \$34.80$$
$$EE|11 = \$36.60$$
$$EE|12 = \$40.00$$

The optimal action which minimizes expected expense is to prepare 9 meals.

4-25   Using the criterion of maximum likelihood, we first select
        the outcome which has the highest probability of occurring.
        This is associated with a demand of 4 golf bags
        (probability of .4).
        Now, we select the highest payoff associated with this
        outcome--in this case, the maximum payoff is $100 if we
        stock 4 golf bags. The action of stocking 4 golf bags is
        an optimal action for a maximum likelihood criterion.

4-26   From equation (4-3), the combined mean is:

$$\hat{\mu} = \frac{\dfrac{200}{50^2} + \dfrac{160}{70^2}}{\dfrac{1}{50^2} + \dfrac{1}{70^2}}$$

$\hat{\mu}$ = 186.486 or 186,486 miles.

From equation (4-4), the combined standard deviation is:

$$\hat{\sigma} = \frac{1.4142136}{\sqrt{\dfrac{1}{50^2} + \dfrac{1}{70^2}}}$$

$\hat{\sigma}$ = 57.539 or 57,539 miles.

4-27   We use equations (4-3) and (4-4) to compute a combined mean
        and standard deviation.

com. est. of mean $= \dfrac{(230)(1/60)^2 + (280)(1/50)^2 + (220)(1/60)^2}{1/60^2 + 1/50^2 + 1/60^2}$

= 248 units.

and,

combined standard deviation $= \dfrac{\sqrt{3}}{\sqrt{1/60^2 + 1/50^2 + 1/60^2}}$

= 56 units.

4-28   From question a, where p = .9, we find:

        Utility of $20,000 = (.9)(10) + (.1)(0) = 9

From question b, where p = .8, we find:

        Utility of $10,000 = (.8)(10) + (.2)(0) = 8

From question c, where p = .4, we find:

Utility of -$10,000 = (.4)(10) + (.6)(0) = 4

Jamie's utility curve looks something like this:

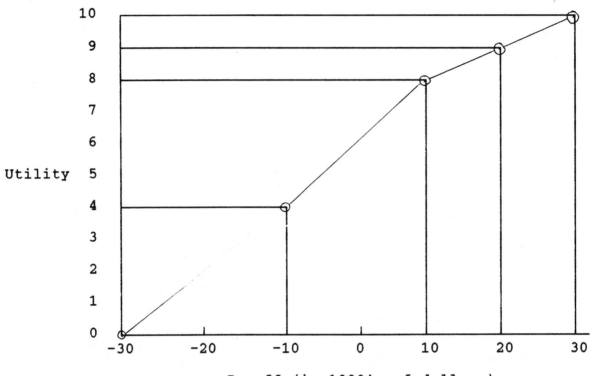

Payoff (in 1000's of dollars)

This curve shows Jamie to be slightly risk averse because his utility curve bows upward above the expected value line connecting the end points of the curve.

4-29 The utility curve would be approximately as follows:

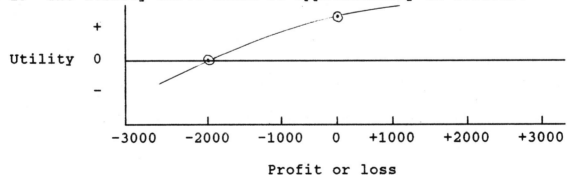

Profit or loss

4-30 The table of conditional utility values is as follows:

Possible outcomes	Prob	Possible actions					
		all A	all B	½A	½B	½A & ½B	none
A win; B win	.36	1	1	.9	.9	1	.4
A win; B lose	.24	1	0	.9	.2	.7	.4
A lose; B win	.24	0	1	.2	.9	.7	.4
A lose; B lose	.16	0	0	.2	.2	0	.4

Now, for each action we may compute the expected utility.

$$EU|\text{all A} = (.36)(1) + (.24)(1) + (.24)(0) + (.16)(0) = .600$$

$$EU|\text{all B} = (.36)(1) + (.24)(0) + (.24)(1) + (.16)(0) = .600$$

$$EU|\text{½A} = (.36)(.9) + (.24)(9) + (.24)(2) + (.16)(.2) = .620$$

$$EU|\text{½B} = (.36)(.9) + (.24)(2) + (.24)(9) + (.16)(.2) = .620$$

$$EU|\text{½A \& ½B} = (.36)(1) + (.24)(.7) + (.24)(.7) + (.16)(0) = .696$$

$$EU|\text{none} = .40$$

The optimal action which maximizes utility is to invest half the $10,000 in A and half in B.

4-31 We let c = commercial property; and s = stocks. The table of conditional utility values is:

Possible outcomes	Prob	Possible actions					
		all C	all S	½C	½S	½C & ½S	none
C win; S win	.15	1	1	.8	.8	1	.4
C win; S lose	.35	1	0	.8	.2	.6	.4
C lose; S win	.15	0	1	.2	.8	.6	.4
C lose; S lose	.35	0	0	.2	.2	0	.4

Now, we compute the expected utility for each action:

$$EV|\text{all C} = (.15)(1) + (.35)(1) + (.15)(0) + (.35)(0) = .50$$

$$EV|\text{all S} = (.15)(1) + (.35)(0) + (.15)(1) + (.35)(0) = .30$$

$$EV|\text{½C} = (.15)(.8) + (.35)(.8) + (.15)(.2) + (.35)(.2) = .50$$

$$EV|\text{½S} = (.15)(.8) + (.35)(.2) + (.15)(.8) + (.35)(.2) = .38$$

$$EV|\text{½C \& ½S} = (.15)(1) + (.35)(.6) + (.15)(.6) + (.35)(0) = .45$$

$$EV|\text{none} = .40$$

The investor's optimal actions to maximize utility are to either invest all in commercial property or invest half in commercial property.

4-32 The subjective estimate given by June Baer is:

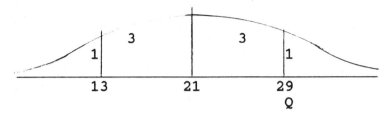

Point Q is where $\frac{1+3+3}{1+3+3+1}$ = .875 (area lying to the left).

From Appendix Table 1, we find point Q is about 1.15 standard deviations to the right of the mean. June's estimate of standard deviations is therefore:

$$1 \text{ standard deviation} = \frac{8}{1.15} = 6.957 \text{ passengers}$$

Our two estimates are now:

Source	Mean	Std. dev.	(Std. dev.)²	$\frac{1}{(\text{Std. dev.})^2}$
Other airline	18	7.4	54.76	.01826
June Baer	21	6.957	48.40	.02066

Using equation (4-3), we find the combined mean:

$$\text{combined mean} = \frac{(18)(.01826) + (21)(.02066)}{.01826 + .02066}$$
$$= 19.59$$

Now, using equation (5-4), we obtain the combined standard deviation:

$$\text{combined std. dev.} = \frac{\sqrt{2}}{\sqrt{.01826 + .02066}} = 7.17$$

4-33 The estimates are generally as follows:

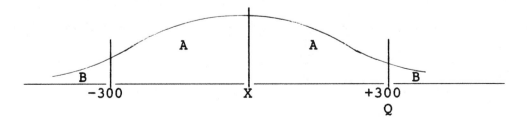

For each supervisor, the estimated average operating hours is an estimate of point X. The odds given by each supervisor are the ratio A:B.

Now we may estimate the number of standard deviations point Q is to the right of the mean, X, as follows:

Superv.	Estimate of mean	Area to the left of point Q	From App. Table 1 Point Q is Z std. dev. from mean	Est. of std.dev.
1	1200	11/12=.9167	1.38	300/1.38=217.4
2	1400	11/16=.6875	0.49	300/.49=612.2
3	2000	3/4=.75	0.67	300/.67=447.8
4	1000	13/18=.7222	0.59	300/.59=508.5
5	1600	7/10=.7000	0.52	300/.52=576.9

4-34

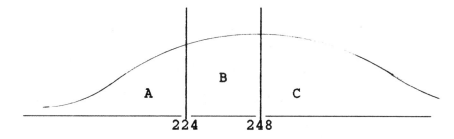

We wish to find A, the area to the left of 224 units. The number of standard deviations between 224 and 248 is:

$$Z = \frac{248-224}{56} = .4286 \approx .43$$

When we look up a Z = .43 in Appendix Table 1, we are reading the area to the left of a point which is .43 standard deviations to the right of the mean. This is the mirror image of the area (B + C). We read this value B + C = .66640.

Therefore, area A = 1 - .66640 = .3336 or about 1/3.

4-35

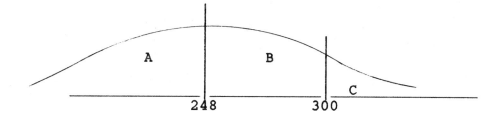

We wish to find area C, the area to the right of 300 units. The number of standard deviations between 248 and 300 is:

$$Z = \frac{300-248}{56} = .9286 \approx .93$$

When we look up a Z = .93 in Appendix Table 1, we are reading the area (A + B), which is .82381.

Therefore, area C = 1 - .82381 = .17619.

4-36

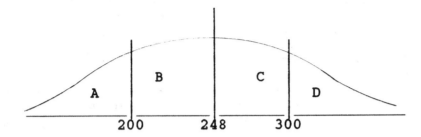

From the previous problem (4-35) the area to the right of 300 units is .17619 (this is shown above as area D).

We now find that 200 units is to the left of the mean by

$$Z = \frac{248 - 200}{56} = .8571 \approx .86 \text{ standard deviations}$$

From Appendix Table 1 at Z = .86 we read .80511, which is the area of (B + C + D). Therefore, area A = 1 - .80511 = .19489
The probability we are looking for is area (B + C), which represents sales between 200 and 300 units.
Area (B + C) = 1 - A - D = 1 - .19489 - .17619 = .62892 or about 63%.

4-37

| Criterion | Choice | | Profit | Person |
	Row	Column		
Maximax	Boom	Complex	85	Al
Maximin	Bust	Simple	5	Betty
Minimax regret	Boom	Medium	25 regret	Carl

| | Regret Values | | |
	Complex	Medium	Simple
Boom	0	25	65
Stable	5	0	20
Bust	35	5	0

4-38   The measures of realism are:

Decision	Measure of realism
Complex	.6(85) + .4(-30) = 39
Medium	.6(60) + .4(0) = 36
Simple	.6(20) + .4(5) = 14

The optimum decision is to go with the complex version as
Al has recommended.

4-39   Assigning probabilities of .33 to each state of nature, the
        expected value of the three possible decisions are:

Decision	Expected Value
Complex	.33(85) + .33(25) + .33(-30) = 26.4
Medium	.33(60) + .33(30) + .33(0) = 29.7
Simple	.33(20) + .33(10) + .33(5) = 11.6

The optimum decision is to adopt the medium product, and
this is consistent with Carl's decision.

4-40   In this problem, the students may have to review their
        understanding of developing posterior probabilities with
        more than two elementary events (Chapter 2 of the text).

We define: B = blown engine
            M = complete overhaul
            m = minor maintenance

We first construct the following table:

Event	P(event)	P(>175|event)	P(>175 and event)
B	.20	.70	.14
M	.30	.60	.18
m	.50	.10	.05
			P(>175) = .37

Our revised probabilities of the three events given that
our speed was in excess of 175 mph are:

$$P(B|>175) = \frac{P(B \text{ and } >175)}{P(>175)} = \frac{.14}{.37} = .378$$

$$P(M|>175) = \frac{P(M \text{ and } >175)}{P(>175)} = \frac{.18}{.37} = .486$$

$$P(m|>175) = \frac{P(m \text{ and } >175)}{P(>175)} = \frac{.05}{.37} = .135$$

Now, we may compute the expected cost, EC.

$$EC|{>}175 = (.378)(5000) + (.486)(2000) + (.135)(0)$$
$$= \$2862.$$

4-41 The minimum probability is:

$$p = \frac{ML}{MP+ML} = \frac{3}{2+3} = .6$$

Our stock point is 1 - .6 = .4, or an area of .1 to the
left of the mean. From Appendix 1, at an area of .600, we
have about 0.26 standard deviations. We should stock:

$$\mu - .26\sigma = 600 - (.26)(250) = 535 \text{ shirts.}$$

4-42 We define the breakeven probability as p. Our table of
conditional profit is:

| Possible | Possible actions | |
event	out of town	in town
breakdown	20	60
no breakdown	200	90

Now we lay out expected value equations for the actions.
$$EV|\text{out of town} = 20p + 200(1-p)$$
$$EV|\text{in town} \quad = 60p + 90(1-p)$$

Our breakeven condition is met when the two expected values
are equal. Setting the two equations equal and solving for
p, we obtain:

$$20p + 200(1-p) = 60p + 90(1-p)$$
$$20p + 200 - 200p = 60p + 90 - 90p$$
$$150p = 110$$
$$p = .733$$

He will be indifferent when the probability of breakdown is
.733.

4-43 First we create a payoff table of conditional profits:

| Decision maker's | States of nature, price/share at exp. | | | | | |
alternatives	42	48	52	56	60	64
2-month option	-400	-400	0	400	800	1200
4-month option	-800	-800	-400	0	400	800
Neither option	0	0	0	0	0	0

The conditional profits (100 shares) were computed as follows:

Alternat.	State of nature selling price	Purch. stock	Purch. option	Net gain or loss
2-month	4200	*	400	-400
2-month	4800	*	400	-400
2-month	5200	4800	400	0
2-month	5600	4800	400	400
2-month	6000	4800	400	800
2-month	6400	4800	400	1200
4-month	4200	*	800	-800
4-month	4800	*	800	-800
4-month	5200	4800	800	-400
4-month	5600	4800	800	0
4-month	6000	4800	800	400
4-month	6400	4800	800	800

Now we convert the payoff table to values of utility:

Decision maker's alternatives	States of nature, price/share at exp.					
	42	48	52	56	60	64
2-month option	.1	.1	.6	.7	.8	1.0
4-month option	0	0	.1	.6	.7	.8
Neither option	.6	.6	.6	.6	.6	.6

The expected values of utility are:

Alternative	Expected value of utility
2-month option	(.1)(.05) + (.1)(.1) + (.6)(.15) + (.7)(.2) + (.8)(.5) + (1.0)(0) = .645
4-month option	(0)(0) + (0)(.05) + (.1)(.10) + (.6)(.15) + (.7)(.30) + (.8)(.40) = .630
Neither option	= .600

The investor should purchase 100 options to expire in 2 months.

4-44 First, we determine the distribution of each broker, we assume that the selling price in 6 months is normally distributed.

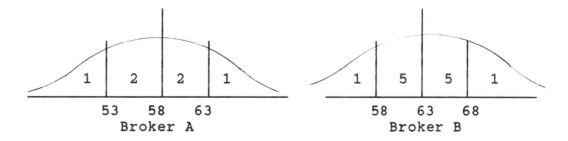

Broker A   Broker B

69

For Broker A, the area to the left of $63 a share is:

$$\frac{1 + 2 + 2}{1 + 2 + 2 + 1} = .8333$$

And from Appendix Table 1, we find that this corresponds to a .97 standard deviation. Consequently, for Broker A, one standard deviation is:

$$\frac{5}{.97} = \$5.15/\text{share}$$

For Broker B, the area to the left of $68 a share is

$$\frac{1 + 5 + 5}{1 + 5 + 5 + 1} = .9167$$

And from Appendix Table 1, we find that this corresponds to 1.38 standard deviations. Consequently, for Broker B, one standard deviation is:

$$\frac{5}{1.38} = \$3.62/\text{share}$$

We combine broker A's distribution (mean = $58, standard deviation = $5.15) with broker B's distribution (mean = $63, standard deviation = $3.62):

$$\text{Combined mean estimate} = \frac{(58)\dfrac{1}{(5.15)^2} + (63)\dfrac{1}{(3.62)^2}}{\dfrac{1}{(5.15)^2} + \dfrac{1}{(3.62)^2}} = \frac{6.9944}{.1140}$$

$$= \$61.35/\text{share}$$

$$\text{Combined std. dev.} = \sqrt{\frac{\sqrt{2}}{\dfrac{1}{(5.15)^2} + \dfrac{1}{(3.62)^2}}} = \frac{1.4142}{.3377}$$

$$= \$4.19/\text{share}$$

Now we compute the probability that the price of Warner will be $60 or greater. The value $60 is less than the mean ($61.35) by:

$$\frac{61.35 - 60}{4.19} = .32 \text{ standard deviations}$$

From Appendix Table 1, this corresponds to an area of .62552. Therefore, the probability of selling at $60 or more is 62.552%, which is greater than our requirement of 60%. You should buy the stock.

CHAPTER 5

DECISION MAKING

USING

PROBABILITIES II

5-1 Using the techniques presented in Chapter 4, we find the
estimated distribution is:

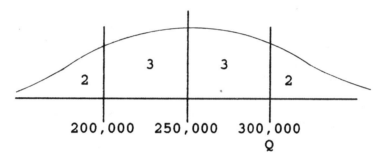

The area to the left of point Q is $\dfrac{2 + 3 + 3}{2 + 3 + 3 + 2}$ = .8000.

From Appendix Table 1 we read Z ≈ .84 standard deviations.

Therefore, 1 std. dev. = $\dfrac{300,000 - 250,000}{.84}$ = 59,524 units.

At a savings of 6 cents per unit, we would have to produce:
$\dfrac{12,000}{.06}$ = 200,000 units in order to offset the cost.

The breakeven point of 200,000 is 50,000 units to the left
of the mean or:

$$Z = \frac{50,000}{59,524} = .84 \text{ standard deviations.}$$

This area, we know from before, is .8000. The probability
of producing less than 200,000 units is 1 - .8 = .20,
or 20%.

5-2 We compute the breakeven point using equation (5-1).

$$B.E. = \frac{250,000}{11 - 6.60} = 56,818.18 \text{ units}$$

The expected profit is computed using the equation:

    Expected profit = expected sales x contribution/unit
                      - fixed cost
    Expected profit = (200,000)(11 - 6.60) - 50,000
    Expected profit = $630,000 per year

ACME will lose money if sales are below 56,818 units or Area A.

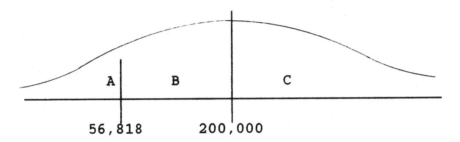

A sales volume of 56,818 is $Z = \dfrac{200,000 - 56,818}{85,000} = 1.68$ standard deviations below the mean. From Appendix Table 1 we read the area (B + C) as .95352.

Therefore, the probability of losing money on this product is 1 - .95352 = .04648, or about 4.6%.

5-3 In order to break even on the fixed cost, the plant must produce $\frac{840,000}{5} = 168,000$ units.

The estimated distribution of production is:

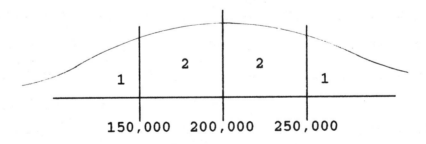

The area to the left of $Q = \dfrac{1 + 2 + 2}{1 + 2 + 2 + 1} = .83333$

From Appendix Table 1 we read Z = .97.

Therefore, 1 std. dev. = $\dfrac{250,000 - 200,000}{.97}$ = 51,546.39 units.

Now our problem is to find the probability of operating below breakeven which is area A in the curve:

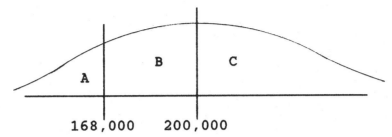

The breakeven is left of the mean by Z = $\dfrac{200,000 - 168,000}{51,546.39}$

so, Z = .62 standard deviations.

From Appendix Table 1 we read area (B + C) = .73237.

Area A = 1 - .73237 = .26763 or about 26.76%.

5-4   Twice the cost of the proposal is $250,000, so at a contribution of $.05 per yard, then sales must be at least $\dfrac{250,000}{.05}$ = 5 million yards.

The projected sales, in millions of yards, are:

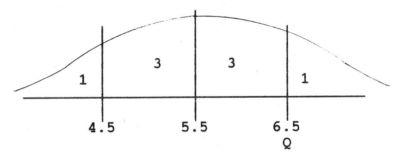

The area to the left of Q = $\dfrac{1 + 3 + 3}{1 + 3 + 3 + 1}$ = .875, which

from Appendix Table 1 is Z = 1.15 standard deviations.

Therefore, 1 std. dev. = $\dfrac{6.5 - 5.5}{1.15}$ = .8696 million yards.

Now our problem is to find areas B and C to the right of the targeted point.

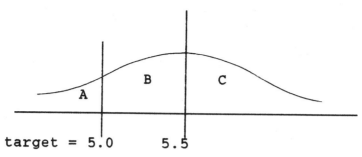

target = 5.0   5.5

At $Z = \dfrac{5.5 - 5.0}{.8696} = .575$, we read area (B + C) = .71735

There is better than a 60% probability of making twice the proposal cost or more.

5-5   The contribution per undergraduate student is:

5000 - 4000 = $1000 per student

The expected profit for the undergraduate program is:

Expected profit = expected enrollment x contribution
- fixed cost
Expected profit = (11,000)(1,000) - 10,000,000
= $1,000,000 (Part a)

At a cost of $1800 per graduate student, the $1,000,000 profit can accommodate:

Breakeven grad. students = $\dfrac{1,000,000}{1800}$ = 556 students
(Part b)

Given the undergraduate enrollment distribution:

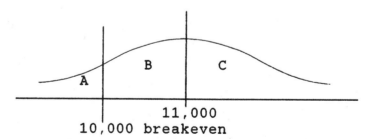

11,000
10,000 breakeven

The breakeven number of undergrads is $\dfrac{10,000,000}{1,000}$ = 10,000 students

This is $\dfrac{11,000 - 10,000}{800}$ = 1.25 standard deviations to the left of the mean

From Appendix Table 1 we read area (B + C) = .89435.

74

Therefore, area A (the probability of a loss) = 1 - .89435
        = .10565 (Part c).

In order to accommodate 1500 graduate students each of whom
costs $1800, we need a profit from the undergraduate
program of:

    (1500)(1800) = $2,700,000

Therefore, we will need:

    Expected profit = Undergrads x contribution/student
                      - fixed costs
        2,700,000 = 1000 x Undergrads - 10,000,000
        Undergrads = 12,700 students

5-6   From Appendix Table 1, we find that the area to the right
of the breakeven point (3125 units) is .9503, or about 95%.
Therefore, there is a 95% probability that usage of IF
modules will be greater than the make-or-buy breakeven
point.

Now we consider the second question regarding the company
policy of producing only when usage has greater than 50%
probability of being 1.5 standard deviations above the
make-or-buy breakeven point.

Usage at 1.5 standard deviations above breakeven is

    Policy point = breakeven point + 1.5 (std. dev.)
               = 3125 + (1.8)(525) = 4070 units

Since this usage (4070 units) is to the right of the
distribution's mean annual usage, there is less than 50%
probability that usage will be 4070 or higher. Therefore,
according to company policy the IF modules should be bought
from the vendor.

5-7   First, we convert the distribution of sales of citizens
band radios into a distribution of IF module usage:

    Mean annual IF usage = 3800 x 1.05 = 3990 units
    Std. dev. of annual IF usage = 500 x 1.05 = 525 units

We now compute the breakeven point in the make-or-buy
decision:

$$\text{Breakeven point} = \frac{\text{total fixed cost}}{\text{buy cost/unit} - \text{variable cost/unit}}$$

$$= \frac{25,000}{20 - 12} = 3125 \text{ units}$$

The breakeven point (3125 units) is to the left of the mean annual usage (3990 units) by 865 units:

$$\text{Std. dev. to the left} = \frac{865}{525} = 1.648 \text{ std. dev.}$$

The expected annual saving is

$$
\begin{aligned}
\text{Expected annual saving} &= \text{expected usage x (buy cost} - \text{variable cost)} - \text{fixed cost} \\
&= 3990(20 - 12) - 25{,}000 \\
&= \$6920/\text{year}
\end{aligned}
$$

In order to compute the expected loss, we need to determine the loss per unit of usage below the breakeven usage of 3125 units. This loss per unit is the difference between the buy cost per unit and the variable production cost per unit, or \$20 per unit - \$12 per unit. Hence, the loss per unit for usage less than 3125 units is \$8 per unit.

Now we compute the number of standard deviations between the mean usage (3990 units) and the breakeven usage (3125 units):

$$\frac{3990 - 3125}{525} = 1.648 \text{ std. dev.}$$

When we refer to Appendix 3, we find that the unit normal loss integral value is .02074.

The expected loss is then computed as the product of the unit loss times the standard deviation of usage times the unit normal loss integral value:

$$
\begin{aligned}
\text{Expected loss} &= \$8 \times 525 \times .02074 \\
&= \$87.11
\end{aligned}
$$

5-8 At a price of \$130 per set, the breakeven point (BE) is

$$
\begin{aligned}
\text{BE at } \$130 &= \frac{\text{total fixed cost}}{\text{price/unit} - \text{variable cost/unit}} \\
&= \frac{125{,}000}{130 - 60} = 1786 \text{ sets}
\end{aligned}
$$

and

$$\text{BE at } \$140 = \frac{125{,}000}{140 - 60} = 1563 \text{ sets}$$

The expected values of profit (EP) are

```
        EP at $130 = expected sales x contribution/unit
                     - fixed cost
                   = 4000 x $70 - $125,000
                   = $155,000/yr

and   EP at $140 = 3200 x $80 - $125,000
                 = $131,000/yr
```

The required annual return on investment is

```
        Required return = .15 x $400,000 = $60,000/yr
```

Now we convert the standard deviations on sales into standard deviations of total contribution:

```
        Std. dev. at $130 = 450 sets x $70 contribution/set
                          = $31,500

and   Std. dev. at $140 = 300 sets x $80 contribution/set
                        = $24,000
```

The required return, $60,000, lies to the left of both profit means ($155,000 at a price of $130 and $131,000 at a price of $140). Standard deviations to the left are

$$\text{Std. dev. to left at \$130} = \frac{155,000 - 60,000}{31,500} = 3.02$$

$$\text{Std. dev. to left at \$140} = \frac{131,000 - 60,000}{24,000} = 2.96$$

which from Appendix Table 1 corresponds to areas:

```
        Area at $130 = .99874
        Area at $140 = .99846
```

With either price there is better than 99% probability that the required 15% return will be satisfied. The company should proceed with this venture and sell the product at $130 per pair, because the expected profit is higher at that price.

5-9

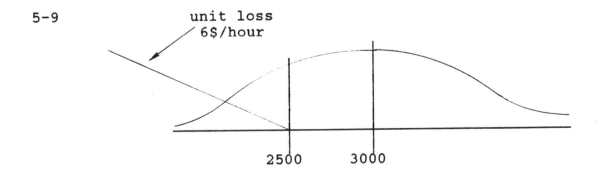

Step 1. $Z = \dfrac{3000 - 2500}{800} = .625$ standard deviations.

Step 2. From Appendix Table 4, we read the unit lost integral, UNLI = .1620

Step 3. The expected loss is: ($6)(800)(.1620) = $777.60

5-10 Our distribution is:

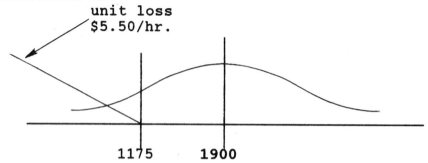

Step 1. Determine the number of standard deviations between the mean and the breakeven.

$Z = \dfrac{1900 - 1175}{400} = 1.81$ standard deviations

Step 2. From Appendix Table 3, we read a unit loss integral value of .01392

Step 3. Compute the total expected loss as:

Expected loss = (5.50)(400)(.01392) = $30.62

5-11 Step 1. We find now:

$Z = \dfrac{1900 - 1175}{170} = 4.26$ standard deviations

Step 2. From Appendix Table 3, we read:

UNLI = .000002188

Step 3. The new expected loss is:

Expected loss = (5.50)(170)(.000002188) = $.0020

Therefore, the new information is worth EVSI = 30.62 −.0020 ≈ $30.62. And, for a cost of $50, it would not pay to develop the new information.

5-12 The procedure is as follows:

| Step 1 | Step 2 |
| Expected loss | Expected profit |

a. $\dfrac{1900-1175}{400} = 1.81$ std. dev.   a. Also 1.81 std. dev.

b. From Appendix Table 3   b. Also, UNLI = .01392
   UNLI = .01392   .01392
                                                +1.81
                                               ─────────
                                                1.82392

c. Expected loss: c. Expected profit:
   (5.50)(400)(.01392) =   (8)(400)(1.82392) =
        $30.62 $5836.54

Subtracting the two results gives:

   Expected net profit = 5836.54 - 30.62 = $5805.92

At 14% of the $80,000 investment our required return is $11,200, which is greater than the expected net profit of $5805.92. Consequently, the company should not consider purchasing the machine.

5-13

| Step 1 | Step 2 |
| Expected loss | Expected profit |

a. $\dfrac{3600-2800}{300} = 2.67$ std. dev.   a. Also 2.67 std. dev.

b. From Appendix Table 3   b. Also, UNLI = .001169
   UNLI = .001169   .001169
                                                +2.67
                                               ─────────
                                                2.671169

c. Expected loss: c. Expected profit:
   (8)(300)(.001169) =   (14)(300)(2.671169) =
        $2.81 $11,218.91

Subtracting the two results gives:

   Expected net profit = 11,218.91 - 2.81 = $11,216.10

5-14 From the estimates given and assuming demand is normally distributed:

Daily mean = 10 units/day and odds of 3:1 that demand is within 6 to 14 units/day. We find point Q on the distribution:

$$Q = \frac{1 + 3 + 3}{1 + 3 + 3 + 1} = .875 \text{ where } Q = 14 \text{ units rented}$$

From Appendix 1 at .875 area, we read z = 1.15 std. dev.

Consequently, 1 std. dev. = $\dfrac{14 - 10}{1.15}$ = 3.48 units

On an annual basis μ = (10)(360) = 3600 units

σ = (3.48)(360) = 1252.8 units

From Appendix 3 at 1.15 std. dev., we read UNLI = .06210

Expected loss	Expected profit
(35)(1252.8)(.06210)	(40)(1252.8)(1.15 + .06210)
= $2723	= $60,741

Expected net profit = 60,741 − 2,723 = $58,018 per year

5-15   With the revised estimate of (2.3)(360) = 828 per year as our std. dev., we have:

$Z = \dfrac{14 - 10}{2.3}$ = 1.74 standard deviations

UNLI = .01658

Expected loss = (35)(828)(.01658) = $480 per year

The reduction is $2,723 − 480 = $2,243 per year, which is greater than the $1500 cost of the survey.

5-16   The expected life of a cutter head is:

Expected life = (.05)(300) +(.15)(600) + (.50)(900)
         + (.30)(1200)
        = 915 hours

If no regular replacement: Cost = (1000/915)($280)(300)
             = $91,803.28 per period

We have arbitrarily assigned the number of cutters to be 1000.
N_0 = 1000
Our equations are:

N_1 = (1000)(.05)   = 50.0
N_2 = (1000)(.15) + (50)(.05)   = 152.5
N_3 = (1000)(.50) + (50)(.15) + (152.5)(.05)= 515.125
N_4 = (1000)(.30) + (50)(.50) + (152.5)(.15)
             + (515.125)(.05) = 373.63125

The costs of the alternatives are:

Replacement at end of	Cost of Replacing 1000 at $30	Expected Failures	Cost of Replacing Failures at $280	Total Cost	Cost per 300 hrs
300 hours	30,000	50.00	14,000	44,000	44,000
600 hours	30,000	202.50	56,700	86,700	43,350
900 hours	30,000	717.625	200,935	230,935	76,978
1200 hours	30,000	1091.25625	305,552	335,552	83,888

We should replace all the cutters after each 600 hours of use.

5-17

$$\text{Expected life} = (1)(.10) + (2)(.05) + (3)(.05) + (4)(.50) + (5)(.30)$$
$$= 3.85 \text{ months}$$

If no regular replacement is made for the 600 loaders, the expected cost is:

$$\text{Cost} = (600/3.85)(80) = \$12,467.53 \text{ per month}$$

With $N_0 = 600$, our equations for monthly failures are:

$$N_1 = (600)(.10) = 60.00$$
$$N_2 = (600)(.05) + (60)(.10) = 36.00$$
$$N_3 = (600)(.05) + (60)(.05) + (36)(.10) = 36.60$$
$$N_4 = (600)(.50) + (60)(.05) + (36)(.05) + (36.6)(.10) = 308.46$$
$$N_5 = (600)(.30) + (60)(.50) + (36)(.05) + (36.6)(.05) + (308.46)(.10) = 244.476$$

The costs of the alternatives are:

Replacement at end of	Cost of Replacing 600 at $40	Expected Failures	Cost of Replacing Failures at $80	Total Cost	Cost per month
1 mo.	24,000	60.000	4,800	28,800	28,800
2 mo.	24,000	96.000	7,680	31,680	15,840
3 mo.	24,000	132.600	10,608	34,608	11,536
4 mo.	24,000	441.060	35,285	59,285	14,821
5 mo.	24,000	685.536	54,843	78,843	15,769

The optimal policy is to replace all loaders at the end of each three-month period.

5-18   Expected life = (1)(.10) + (2)(.10) + (3)(.20)
                        + (4)(.30) + (5)(.30)
                      = 3.6 months

If no regular replacement is made for the 2000 tires, the expected cost is:

Cost = (2000/3.6)(80) = \$44,444.44 per month

With N_0 = 2000, our equations for monthly failures are:

$$
\begin{aligned}
N_1 &= (2000)(.10) & &= 200.00 \\
N_2 &= (2000)(.10) + (200)(.10) & &= 220.00 \\
N_3 &= (2000)(.20) + (200)(.10) + (220)(.10) & &= 442.00 \\
N_4 &= (2000)(.30) + (200)(.20) + (220)(.10) + \\
    & \qquad (442)(.10) & &= 706.20 \\
N_5 &= (2000)(.30) + (200)(.30) + (220)(.20) + \\
    & \qquad (442)(.10) + (706.2)(.10) & &= 818.82
\end{aligned}
$$

The costs of the alternatives are:

Replacement at end of	Cost of Replacing 2000 at \$65	Expected Failures	Cost of Replacing Failures at \$80	Total Cost	Cost per month
1 mo.	130,000	200.00	16,000	146,000	146,000
2 mo.	130,000	420.00	33,600	163,600	81,800
3 mo.	130,000	862.00	68,960	198,960	66,320
4 mo.	130,000	1568.20	125,456	255,456	63,864
5 mo.	130,000	2387.02	190,962	320,962	64,192

The optimal policy is to continue replacement when worn.

5-19   The expected life of a filter unit in hundreds of hours is:

EL = (1)(.01) + (2)(.02) + (3)(.15) + (4)(.30) +
     (5)(.52) = 4.3 hundred hours

If the filters are replaced as they fail, the expected cost is:

EC = (60/4.3)(1000) = \$13,953 per 100 hours

For periodic replacement with N_0 = 60, failures per 100 hours are:

$$
\begin{aligned}
N_1 &= (60)(.01) & &= 0.600 \\
N_2 &= (60)(.02) + (0.6)(.01) & &= 1.206 \\
N_3 &= (60)(.15) + (0.6)(.02) + (1.206)(.01) & &= 9.024 \\
N_4 &= (60)(.30) + (0.6)(.15) + (1.206)(.02) \\
    & \qquad + (9.024)(.01) & &= 18.204 \\
N_5 &= (60)(.52) + (0.6)(.30) + (1.206)(.15) \\
    & \qquad + (9.024)(.02) + (18.204)(.01) & &= 31.923
\end{aligned}
$$

82

The costs of the alternatives are:

Replacement at end of	Cost of Replacing 60 at $20	Expected Failures	Cost of Replacing Failures at $1000	Total Cost	Cost per 100 hrs
1 hundred-hrs	1200	0.600	600	1,800	1,800
2	1200	1.806	1,806	3,006	1,503
3	1200	10.830	10,830	12,030	4,010
4	1200	29.034	29,034	30,234	7,559
5	1200	60.957	60,957	62,157	12,431

The most cost effective policy is to replace all filters at the end of each 200 hours of operation.

5-20

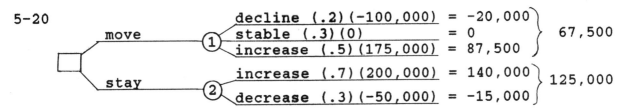

```
                        decline (.2)(-100,000) = -20,000 ⎫
            move        stable  (.3)(0)         = 0        ⎬ 67,500
                   ①   increase (.5)(175,000)  = 87,500   ⎭
  ☐
            stay        increase (.7)(200,000)  = 140,000 ⎫ 125,000
                   ②   decrease (.3)(-50,000)  = -15,000  ⎭
```

The expected value of the decision to stay ($125,000) is higher, so Harry should stay.

5-21

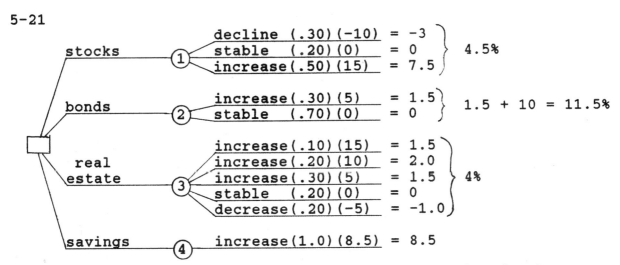

```
            stocks      decline (.30)(-10)  = -3    ⎫
                   ①   stable  (.20)(0)    = 0      ⎬ 4.5%
                        increase(.50)(15)   = 7.5   ⎭

            bonds       increase(.30)(5)    = 1.5   ⎫ 1.5 + 10 = 11.5%
                   ②   stable  (.70)(0)    = 0      ⎭

  ☐                     increase(.10)(15)   = 1.5   ⎫
            real        increase(.20)(10)   = 2.0   ⎪
            estate      increase(.30)(5)    = 1.5   ⎬ 4%
                   ③   stable  (.20)(0)    = 0      ⎪
                        decrease(.20)(-5)   = -1.0  ⎭

            savings     increase(1.0)(8.5)  = 8.5
                   ④
```

The investment with the highest expected value is the bonds.

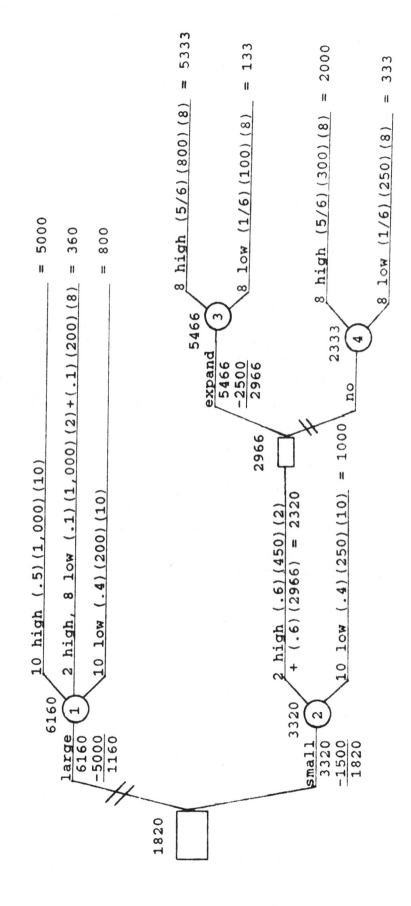

The expected value of a large plant is $1,160,000, whereas the expected value of a small plant is $1,820,100. Therefore, the small plant should be built. If demand is high in the first two years, the plant should be expanded.

5-23 First we compute the posterior probabilities.

Favorable report

Event	P(event)	P(report|event)	P(report,event)	P(event|report)
Low	.2	.2	.04	.07
Moderate	.5	.6	.30	.49
High	.3	.9	.27	.44

P(favorable) = .61

Unfavorable report

Event	P(event)	P(report|event)	P(report,event)	P(event|report)
Low	.2	.8	.16	.41
Moderate	.5	.4	.20	.51
High	.3	.1	.03	.08

P(unfavorable) = .39

payoffs

```
                                                      sell patents          1-.25=.75
                            (.61)
                  favorable  [4]
                  3.644                        low  (.07)  -2.5-.25=-2.75
                                    produce (6) mod. (.49)   1.3-.25=1.05
                                    3.644     high (.44)     7.8-.25=7.55
        survey (2)
        2.515                                 sell patents          .75
                            (.39)
                  unfavorable [5]
                  .75                          low  (.41     -2.75
                                    produce (7) mod. (.51)    1.05
                                    .012      high (.08)      7.55

                                              sell patents         1.00
 [1]
                  no survey  [3]              low  (.20)     -2.50
                  2.490             produce (8) mod. (.50)    1.30
                                    2.490     high (.30)      7.80
```

The optimum course of action is to conduct the survey. If
the survey result is favorable, the product should be
produced. If the survey is unfavorable, the product should
not be produced, and the patents should be sold.

5-24

a. $\begin{bmatrix} 7 & -9 \\ 4 & \boxed{-2} \end{bmatrix}$ Strategy X,2; Y,2; game value: -2

b. No saddle point

c. $\begin{bmatrix} \boxed{1} & 3 \\ -2 & 4 \end{bmatrix}$ Strategy X,1; Y,1; game value: 1

d. No saddle point

e. No saddle point

f. $\begin{bmatrix} 5 & \boxed{3} \\ 2 & 1 \end{bmatrix}$ Strategy X,1; Y,2; game value: 3

5-25

$$\begin{array}{c} \\ Q \\ 1-Q \end{array} \begin{array}{cc} P & 1-P \\ \begin{bmatrix} 8 & -3 \\ -4 & 2 \end{bmatrix} \end{array}$$

Our equation for X's strategy is:

$$8Q + (-4)(1-Q) = -3Q + 2(1-Q)$$
$$Q = 6/17$$
$$\text{and, } 1-Q = 11/17$$

For player Y, the equation is:

$$8p + (-3)(1-P) = -4P + 2(1-P)$$
$$P = 5/17$$
$$\text{and, } 1-P = 12/17$$

5-26 The expected payoff equation is:

$$5/17[(8)(6/17) + (-4)(11/17)] + 12/17[(-3)(6/17) + (2)(11/17)]$$
$$5/17(4/17) + 12/17(4/17) = 68/289.$$

The value of the game is 4/17.

5-27 The joint probability for each payoff is:

Payoff value	Strategies which produce this payoff	Probability of this payoff
8	Row 1, col 1	(6/17)(5/17) = 30/289
-3	Row 1, col 2	(6/17)(12/17) = 72/289
-4	Row 2, col 1	(11/17)(5/17) = 55/289
2	Row 2, col 2	(11/17)(12/17) = 132/289
		1.0

Now we multiply each payoff by its probability and sum these results:

Payoff	Prob	Result
8	30/289	240/289
-3	72/289	-216/289
-4	55/289	-220/289
2	132/289	240/289
		68/289 = 4/17 game value

5-28

$$\begin{array}{cc} & \begin{array}{cc} P & \quad 1-P \end{array} \\ \begin{array}{c} Q \\ 1-Q \end{array} & \begin{bmatrix} -5 & 10 \\ 8 & 3 \end{bmatrix} \end{array}$$

For the offense: $-5Q + 8(1-Q) = 10Q + 3(1-Q)$
$$Q = .25 \text{ (pass)}$$
$$1-Q = .75 \text{ (rush)}$$

For the defense: $-5P + 10(1-P) = 8P + 3(1-P)$
$$P = .35 \text{ (Blue)}$$
$$1-P = .65 \text{ (Green)}$$

Using joint probabilities, we find the value of the game.

Payoff value	Strategies which produce this payoff	Probability of this payoff
-5	Row 1, col 1	(.25)(.35) = .0875
10	Row 1, col 2	(.25)(.65) = .1625
8	Row 2, col 1	(.75)(.35) = .2625
3	Row 2, col 2	(.75)(.65) = .4875

Payoff x Prob. of payoff

-5	.0875	= -.4375
10	.1625	= 1.6250
8	.2625	= 2.1000
3	.4875	= 1.4625
		4.7500 = yards value of the game

5-29 a. Player Y will not play column 1 because his payoffs are
           equal to or better with column 2 regardless of the row.
           This reduces the matrix to:

$$\begin{bmatrix} 5 & 3 \\ 2 & -2 \\ 4 & 8 \end{bmatrix}$$

Now, we find player X will not play row 2 because his
payoffs are better with either row 1 or 3. Now our
matrix becomes:

$$\begin{bmatrix} 5 & 3 \\ 4 & 8 \end{bmatrix}$$

There is no saddle point.

The optimum strategies are

$$\begin{array}{cc} & P \quad\ 1-P \\ \begin{array}{c} Q \\ 1-Q \end{array} & \begin{bmatrix} 5 & 3 \\ 4 & 8 \end{bmatrix} \end{array}$$

Our equation for X's strategy is:

$$5Q + 4(1-Q) = 3Q + 8(1-Q)$$
$$4 + Q = 8 - 5Q$$
$$6Q = 4$$
$$Q = 2/3$$
$$\text{and, } 1-Q = 1/3$$

For Y, the equation is

$$5P + 3(1-P) = 4P + 8(1-P)$$
$$3 + 2P = 8 - 4P$$
$$6P = 5$$
$$P = 5/6$$
$$\text{and, } 1-P = 1/6$$

Using joint probabilities, we find the value of the game.

Payoff value	Strategies which produce this payoff	Probability of this payoff
5	Row 1, col. 1	(2/3)(5/6) = 10/18
3	Row 1, col. 2	(2/3)(1/6) = 2/18
4	Row 2, col. 1	(1/3)(5/6) = 5/18
8	Row 2, col. 2	(1/3)(1/6) = 1/18

Payoff x Prob. of payoff

Payoff	Prob. of payoff	
5	10/18	= 50/18
3	2/18	= 6/18
4	5/18	= 20/18
8	1/18	= 8/18
		84/18 = game value

b. Player X will not play row 2 because each payoff is less than the corresponding payoff in row 1. The reduced matrix is:

$$\begin{bmatrix} 5 & 2 & 7 \\ -3 & -1 & 8 \end{bmatrix}$$

Player Y will not play column 3 because his payoff is better for either column 1 or 2. Now the matrix becomes:

$$\begin{bmatrix} 5 & ②\ \\ -3 & -1 \end{bmatrix}$$

The strategies are X,1; Y,2; game value: 2

Note: It can also be shown for this problem that the 2 x 2 matrix can reduce to:

$$\begin{bmatrix} 5 & ②\ \\ -5 & 1 \end{bmatrix}$$ The strategies and game value are the
                                    same.

c. Player X is indifferent to rows 1 or 2 since they have identical payoffs. We eliminate one of the rows to obtain:

$$\begin{bmatrix} 3 & 2 & 7 \\ -4 & 3 & 3 \end{bmatrix}$$

Player Y will not play column 3. We now have:

$$\begin{bmatrix} 3 & 2 \\ -4 & 3 \end{bmatrix}$$

There is no saddle point.

The optimum strategies are

$$\begin{array}{cc} & P \quad\quad 1-P \\ \begin{array}{c} Q \\ 1-Q \end{array} & \begin{bmatrix} 3 & 2 \\ -4 & 3 \end{bmatrix} \end{array}$$

Our equation for X's strategy is:

$$3Q + (-4)(1-Q) = 2Q + 3(1-Q)$$
$$-4 + 7Q = 3 - Q$$
$$8Q = 7$$
$$Q = 7/8$$
$$\text{and, } 1-Q = 1/8$$

For Y, the equation is

$$3P + 2(1-P) = -4P + 3(1-P)$$
$$2 + P = 3 - 7P$$
$$8P = 1$$
$$P = 1/8$$
$$\text{and, } 1-P = 7/8$$

Using joint probabilities, we find the value of the game.

Payoff value	Strategies which produce this payoff	Probability of this payoff
3	Row 1, col 1	(7/8)(1/8) = 7/64
2	Row 1, col 2	(7/8)(7/8) = 49/64
-4	Row 2, col 1	(1/8)(1/8) = 1/64
3	Row 2, col 2	(1/8)(7/8) = 7/64

<u>Payoff</u> x <u>Prob. of payoff</u>

3	7/64	= 21/64
2	49/64	= 98/64
-4	1/64	= -4/64
3	7/64	= <u>21/64</u>
		136/64 = 17/8 = game value

5-30   Player X will not play row 2; it is dominated by row 1. This leaves:

$$\begin{bmatrix} 8 & -3 & 7 \\ -2 & 2 & -3 \end{bmatrix}$$

Player Y will not play column 1; it is dominated by column 3. Our reduced 2 x 2 matrix is:

$$\begin{bmatrix} -3 & 7 \\ 2 & -3 \end{bmatrix}$$

Since there is no saddle point, we have a mixed strategy game.

Now computing the optimum mixed strategies:

$$
\begin{array}{cc}
 & \begin{array}{cc} P & 1-P \end{array} \\
\begin{array}{c} Q \\ 1-Q \end{array} &
\left[\begin{array}{cc} -3 & 7 \\ 2 & -3 \end{array} \right]
\end{array}
$$

Our equation for X's strategy is:

$$
\begin{aligned}
-3Q + 2(1-Q) &= 7Q - 3(1-Q) \\
2 - 5Q &= -3 + 10Q \\
15Q &= 5 \\
Q &= 1/3 \\
\text{and, } 1-Q &= 2/3
\end{aligned}
$$

For Y, the equation is:

$$
\begin{aligned}
-3P + 7(1-P) &= 2P - 3(1-P) \\
7 - 10P &= -3 + 5P \\
15P &= 10 \\
P &= 2/3 \\
\text{and, } 1-P &= 1/3
\end{aligned}
$$

5-31 We find the value of the game using joint probabilities.

Payoff value	Strategies which produce this payoff	Probability of this payoff
-3	Row 1, col. 1	$(1/3)(2/3) = 2/9$
7	Row 1, col. 2	$(1/3)(1/3) = 1/9$
2	Row 2, col. 1	$(2/3)(2/3) = 4/9$
-3	Row 2, col. 2	$(2/3)(1/3) = 2/9$
		$= 1$

Payoff x Prob. of payoff

-3	2/9	= -6/9
7	1/9	= 7/9
2	4/9	= 8/9
-3	2/9	= -6/9
		3/9 = 1/3 = value of the game

5-32 The decision tree is:

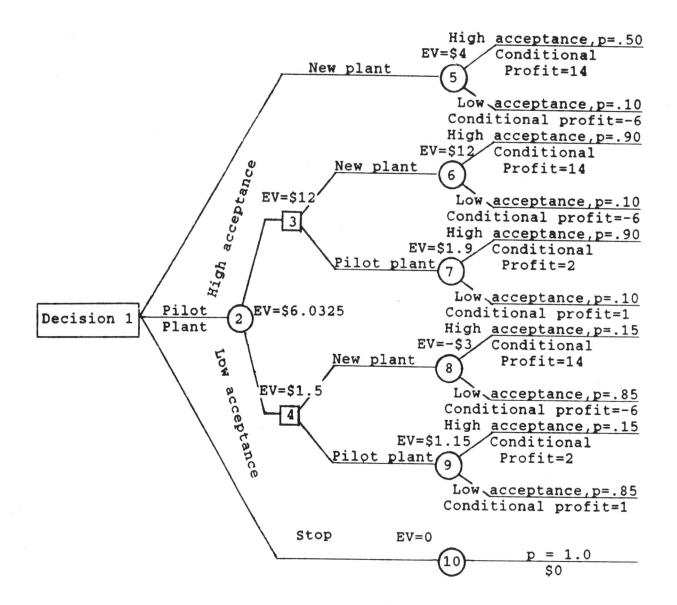

Note that the branches leading to nodes 7 and 8 may be
pruned away. Motor City's optimal decision is to
reconfigure the existing plant facility into a pilot plant
and produce for the coming model year on a limited basis.
The value of information from the pilot plant is $6.0325
million minus $4 million, or $2.0325 million. The cost of
reconfiguring the pilot plant is only $1 million. After
observing consumer behavior for the new pilot models, Motor
City's decision is straightforward. If acceptance is high,
build a new plant; however, if acceptance is low,
production should be continued with the pilot plant.

5-33 First the prior probability estimates are revised based
      upon the observed outcome—— the passage of the new law.

Elementary event	Probability of elementary event	P(law|event)	P(law,event)
Low acceptance	.85	.10	.085
High acceptance	.15	.90	.135
		P(law) =	.220

The new posterior probabilities are

$$P(\text{low acceptance}|\text{law}) = \frac{P(\text{law,low acceptance})}{P(\text{law})}$$

$$= \frac{.085}{.220} = .3864$$

$$P(\text{high acceptance}|\text{law}) = \frac{P(\text{law,high acceptance})}{P(\text{law})}$$

$$= \frac{.135}{.220} = .6136$$

The decision tree at this point is:

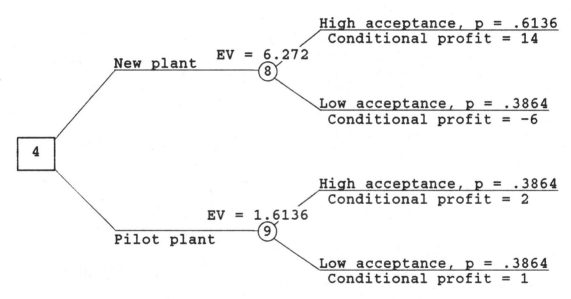

Based on new information, Motor City's optimal decision is
now to proceed with construction of the new plant. The
expected annual profit with this decision is $6.272
million.

5-34 We compute expected profit using the equation:

      Expected profit = expected sales x contribution/unit
                              - fixed cost
      Expected profit = (200,000)(8.95 - 6.29) - 461,000
      Expected profit = $71,000 (Part a)

93

The breakeven point is computed using equation (5-1)

B.E. $= \dfrac{461,000}{8.95 - 6.29} = 173,308$

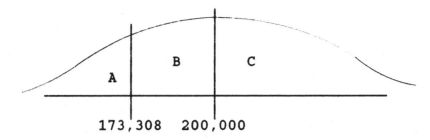

173,308   200,000

The probability of not making breakeven is area A.

We find that the breakeven point is to the left of the mean by:

$$Z = \dfrac{200,000 - 173,308}{40,000} = .67 \text{ standard deviations}$$

From Appendix Table 1 we can read area (B + C) = .74857.

The probability of losing money is 1 − .74857 = .25143 (Part b).

The probability of making a profit between $20,000 and $50,000 is computed by first determining the sales necessary to achieve each of these profit levels.

We use the equation:

Expected profit = expected sales x contribution/unit
− fixed cost

at profit = $20,000
   Sales $= \dfrac{20,000 + 461,000}{2.66} = 180,827$ units

at profit = $50,000
   Sales $= \dfrac{50,000 + 461,000}{2.66} = 192,105$ units

Therefore, we wish to find area B where profits are between 20 and 50 thousand.

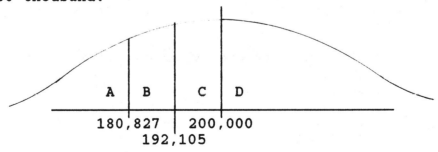

180,827   200,000
192,105

$$\text{at } Z = \frac{200{,}000 - 180{,}827}{40{,}000} = .48, \text{ so areas (BCD)} = .68439$$

$$\text{at } Z = \frac{200{,}000 - 192{,}105}{40{,}000} = .20, \text{ so areas (CD)} = .57926$$

Area B = .68439 - .57926 = .10513 (Part c)

at profit = -$30,000

$$\text{Sales} = \frac{-30{,}000 + 461{,}000}{2.66} = 162{,}030 \text{ units}$$

$$\text{at } Z = \frac{200{,}000 - 162{,}030}{40{,}000} = .95, \text{ so the probability of}$$

profits being -$30,000 or greater is .82894.

Therefore, the probability of losing 30,000 or more is 1 - .82894 = .17106 (Part d).

5-35 Let M = Midtown
J = Jumbo
p = produce
m = meat

		J: p	J: m
M	p	-100	150
	m	150	-200

Now, calling our strategies P and Q we have

	P	1-P
Q	-100	150
1-Q	150	-200

For Midtown: $-100Q + 150(1-Q) = 150Q - 200(1-Q)$

$Q = 7/12$

and, $1-Q = 5/12$

For Jumbo: $-100P + 150(1-P) = 150P - 200(1-P)$

$P = 7/12$

and, $1-P = 5/12$

So, each market should advertize produce seven out of every twelve weeks and meat five out of every twelve weeks.

Using joint probabilities, we find the value of the game.

Payoff value	Strategies which produce this payoff	Probability of this payoff
-100	Row 1, col. 1	(7/12)(7/12) = 49/144
150	Row 1, col. 2	(7/12)(5/12) = 35/144
150	Row 2, col. 1	(5/12)(7/12) = 35/144
-200	Row 2, col. 2	(5/12)(5/12) = 25/144

Payoff x Prob. of payoff

-100	49/144	= -34.03
150	35/144	= 36.46
150	35/144	= 36.46
-200	25/144	= -34.72
		4.17 = game value

In the long run only about 4 shoppers per week are lost to Jumbo Markets.

5-36

Step 1 Expected loss	Step 2 Expected profit
a. $\dfrac{2000 - 1200}{500} = 1.60$ std. dev.	a. Also 1.60 std. dev.
b. From Appendix Table 3 UNLI = .02324	b. Also, UNLI = .02324 $\begin{array}{r} .02324 \\ +1.60 \\ \hline 1.62324 \end{array}$
c. Expected loss: (8.50)(500)(.02324) = $98.77	c. Expected profit: (27)(500)(1.62324) = $21,913.74

Subtracting the two results gives:

Expected net profit = 21,913.74 - 98.77 = $21,814.97

The required return is (.10)(100,000) = $10,000
This would warrant purchase of the machine.

5-37 This problem involves replacement analysis. The data
provided are

N_0 = original number of modules = 60
P_1 = probability of failure during first 100 hr = .10
P_2 = probability of failure during second 100 hr = .15
P_3 = probability of failure during third 100 hr = .20
P_4 = probability of failure during fourth 100 hr = .25
P_5 = probability of failure during fifth 100 hr = .30

The average life expectancy of the 60 modules is

```
.10 x 100 hr =  10 hr
.15 x 200 hr =  30 hr
.20 x 300 hr =  60 hr
.25 x 400 hr = 100 hr
.30 x 500 hr = 150 hr
    Av. life = 350 hr
```

If we replace modules when they fail and start with 60 new
modules, we will replace

$$\frac{60}{350} = .1714 \text{ module/hr}$$

At a replacement cost of $50 per module, the hourly cost
becomes

(.1714)(50) = $8.57/hr, or $857/100 hr

Now we compute the costs if we adopt a periodic replacement
policy. First, we compute the number of modules replaced
every 100 hours:

$N_1 = N_0 \times P_1 = 60 \times .10$ = 6
$N_2 = (N_0 \times P_2) + (N_1 \times P_1)$
$\quad = (60 \times .15) + (6 \times .10)$ = 9.6
$N_3 = (N_0 \times P_3) + (N_1 \times P_2) + (N_2 \times P_1)$
$\quad = (60 \times .20) + (6 \times .15) + (9.6 \times .10)$ = 13.85
$N_4 = (N_0 \times P_4) + (N_1 \times P_3) + (N_2 \times P_2) +$
$\qquad\qquad\qquad\qquad (N_3 \times P_1)$
$\quad = (60 \times .25) + (6 \times .20) + (9.6 \times .15) +$
$\qquad\qquad\qquad\qquad (13.86 \times 1.0)$ = 19.03
$N_5 = (N_0 \times P_5) + (N_1 \times P_4) + (N_2 \times P_3) +$
$\qquad\qquad\qquad\qquad (N_3 \times P_2) + (N_4 \times P_1)$
$\quad = (60 \times .30) + (6 \times .25) + (9.6 \times .20) +$
$\qquad\qquad (13.86 \times .15) + (19.03 \times .10)$ = 25.40

97

Now we compare alternatives.

Replace at at end of	Cost of replacing 60 modules at $35 each	Cost of replacing failed modules at $50 each			Total cost	Cost per 100 hr
100 hr	$2100	6 x 50 =	$ 300		$2400	$2400
200 hr	2100	15.6 x 50 =	780		2880	1440
300 hr	2100	29.46 x 50 =	1473		3573	1191
400 hr	2100	48.49 x 50 =	2425		4525	1131
500 hr	2100	73.89 x 50 =	3695		5795	1159

For this example the expected replacement cost of $857 per 100 hours, which we incur if modules are replaced when they fail, is less costly than a periodic replacement policy.

5-38 Y will not play column 4; it is dominated by column 2. This leaves:

$$\begin{bmatrix} 3 & 2 & -1 \\ 2 & 3 & 2 \\ 1 & -4 & -2 \\ 4 & -1 & -1 \end{bmatrix}$$

X will not play row 3; it is dominated by row 2. This leaves:

$$\begin{bmatrix} 3 & 2 & -1 \\ 2 & 3 & 2 \\ 4 & -1 & -1 \end{bmatrix}$$

Y will not play column 1; it is dominated by column 3. This leaves:

$$\begin{bmatrix} 2 & -1 \\ 3 & 2 \\ -1 & -1 \end{bmatrix}$$

X will not play either row 1 or row 3; both are dominated by row 2. This leaves:

$$\begin{bmatrix} 3 & 2 \end{bmatrix}$$

Y will not play column 1; it is dominated by column 2. This leaves the saddle point. Our problem has a' saddle point circled below:

$$\begin{bmatrix} 3 & 2 & -1 & 3 \\ 2 & 3 & ② & 5 \\ 1 & -4 & -2 & -3 \\ 4 & -1 & -1 & 1 \end{bmatrix}$$

5-39

| | Step 1
Expected loss | Step 2
Expected profit |

a. $\dfrac{10,000 - 8000}{1500} = 1.333$ std. dev.   a. Also 1.333 std. dev.

b. From Appendix Table 3:
      .04270

b. From Appendix Table 3:
      .04270

c. Adding: .04270 +
   1.33333 = 1.37603

d. Expected loss:
   (30)(1500)(.04270) =
   $1,921.50

d. Expected profit:
   (40)(1500)(1.37603) =
   $82,561.80

Expected net profit = 82,561.80 - 1,921.50 = $80,640.30

The offer is eight times the expected annual net profit so:

Offer = (8)(80,640.30) = $645,122.40

5-40

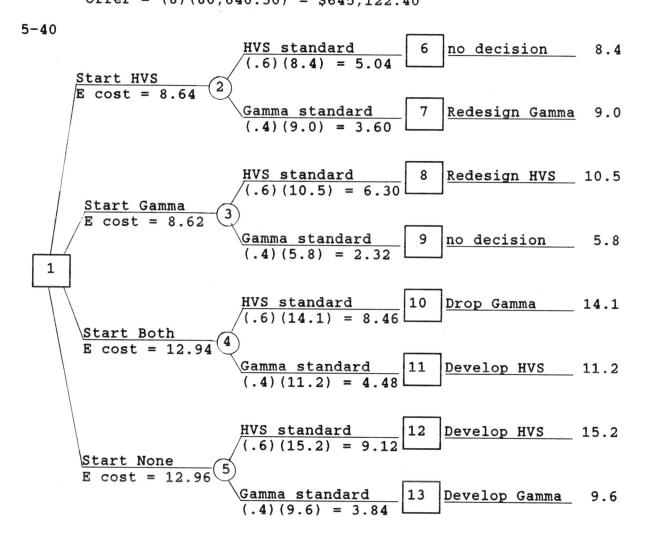

The decision with the lowest expected cost ($8.62 million) is to start development of the Gamma Max design at the current time. This is only slightly better than the decision to start developing the HVS unit, however (cost $8.64 million).

5-41 First we compute posterior probabilities:

		Prefer Soonery Survey Result	
Event	P(event)	P(Soonery|event)	P(Soonery,event)
HVS	.4	.20	.12
Gamma Max	.6	.75	.30
		P(Soonery) =	.42

P(HVS standard\|prefer Soonery)   = .12 ÷ .42 = .286
P(Gamma standard\|prefer Soonery) = .30 ÷ .42 = .714

		Prefer Mitzy Bishi Survey Result	
Event	P(event)	P(Mitzy|event)	P(Mitzy,event)
HVS	.6	.80	.48
Gamma Max	.4	.25	.10
		P(Mitzy Bishi) =	.58

P(HVS standard\|prefer Mitzy Bishi)   = .48 ÷ .58 = .828
P(Gamma standard\|prefer Mitzy Bishi) = .10 ÷ .58 = .172

Since the decision involving starting the design of both Gamma and HVS as well as the decision involving waiting 6 months to decide are all dominated, we consider only decisions "Start HVS design" and "Start Gamma design" in the tree on the following page.

Referring to the decision tree, we observe that the .5 million dollar cost of the survey is worth the money. The company should take the survey. If the results of the survey are "prefer Soonery," then Xerxes should initiate development using the Gamma Max standard. On the other hand, if the survey results are "prefer Mitzy Bishi," development should be initiated using the HVS standard.

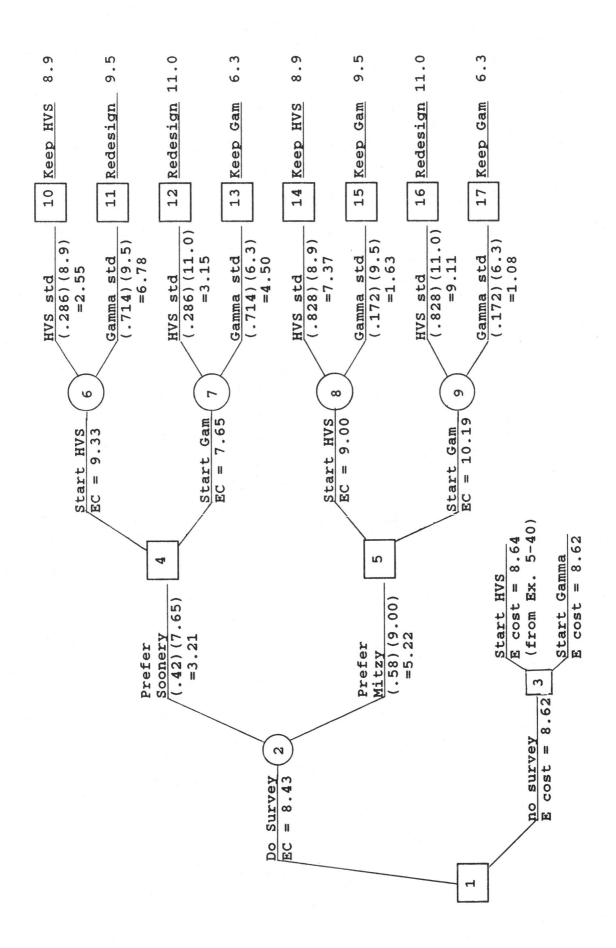

101

CHAPTER 6

INVENTORY I

6-1

Classifi-cation	SKU Number	% of total number	Total Value	% of total value
A	1,8	10	7,004,000	69.98
B	3,5,7,12,16,20	30	2,003,500	20.02
C	2,4,6,9,10,11,13,14, 15,17,18,19	60	1,001,200	10.00

6-2

Classifi-cation	SKU Number	% of total number	Total value	% of total value
A	J-620	12.5	120,000	61.71
B	H-206 KLJ-160	25.0	53,700	27.62
C	F-2130 M-14562 012-76 Z-321 LX-002	62.5	20,750	10.67

6-3 Using equation (6-1):

$$N_0 = \sqrt{\frac{AC}{2P}} = \sqrt{\frac{(220,000)(.18)}{(2)(30)}} = 25.69 \text{ orders per year}$$

6-4 Using equation (6-3):

$$N_\$ = \sqrt{\frac{2AP}{C}} = \sqrt{\frac{(2)(28,000)(48)}{.23}} = \$3418.62 \text{ per order}$$

6-5   Given: A = $96,000 per year
                P = $45 per order
                C = .22 of value per year

We can use equation (6-2) to determine the optimum number
of months' supply:

$$N_d = 12\sqrt{\frac{2P}{AC}} = 12\sqrt{\frac{(2)(45)}{(96,000)(.22)}} = .784 \text{ month's supply}$$

6-6   We use equation (6-2) with:

        A = (5400)(365) = $1,971,000 per year
        P = $55 per order
        C = .28
        R = $365 per unit

$$N_u = \sqrt{\frac{2AP}{R^2C}} = \sqrt{\frac{(2)(1,971,000)(55)}{(365)^2(.28)}} = 76 \text{ units per order}$$

6-7   We may use equation (6-1).

$$N_o = \sqrt{\frac{AC}{2P}} = \sqrt{\frac{(1,971,000)(.28)}{(2)(55)}} = 70.83 \text{ orders per year}$$

Alternatively, we could have proceeded directly using our
result from exercise 6-6, which was N_u = 76 units per
order. If we order 76 units each time we order, and
require 5400 units per year, then:

$$N_o = \frac{5400}{76} = 71.05 \text{ orders per year (difference due to}$$
$$\text{rounding)}$$

6-8   To find the optimum number of units per order, we use
       equation (6-2) where:

        A = (9000)(8) = $72,000 per year
        P = $40 per order
        C = .20 of value per year
        R = $8 per unit

$$N_u = \sqrt{\frac{2AP}{R^2C}} = \sqrt{\frac{(2)(72,000)(40)}{(8)^2(.20)}} = 671 \text{ units}$$

Since the containers require 10 ft² of space, the required
space for 671 units is:

        Area = (671)(10) = 6710 ft².

With the 5000 ft² restriction, at most $\frac{5000}{10} = 500$
containers may be ordered.

We now evaluate the costs of the alternatives:

Alter- native	Annual ordering cost (AP/RN_u)	Annual Carrying cost ($RCN_u/2$)	Total annual cost
671/order	$\dfrac{(72,000)(40)}{(8)(671)} = 537$	$\dfrac{(8)(.20)(671)}{2} = 537$	1074
500/order	$\dfrac{(72,000)(40)}{(8)(500)} = 720$	$\dfrac{(8)(.20)(500)}{2} = 400$	1120

Adding the additional storage area would save \$46 per year, and it is not justified economically.

The daily demand is $\dfrac{9000}{300} = 30$ units/day.

The 500 unit capacity represents $\dfrac{500}{30} = 16.67$ days supply.

6-9   To compute the optimum order size with gradual receipt of inventory, we use equation (6-5) where:

$X = 50$ containers per day receipt rate

$y = \dfrac{9000}{365}$ containers per day use rate

$$N_u = \sqrt{\dfrac{2UP}{RC(1-y/x)}} = \sqrt{\dfrac{(2)(9000)(40)}{(8)(.20)\left(1-\dfrac{9000}{(365)(50)}\right)}}$$

$= 942$ units per order

The maximum number stored in inventory would be:

$$N_u(1-y/x) = 942\left(1-\dfrac{9000}{(365)(50)}\right) = 477 \text{ units}$$

Under this system the maximum inventory level of 477 units can be accommodated with the available area.

The costs of the system are:

Annual ordering $= UP/N_u = (9000)(40)/942 = \$382$

Annual carrying $= RCN_u(1-y/x)/2$
$$= (8)(.20)(942)\left(1-\dfrac{9000}{(365)(50)}\right)/2$$
$$= \$382$$

Total annual costs $= 382 + 382 = \$764$ per year.

Compared to the \$1120 annual cost of the present system, this is an attractive plan.

Daily demand is 30 units/day.
The order of 942 units then represents 942/30 = 31.4 day's
supply.

6-10   Using equation (6-2), we find the optimum order size.

$$N_u = \sqrt{\frac{2AP}{R^2C}} = \sqrt{\frac{(2)(14000)(80)(30)}{(80)^2(.25)}} = 205 \text{ units per order}$$

The number of units requires a storage area of:

(205)(16) = 3280 ft²

Therefore, the current storage area is sufficient.

6-11   Given: A = $9,800 per year
                  P = $55 per order
                  C = .26 of value per year

Using equation (6-2) to find the optimum number of day's
supply:

$$N_d = 365\sqrt{\frac{2P}{AC}} = 365\sqrt{\frac{(2)(55)}{(9800)(.26)}} = 75.84 \text{ days supply}$$

This policy is within the 90-day shelf-life recommendation.

6-12   Given: A = $30,000 per year
                  P = $30 per year
                  C = .28 of value per year

Using equation (6-3) to find the optimum dollars per order:

$$N_s = \sqrt{\frac{2AP}{C}} = \sqrt{\frac{(2)(30,000)(30)}{.28}} = \$2535.46$$

This is not enough to ensure the visit by Dr. Lock.

6-13   Given: N_u = 1000 units
                  C = .32 of value per year
                  P = $58 per order
                  R = $120 per unit

Using equation (6-4) we solve for the annual dollar value
A:

$$N_u{}^2 = \frac{2AP}{R^2C}$$

$$(1000)^2 = \frac{(2)(58)A}{(120)^2(.32)}$$

$$A = \frac{(1000)^2(120)^2(.32)}{(2)(58)} = \$39,724,138 \text{ per year.}$$

6-14   Given for last year: N_o = 9.3 orders per year
 C = .30 of value per year
 P = \$46 per order

Using equation (6-1) to find annual dollar value A:

$$N_o{}^2 = \frac{AC}{2P}$$

$$(9.3)^2 = \frac{.30A}{(2)(46)}$$

$$A = \frac{(9.3)^2(2)(46)}{.30} = \$26,523.60$$

Next year A = (26,523.60)(1.20) = \$31,828.32

$$N_o = \sqrt{\frac{AC}{2P}} = \sqrt{\frac{(31,828.32)(.30)}{(2)(46)}} = 10.19 \text{ orders per year.}$$

6-15   Given: P = (.25)(9) + .50 = \$2.75 per order
 A = (5)(365)(3) = \$5,475 per year
 C = .085
 R = \$3 per unit

We use equation (6-3) to find the number of days' supply per order.

$$N_d = \sqrt{\frac{266,450P}{AC}} = \sqrt{\frac{(266,450)(2.75)}{(5475)(.085)}} = 40 \text{ days}$$

6-16   In this problem we use equation (6-5) from which we can compute the optimum order size given a gradual delivery of inventory.

 x = 12 tires/day
 y = 900/360 tires/day
 so (1-y/x) = .791667

$$N_u = \sqrt{\frac{2UP}{RC(1 - y/x)}} = \sqrt{\frac{(2)(900)(60)}{(260)(.24)(.791667)}} = \begin{array}{l} 47 \text{ tires} \\ \text{per order} \end{array}$$

Since 900 tires are required in a year, the company needs to place $900/47 = 19.149$ orders per year.

6-17   In this problem the average inventory held is $N_u/4$ rather than $N_u/2$. This means we can modify equation (6-2) to be:

$$N_u = \sqrt{\frac{4AP}{R^2C}} \quad \begin{array}{l} \text{where A} = (600)(180) = \$108,000 \\ \qquad\quad\; C = (12)(.02) = .24 \text{ of value/year} \end{array}$$

$$N_u = \sqrt{\frac{(4)(108,000)(85)}{(180)^2(.24)}} = 69 \text{ barrels per order}$$

6-18   We solve this problem as we solved the sample problem given in Section 6 of the text.

Week	Beginning Inventory	Demand	Net requirements	Cumulative requirements
1	100	40	0	0
2	60	50	0	0
3	10	55	45	45
4		70	70	115
5		80	80	195
6		65	65	260
7		60	60	320
8		50	50	370
9		45	45	415

Carrying cost = $(58.60)(.0225) = \$1.3185$ per month per unit. Or, carrying cost = $(1.3185)(12/52) = \$0.3043$ per week per unit. We now pick some alternatives on ordering. These can be to order 45 units, 115 units, and 195 units.

Number ordered	Carrying cost	Ordering cost
45	All used in third week = $0	37.50
115	70 held 1 week = $21.30	37.50
195	$21.30 plus 80 held 2 weeks = $69.99	37.50

We wish to order as many units as necessary to make carrying and holding costs equal. This is something greater than 115 and less than 195 units. We interpolate to find this order level as follows:

$$115 + \frac{37.50 - 21.30}{(.3043)(2)} = 142 \text{ units}$$

The order size should be 142 units.

6-19 We follow the procedure given in Section 6 of the text.

Week	Beginning inventory	Demand	Net requirements	Cumulative requirement
1	120	45	0	0
2	75	60	0	0
3	15	35	20	20
4		70	70	90
5		80	80	170
6		60	60	230
7		70	70	300
8		50	50	350
9		55	55	405

Carrying cost = (92.40)(.03) = \$2.772 per month per unit
or, carrying cost = (2.772)(12/52) = \$0.6397 per week per unit.

We now select several ordering alternatives:
Order 20, 90, or 170 units.

Number ordered	Carrying cost	Ordering cost
20	All units used in the third week = \$0	\$70
90	70 held 1 week = \$44.78	\$70
170	\$44.78 plus 80 held 2 weeks = \$147.13	\$70

Since we wish to make ordering and carrying costs equal,
our order point lies between 90 and 170 units. We
interpolate to get:

$$90 + \frac{70 - 44.78}{(.6397)(2)} = 110 \text{ units to order.}$$

6-20 With 60 units, or 2 weeks' demand, on hand initially, the
requirements for the first 6 weeks are:

Week	Net requirements
1	0
2	0
3	30
4	30
5	30
6	30

We now use an iterative approach. First the carrying costs are computed for a few arbitrary alternatives-- carry stock for 3, 4, 5, or six weeks' use.

Number of sets bought		Carrying cost, $/6 weeks
30	all units sold by week 3	= $0
60	30 units held 1 week (30)(.13/41)(400)	= $30
90	$60 (above) plus 30 units held 2 weeks (30)(.13/52)(400)(2)	= $60

We need not compute the past 5 weeks' usage since it is seen that our holding costs are now greater ($60) than the ordering cost ($30). The comparison of costs is:

Number of sets bought	Carrying cost	Ordering cost
30	$0	$30
60	$30	$30
90	$60	$30

Since for an optimal EOQ system holding costs and ordering costs are equal, we take the heuristic approach here of stocking 60 units, or 2 weeks' demand, where the estimated carrying cost ($30) equals the estimated ordering cost ($30).

6-21   This problem is solved using the procedures explained in Section 7 of the text.

Item	A	$\sqrt{A}$	Number of orders	N_s	A/N_s
A	120,000	346.41	5	24,000	5
B	80,000	282.84	6	13,333	6
C	50,000	223.61	6	8,333	6
D	24,000	154.92	4	6,000	4
E	10,500	102.47	8	1,313	8
F	5,200	72.11	6	867	6
G	2,400	48.99	7	343	7
H	1,100	33.17	8	138	8
I	900	30.00	6	150	6
J	300	17.32	6	50	6
		$\Sigma\sqrt{A} = 1,311.84$		$\Sigma N_s = 54,527$	$\Sigma A/N_s = 62$

From equation (6-7)

$$X = \frac{\Sigma\sqrt{A}}{\Sigma(A/N_s)} = \frac{1311.84}{62} = 21.1587$$

We now compute the minimum average inventory without increasing the purchasing work load using equation (6-6).

Item	$N_\$ = X \sqrt{A}$	Avg. inventory ($N_\$/2$)	Orders/year $A/N_\$$
A	7,329.59	3,664.80	16.37
B	5,984.53	2,992.27	13.37
C	4,731.30	2,365.65	10.57
D	3,277.91	1,638.96	7.32
E	2,168.13	1,084.07	4.84
F	1,525.75	762.88	3.41
G	1,036.56	518.28	2.32
H	701.83	350.92	1.57
I	634.76	317.38	1.42
J	366.47	183.24	0.82
		$13,878.45	62.01

With the old system where $\Sigma N_\$ = \$54{,}527$, the average inventory value was

$$\frac{54{,}527}{2} = \$27{,}263.5$$

The improvement is:

$$\frac{27{,}263.50 - 13{,}878.45}{27{,}263.50} = 49.1\% \text{ (Part a)}$$

Now, we will explore the minimum average inventory possible with a 25% increase in orders.

$$1.25 \ \Sigma A/N_\$ = 1.25(62) = 77.5 \text{ orders per year}$$

Now, from equation (6-7), the new value of X is:

$$X = \frac{E \sqrt{A}}{\Sigma(A/N_\$)} = \frac{1311.84}{77.5} = 16.9270$$

This means our new value of $X\Sigma \sqrt{A}$ is:

$$N_\$ = (16.9270)(1311.84) = \$22{,}205.52$$

and our new average inventory value is:

$$N_\$/2 = 22{,}205.52/2 = \$11{,}102.76 \text{ (Part b)}$$

This represents a reduction of:

$$\frac{13{,}878.45 - 11{,}102.76}{13{,}878.45} = 20\%$$

Now, we explore the question of reducing the number of orders when average inventory is allowed to be increased by 10%. By raising average inventory, which is $N_\$/2$, by 10%, we in effect are increasing X by 10%. The new value of X is then:

$$X = (21.1587)(1.10) = 23.2746$$

From equation (6-7), the new number of orders per year, which is $\Sigma A/N_\$$, becomes:

$$\Sigma A/N_\$ = \frac{\Sigma \sqrt{A}}{X} = \frac{1311.84}{23.2746} = 56.3636$$

The reduction is $\dfrac{62 - 56.3636}{62} = 9.1\%$ (Part c)

6-22 We follow the procedure given in Section 7 of the text.

SKU	A	$\sqrt{A}$	Number of orders	$N_\$$	$A/N_\$$
1	721,000	849.12	6	120,167	6
2	461,000	678.97	5	92,200	5
3	207,000	454.97	8	25,875	8
4	91,000	301.66	3	30,333	3
5	54,000	232.38	4	13,500	4
6	26,000	161.25	9	2,889	9
7	10,000	100.00	10	1,000	10
		$\Sigma \sqrt{A}$ = 2,778.35		$\Sigma N_\$$ = 285,964	$\Sigma A/N_\$$ = 45

From equation (6-7)

$$X = \frac{\Sigma \sqrt{A}}{\Sigma A/N_\$} = \frac{2778.35}{45} = 61.7411$$

Without increasing number of orders, the minimum average inventory values are:

SKU	$N_\$ = X\sqrt{A}$	Avg. inv. ($N_\$/2$)	Orders/year $A/N_\$$
1	52,425.60	26,212.80	13.75
2	41,920.35	20,960.18	11.00
3	28,090.35	14,045.18	7.37
4	18,624.82	9,312.41	4.89
5	14,347.40	7,173.70	3.76
6	9,955.75	4,977.88	2.61
7	6,174.11	3,087.06	1.62
		85,769.21	45.00

With the old system where $\Sigma N_\$ = \$285,964$, the average inventory value was $285,964/2 = \$142,982$.
The improvement is:

$$\frac{142,982 - 85,769.21}{142,982} = 40\% \quad \text{(Part a)}$$

By increasing the number of orders by 25% we have:

$$1.25\Sigma A/N_\$ = (1.25)(45) = 56.25 \text{ orders per year}$$

From equation (6-7), the new value of X is:

$$X = \frac{\Sigma\sqrt{A}}{\Sigma A/N_\$} = \frac{2778.35}{56.25} = 49.3929$$

Our new value of $X\Sigma\sqrt{A}$ is:

$$N_\$ = (49.3929)(2778.35) = \$137,230.73$$

And, our new average inventory value becomes:

$$N_\$/2 = 137,230.73/2 = \$68,615.37 \quad \text{(Part b)}$$

This is an additional reduction of:

$$\frac{85,769.21 - 68,615.37}{85,769.21} = 20\%$$

If we allow a 20% increase in average inventory value, then X increases to:

$$X = (61.7411)(1.20) = 74.0893$$

From equation (6-7) the value of $\Sigma A/N_\$$, the new number of orders, becomes:

$$\Sigma A/N_\$ = \frac{\Sigma\sqrt{A}}{X} = \frac{2778.35}{74.0893} = 37.50$$

The reduction becomes:

$$\frac{45 - 37.5}{45} = 16.67\% \quad \text{(Part c)}$$

6-23 Following the procedure of Section 7 of the text:

Item	A	$\sqrt{A}$	Number of orders A/N	$N_\$$
leather	200,000	447.21	4	50,000
v. soles	40,000	200.00	2	20,000
r. soles	30,000	173.21	2	15,000
lining	30,000	173.21	2	15,000
l. laces	4,000	63.25	2	2,000
c. laces	2,000	44.72	2	1,000
		$\Sigma\sqrt{A} = 1,101.60$	$\Sigma A/N_\$ = 14$	$\Sigma N_\$ = 103,000$

From equation (6-7):

$$X = \frac{\Sigma\sqrt{A}}{\Sigma A/N_\$} = \frac{1101.60}{14} = 78.6857$$

With a constant number of orders, the minimum average inventory becomes:

Item	$N_\$ = X\sqrt{A}$	Avg. inv. ($N_\$/2$)	Orders per year A/$N_\$$
leather	35,189.04	17,594.52	5.68
v. soles	15,737.14	7,868.57	2.54
r. soles	13,629.15	6,814.58	2.18
lining	13,629.15	6,814.58	2.18
l. laces	4,976.87	2,488.44	0.80
c. laces	3,518.83	1,759.42	0.57
		43,340.11	13.95

Compared to the old system, where $\Sigma N_\$/2 = \$51,500$, our new average inventory value of $43,340.11 represents a 15.84% improvement.

6-24 In this problem we wish to decrease the number of setups by 20%. Let us use the procedure of Section 7 in the text and simply follow the same computations, but we will arbitrarily reduce each of the setups by 20%. This gives us the following:

SKU	A	$\sqrt{A}$	Setups x .80	$N_\$$	Current value of $N_\$$ A/current setups
FS	80,000	282.84	4.0	20,000	16,000
BS	50,000	223.61	6.4	7,813	6,250
MC	30,000	173.21	9.6	3,125	2,500
TR	20,000	141.42	8.0	2,500	2,000
MR	10,000	100.00	7.2	1,389	1,111
TT	5,000	70.71	8.0	625	500
AS	1,000	31.62	4.8	208	167
		$\Sigma\sqrt{A}=1,023.41$	$\Sigma A/N_\$=48.0$	$N_\$=35,660$	$28,528

Current average inventory value = ($\frac{1}{2}$)(28,528) = $14,264

From equation (6-7):

$$X = \frac{\Sigma\sqrt{A}}{\Sigma A/N_s} = \frac{1023.41}{48.00} = 21.3210$$

Now, given the 20% reduction to 48 setups, the minimum average inventory values are:

SKU	$N_s = X\sqrt{A}$	Ave. inv. N$/2	Setups A/N$
FS	6,030.44	3,015.22	13.27
BS	4,767.60	2,383.80	10.49
MC	3,693.02	1,846.51	8.12
TR	3,015.22	1,507.61	6.63
MR	2,132.10	1,066.05	4.69
TT	1,507.61	753.81	3.32
AS	674.17	337.09	1.48
		$10,910.09	48.00

We have not only been able to reduce the number of setups by 20% to become 48 setups per year but have also reduced average inventory value from $14,264 to $10,910.09 for a 23.51% reduction.

6-25   d = 21900/300 = 73 units per day

$$N_u = \sqrt{\frac{2US}{RC(1 - d/p)}} = \sqrt{\frac{(2)(21900)(300)}{(350)(.28)(1 - 73/300)}} = 421 \text{ units}$$

N_r = 21900/421 = 52.02 production runs per year.

Production run length = 421/300 = 1.403 days.

The maximum inventory level = 421 - (73)(1.403) = 319 units.

The total annual inventory costs are:
  Annual holding cost = (319/2)(350)(.28)= 15,631
  Annual setup cost   = (52.02)(300)   = 15,606
                                  TOTAL = $31,237 per year

6-26 $N_u = \sqrt{\dfrac{2US}{RC(1 - d/p)}}$,   or $N_u{}^2 = \dfrac{2US}{RC(1 - d/p)}$

$$(2600)^2 = \frac{(2)(30,000)(135)}{R(.28)(1 - 100/200)}$$

114

$$6,760,000R = \$57,857,143$$
$$R = \$8.56 \text{ per unit, which is the implied cost of stock item B.}$$

6-27 First we compute costs with an aggregate policy:

$$A = (6000)(80) = \$480,000/\text{yr}$$

$$N_u = \sqrt{\frac{2AP}{R^2 C}} = \sqrt{\frac{(2)(\$480,000)(\$35)}{(\$80/\text{unit})^2 (.24/\text{yr})}}$$

$$= 148 \text{ units/order}$$

The number of orders per year, N_o, is:

$$N_o = \frac{\text{units/yr}}{N_u} = \frac{6000}{148} = 40.54 \text{ orders/year}$$

The annual total costs (T.C.) for an aggregate policy are:

$$\text{T.C.} = (N_u/2)RC + N_o P$$

$$= \frac{148}{2}(80(.24) + (40.54)(35) = 1420.80 + 1418.90$$

$$= \$2839.70$$

Now with a split policy we will use the subscript s to denote summer and w to denote winter. Further, we will let demand be on a monthly basis, and so C=.02 per month. For a summer season:

$$A_s = (780)(80) = \$62,400/\text{mo.}$$

$$N_{us} = \sqrt{\frac{2A_s P}{R^2 C}} = \sqrt{\frac{2(\$62,400)(\$35)}{(\$80/\text{unit})^2 (.02/\text{mo.})}} = 185 \text{ units}$$

And the number of orders during a 5-month summer season, N_{os}, is:

$$N_{os} = \frac{\text{units/mo x 5 mo.}}{N_s} = \frac{(780 \text{ units/mo.})(5 \text{ mo.})}{185 \text{ units}}$$

$$= 21.08 \text{ orders}$$

For a winter season:

$$A_w = (300)(80) = \$24,000/\text{mo.}$$

$$N_{uw} = \sqrt{\frac{2A_w P}{R^2 C}} = \sqrt{\frac{2(\$24,000)(\$35)}{(80)^2 (.02)}} = 115 \text{ units}$$

And the number of orders is:

$$N_{ow} = \frac{(300)(7)}{115} = 18.26 \text{ orders}$$

The total annual costs for a split policy are:

$$T.C. = \frac{N_{us}}{2} RC_s + \frac{N_{uw}}{2} RC_w + N_{os}P + N_{ow}P$$

$$= (185/2)(80)(.10) + (115/2)(80)(.14) + (21.08)(35) + (18.26)(35)$$

$$= 740.00 + 644.00 + 737.80 + 639.10$$

$$= \$2760.90/\text{yr}$$

where $C_s = (.02)(5 \text{ mo})$
$C_w = (.02)(7 \text{ mo})$

The amount saved (A.S.) by going to a split plan is:

$$\begin{aligned} A.S. &= 2839.70 - 2760.90 \\ &= \$78.80/\text{yr}. \end{aligned}$$

6-28   First we compute $\Sigma\sqrt{A}$:

$$\Sigma\sqrt{A} = \sqrt{60,000} + \sqrt{90,000} + \sqrt{30,000} + \sqrt{80,000}$$
$$= 245 + 300 + 173 + 283 = 1001$$

Since $\Sigma(A/N_s) = 11$, which is the number of orders per year total, the value of X, where $X = \Sigma\sqrt{A}/\Sigma(A/N_s)$, becomes $X = 1001/11 = 91$, which is assumed constant for each of the four SKUs. Now we find the near optimal dollar value for each of the SKUs, $N_s = X\sqrt{A}$, as well as the resulting new average inventory balance figures and number of orders per year.

SKU	$\sqrt{A}$	$N_s = X\sqrt{A}$, $/order	Avg. inv. $N_s/2$	No. orders/yr A/N_s
½ HP	245	$22,295	$11,147.50	2.69
1 HP	300	27,300	13,650.00	3.30
2 HP	173	15,743	7,871.50	1.91
6 HP	283	25,753	12,876.50	3.10
			$45,545.50	11.00

With this plan, the Freehold average inventory balance has been reduced by $50,000 - $45,545.50, or $4,454.50, without increasing purchasing workload.

116

6-29 First, we compute $\Sigma N_\$$:

$$\Sigma N_\$ = \$20,000 + \$30,000 + \$10,000 + \$40,000$$
$$= \$100,000$$

And since $\Sigma\sqrt{A} = 1001$ from Problem 6-28, we compute X as:

$$X = \frac{\Sigma N_\$}{\Sigma\sqrt{A}} = \frac{100,000}{1001}$$

$$= 99.90, \text{ which is assumed constant for each of the four SKUs.}$$

Now we find the near optimal dollar value for each of the SKUs as well as the resulting new average inventory balance figures and number of orders per year:

SKU	$\sqrt{A}$	$N_\$ = X\sqrt{A}$, \$/order	Avg. inv. $N_\$/2$	No. orders/yr $A/N_\$$
½ HP	245	24,475.50	\$12,237.75	2.45
1 HP	300	29,970.00	14,985.00	3.00
2 HP	173	17,282.70	8,641.35	1.74
6 HP	283	28,271.70	14,135.85	2.83
			\$50,000.00	10.02

The number of orders placed at Newark has been reduced from 11 orders to 10.02 without increasing the annual holding costs.

6-30 From exercise (6-28) we determined:

$$X = \frac{\Sigma\sqrt{A}}{\Sigma A/N_\$} = \frac{1001}{11} = 91$$

Now with 15 orders/year allowed instead of 11, we have:

$$X = \frac{1001}{15} = 66.73$$

SKU	$\sqrt{A}$	$N_\$ = X\sqrt{A}$, \$ per order	Avg. inv. $N_\$/2$	No. orders/yr $A/N_\$$
½ HP	245	16,349	8,174.5	3.67
1 HP	300	20,019	10,009.5	4.50
2 HP	173	11,544	5,772.0	2.60
6 HP	283	18,885	9,442.5	4.24
			33,398.5	15.01

From exercise (6-28), the average inventory was valued at $45.545.50. The savings due to the 36% increase in orders per year is:

$$\$45,545.50 - 33,398.50 = \$12,147$$

The savings, of course, results at the expense of our adding four more orders per year from 11 to 15, the cost of which is not known by the company.

6-31 The high level of sales is:

$$(6000)(1.20) = 7200 \text{ units/yr}$$

And the low level of sales is:

$$(600)(.80) = 4800 \text{ units/yr}$$

At U = 7200 units per year, the order quantity N_u and the number of orders N_o are:

$$N_u = \sqrt{\frac{2AP}{R^2C}} = \sqrt{\frac{(2)(\$2,160,000)(40)}{(300)^2(.16)}} = 110 \text{ units}$$

$$N_o = \frac{A_u}{N_u} = \frac{7200}{110} = 65.45 \text{ orders/yr}$$

At U = 4800 units per year,

$$N_u = \sqrt{\frac{(2)(\$1,440,000)(40)}{(300)^2(.16)}} = 89 \text{ units}$$

$$N_o = \frac{4800}{89} = 53.93$$

At U = 6000 units per year:

$$N_u = \sqrt{\frac{(2)(\$1,800,000)(40)}{(300)^2(.16)}} = 100 \text{ units}$$

N_o (at sales of 7200) = 72 orders per year, and N_o (at sales of 4800) = 48 orders per year. We now compute these costs for ordering 100 units at the high and low sales figures and compare these costs with an optimal policy at each level of sales.

At sales of 7200 units per year,

	Optimal order 110 units	Order 100 units
Carrying cost	$(110/2)(300)(.16)=\$2640/yr$	$(100/2)(300)(.16)=\$2400/yr$
Ordering cost	$(65.45)(40)=\underline{2618/yr}$ TOTALS $\$5258/yr$	$(72)(40)=\underline{2880/yr}$ $\$5280/yr$

Cost difference = $5280 - $5228 = $52/yr

At sales of 4800 units per year,

	Optimal order 89 units	Order 100 units
Carrying cost	$(89/2)(300)(.16)=\$2136/yr$	$(100/2)(300)(.16)=\$2400/yr$
Ordering cost	$(53.93)(40)=\underline{2157/yr}$ TOTALS $\$4293/yr$	$(48)(40)=\underline{1920/yr}$ $\$4320/yr$

Cost difference = $4320 - $4293 = $27/yr

Fortunately, due to the square root nature of the EOQ model, we find that the model is not overly sensitive to changes in demand. Even for variations of ±20% in annual demand, we can hold to a policy of always ordering 100 units per order and be no more than $52 higher than the optimal order quantity costs.

6-32   Using equation (6-5):

$$N_u{}^2 = \frac{2UP}{RC\,(1-y/x)}$$

When y = x, the factor (1-y/x) becomes zero. This implies that the optimal order quantity, N_u, is infinitely large.

6-33

Class	SKU	% of total Number	Total Value	% of total Value
A	K-92 H-92 L-03	25.00	27,650.00	73.39
B	A-27 B-34 D-07 H-17 H-27	41.67	8,536.50	22.57
C	C-93 G-23 K-83 M-09	33.33	1,642.50	4.34

119

6-34 Following the procedure in Section 6 of the text:

Week	Beginning Inventory	Demand	Net Reqm'ts	Cumulative Reqm'ts
1	60	25	0	0
2	35	25	0	0
3	10	25	15	15
4		30	30	45
5		30	30	75
6		35	35	110
7		35	35	145
8		40	40	185

Carrying costs = (50)(.005) = $0.25 per week per copy

We now select a few ordering policies: 15, 45, 75, and 110 copies:

Number Ordered	Carrying cost	Ordering cost
15	All units used in the third week = $ 0	$40
45	30 held one week = $ 7.50	$40
75	7.50 plus 30 held two weeks = $22.50	$40
110	22.50 plus 35 held 3 weeks = $48.75	$40

Since we wish to make ordering and carrying costs equal, we interpolate to get:

$$75 + \frac{40 - 22.50}{(.25)(3)} \approx 98 \text{ copies to order}$$

6-35 We use equation 6-4:

1980 data
N_μ = 350 units
A = $60,000 per year
R = $12 per unit

$$N_\mu{}^2 = \frac{2AP}{R^2 C}$$

$$\frac{2P}{C} = N_\mu{}^2 \frac{R^2}{A} = \frac{(350)^2 (12)^2}{60,000} = 294$$

<u>1990 data</u>
A = $120,000   (double cost with same units/year usage)
R = $24 per unit (double cost)
$\frac{2P}{C}$ = 294 (unchanged)

$$N_\mu = \sqrt{\frac{2AP}{R^2 C}} = \sqrt{\frac{(120,000)(294)}{24^2}} = 247 \text{ units}$$

This is a reduction of 350 - 247 = 103 units or about 30%.

6-36   Using equation 6-10:

$$N_\mu = \sqrt{\frac{2US}{RC(1 - d/p)}} = \sqrt{\frac{(2)(90,000)(600)}{(50)(.18)(1 - 300/1800)}}$$

N_μ = 3795 units

Since 1800 units are produced per day, 3795 units will require 3795/1800 = 2.11 days of production.

7-1 First we compute the expected total annual stockout costs
for the two alternatives.

ROP	Prob. of being out	Number short	Expected Annual cost		Total annual Stockout cost
250	.04 when 260	10	(10)(.04)(200)(10) =	800	
	.02 when 280	30	(30)(.02)(200)(10) =	1,200	
					$2,000/yr.
220	.06 when 240	20	(20)(.06)(200)(10) =	2,400	
	.04 when 260	40	(40)(.04)(200)(10) =	3,200	
	.02 when 280	60	(60)(.02)(200)(10) =	2,400	
					$8,000/yr.

The savings in carrying cost when reducing from a ROP of
250 units down to 220 units is:

(30)(20) = $600 per year

Since the stockout cost increase ($6000) is larger than the
carrying cost savings ($600), the ROP should remain at 250.

7-2 The number of orders per year is:

$$\frac{(4 \text{ units/day})(250 \text{ days})}{100 \text{ units/order}} = 10 \text{ orders/year.}$$

The average demand in the reorder period is:

(4 units/day)(25 days) = 100 units

The expected annual stockout costs are:

ROP	SS	Prob. of being out	Number short	Expected annual cost	T.C.
100	0	.20 when 125	25	(25)(.20)(20)(10) = $1,000	
		.15 when 150	50	(50)(.15)(20)(10) = 1,500	
		.10 when 175	75	(75)(.10)(20)(10) = 1,500	
					$4,000/yr
125	25	.15 when 150	25	(25)(.15)(25)(10) = $ 750	
		.10 when 175	50	(50)(.10)(20)(10) = 1,000	
					$1,750/yr
150	50	.10 when 175	25	(25)(.10)(20)(10) = $ 500	
					$ 500/yr
175	75	none	--	----	$ 0/yr

The total annual costs of the safety stock are:

ROP	SS	Expected stockout	Carrying cost	Total annual cost
100	0	4,000	0	$4,000/yr.
125	25	1,750	(25)(5) = 125	$1,875/yr.
150	50	500	(50)(5) = 250	$ 750/yr.
175	75	0	(75)(5) = 375	$ 375/yr.

The optimal policy is to set the ROP at 175 units.

7-3 We first compute the expected annual stockout costs:

ROP	SS	Prob. of being out	Number short	Expected annual cost	T.C.
30	0	.10 when 32	2	(2)(.10)(100)(10) = 200	
		.05 when 35	5	(5)(.05)(100)(10) = 250	
		.01 when 36	6	(6)(.01)(100)(10) = 60	
					$510/yr
32	2	.05 when 35	3	(3)(.05)(100)(10) = 150	
		.01 when 36	4	(4)(.01)(100)(10) = 40	
					$190/yr
35	5	.01 when 36	1	(1)(.01)(100)(10) = 10	
					$ 10/yr
36	6	none	-	----	$ 0/yr

123

The total annual costs of the safety stock are:

ROP	SS	Expected stockout	Carrying cost			Total annual cost
30	0	510			0	$510/yr.
32	2	190	(2)(18)	=	36	$226/yr.
35	5	10	(5)(18)	=	90	$100/yr.
36	6	0	(6)(18)	=	108	$108/yr.

The optimal reorder point should be 35 units. The expected annual stockout cost is $10 per year, or one stockout ($100 bill) in ten years time.

7-4   For the two alternatives, we compute the expected annual stockout costs.

ROP	Prob. of being out	Number short	Expected Annual Cost	T.C.
105	.02 at 115	10	(10)(.02)(200)(10)=$ 400	$400/yr
80	.08 at 85	5	(5)(.08)(200)(10) =$ 800	
	.06 at 95	15	(15)(.06)(200)(10)= 1,800	
	.04 at 105	25	(25)(.04)(200)(10)= 2,000	
	.02 at 115	35	(35)(.02)(200)(10)= 1,400	$6,000/yr

The savings in carrying costs for dropping from a ROP of 105 to a ROP of 80 is:

(25 units)($25/unit-yr.) = $625 per year

Since the additional expected stockout cost (6000 - 400) of $5,600 per year is greater than the savings in carrying the additional safety stock of $625 per year, the hospital should not drop the reorder point.

7-5   The stockout cost is:

(30 sandwiches/ham)($5/sandwich) = $150/ham

We compute the expected annual stockout cost for each possible ROP where the total number of past reorder periods = (10 yrs.)(30/yr.) = 300.

ROP	SS	Prob. of being out	Number short	Expected annual cost	T.C.
15	0	.10 at 17	2	(2)(.10)(150)(30)=$ 900	
		.05 at 20	5	(5)(.05)(150)(30)= 1,125	
		.01 at 25	10	(10)(.01)(150)(30)= 450	
					$2,475/yr
17	2	.05 at 20	3	(3)(.05)(150)(30)=$ 675	
		.01 at 25	8	(8)(.01)(150)(30)= 360	
					$1,035/yr
20	5	.01 at 25	5	(5)(.01)(150)(30)=$ 225	
					$ 225/yr
25	10	none	--	-------	$ 0/yr

The total annual costs of the safety stock are:

ROP	SS	Expected stockout	Carrying cost	Total annual cost
15	0	2,475	0	$2,475/yr.
17	2	1,035	(2)(5) = 10	$1,045/yr.
20	5	225	(5)(5) = 25	$ 250/yr.
25	10	0	(10)(5) = 50	$ 50/yr.

The restaurant should reorder at 25 canned hams. The safety stock is 10 hams and they should never expect to pay the $5 stock out premium.

7-6   The mean demand in the reorder lead time is:
        (5 kits/day)(20 days) = 100 kits.

We compute the expected annual stockout for each ROP alternative.

ROP	SS	Prob. of being out	Number short	Expected annual stockout cost	T.C.
100	0	.20 at 120	20	(20)(.20)(30)(6) =$720	
		.08 at 140	40	(40)(.08)(30)(6) = 576	
		.02 at 160	60	(60)(.02)(30)(6) = 216	
					$1,512/yr
120	20	.08 at 140	20	(20)(.08)(30)(6) =$288	
		.02 at 160	40	(40)(.02)(30)(6) = 144	
					$ 432/yr
140	40	.02 at 160	20	(20)(.02)(30)(6) =$ 72	
					$ 72/yr
160	60	none	--	---------	$ 0/yr

Now, we compute total annual cost of the safety stock for each alternative ROP:

ROP	SS	Exp. stockout cost	Carrying cost	Total annual cost
100	0	1,512	0	$1,512/yr.
120	20	432	(20)(8) = 160	$ 592/yr.
140	40	72	(40)(8) = 320	$ 392/yr.
160	60	0	(60)(8) = 480	$ 480/yr.

The optimal ROP is 140 units where SS = 40 units.

7-7   A safety stock of 64 gears is a reorder point, which is $Z = 64/50 = 1.28$ standard deviations to the right of the mean. From Appendix Table 1, we find the area .89973, which is the probability of not stocking out. Therefore, stockouts will occur 10% of the time during reorder periods.

7-8   From Appendix Table 1 we find the area .95 is about 1.645 standard deviations to the right of the mean. This gives a safety stock of (1.645)(50) = 82 units.

7-9   At the current service level of 80 percent we find from Appendix Table 1 that the safety stock represents about .84 standard deviations or (.84)(80) = 67.2 units.

At a proposed service level of 99 percent, we find that we are about 2.33 standard deviations or (2.33)(80) = 186.4 units of stock above the mean. So, to go from 80 to 99% service level, we must add 186.4 - 67.2 = 119.2 units of stock, which costs (119.2)(6) = $715.20 per year in additional carrying costs. Therefore, they should not make the change.

7-10   The safety stock of 24 units is to the right of the mean by:

$$Z = 24/26 = 0.923 \text{ standard deviations.}$$

From Appendix Table 1 we read the area .82199. Therefore, the probability of stocking out in the reorder lead time is 1 - .82199 = about 17.8%.

7-11 Our distribution is:

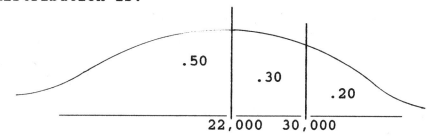

We look in Appendix Table 1 at an area of .8000 and find the attendance of 30,000 people is about Z = 0.84 standard deviations.

Therefore, 1 std. dev. = $\dfrac{30,000 - 22,000}{.84}$ = 9,523.81

Again at an area of .9500, we find Z = 1.645.
The number of customers we should allow for becomes:

μ + (1.645)(9523.91) = 22,000 + 15,667 or 37,667
customers.

7-12 The distribution is:

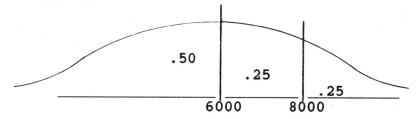

At 8000 fans, the area is .75. From Appendix Table 1 this point is found to be Z = .674 standard deviations.
Therefore, 1 std. dev. = 8,000 - 6,000/.674 = 2967.36 fans.

At 95%, we find Z = 1.645 so our seating capacity should be:

6000 + (1.645)(2967.36) = 10,881 fans.

7-13 Currently with a reorder point of 80 games, the service level during the reorder lead time is:

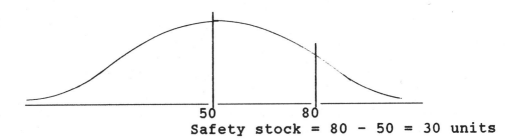

Safety stock = 80 - 50 = 30 units

$$Z = \frac{80-50}{25} = 1.2 \text{ standard deviations}$$

From Appendix Table 1 the area is .88493 which corresponds to a service level of 1 - .88493 = .11507 or about 11.5%.

To yield a service level of 99%, the reorder point must be about 2.33 standard deviations to the right of the mean, and:

Reorder point = 50 + (2.33)(25) = 108 games

The increased holding cost for 108 - 80 = 28 additional units of safety stock is:
Additional cost = (28)(10)(.22) = $61.60 per year.

7-14 Since the service level in the reorder lead time is 95%, we find from Appendix Table 1 that the reorder point lies about 1.64 standard deviations to the right of the mean. This represents 1.64σ units of safety stock where σ is the unknown standard deviation. The safety stock is known to be 180 - 140 = 40 units. Therefore:

1.64σ = 40 units
σ = 24.4 units.

7-15 Our first step is to order the trigger EOQ item which is an order of 500 cartons of SKU item C. This leaves 1100 cartons remaining to fill the truck. In the next step we examine the stock level above the reorder point expressed as a percent of the reorder point. We rank these from lowest to highest.

SKU	ROP	Level above ROP	% above ROP	Ranking
A	400	100	25.00	4
B	300	50	16.67	3
D	500	50	10.00	2
E	100	5	5.00	1
F	75	25	33.33	5
G	50	50	100.00	6
H	40	160	400.00	7

Our order should be:

SKU Item	Cartons
C	500
E	200
D	500
B	300
A	100
	TOTAL = 1600 cartons ordered

7-16 Two items are at their reorder point and will be shipped:

Item	Trigger EOQ	Volume (ft^3)
Pennants	19	(30)(19) = 570
Backpack	18	(56)(18) = 1008
		1578

There is 4,000 − 1,578 = 2,422 ft^3 remaining for other items. The rankings of these items are:

Item	ROP	Level above ROP	% above ROP	Ranking
Desk lamp	20	7	35	3
Waste basket	18	4	22	1
Stuffed dolphin	23	6	26	2
Sweatshirt	20	9	45	4
Beverage cooler	10	8	80	5

We order the following:

Item	Line Item EOQ	Volume	Remaining volume from 2,422 ft^3
Waste basket	16	(58)(16) = 928	1,494
Stuffed dolphin	18	(48)(18) = 864	630
Desk lamp	18	(60)(18) =1080	

129

Since the line item EOQ for desk lamps of 18 cases is greater than the 630 ft³ still available, we reduce its order level to 630/60 = 10.5 or 10 cases.

7-17   The order is triggered by the 2 inch metal rivets for which we order the EOQ amount of 2,500 cartons. We express the other SKU's as stock level above ROP expressed as a percent of ROP and rank them from lowest to highest.

SKU	ROP	Level above ROP	% above ROP	Ranking
#10 screw	1,500	500	33.33	3
8-32 H.B.	800	40	5.00	1
#4 screw	1,400	700	50.00	4½
5/16 L.W.	1,000	500	50.00	4½
3" pop	500	300	60.00	6
1" hex	100	100	100.00	7½
10/32 hex	2,800	200	7.14	2
7/16 F.W.	1,500	1,500	100.00	7½

Our order should be:

SKU Item	Cartons
2" metal rivets	2,500
8/32 x 1½" hex bolts	1,000
10/32 x 2" hex bolts	5,000
#10 sheet metal screw	1,500
	TOTAL = 10,000 cartons

7-18   The casual sweater has reached its reorder point, so the trigger EOQ quantity of 20 sweaters are to be ordered at a cost of (20)(18) = $360, leaving $1640 to be ordered from the set of remaining sweater styles.

The rankings are:

Item	ROP	Level above ROP	% above ROP	Ranking
V-neck	22	5	23	2
Ski	30	21	70	7
Turtleneck	26	9	35	3
Buttoned	15	9	60	6
Vest	14	5	36	4
Hip-length	26	4	15	1
Collared	18	8	44	5

We order the following:

Item	Line item EOQ	Cost	Remaining cost from $1640
Hip-length	14	(14)(43) = 602	1038
V-neck	15	(15)(20) = 300	738
Turtleneck	18	(18)(35) = 630	108
Vest	8	(8)(20) = 160 min. order satisfied	

7-19 Given: U = 200 units
C = \$50
P = \$30
V = \$40

Using equation (7-6) and (7-7):

$$N_u = \sqrt{\left(\frac{2UP}{C}\right)\left(\frac{C+V}{V}\right)} = \sqrt{\frac{(2)(200)(30)}{50} \times \frac{50+40}{40}} = 23 \text{ units}$$

$$B = N_u\left(\frac{C}{C+V}\right) = (23)\left(\frac{50}{50+40}\right) = 13 \text{ units}$$

7-20 Given: U = 400 units
C = \$10
P = \$35
V = \$20

Current EOQ model:

$$N_u = \sqrt{\frac{2UP}{C}} = 53 \text{ bibles}$$

$$N_o = \frac{U}{N_u} = \frac{400}{53} = 7.55 \text{ orders per year}$$

Annual cost $= \frac{N_u}{2}C + N_o P = \frac{53}{2}(10) + (7.55)(35) = \$529.15$

With the backorder model, using equation (7-6) and (7-7):

$$N_u = \sqrt{\frac{(2)(400)(35)}{10} \times \frac{10+20}{20}} = 65 \text{ bibles}$$

$$B = (65)\frac{10}{10+20} = 22 \text{ bibles}$$

From equation (7-5), the annual costs are:

Annual carrying cost $\dfrac{(N_u - B)^2}{2N_u} C = \dfrac{(65-22)^2}{(2)(65)} (10) = 142.23$

Annual order cost $\dfrac{U}{N_u} P = \dfrac{400}{65} (35) = 215.38$

Annual backorder cost $\dfrac{B^2 V}{2N_u} = \dfrac{(22)^2(20)}{(2)(65)} = \underline{74.46}$

$\text{TOTAL} = \$432.07$

The annual savings is $529.15 - 432.07 = \$97.08$.

7-21 We solve this problem using equation (7-6) and (7-7).

Given: U = 60 units
         P = \$50 per order
         C = \$70 per sofa per year
         V = \$20 per sofa backordered per year

$$N_u = \sqrt{\left(\dfrac{2UP}{C}\right)\left(\dfrac{C+V}{V}\right)} = \sqrt{\dfrac{(2)(60)(50)}{70} \times \dfrac{70+20}{20}} = 20 \text{ units per order}$$

$$B = N_u \dfrac{C}{C+V} = (20) \dfrac{70}{70+20} = 16 \text{ units backordered}$$

The total annual cost is obtained from equation (7-5):

$$\text{Cost} = \dfrac{(N_u - B)^2}{2N_u} C + \dfrac{UP}{N_u} + \dfrac{B^2 V}{2N_u}$$

$$\text{Cost} = \dfrac{(20-16)^2}{(2)(20)} (70) + \dfrac{(60)(50)}{20} + \dfrac{(16)^2(20)}{(2)(20)}$$

$$\text{Cost} = \$306.$$

7-22 To find the optimal policy, we use the backorder model given by equations (7-6) and (7-7).

$$N_u = \sqrt{\left(\dfrac{2UP}{C}\right)\left(\dfrac{C+V}{V}\right)} = \sqrt{\left(\dfrac{(2)(72)(200)}{4,000}\right)\left(\dfrac{4,000+300}{300}\right)}$$

$$= 10 \text{ trucks/order}$$

$$B = N_u \dfrac{C}{C+V} = (10) \dfrac{4,000}{4,000+300} = 9 \text{ trucks/order}$$

With this plan, the total annual costs are given by equation (7-5) as:

$$\text{Total annual costs} = \frac{(N_u - B)^2}{2N_u}C + \frac{UP}{N_u} + \frac{B^2 V}{2N_u}$$

$$= \frac{(10 - 9)^2}{(2)(10)}(4,000) + \frac{(72)(200)}{10} + \frac{(9)^2(300)}{(2)(10)}$$

$$= \$2,855/\text{yr}.$$

With the current plan, we assume that none of the trucks are backordered.

```
Annual ordering cost = (12)(200)     = $  2,400
Annual carrying cost = (6/2)(4,000) = $ 12,000
               Total annual costs = $ 14,400/yr.
```

The new ordering plan would save 14,400 - 2,855 = $11,545 per year.

7-23 We compute the optimal number of orders per year using equation (6-1):

$$N_0 = \sqrt{\frac{AC}{2P}} = \sqrt{\frac{(80,000)(.28)}{(2)(40)}} = 16.7332 \text{ orders/year}$$

The current total annual costs are:

```
Annual ordering = (16.7332)(40)            = $    669.33
Annual carrying = the same as ordering = $    669.33
Annual purchase =                          = $80,000.00
                              TOTAL = $81,338.66
```

If four orders are placed per year, the order size will be

$$\frac{(.99)(80,000)}{4} = \$19,800 \text{ per order}.$$

The average inventory will be

$$\frac{19,800}{2} = \$9,900.$$

The annual costs would be:

```
Annual ordering = (4)(40)            = $    160.00
Annual carrying = (9,900)(.28)    = $  2,772.00
Annual purchase = (.99)(80,000) = $79,200.00
                              TOTAL = $82,132.00
```

Therefore, it is more cost effective to reject the discount and continue using the EOQ approach.

To find a counteroffer, we will look for a point of indifference or a discount which will result in costs which are equal to the current EOQ system costs of $81,338.66. We call this discount, 1 - X, where:

Annual ordering = $160.00

Annual carrying = $\frac{(X)(80,000)}{4}$ x $\frac{(.28)}{2}$ = 2800X

Annual purchase = $80,000X

$$160 + 2800X + 80,000X = \$81,338.66$$
$$X = .98$$

So, any discount greater than 2% should be accepted.

7-24 Using equation (6-1), we compute the optimal number of orders per year.

$$N_0 = \sqrt{\frac{AC}{2P}} = \sqrt{\frac{(75,000)(.25)}{(2)(45)}} = 14.43375 \text{ orders per year.}$$

The current total annual costs are:

Annual ordering = (14.43375)(45)	= $	649.52
Annual carrying = the same	= $	649.52
Annual purchase	= $75,000.00
	TOTAL = $76,299.04

If four orders are placed per year, the order size will be (.985)(75,000)/4 = $18,468.75 per order.

The average inventory will be $18,468.75/2 = $9,234.375.

The annual costs would be:

Annual ordering = (4)(45)	= $	180.00
Annual carrying = (9,234.375)(.25)	= $	2,308.59
Annual purchase = (.985)(75,000)	= $73,875.00
	TOTAL = $76,363.59

In this case we would reject the discount. Our offer to them is a discount rate which would result in our being indifferent (where total costs are $76,299.04). We call the discount 1 - X where:

Annual ordering = $180.00

Annual carrying = $\frac{(75,000)(X)}{4}$ $\frac{(.25)}{2}$ = 2343.75X

134

Annual purchase = 75,000X

$$180 + 2343.75X + 75,000X = \$76,299.04$$
$$X = .9842$$

So, any discount greater than about 1.6% should be accepted.

7-25　For supplier A who sells any quantity at \$125 per barrel, we compute our EOQ using equation (7-2) where A = (125)(1500) = \$187,500 per year:

$$N_u = \sqrt{\frac{2AP}{R^2 C}} = \sqrt{\frac{(2)(187,500)(75)}{(125)^2(.20)}} = 95 \text{ barrels per order.}$$

For supplier B, our optimal order is:

$$N_u = \sqrt{\frac{2AP}{R^2 C}} = \sqrt{\frac{(2)(120)(1500)(75)}{(120)^2(.20)}} = 97 \text{ barrels per order}$$

For supplier C, our optimal order quantity is:

$$N_u = \sqrt{\frac{2AP}{R^2 C}} = \sqrt{\frac{(2)(118)(1500)(75)}{(118)^2(.20)}} = 98 \text{ barrels per order}$$

Since the optimal order quantity for supplier B (97 barrels) is above the 80 barrel minimum, we can qualify for the \$120 price and still order optimally. For this reason we can eliminate supplier A who sells for \$120 per barrel. We now compare the annual costs with suppliers B and C.

	Supplier B	Supplier C
Order quantity	97 bbls	150 bbls
No. orders/year	15.4639	10
Annual ordering	(15.4639)(75) =1,159.79	(10)(75) = 750.00
Annual carrying	(97/2)(120)(.20) =1,164.00	(150/2)(118)(.20)= 1,770.00
Annual purchase	(120)(1500) =180,000.00	(118)(1500)= 177,000.00
TOTALS	=\$182,323.79	\$179,520.00

The most effective alternative is supplier C.

7-26　The current optimal number of orders per year is computed with equation (6-1):

$$N_o = \sqrt{\frac{AC}{2P}} = \sqrt{\frac{(9,000)(.16)}{(2)(40)}} = 4.24264 \text{ orders/year}$$

135

We compare the costs of the two alternatives:

	Present	Proposed
Order quant.	9,000/4.24264 =$2,121.32	(.97)(9,000)/3 =$2,910.00
No. orders/yr.	4.24264	3

Ann. ordering	(4.24264)(40) = 169.71	(3)(40) =	120.00
Ann. carrying	(2,121.32/2)(16)= 169.71	(2,910/2)(.16)=	232.80
Ann. purchase	$9,000.00	(.97)(9,000)=	8,730.00

TOTALS = $9,339.42 $9,082.80

The hospital should order 3 times a year and take the 3% discount.

7-27   The net requirements are:

Component	Number needed	Number on hand	Net new requirements
0025	600	56	544
1027	544	23	521
1028	544	22	522
1029	544	1000	0
1030	544	87	457
1031	544	720	0
2079	914	200	714
2080	457	156	301

7-28   The order release and production release schedule is:

Step in process	Completion	Release
1. Desk lamp complete	20	
Lead time	-3	
Assemble desk lamp		17
2. Shade	17	
Lead time	-2	
Manufacture shade		15
3. Ceramic base	17	
Lead time	-3	
Manufacture ceramic base		14
4. Switch assembly	17	
Lead time	-1	
Assemble switch assembly		16
5. Insulator	16	
Lead time	-6	
Order insulator		10
6. 3-way switch	16	
Lead time	-5	
Order 3-way switch		11

7-29   The net requirements are:

Component	Number needed	Number on hand	Net new requirements
0017	825	85	740
1023	740	91	649
1024	740	23	717
1043	740	17	723
1097	740	14	726
2013	649	45	604
2014	717	64	653

7-30   The order release and production release schedule is:

Step in process	Completion	Release
1. Pliers/Box complete	10	
Lead time	-1	
Assemble pliers/Box		9
2. Left grip complete	9	
Lead time	-2	
Assemble left grip		7
3. Right grip complete	9	
Lead time	-2	
Assemble right grip		7
4. Packing box complete	9	
Lead time	-3	
Order box		6
5. Screws complete	9	
Lead time	-3	
Order screws		6
6. Left insulator complete	7	
Lead time	-4	
Order left insulator		3
7. Right insulator complete	7	
Lead time	-4	
Order right insulator		3

7-31

Component	Number needed to assemble 800 units of A	Number on hand	Net new requirement
B	800	50	750
C	800	100	700
D	800	20	780
E	(800 − 100)(2) = 1400	600	800
F	(800 − 100)(3) = 2100	1200	900

The order release and production release schedule is:

Step in process	Must be completed by week:
Item B completed	60
- Lead time for B	- 3
Start B production	57
Item D completed	60
- Lead time for D	- 1
Order D	59
Item C completed	60
- Lead time for C	- 2
Start C production	58
Item E completed	58
- Lead time for E	- 4
Start E production	54
Item F completed	58
- Lead time for F	- 6
Order F	52

7-32 The net requirements are:

Component	Number needed	Number on hand	Net new requirements
0094	50	21	29
1116	29	8	21
1214	29	12	17
1219	29	16	13
1347	29	0	29
2837	21	16	5
2214	(3)(21)=63	43	20
2305	13	4	9
3219	(2)(9)+(1)(13)=31	20	11

7-33 The schedule of releases to production is:

Step in process	Completion	Release
1. Special jig completed	12	
Lead time	-3	
Start jig assembly		9
2. Housing assembly completed	9	
Lead time	-2	
Start housing assembly		7
3. Clamp assembly completed	9	
Lead time	-4	
Start clamp assembly		5
4. Control assembly completed	9	
Lead time	-3	
Start control assembly		6

(Continued)

```
5. Packing crate completed         9
     Lead time                     -1
     Start packing crate                          8
6. Casting completed               7
     Lead time                     -2
     Start casting                                 5
7. Sleeve completed                7
     Lead time                     -1
     Start sleeve                                  6
8. Electronics package completed   6
     Lead time                     -2
     Start electronics package                     4
9. Digital counter completed       4(lesser of 4 or 6)
     Lead time                     -3
     Start digital counter                         1
```

7-34   Two of the six items have reached their reorder point--
        copper plate and wrought iron. These will be ordered at
        their trigger levels:

```
          Copper plate:      800 kg
          Wrought iron:     2000 kg
                            2800 kg
```

This leaves another 1200 kilograms of metal to be ordered
in order to meet the 400-kilogram minimum.

Now we compute the percentage above reorder point of the
remaining four items:

Item	Amount over ROP	Percentage over ROP	Order of selection
Rolled steel	200 kg	20%	1
Brass	600 kg	100%	3
Aluminum	300 kg	100%	3
Copper pipe	50 kg	25%	2

We take the two trigger items and add to them additional
items in order of selection: (1) rolled steel, (2) copper
pipe, and (3) brass or aluminum, until the minimum 400-
kilogram order is met. The order is:

Item	Quantity ordered
Copper plate	800 kg
Wrought iron	2000 kg
Rolled steel	1050 kg
Copper pipe	150 kg

139
```
```

7-35 Knowing the mean usage of 150 tons and knowing that in 70% of the cases 200 tons or less will be used, we can determine the standard deviation of annual usage. From Appendix Table 1 we find that when 70% of the area lies to the left, we are about .52 standard deviations to the right of the mean.

$$.52 \text{ std. dev.} = 200 - 150 = 50 \text{ tons}$$
$$1 \text{ std. dev.} = 50/.52 = 96.15 \text{ tons}$$

Appendix, Table 1 also tells us that a 95% service level is equivalent to about 1.64 standard deviations. The 95% service-level usage then is:

$$\text{Usage at 95\% service level} = 150 + (1.64)(96.15)$$
$$= 308 \text{ tons}$$

With a safety stock of 308 - 150 = 158 tons, the annual storage costs are:

$$\text{Annual expected storage cost of safety stock} = (158)(15)$$
$$= \$2370$$

7-36 First, we compute the EOQ order quantity under the old procedure:

$$N_u = \sqrt{\frac{2AP}{R^2 C}} = \sqrt{\frac{2(\$600,000)(50)}{(10,000)^2 (.15)}} = 2 \text{ tractors/order}$$

The annual holding costs are:

$$\text{Annual holding costs} = 1/2 N_u RC = (2/2)(1500) = \$1500/\text{yr}$$

The total price reduction of 60 tractors is then $1500, or on a per-unit basis:

$$\text{Price reduction} = \frac{\$1500}{60} = \$25/\text{tractor}.$$

7-37 The optimum order quantity is:

$$N_u = \sqrt{\frac{2AP}{R^2 C}} = \sqrt{\frac{(2)(\$54,000)(30)}{(60)^2 (.26)}} = 59 \text{ lamps}$$
$$\text{where } A = (900)\$60 = \$54,000$$

At a service level of 90% we find from the normal distribution table in Appendix Table 1 the value of 1.28 standard deviations. Therefore, the safety stock is:

$$\text{Safety stock} = (1.28)(4) = 5 \text{ lamps}$$

$$\text{Reorder point} = 10 + 5 = 15 \text{ lamps}$$

The annual costs are:

Annual holding cost = $1/2 N_u RC$ = (59/2)(60)(.26) = $460.20/yr

Annual ordering cost = UP/N_u = (900/59)(30) = 457.63/yr

Annual holding cost of safety stock = (S.S.)(RC) =
(5)(60)(.26) = <u>78.00/yr</u>
Total annual costs = $995.83/yr

7-38 The economic lot size is:

$$N_u = \sqrt{\frac{2US}{RC(1-d/p)}} = \sqrt{\frac{(2)(8000)(500)}{(2)(1-26/100)}} = 735 \text{ units}$$

The optimum number of setups per year is:

$$N_o = \frac{A_u}{N_u} = \frac{8000}{735} = 10.88 \text{ setups/year}$$

We now evaluate the stockout costs for each possible level of safety stock:

Reorder point	Safety stock	Prob. of being out	Number short	Expected annual cost	
130	0	.10 at 140 use	10	(10)(.10)(600)(10.88)=$	6528.00
		.06 at 150 use	20	(20)(.06)(600)(10.88)=	7833.60
		.02 at 160 use	30	(30)(.02)(600)(10.88)=	3916.80
		.01 at 170 use	40	(40)(.01)(600)(10.88)=	<u>2611.20</u>
				Total annual stockout cost =	$20,889.60
140	10	.06 at 150 use	10	(10)(.06)(600)(10.88)=$	3916.80
		.02 at 160 use	20	(20)(.02)(600)(10.88)=	2611.20
		.01 at 170 use	30	(30)(.01)(600)(10.88)=	<u>1958.40</u>
				Total annual stockout cost =	$ 8486.40
150	20	.02 at 160 use	10	(10)(.02)(600)(10.88)=$	1305.60
		.01 at 170 use	20	(20)(.01)(600)(10.88)=	<u>1305.60</u>
				Total annual stockout cost =	$ 2611.20
160	30	.01 at 170 use	10	(10)(.01)(600)(10.88)=$	<u>652.80</u>
				Total annual stockout cost =	$ 652.80
170	40	0		Total annual stockout cost =	$ 0

Now we add the carrying cost of the safety stock to the annual expected stockout cost to develop a total annual cost for each safety stock option:

141

Reorder point	Safety stock	Annual carrying costs of safety stock	Exp. annual stockout, $	Total annual cost, $/yr
130	0	0	20,890	20,890
140	10	200	8,486	8,686
150	20	400	2,611	3,011
160	30	600	653	1,253
170	40	800	0	800

The optimum policy is to carry a safety stock of 40 shafts and reorder when stock level dips to a reorder point of 170 shafts.

7-39   The annual demand in dollars for the various discounts are:

R	A
$40.00 per unit	$80,000 per year
39.50	79,000
39.00	78,000

for 99 or less:

$$N_\mu = \sqrt{\frac{(2)(80,000)(40)}{(40)^2(.20)}} = 141 \text{ dozen}$$

Since they already qualify for a discount for ordering more than 100, we now compute:

for the 100 to 499 dozen:

$$N_\mu = \sqrt{\frac{(2)(79,000)(40)}{(39.50)^2(.20)}} = 142 \text{ dozen}$$

Comparing the two policies:

	Policy 1 (Order 142 dozen)	Policy 2 (Order 500 dozen)
Hold. cost	(142/2)(39.50)(.20)=560.90	(500/2)(39.00)(.20)=1,950.00
Order. cost	(2000/142)(40)=563.38	(2000/500)(40)= 160.00
Purch. cost	= 79,000.00	= 78,000.00
	80,124.28	80,110.00

Policy 2 is slightly less costly.

7-40   We use equation 6-4:

$$\text{Trigger EOQ} = \sqrt{\frac{(2)(8000)(23)(100)}{(23)^2(.23)}} = 550 \text{ units}$$

$$\text{Line item EOQ} = \sqrt{\frac{(2)(8000)(23)(40)}{(23)^2(.23)}} = 348 \text{ units}$$

7-41 Using equations (7-6) and (7-7), we have:

$$N_u = \sqrt{\left(\frac{(2)(180)(85)}{700}\right)\left(\frac{700 + 150}{150}\right)} = 15.74 \text{ or } 16 \text{ units}$$

$$B = (15.74) \frac{700}{700 + 150} = 12.96 \text{ or } 13 \text{ units}$$

The total annual cost from equation (7-5) is:

$$\text{Cost} = \frac{(16 - 13)^2}{(2)(16)} (700) + \frac{(180)(85)}{16} + \frac{(13)^2(150)}{(2)(16)}$$

$$= 196.88 + 956.25 + 792.19 = \$1945.32 \text{ per year}$$

7-42 The net requirements are:

Component	Number needed		Number on hand	Net new requirements
0055	1000		210	790
1023	790		144	646
1182	790		612	178
1229	790		92	698
1488	790		0	790
1551	790		0	790
2331	(2)(790) =	1580	965	615
2699	790 + 790 =	1580	29	1551
2786	(2)(790) =	1580	155	1425
2866	(2)(646) =	1292	312	980
2965	646		3016	0

7-43 The schedule of production or order release data is:

Step in Process	Completion	Release
1. Radio set completed	18	
Lead time P.N. 0055	-2	
Start radio set assembly		16
2. Ear phone set completed	16	
Lead time P.N. 1023	-1	
Start ear phone set assembly		15
3. Power supply completed	16	
Lead time P.N. 1182	-6	
Order power supply		10
4. Canister completed	16	
Lead time P.N. 1229	-7	
Order canister		9

(Continued)

143

5.	Tuner assembly completed	16	
	Lead time P.N. 1488	-3	
	Start tuner assembly		13
6.	Amplifier assembly completed	16	
	Lead time P.N. 1551	-4	
	Start amplifier assembly		12
7.	Module 68G competed	13	
	Lead time P.N. 2331	-8	
	Order module 68G		5
8.	Module 73G completed (lesser of 12 or 13)	12	
	Lead time P.N. 2699	-6	
	Order module 73G		6
9.	Module 79H completed	12	
	Lead time P.N. 2786	-10	
	Order module 79H		2
10.	Ear speaker assembly completed	15	
	Lead time P.N. 2866	-12	
	Order ear speaker assembly		3
11.	Head set assembly completed	15	
	Lead time P.N. 2965	-5	
	Order head set assembly		10

CHAPTER 8

LINEAR PROGRAMMING I:
SOLUTION METHODS

Note: In this chapter, the symbol Θ is used to represent the value of the objective function and * is used to denote the optimum solution.

8-1   We define: R = number of Jack Rice bats
                   G = number of Mitch Gedman bats

       Objective: Maximize weekend contribution = 9R + 8G
          S.T.   30R + 25G ≤ 1200   minutes lathe time available
                          R ≥ 25   commitment for Rice bats
                       R, G ≥ 0   nonnegativity

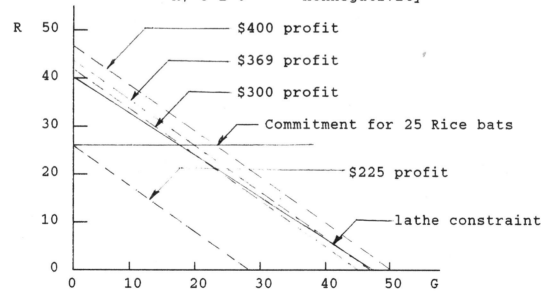

Point A
R = 25; G = 0
Θ = (9)(25) + (8)(0) = $225

Point B
R = 40; G = 0
Θ = (9)(40) + (8)(0) = $360

Point C
R = 25; G = 18
Θ = (9)(25) + (8)(18) = $369*

8-2   The isoprofit lines are shown on the graph above.

Isoprofit line	Status
$225	feasible; suboptimal
$300	feasible; suboptimal
$369	feasible; optimal
$400	nonfeasible

8-3   We define: X = number of minutes to operate machine X
                        Y = number of minutes to operate machine Y

Objective: Minimize cost = 2X + 3Y
  S.T.   X/30 + Y/25 = 40   required units of Product A
                X ≤ 600   minutes of Machine X time
              X,Y ≥ 0   nonnegativity

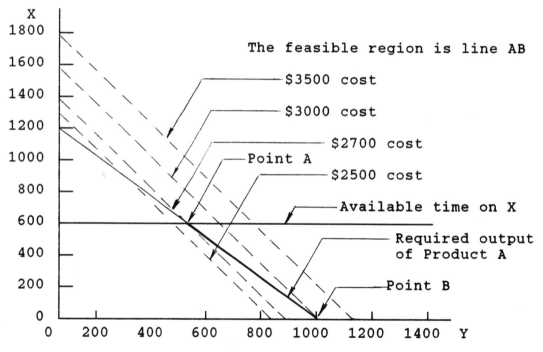

The feasible region is line AB

Point A
X = 600; Y = 500
Θ = (2)(600) + (3)(500) = $2700*

Point B
X = 0; Y = 1000
Θ = (2)(0) + (3)(1000)
    = $3000

146

8-4   The isocost lines are shown on the graph above.

Isocost line	Status
$2500	nonfeasible
$2700	feasible; optimal
$3000	feasible; suboptimal
$3500	nonfeasible unless the first constraint is expressed as a $\geq$ constraint. Suboptimal in either case

8-5   We let: Y = liters Yeltzflux in one liter of storage
       liquid mix
            Z = liters Zinderfud in one liter of storage
       liquid mix

    Obj: minimize 1.25Y + 1.38Z

    S.T.   .3Y + .6Z $\geq$ .3 liters   min Algine
            .3Y + .6Z $\leq$ .4 liters   max Algine
            .4Y + .1Z $\geq$ .2 liters   min Bendroll
            .4Y + .1Z $\leq$ .3 liters   max Bendroll
                 Y, Z $\geq$ 0   nonnegativity

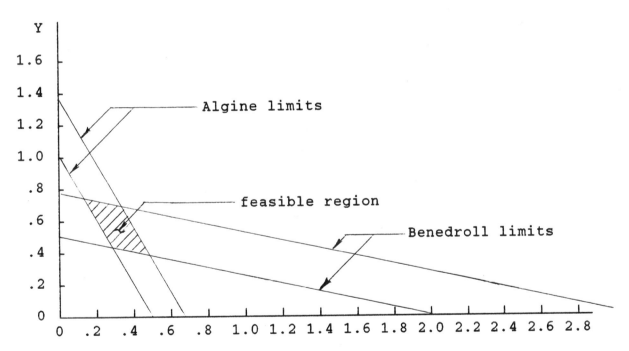

    The optimum is at the intersection of constraints #1 and
    #3:

            .3Y + .6Z = .3
            .4Y + .1Z = .2

Solving simultaneously, we get: Y = .4286 liters
                                   Z = .2857 liters

Amount of Dud = 1 - .4286 - .2857 = .2857 liters;
        cost = (1.25)(.4286) + (1.38)(.2857) = $0.93/liter

8-6   a.   The optimal solution was such that there was slack of
           .1 liter in the constraint: .3Y + .6Z ≤ .4 liters
           max Algine.

           Consequently, raising the RHS to .6 liters will not
           change the optimum solution; it would only change the
           slack in the above constraint.

      b.   We repeat a portion of the graphical solution from
           Exercise 8-5:

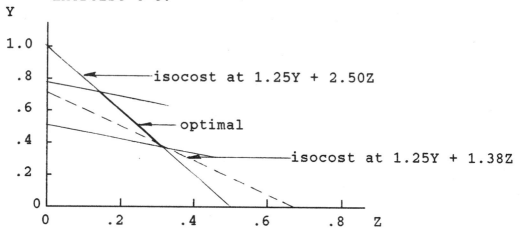

The isocost lines for both $1.38 and $2.50 per liter
for Zinderfud are shown. The one for $2.50 lies on the
constraint line for minimum Algine, thus indicating
alternative optimum solutions along this line and
otherwise within the feasible region. This agrees with
the computer output of $2.50 as the upper bound for
Zinderfud's cost.

      c.   A change in this constraint will affect the optimum
           solution since the original optimum lay on the .4Y +
           .1Z ≥ .2 liters constraint line.

           To obtain the new optimal we solve simultaneously:

                  .3Y + .6Z = .3
                  .4Y + .1Z = .3

           The result is: Y = .7143; Z = .1429; and cost =
           $1.09 per liter.

148

8-7   We define: B = number of bookcases
                     T = number of tables

       Objective: Maximize profit = 6B + 5T
          S.T. 4B + 3T ≤ 40 hours   cutting constraint
                4B ⊤ 5T ≤ 30 hours   finishing constraint
                   B,T ≤ 0   nonnegativity constraints

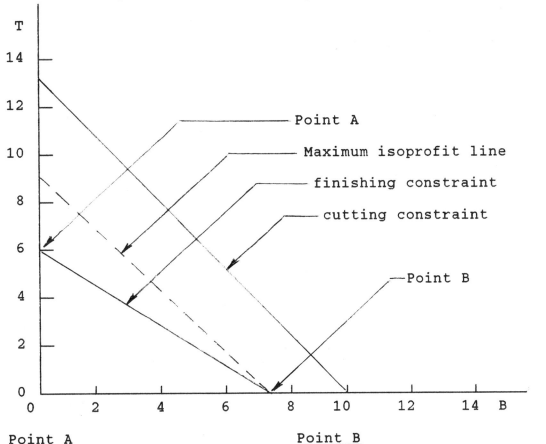

Point A   Point B
T = 6; B = 0   T = 0; B = 7.5
Θ = (6)(0) + (5)(6) = $30   Θ = (6)(7.5) + (5)(0) = $45*

The optimum plan is to produce 7.5 bookcases and no tables
for a profit of $45.

8-8   We define: T = number of turntables
                  C = number of cassette players

       Objective: Maximize profit = 10T + 6C
          S.T.   12T + 4C ≤ 60 hours   assembly constraint
                  4T + 8C ≤ 40 hours   bench check constraint
                    T,C ≥ 0   nonnegativity constraints

149

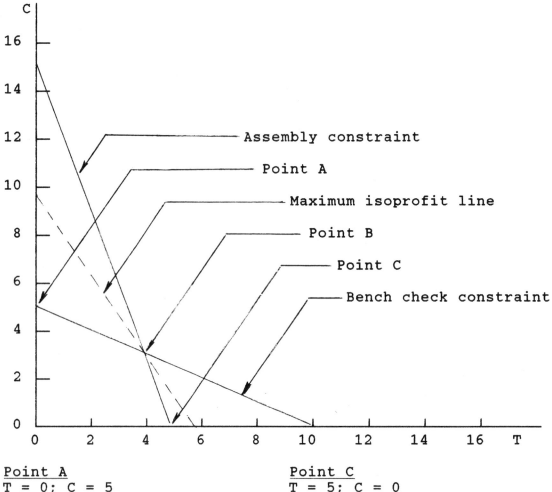

Point A
T = 0; C = 5
Θ = (10)(0) + (6)(5) = $30

Point C
T = 5; C = 0
Θ = (10)(5) + (6)(0) = $50

Point B
We solve simultaneously
12T + 4C = 60
 4T + 8C = 40
T = 4; C = 3
Θ = (10)(4) + (6)(3) = $58*

Therefore, we should produce 4 turntables and 3 cassette players for a $58 profit.

8-9   We define: D = number of 7-lb bags of Diet-Sup
                   G = number of 3-lb bags of Gro-More

       Objective: Maximize profit = 1.5D + 1.1G
                   S.T.   4D + 2G ≤ 700 pounds   protein constraint
                          3D + 1G ≤ 500 pounds   carbohydrate
                          D,G ≥ 0   nonnegativity

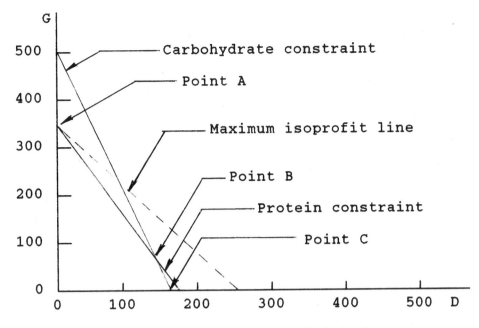

Point A

Carbohydrate constraint

Maximum isoprofit line

Point B

Protein constraint

Point C

Point A
D = 0; G = 350
Θ = (1.5)(0) + (1.1)(359)
  = $385*

Point C
D = 166 2/3; G = 0
Θ = (1.5)(166 2/3) +(1.1)(0)
  = $250

Point B
We solve simultaneously
4D + 2G = 700
3D + 1G = 500
D = 150; G = 50
Θ = (1.5)(150) + (1.1)(50) = $280

The optimal plan is to make 350 bags of Gro-More and no Diet-Sup for a profit of $385.

8-10 We define: S = number of ounces of Silent Flower
              M = number of ounces of Mood Swing

Objective: Maximize profit = 9S + 6M
    S.T. .2S + .1M ≤ 48 ounces E_1 constraint
          .3S + .1M ≤ 30 ounces E_2 constraint
          .5S + .8M ≤ 60 ounces E_3 constraint
              S,M ≥ 0   nonnegativity

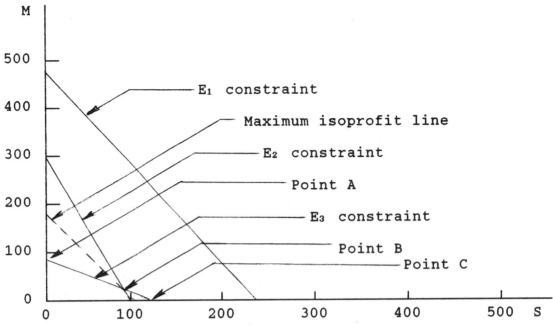

Point A
S = 0; M = 75
Θ = (9)(0) + (6)(75) = $450

Point C
S = 100; M = 0
Θ = (9)(100) + (6)(0) = $900

Point B
We simultaneously solve the E_2 and E_3 constraint equations
.3S + .1M = 30
.5S + .8M = 60
S = 1800/19; M = 300/19
Θ = (9)(1800/19) + (6)(300/19) = $947.37*

The optimum solution is to produce 94.74 oz of Silent
Flower and 15.79 oz of Mood Swing for a profit
of $947.37.

8-11   At 8% defective there are (.08)(5000) = 400 defects per
       week, while at 2% defective there are (.02)(5000) = 100
       defects per week. Therefore, 300 defective units must be
       caught each week.

       We define: E = number of experienced inspectors
                  I = number of inexperienced inspectors

       Objective: Minimize weekly cost = 360E + 260I
          S.T. 60E + 50I $\geq$ 300   (can be expressed as an equality)
                       E $\leq$ 3   limit on experienced people
                     E,I $\geq$ 0   nonnegativity

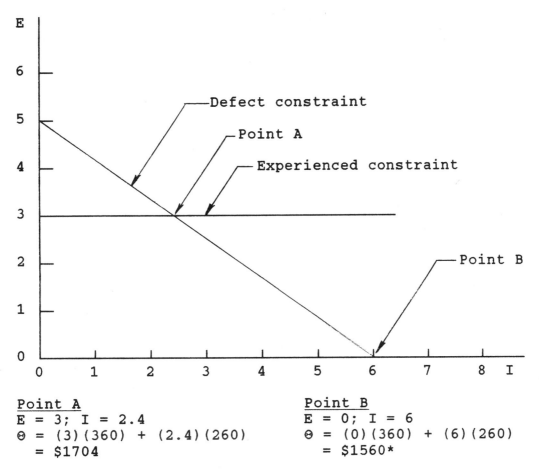

Point A
E = 3; I = 2.4
Θ = (3)(360) + (2.4)(260)
  = $1704

Point B
E = 0; I = 6
Θ = (0)(360) + (6)(260)
  = $1560*

The optimum solution is to hire 6 inexperienced inspectors
and 0 experienced inspectors at a weekly cost of $1560.

8-12 Referring to the graph shown above with Exercise 8-10, we
      see that alternative optima would exist if both points A
      and B (as well as those solutions on the line segment
      connecting them) are optimal. Defining X as the breakeven
      wage of the experienced inspectors, we have:

Point A
3X + (2.4)(260)

Point B
(6)(260) = $1560

Solving for X:
     3X + 624 = 1560
            X = $312 per week

At a wage of $312 per week, the isocost line would fall
directly on the line segment between points A and B.

8-13   We define: A = number of bolts from mill A
               B = number of bolts from mill B

       Objective: Maximize profit = 8A + 6B
           S.T. .4A + .2B ≤ 1600 bolts   fabric constraint
                 .1A + .2B ≤ 2800 bolts   discount constraint
                 .3A + .4B ≤ 2600 bolts   mail constraint
                       A,B ≥ 0   nonnegativity

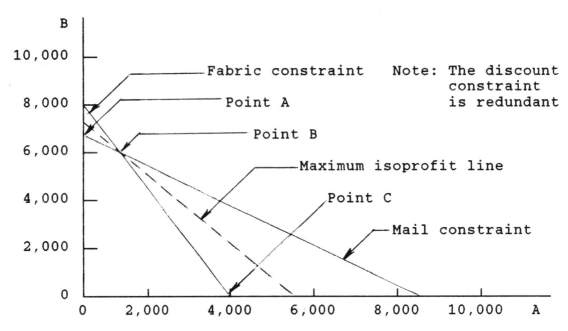

Point A   Point C
A = 0; B = 6500   A = 4000; B = 0
Θ = (8)(0) + (6)(6500)   Θ = (8)(4000) + (6)(0)
  = $39,000   = $32,000

Point B
We solve simultaneously:
.4A + .2B = 1600
.3A + .4B = 2600
A = 1200; B = 5600
Θ = (8)(1200) + (6)(5600) = $43,200*

8-14   We define: W = number of western movie ads
               R = number of romance movie ads

       Objective: Maximize number of serious buyers = 800W + 1000R
           S.T. 6500W + 5600R ≤ $20,000   budget constraint
                           W ≤ 2 ads   advertising limit
                           R ≤ 2 ads   advertising limit
                       W,R ≥ 0   nonnegativity

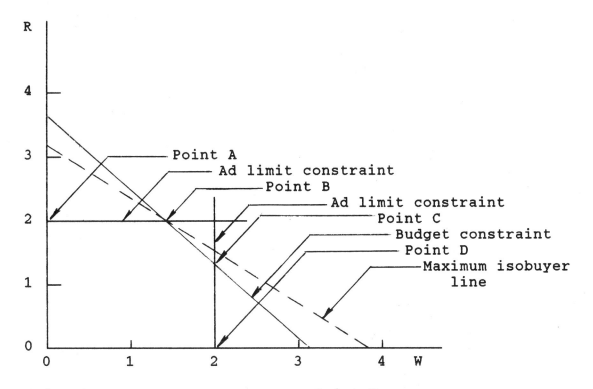

Point A
W = 0; R = 2
Θ = (800)(0) + (1000)(2)
  = 2000 buyers

Point D
W = 2; R = 0
Θ = (800)(2) + (1000)(0)
  = 1600 buyers

Point B
W = 1.354; R = 2
Θ = (800)(1.354) + (1000)(2)
  = 3083 buyers*

Point C
W = 2; R = 1.25
Θ = (800)(2) + (1000)(1.25)
  = 2850 buyers

Since the problem calls for an integer solution (i.e., no
fractions of an ad) we round off to 2 romance movie ads
and 1 western movie ad. The exposure is to 2800 serious
buyers at a cost of $17,700.

8-15   We define: P = pounds of peanuts per pound of mix
                  S = pounds of soybeans per pound of mix

Although the objective function is not specified in the
problem, we could try to minimize the total weight of
peanuts and soybeans in the mix as follows:

Objective: Minimize weight = P + S
    S.T.   P + S ≤ .5 pounds   for a profit
    50P + 100S ≥ 50 grams   Protein requirement
     40P + 15S ≥ 20 mg   Niacin requirement
           P,S ≥ 0   Nonnegativity

155

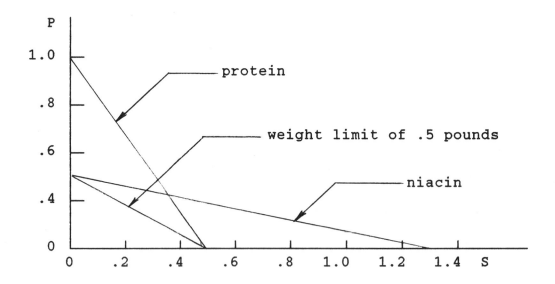

The problem is infeasible. More than half a pound of peanuts and soybeans would have to be added in order to meet the nutrition constraints.

8-16 We define: P_1 = number of Stanley Steamers produced per day
                    P_2 = number of Model T's produced per day

Objective: Maximize total contribution = $8P_1 + 10P_2$
      S.T. $7P_1 + 4P_2 \leq 420$ min/day   Machine X
             $4P_1 + 15P_2 \leq 600$ min/day   Machine Y
            $10P_1 + 16P_2 \leq 840$ min/day   Machine Z
                         $P_1 \geq 0$ all i   Nonnegativity

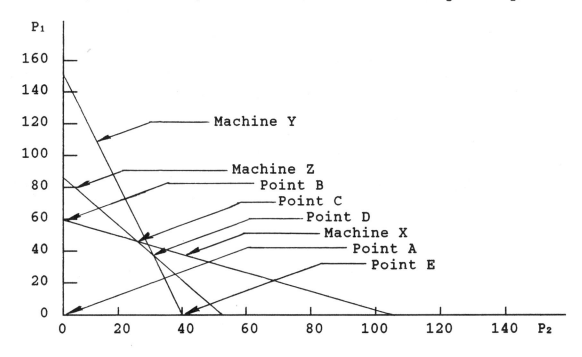

156

Now we determine the objective function for the five points:

Point	Value of P_1	Value of P_2	Value of Z, $/day	
A	0	0	8(0) + 10(0)	= 0
B	60	0	8(60) + 10(0)	= 480
C	46.67	23.33	8(46.67) + 10(23.33)	= 606.7
D	34.88	30.70	8(34.88) + 10(30.70)	= 586.0
E	0	40	8(0) + 10(40)	= 400

The optimum solution is to produce 46.67 units per day of Stanley Steamers and 23.33 units per day of Model T's for a total contribution of $606.67 per day.

8-17   We define B = number of blocks purchased
                 P = number of planks purchased
       where: contribution/block = $0.50 - $0.25 = $0.25
                    contribution/plank = $5.00 - $4.00 = $1.00

Objective: Maximize contribution = .25B + 1P
    S.T.   .5B + 1P ≤   60 cubic feet   Volume constraint
          80B + 40P ≤ 4000 pounds   Weight constraint
               B,P ≥ 0   Nonnegativity

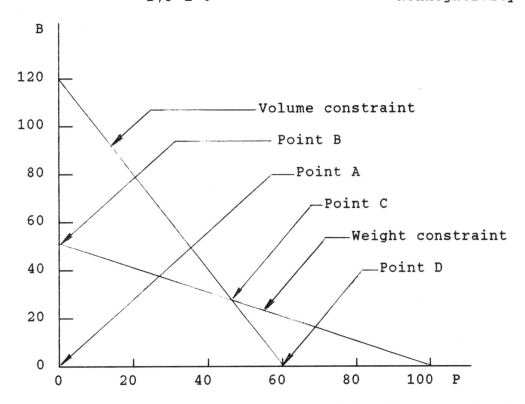

Now we determine the value of the objective function for each of the four points:

Point	Value of B	Value of P	Value of Z, $	
A	0	0	.25(0) + 1(0)	= 0
B	50	0	.25(50) + 1(0)	= 12.50
C	26 2/3	46 2/3	.25(26 2/3) + 1(46 2/3)	= 53.33
D	0	60	.25(0) + 1(60)	= 60.00

The optimum solution is to buy 60 planks for which Joe will
realize a profit of $60. No blocks should be purchased.
The entire 60 cubic feet of capacity will be used up, and
2400 pounds of the 4000 pound weight capacity will be taken
up, leaving a slack of 1600 pounds in the weight
constraint.

8-18   The only change to the problem is the objective function,
which now reads:

Objective: Maximize Z = .35B + .50P

Since the constraint set is unchanged, the four points are:

Point	Value of B	Value of P	Value of Z, $	
A	0	0	.35(0) + .50(0)	= 0
B	50	0	.35(50) + .50(0)	= 17.50
C	26 2/3	46 2/3	.35(26 2/3) + .50(46 2/3)	= 32.67
D	0	60	.35(0) + .50(60)	= 30.00

The optimum solution is point C at a profit of $32.67.

8-19   We define: T = number of of Tourglides produced/week
                  S = number of Slipstreams produced/week
                  L = number of Lightskims produced/week
                  C = number of Competitors produced/week

Objective: Maximize weekly output = 1T + 1S + 1L + 1C
    S.T. $3.0T + 2.8S + 2.5L + 2.3C \le 200$ lb/wk fiberglass
            $1.7T + 1.6S + 1.7L + 1.8C \le 130$ pints/wk bonding
            $4.3T + 4.6S + 4.2L + 5.1C \le 240$ hours/wk labor
            $1.6T + 1.5S + 1.7L + 1.9C \le 160$ hours/wk machine
                        $T,S,L,C \ge 0$ nonnegativity

The optimum solution is:
T = 0; S=0; L = 57.14; C = 0
Weekly output = 57.14 pairs of skis per week
The labor constraint is the only one constraining the
solution.

8-20 (a) The objective is to maximize total weekly contribution.

Maximize: $9T + 12S + 12L + 12C$

The optimum solution is:
$T = 0$; $S = 0$; $L = 57.14$; $C = 0$
Weekly contribution = \$685.71

(b) The objective is to maximize machine usage.

Maximize: $1.6T + 1.5S + 1.7L + 1.9C$

The optimum solution is:
$T = 0$; $S = 0$; $L = 57.14$; $C = 0$
Weekly machine usage = 97.14 hours

(c) The objective is to minimize labor usage.

Minimize: $4.3T + 4.6S + 4.2L + 5.1C$

If this were the objective function, with all constraints being of the $\leq$ type, the optimum solution would turn out to be to produce nothing (T, S, L, and C are all zero). This gives the optimum solution value of using zero labor hours per week.

8-21 We define: X_1 = number reporting at 00:01
X_2 = number reporting at 04:01
X_3 = number reporting at 08:01
X_4 = number reporting at 12:01
X_5 = number reporting at 16:01
X_6 = number reporting at 20:01

Objective: Minimize people = $X_1 + X_2 + X_3 + X_4 + X_5 + X_6$

S.T.			
X_1	$+ X_6 \geq 3$	00:01-01:00
$X_1 + X_2$	≥ 5	04:01-08:00
$X_2 + X_3$	≥ 13	08:01-12:00
$X_3 + X_4$	≥ 8	12:01-16:00
$X_4 + X_5$	≥ 19	16:01-20:00
$X_5 + X_6$	≥ 10	20:01-24:00
$X_1 \geq 0$ for all i		

The optimum solution is:
$X_1 = 3$: $X_2 = 13$; $X_3 = 0$; $X_4 = 9$; $X_5 = 10$; $X_6 = 0$
Total required people = 35

8-22 We define: A_1 = number of A buses on route 1
                 A_2 = number of A buses on route 2
                 A_3 = number of A buses on route 3
      similarly, B_1 = number of B buses on route i (i = 1,2,3)
                 C_1 = number of C buses on route i (i = 1,2,3)
                 U_1 = number of lost passengers on route 1
                 U_2 = number of lost passengers on route 2
                 U_3 = number of lost passengers on route 3
      where U_1, U_2, and U_3 are in thousands of passengers

      Objective: Minimize total cost/year = $18A_1 + 24A_2 + 20A_3$
                      $+ 18B_1 + 22B_2 + 19B_3 + 18C_1 + 26C_2 + 24C_3$
                      $+ 40U_1 + 28U_2 + 32U_3$
          S.T. $A_1 + A_2 + A_3 \leq 18$ buses   avail. of A buses
                $B_1 + B_2 + B_3 \leq 7$ buses   avail. of B buses
                $C_1 + C_2 + C_3 \leq 31$ buses   avail. of C buses
          $18A_1 + 20B_1 + 6C_1 + U_1 = 300$ pass. rte 1
          $20A_2 + 23B_2 + 8C_2 + U_2 = 400$ pass. rte 2
          $19A_3 + 21B_3 + 8C_3 + U_3 = 200$ pass. rte 3
                    All variables ≥ 0 nonnegativity

8-23 We define: GP = Units of Graphiteen produced
                 FP = Units of Fibreglow produced
                 WP = Units of Woodgloss produced
                 GV = Units of Graphiteen purchased from vendor
                 FV = Units of Fibreglow purchased from vendor
                 WV = Units of Woodgloss purchased from vendor

      Objective: Maximize profit = $122GP + 138FP + 154WP$
                      $+ 12GV + 6FV + 8WV$
          S.T. $17GP + 14FP + 12WP \leq 10,800$ min   Mach. A
               $12GP + 10FP + 19WP \leq 9,600$ min   Mach. B
                      $GP + GV \geq 220$ units   Graphiteen
                      $FP + FV \geq 310$ units   Fibreglow
                      $WP + WV \geq 40$ units   Woodgloss
                           $GV \leq 40$ units   Graph. avail
                           $FV \leq 80$ units   Fibre. avail
                 All variables ≥ 0 Nonnegativity

8-24 We define: S_1 = no. of plywood sheets Sue produces/day
                 S_2 = no. of pressboard sheets Sue produces/day
                 A_1 = no. of plywood sheets Al produces/day
                 A_2 = no. of pressboard sheets Al produces/day

      Sue's rates are: 1/12 day per sheet of plywood
                       1/10 day per sheet of pressboard
      Al's rates are: 1/10 day per sheet of plywood
                       1/9 day per sheet of pressboard

Objective: Maximize profit = $5S_1 + 5A_1 + 8S_2 + 8A_2$
S.T. $1/12S_1 + 1/10S_2 \leq 1$ Sue's daily output
      $1/10A_1 + 1/9\ A_2 \leq 1$ Al's daily output
      All variables ≥ 0 Nonnegativity

The optimum solution is:
$S_1 = 0$; $A_1 = 0$; $S_2 = 10$; $A_2 = 9$
$\Theta = \$152$ per day

8-25 We define our variables as the number of logs to be cut
      with each of the three cut sequences:

Let X_1 = number of logs cut per day with first sequence
    X_2 = number of logs cut per day with second sequence
    X_3 = number of logs cut per day with third sequence

Output	First Sequence			Second Sequence		
	Number	Revenue	Time	Number	Revenue	Time
1 x 2	17	17	17	22	22	22
2 x 4	7	28	14	0	0	0
2 x 6	3	18	6	0	0	0
4 x 8	0	0	0	8	80	24
Sawdust	8	0.80	--	6	0.60	--
Chips	87	6.09	--	94	6.58	--
	Totals	69.89	37		109.18	46

Output	Third Sequence		
	Number	Revenue	Time
1 x 2	4	4	4
2 x 4	9	36	18
2 x 6	4	24	8
4 x 8	0	0	0
Sawdust	9	0.90	--
Chips	73	5.11	--
	Totals	70.01	30

Objective: maximize profit = $69.89X_1 + 109.18X_2 + 70.01X_3$
S.T. $37X_1 + 46X_2 + 30X_3 \leq 1680$ min   saw time
                        $X_2 \geq 50/8$ logs/day for 4 x 8's
      All variables ≥ 0 Nonnegativity

The optimum solution is:
$X_1 = 0$; $X_2 = 36.52$; $X_3 = 0$
$\Theta = \$3987.44$ per day

CHAPTER 9

LINEAR PROGRAMMING II:
THE SIMPLEX METHOD

9-1   We define: A = tons/week of Type A produced
               B = tons/week of Type B produced

Objective: Maximize contribution = 3A + 4B
      S.T.   2A + 3B ≤ 40 hours/week   Dept. 1
              3A + 3B ≤ 75 hours/week   Dept. 2
      All variables ≥ 0   Nonnegativity

First tableau

C_j	Prod. Mix	Quantity	3 A	4 B	0 S_1	0 S_2
0	S_1	40	2	3	1	0
0	S_2	75	3	3	0	1
	Z_j	$ 0	0	0	0	0
	$C_j - Z_j$		3	4	0	0

We enter variable B in place of variable S_1:

Second tableau

C_j	Prod. Mix	Quantity	3 A	4 B	0 S_1	0 S_2
4	B	40/3	2/3	1	1/3	0
0	S_2	35	1	0	−1	1
	Z_j	$160/3	8/3	4	4/3	0
	$C_j - Z_j$		1/3	0	−4/3	0

We now enter variable A in place of variable B:

Third tableau

C_j	Prod. Mix	Quantity	3 A	4 B	0 S_1	0 S_2
3	A	20	1	3/2	1/2	0
0	S_2	15	0	-3/2	-3/2	1
	Z_j	$60	3	9/2	3/2	0
	$C_j - Z_j$		0	-1/2	-3/2	0

The solution is optimal; we produce 20 tons/week of Type A
for a weekly contribution of $60. There are 15 hours/week
of slack time (S_2 = 15) in Department 2 while Department 1
is used to capacity (S_1 = 0 since it is not in the product
mix). Therefore, we should allocate plant expansion funds
to Department 1 for a potential profit improvement of $3/2
per hour/week of additional capacity.

9-2 Going from the first tableau of exercise 9-1, we enter
variable A in place of variable S_1:

C_j	Prod. Mix	Quantity	3 A	4 B	0 S_1	0 S_2
3	A	20	1	3/2	1/2	0
0	S_2	15	0	-3/2	-3/2	1
	Z_j	$60	3	9/2	3/2	0
	$C_j - Z_j$		0	-1/2	-3/2	0

We find that this solution is identical to the one obtained
in the third tableau of exercise 9-1. This demonstrates
that in this particular problem, we were able to solve the
problem in only one pivot when we violated Step 1, whereas
it takes two pivots when we follow the correct procedure.
The point of this exercise is that Step 1 of Simplex is a
heuristic (a good rule of thumb). In most cases, adherence
to the Step 1 procedure will tend to get us to an optimum
solution in the fewest number of pivots, but this is not
always the case. The simplex procedure can guarantee that
we will always be able to find an optimum solution if there
is one; it does not guarantee we will get there in the most
direct manner.

9-3 Starting from the second tableau of exercise 9-1, we enter
variable A in place of S_2 in violation of Step 2 of the
simplex procedure.

Third tableau

C_j	Prod. Mix	Quantity	3 A	4 B	0 S_1	0 S_2
4	B	-10	0	1	1	-2/3
3	A	35	1	0	-1	1
	Z_j	$65	3	4	1	1/3
	$C_j - Z_j$		0	0	-1	-1/3

This solution, with a profit of $65 per week, appears to be better on the surface than the optimum profit of $60. But, this solution is infeasible; it says we should produce 35 tons/week of Type A and -10 tons/week of Type B fertilizer. We cannot produce negative 10 tons/week of Type B fertilizer. Consequently, we have violated a nonnegativity constraint. The point of this exercise is to demonstrate that by following the Step 2 procedure, we always produce feasible solutions (assuming, of course, there does exist one).

9-4   When our objective is to maximize the total number of units produced, we have:

Objective: Maximize total output = $1X_1 + 1X_2$
    S.T. $6X_1 + 8X_2 \leq 38$ hours   Dept. 1 constraint
            $6X_1 + 12X_2 \leq 42$ hours   Dept. 2 constraint
                $X_1, X_2 \geq 0$ Nonnegativity

First tableau

C_j	Prod. mix	Quantity	1 X_1	1 X_2	0 S_1	0 S_2
0	S_1	38	6	8	1	0
0	S_2	42	6	12	0	1
	Z_j	0	0	0	0	0
	$C_j - Z_j$		1	1	0	0

Going to the second tableau, we can enter either X_1 or X_2. Let us arbitrarily select X_1 to enter in place of variable S_1.

Second tableau

C_j	Prod. Mix	Quantity	1 X_1	1 X_2	0 S_1	0 S_2
1	X_1	19/3	1	4/3	1/6	0
0	S_2	4	0	4	-1	1
	Z_j	19/3	1	4/3	1/6	0
	$C_j - Z_j$		0	-1/3	-1/6	0

164

The solution is optimum when we produce 19/3 units of X_1, which has a contribution of (6)(19/3) = \$38.

When our objective is to maximize total contribution, we have:

Objective: Maximize total contribution = $6X_1 + 14X_2$

First tableau

			6	14	0	0
C_j	Prod. Mix	Quantity	X_1	X_2	S_1	S_2
0	S_1	38	6	8	1	0
0	S_2	42	6	12	0	1
	Z_j	0	0	0	0	0
	$C_j - Z_j$		6	14	0	0

We now enter X_2 in place of variable S_2.

Second tableau

			6	14	0	0
C_j	Prod. Mix	Quantity	X_1	X_2	S_1	S_2
0	S_1	10	2	0	1	-2/3
14	X_2	7/2	1/2	1	0	1/12
	Z_j	\$49	7	14	0	7/6
	$C_j - Z_j$		-1	0	0	-7/6

This solution is optimum. We produce 7/2 units of X_2 for a contribution of \$49.
The difference in contribution between the maximum output and maximum contribution solutions is 49 - 38 = \$11.

9-5   We define: A = pounds of alzene per pound of mix
                   B = pounds of bartomel per pound of mix
                   C = pounds of cathorene per pound of mix

Objective: Minimize cost = 20A + 15B + 10C
       S.T. $3A - 2B - 2C \geq 0$ 3 parts A to 2 parts B and C
                     $B - C \geq 0$ B to C weight ratio
              $A + B + C = 1$ 1 lb of ingred. per 1 lb mix
              $A, B, C \geq 0$ Nonnegativity

After augmenting, we have:

Minimize $Z = 20A + 15B + 10C + MA_1 + MA_2 + MA_3 + 0S_1 + 0S_2$
   S.T. $3A - 2B - 2C + 1A_1 + 0A_2 + 0A_3 - 1S_1 + 0S_2 = 0$
          $0A + 1B - 1C + 0A_1 + 1A_2 + 0A_3 + 0S_1 - 1S_2 = 0$
          $1A + 1B + 1C + 0A_1 + 0A_2 + 1A_3 + 0S_1 + 0S_2 = 1$

165

The optimum solution is:
A = .4; B = .3; C = .3
Θ = $15.50 per pound of mix

9-6   We define: M = number of model M trucks scheduled
                   P = number of model P trucks scheduled

Objective: Minimize cost = 300M + 100P
       S.T. 10M + 5P ≥ 20 tons   Shipping constraint
                    P ≤ 2   trucks   Availability of P

After augmenting, we have:
    Minimize Z = 300M + 100P + MA_1 + $0S_1$ + $0S_2$
       S.T.   10M + 5P + $1A_1$ − $1S_1$ + $0S_2$ = 20
              0M + 1P + $0A_1$ + $0S_1$ + $1S_2$ = 2

Initial tableau

			300	100	M	0	0
C_j	Prod. Mix	Quantity	M	P	A_1	S_1	S_2
M	A_1	20	10	5	1	−1	0
0	S_2	2	0	1	0	0	1
	Z_j	20M	10M	5M	M	−M	0
	$C_j - Z_j$		300−10M	100−5M	0	M	0

We enter variable M and replace A_1 :

Second tableau

			300	100	M	0	0
C_j	Prod. Mix	Quantity	M	P	A_1	S_1	S_2
300	M	2	1	1/2	1/10	−1/10	0
0	S_2	2	0	1	0	0	1
	Z_j	600	300	150	30	−30	0
	$C_j - Z_j$		0	−50	M−30	30	0

We enter variable P and replace S_2 :

Third tableau

			300	100	M	0	0
C_j	Prod. Mix	Quantity	M	P	A_1	S_1	S_2
300	M	1	1	0	1/10	−1/10	−1/2
100	P	2	0	1	0	0	1
	Z_j	500	300	100	30	−30	−50
	$C_j - Z_j$		0	0	M−30	30	50

The solution is optimal. We schedule one M type truck and
two P Type trucks at a cost of $500.

9-7 We note that the constraint $X + Y \geq 1$ is redundant, because of constraint $2X + 2Y \geq 4$. Therefore, we may eliminate the redundant constraint. After adding slack and artificial constraints, our problem becomes:

Objective: Minimize $Z = 2X + 7Y - 3W + MA_1 + MA_2 + 0S_1$
S.T. $3X + 0Y + 2W + 1A_1 + 0A_2 + 0S_1 = 9$
       $2X + 3Y + 0W + 0A_1 + 1A_2 - 1S_1 = 4$

Initial tableau

C_j	Prod. Mix	Quantity	2 X	7 Y	-3 W	M A_1	M A_2	0 S_1
M	A_1	9	3	0	2	1	0	0
M	A_2	4	2	3	0	0	1	-1
	Z_j	13M	5M	3M	2M	M	M	-M
	$C_j - Z_j$		2-5M	7-3M	-3-2M	0	0	M

In the next tableau, we enter variable X. The least positive quotient results in variable A_2 being removed.

Second tableau

C_j	Prod. Mix	Quantity	2 X	7 Y	-3 W	M A_1	M A_2	0 S_1
M	A_1	3	0	-9/2	2	1	-3/2	3/2
2	X	2	1	3/2	0	0	1/2	-1/2
	Z_j	3M+4	2	-9/2M+3	2M	M	-3/2M+1	3/2M-1
	$C_j - Z_j$		0	9/2M+4	-2M-3	0	5/2M+1	-3/2M+1

In the next tableau, we enter variable W and remove variable A_1:

Third tableau

C_j	Prod. Mix	Quantity	2 X	7 Y	-3 W	M A_1	M A_2	0 S_1
-3	W	3/2	0	-9/4	1	1/2	-3/4	3/4
2	X	2	1	3/2	0	0	1/2	-1/2
	Z_j	-1/2	2	39/4	-3	-3/2	13/4	-13/4
	$C_j - Z_j$		0	-11/4	0	M+3/2	M-13/4	M+13/4

We now enter variable Y and remove variable X:

Fourth tableau

C_j	Prod. Mix	Quantity	2 X	7 Y	-3 W	M A_1	M A_2	0 S_1
-3	W	9/2	3/2	0	1	1/2	0	0
7	Y	4/3	2/3	1	0	0	1/3	-1/3
	Z_j	-25/6	1/6	7	-3	-3/2	7/3	-7/3
	$C_j - Z_j$		11/16	0	0	M+3/2	M-7/3	7/3

The solution is now optimal as follows:
W = 9/2; Y = 4/3
θ = -25/6

9-8 This is an example of an unbounded problem. By inspecting the constraints we see that variable X_1 can take on an infinite value. The problem with slack, surplus, and artificial variables added is:

Objective: Maximize $Z = 15X_1 + 10X_2 + 0S_1 - MA_2 + 0S_2$
S.T. $0X_1 + 5X_2 + 1S_1 + 0A_2 + 0S_2 = 25$
      $2X_1 + 1X_2 + 0S_1 + 1A_2 - 1S_2 = 4$

First tableau

			15	10	0	-M	0
C_j	Prod. Mix	Quantity	X_1	X_2	S_1	A_2	S_2
0	S_1	25	0	5	1	0	0
-M	A_2	4	2	1	0	1	-1
	Z_j	-4M	-2M	-M	0	-M	M
	$C_j - Z_j$		2M+15	M+10	0	0	-M

We now enter variable X_1 and replace A_2:

Second tableau

			15	10	0	-M	0
C_j	Prod. Mix	Quantity	X_1	X_2	S_1	A_2	S_2
0	S_1	25	0	5	1	0	0
15	X_1	2	1	1/2	0	1/2	-1/2
	Z_j	30	15	15/2	0	15/2	-15/2
	$C_j - Z_j$		0	5/2	0	-M-15/2	15/2

We now find that variable S_2, with the largest positive $C_j - Z_j$ value of 15/2, should be entered. In performing the Step 2 calculations to find the variable to be replaced, we find:

row S_1: 25 ÷ 0, which approaches infinity

row X_1: 2 ÷ -1/2, which is negative

Variable S_2 is therefore unbounded since it can approach infinity. Since S_2 is the surplus variable in the constraint $2X_1 + 1X_2 \geq 4$, this implies that variable X_1 (which is in the product mix will also approach infinity.

9-9 This is an example of a problem with infeasible constraints. Obviously both constraints cannot be satisfied with variables A and B both being nonnegative. After adding slack and artificial variables, we have:

168

Objective: Maximize $Z = 3A + 4B + 0S_1 - MA_2$
S.T. $2A + 3B + 1S_1 + 0A_2 = 6$
        $1A + 2B + 0S_1 + 1A_2 = 20$

First tableau

C_j	Prod. Mix	Quantity	3 A	4 B	0 S_1	-M A_2
0	S_1	6	2	3	1	0
-M	A_2	20	1	2	0	1
	Z_j	-20M	-M	-2M	0	-M
	$C_j - Z_j$		M+3	2M+4	0	0

Now we enter variable B in place of variable S_1:

Second tableau

C_j	Prod. Mix	Quantity	3 A	4 B	0 S_1	-M A_2
4	B	2	2/3	1	1/3	0
-M	A_2	16	-1/3	0	-2/3	1
	Z_j	8-16M	8/3+M/3	4	4/3+2/3M	-M
	$C_j - Z_j$		-1/3-M/3	0	-4/3-2/3M	0

Since all values in the $C_j - Z_j$ row are negative, and we have a maximization problem, this signals an optimal solution. However, we have an artificial variable, A_2, in the product mix. Consequently, there is no feasible solution to this problem.

9-10   a. An optimal tableau for a maximization problem must contain all zeroes or negative values in the $C_j - Z_j$ row. Therefore, the tableau is optimal.

b. We always find zero values in the $C_j - Z_j$ row beneath the columns associated with those variables in the product mix. In this case X_1, S_2, and S_3 are in the product mix, and the variable columns X_1, S_2, and S_3 all contain zeroes in the $C_j - Z_j$ row. However, variable X_2, which is not in the product mix also has a zero $C_j - Z_j$ value. This means we can enter variable X_2 in another iteration and still not change our optimal profit of $32 per day. In fact, whenever there exists another optimal solution, as in this case, there are an infinite number of optimal solutions. The most X_2 we can enter is the least-positive quotient of the three:

Quantity	X_2	Quotient
4	.75	5.333
4	.05	80
1.4	.175	8

Therefore, we can introduce any amount of X_2 in the continuous range of 0 to 5.333 units per day giving rise to an infinite number of possible solutions.

c. The optimum value of Z is $32 per day.

9-11   Initial tableau

C_j	Prod. Mix	Quantity	1 D	2 F	0 S_1	0 S_2	0 S_3
0	S_1	50	1	3	1	0	0
0	S_2	150	6	9	0	1	0
0	S_3	120	3	8	0	0	1
	Z_j	0	0	0	0	0	0
	$C_j - Z_j$		1	2	0	0	0

We enter variable F in place of variable S_3:

Second tableau

C_j	Prod. Mix	Quantity	1 D	2 F	0 S_1	0 S_2	0 S_3
0	S_1	5	$-1/8$	0	1	0	$-3/8$
0	S_2	15	$21/8$	0	0	1	$-9/8$
2	F	15	$3/8$	1	0	0	$1/8$
	Z_j	30	$3/4$	2	0	0	$1/4$
	$C_j - Z_j$		$1/4$	0	0	0	$-1/4$

Now we enter variable D in place of variable S_2:

Third tableau

C_j	Prod. Mix	Quantity	1 D	2 F	0 S_1	0 S_2	0 S_3
0	S_1	$40/7$	0	0	1	$1/21$	$-3/7$
1	D	$40/7$	1	0	0	$8/21$	$-3/7$
2	F	$90/7$	0	1	0	$-1/7$	$2/7$
	Z_j	$220/7$	1	2	0	$2/21$	$1/7$
	$C_j - Z_j$		0	0	0	$-2/21$	$-1/7$

This is the optimum solution. It may be concluded that the second and third constraints are binding since slacks S_2 and S_3 are not in the product mix. The first constraint is not binding. In fact the first constraint is redundant and could have been deleted.

9-12 Initial tableau

C_j	Product Mix	Quantity	5 A	6 B	0 S_1	0 S_2
0	S_1	12	2	-3	1	0
0	S_2	5	1	0	0	1
	Z_j	0	0	0	0	0
	$C_j - Z_j$		5	6	0	0

We choose to enter variable B. In deciding which variable is to be replaced, we compute theta values as follows:

Row S_1: $\Theta = 12 \div -3 = -4$
Row S_2: $\Theta = 5 \div 0 = $ infinity

Here we find that the least-positive value of Θ is infinitely large. This implies that we can introduce an unlimited number of variable B in place of slack variable S_2. Consequently, the problem is unbounded for variable B.

9-13 After augmenting with slack, surplus, and artificial variables, we have:

Maximize $Z = 6X + 8Y - MA_1 + 0S_1 + 0S_2$
S.T. $2X + 1Y + 1A_1 - 1S_1 + 0S_2 = 20$
$3X + 4Y + 0A_1 + 0S_1 + 1S_2 = 10$

First tableau

C_j	Prod. Mix	Quantity	6 X	8 Y	-M A_1	0 S_1	0 S_2
-M	A_1	20	2	1	1	-1	0
0	S_2	10	3	4	0	0	1
	Z_j	-20M	-2M	-1M	-1M	1M	0
	$C_j - Z_j$		6+2M	8+M	0	-M	0

We enter variable X in place of variable S_2:

Second tableau

C_j	Prod. Mix	Quantity	6 X	8 Y	-M A_1	0 S_1	0 S_2
-M	A_1	40/3	0	-5/3	1	-1	-2/3
6	X	10/3	1	4/3	0	0	1/3
	Z_j	20-40/3M	6	8+5/3M	-M	M	2+2/3M
	$C_j - Z_j$		0	-5/3M	0	-M	-2-2/3M

We find that we have no values greater than zero in the $C_j - Z_j$ row, indicating an optimal solution. Variable A_1, however, is in the product mix valued at 40/3. If we substitute the values $X = 10/3$ and $Y = 0$ into the original constraint equations, we find:

171

$$2X + 1Y \geq 20 \;-->\; (2)(10/3) + (1)(0) = 20/3$$
$$3X + 4Y \geq 10 \;-->\; (3)(10/3) + (4)(0) = 10$$

The second constraint is satisfied, but the first constraint is violated. The presence of an artificial variable in the basis of an optimal tableau signals infeasibility.

9-14 After augmenting, we have:

Minimize $Z = 3X + 4Y + 0S_1 + 0S_2 + MA_3 + 0S_3$
$$\text{S.T.} \quad 3X - 2Y + 1S_1 + 0S_2 + 0A_3 + 0S_3 = 30$$
$$-1X + 2Y + 0S_1 + 1S_2 + 0A_3 + 0S_3 = 40$$
$$6X + 8Y + 0S_1 + 0S_2 + 1A_3 - 1S_3 = 240$$

Initial tableau

C_j	Prod. Mix	Qty.	3 X	4 Y	0 S_1	0 S_2	M A_3	0 S_3
0	S_1	30	3	-2	1	0	0	0
0	S_2	40	-1	2	0	1	0	0
M	A_3	240	6	8	0	0	1	-1
	Z_j	240M	6M	8M	0	0	M	-M
	$C_j - Z_j$		3-6M	4-8M	0	0	0	M

We enter variable Y in place of S_2:

Second tableau

C_j	Prod. Mix	Qty.	3 X	4 Y	0 S_1	0 S_2	M A_3	0 S_3
0	S_1	70	2	0	1	1	0	0
4	Y	20	-1/2	1	0	1/2	0	0
M	A_3	80	10	0	0	-4	1	-1
	Z_j	80M+80	10M-2	4	0	2-4M	M	-M
	$C_j - Z_j$		5-10M	0	0	4M-2	0	-M

We enter variable X in place of A_3:

Third tableau

C_j	Prod. Mix	Qty.	3 X	4 Y	0 S_1	0 S_2	M A_3	0 S_3
0	S_1	54	0	0	1	9/5	-1/5	1/5
4	Y	24	0	1	0	3/10	1/20	-1/20
3	X	8	1	0	0	-2/5	1/10	-1/10
	Z_j	120	3	4	0	0	1/2	-1/2
	$C_j - Z_j$		0	0	0	0	M-1/2	1/2

The solution is optimal. A second optimal solution can be
developed by entering variable S_2, which is not in the
present product mix but has a zero valued $C_j - Z_j$. Variable
S_2 enters in place of variable S_1.

Alternative optimal solution

C_j	Prod. Mix	Qty.	3 X	4 Y	0 S_1	0 S_2	M A_3	0 S_3
0	S_2	30	0	0	5/9	1	-1/9	1/9
4	Y	15	0	1	-1/6	0	1/12	-1/12
3	X	20	1	0	2/9	0	1/18	-1/18
	Z_j	120	3	4	0	0	1/2	-1/2
	$C_j - Z_j$		0	0	0	0	M-1/2	1/2

9-15 After augmenting, we have:

Maximize $Z = 9R + 8G + 0S_1 - MA_2 + 0S_2$
S.T. $30R + 25G + 1S_1 + 0A_2 + 0S_2 = 1200$
$1R + 0G + 0S_1 + 1A_2 - 1S_2 = 25$

Initial tableau

C_j	Prod. Mix	Qty.	9 R	8 G	0 S_1	-M A_2	0 S_2
0	S_1	1200	30	25	1	0	0
-M	A_2	25	1	0	0	1	-1
	Z_j	-25M	-M	0	0	-M	M
	$C_j - Z_j$		M+9	8	0	0	-M

We enter variable R in place of A_2:

C_j	Prod. Mix	Qty.	9 R	8 G	0 S_1	-M A_2	0 S_2
0	S_1	450	0	25	1	0	30
9	R	25	1	0	0	1	-1
	Z_j	225	9	0	0	9	-9
	$C_j - Z_j$		0	8	0	-M-9	9

We enter variable G in place of S_1:

C_j	Prod. Mix	Qty.	9 R	8 G	0 S_1	-M A_2	0 S_2
8	G	18	0	1	1/25	0	6/5
9	R	25	1	0	0	1	-1
	Z_j	369	9	8	8/25	9	3/5
	$C_j - Z_j$		0	0	-8/25	-M-9	-3/5

The solution is optimal.

173

9-16   After augmenting, we have:

Minimize $Z = 2X + 3Y + MA_1 + 0S_2$
  S.T. $1/30X + 1/25Y + 1A_1 + 0S_2 = 40$
               $1X +   0Y + 0A_1 + 1S_2 = 600$

Initial tableau

C_j	Prod. Mix	Quantity	2 X	3 Y	M A_1	0 S_2
M	A_1	40	1/30	1/25	1	0
0	S_2	600	1	0	0	1
	Z_j	40M	M/30	M/25	M	0
	$C_j - Z_j$		2−M/30	3−M/25	0	0

We enter variable X in place of S_2:

Second tableau

C_j	Prod. Mix	Quantity	2 X	3 Y	M A_1	0 S_2
M	A_1	20	0	1/25	1	−1/30
2	X	600	1	0	0	1
	Z_j	20M+1200	2	M/25	M	2−M/30
	$C_j - Z_j$		0	3−M/25	0	−2+M/30

We enter variable Y in place of A_1:

Third tableau

C_j	Prod. Mix	Quantity	2 X	3 Y	M A_1	0 S_2
3	Y	500	0	1	25	−5/6
2	X	600	1	0	0	1
	Z_j	2700	2	3	75	−1/2
	$C_j - Z_j$		0	0	M−75	1/2

The solution is optimal.

9-17   After augmenting, we have:

Maximize $Z = 6B + 5T + 0S_1 + 0S_2$
      S.T. $4B + 3T + 1S_1 + 0S_2 = 40$
             $4B + 5T + 0S_1 + 1S_2 = 30$

Initial tableau

| | | | 6 | 5 | 0 | 0 |
C_j	Prod. Mix	Quantity	B	T	S_1	S_2
0	S_1	40	4	3	1	0
0	S_2	30	4	5	0	1
	Z_j	0	0	0	0	0
	$C_j - Z_j$		6	5	0	0

We enter variable B in place of S_2:

Second tableau

| | | | 6 | 5 | 0 | 0 |
C_j	Prod. Mix	Quantity	B	T	S_1	S_2
0	S_1	10	0	-2	1	-1
6	B	15/2	1	5/4	0	1/4
	Z_j	45	6	15/2	0	3/2
	$C_j - Z_j$		0	$-5/2$	0	$-3/2$

The solution is optimal.

9-18   After augmenting, we have:

Maximize $Z = 10T + 6C + 0S_1 + 0S_2$
   S.T. $12T + 4C + 1S_1 + 0S_2 = 60$
           $4T + 8C + 0S_1 + 1S_2 = 40$

Initial tableau

| | | | 10 | 6 | 0 | 0 |
C_j	Prod. Mix	Quantity	T	C	S_1	S_2
0	S_1	60	12	4	1	0
0	S_2	40	4	8	0	1
	Z_j	0	0	0	0	0
	$C_j - Z_j$		10	6	0	0

We enter variable T in place of S_1:

Second tableau

| | | | 10 | 6 | 0 | 0 |
C_j	Prod. Mix	Quantity	T	C	S_1	S_2
10	T	5	1	1/3	1/12	0
0	S_2	20	0	20/3	$-1/3$	1
	Z_j	50	10	10/3	5/6	0
	$C_j - Z_j$		0	8/3	$-5/6$	0

We enter variable C in place of S_2:

175

Third tableau

C_j	Prod. Mix	Quantity	10 T	6 C	0 S_1	0 S_2
10	T	4	1	0	1/10	-1/20
6	C	3	0	1	-1/20	3/20
	Z_j	58	10	6	7/10	4/10
	$C_j - Z_j$		0	0	-7/10	-4/10

The solution is optimal.

9-19 After augmenting, we have:

Minimize $Z = 360E + 260I + MA_1 + 0S_1 + 0S_2$
S.T. $60E + 50I + 1A_1 - 1S_1 + 0S_2 = 300$
$1E + 0I + 0A_1 + 0S_1 + 1S_2 = 3$

Initial tableau

C_j	Prod. Mix	Qty.	360 E	260 I	M A_1	0 S_1	0 S_2
M	A_1	300	60	50	1	-1	0
0	S_2	3	1	0	0	0	1
	Z_j	300M	60M	50M	M	-M	0
	$C_j - Z_j$		300-60M	260-50M	0	M	0

We enter variable E in place of S_2:

Second tableau

C_j	Prod. Mix	Qty.	360 E	260 I	M A_1	0 S_1	0 S_2
M	A_1	120	0	50	1	-1	-60
360	E	3	1	0	0	0	1
	Z_j	1080+120M	360	50M	M	-M	360-60M
	$C_j - Z_j$		0	260-50M	0	M	60M-360

We enter variable I in place of A_1:

Third tableau

C_j	Prod. Mix	Qty.	360 E	260 I	M A_1	0 S_1	0 S_2
260	I	12/5	0	1	1/50	-1/50	-6/5
360	E	3	1	0	0	0	1
	Z_j	1704	360	260	26/5	-26/5	48
	$C_j - Z_j$		0	0	M-26/5	26/5	-48

We enter variable S_2 in place of E:

176

Fourth tableau

C_j	Prod. Mix	Qty.	360 E	260 I	M A_1	0 S_1	0 S_2
260	I	6	6/5	1	1/50	-1/50	0
0	S_2	3	1	0	0	0	1
	Z_j	1560	312	260	26/5	-26/5	0
	$C_j - Z_j$		48	0	M-26/5	26/5	0

The solution is optimal.

9-20 After augmenting, we have:

Minimize $Z = 1P + 1S + 0S_1 + MA_2 + 0S_2 + MA_3 + 0S_3$

S.T.
$$1P + 1S + 1S_1 + 0A_2 + 0S_2 + 0A_3 + 0S_3 = 0.5$$
$$50P + 100S + 0S_1 + 1A_2 - 1S_2 + 0A_3 + 0S_3 = 50$$
$$40P + 15S + 0S_1 + 0A_2 + 0S_2 + 1A_3 - 1S_3 = 20$$

Initial tableau

C_j	P.M.	Qty.	1 P	1 S	0 S_1	M A_2	0 S_2	M A_3	0 S_3
0	S_1	0.5	1	1	1	0	0	0	0
M	A_2	50	50	100	0	1	-1	0	0
M	A_3	20	40	15	0	0	0	1	-1
	Z_j	70M	90M	115M	0	M	-M	M	-M
	$C_j - Z_j$		1-90M	1-115M	0	0	M	0	M

We enter S in place of S_1 (note· variable A_2 could also be replaced).

Second tableau

C_j	P.M.	Qty.	1 P	1 S	0 S_1	M A_2	0 S_2	M A_3	0 S_3
1	S	0.5	1	1	1	0	0	0	0
M	A_2	0	-50	0	-100	1	-1	0	0
M	A_3	12.5	25	0	-15	0	0	1	-1
	Z_j	.5+12.5M	1-25M	1	1-115M	M	-M	M	-M
	$C_j - Z_j$		25M	0	115M-1	0	M	0	M

At this point we note that there are no negative values in the $C_j - Z_j$ row, thus indicating an optimal solution. However, artificial variables exist in the product mix. Consequently, the solution is infeasible.

CHAPTER 10

LINEAR PROGRAMMING III:
BUILDING LP MODELS AND
INTERPRETING SOLUTIONS

10-1 We define: F = number of ads on WFRA
                S = number of ads on WSMB
                K = number of ads on WKYT
                L = number of ads on WLAW

Maximize: total listener count = 32F + 45S + 14K + 20L
                                              (in thousands)
       S.T. 60F + 74S + 46K + 52L ≤ $5000   budget constraint
             F   ≤ 34   maximum on WFRA
                 S   ≤ 29   maximum on WSMB
                     K   ≤ 44   maximum on WKYT
                         L ≤ 30   maximum on WLAW
             F,S,K,L ≥ 0   nonnegativity

The optimal solution is: F = 34 ads; S = 29 ads; and
L = 15.6538 ads (which may be rounded down to 15 ads). The
total listener count is 2706.0769 thousand with the noninteger value of variable L.

10-2 We define: C = number of cosmetic patients per week
                D = number of dermatology patients per week
                Θ = number of orthopedic patients per week
                N = number of neurosurgery patients per week

Maximize: Weekly contribution = 200C + 150D + 150Θ + 250N
       S.T.   5C + 5D + 2Θ + 4N ≤ 200   hr/wk lab
               2C + 8D + 1Θ + 5N ≤ 140   hr/wk X-ray
               1C + 10D   + 8N ≤ 110   hr/wk therapy
               4C + 8D + 16Θ + 10N ≤ 240   hr/wk surgery
              10C + 14D + 8Θ + 12N ≤ 320   hr/wk physician
              10C   + 8Θ   ≤ 120   hr/wk cos.& ortho.
                         C,D,Θ,N ≥   0   nonnegativity

The optimal solution is: C = 7.9710; Θ = 5.0362;
N = 12.7536 for a weekly contribution Z = $5538.0430.

10-3 We define: E = number of expert machinists hired
                 N = number of normal machinists hired
                 A = number of apprentice machinists hired

      Maximize: Output rate = 20E + 16N + 12A (pieces/day)
          S.T. 80E + 60N + 40A ≤ $800 per day budget
                E   ≤   2 people   avail. of E
                      N   ≤   7 people   avail. of N
                           A ≤   9 people   avail. of A
                10E + 6N + 1A ≥   60 man-yr experience
                        E,N,A ≥   0   nonnegativity

The optimal solution is: E = .25; N = 7; A = 9, which is of
course noninteger, so E can be rounded down to zero or the
problem can be solved again as an integer problem.
Z = 225 pieces per day for the noninteger solution.

10-4 We define: A = $1000's invested in plan A
                 B = $1000's invested in plan B
                 C = $1000's invested in plan C
                 D = $1000's invested in plan D

      Maximimize: Expected yield = .2A + .1B + .15C + .1D
          S.T. 1A + 1B + 1C + 1D ≤ 250   budget
                8A + 4B + 10C   ≤ 1000   risk units
                A   ≤ 100   limit plan A
                     B   ≤   50   limit plan B
                          C   ≤   50   limit plan C
                               D ≤ 150   limit plan D
                     A,B,C,D ≥   0   nonnegativity

The optimal solution is: A = 100; C = 20; D = 130
Yield = Z = $36 thousand.

10-5 We define: A = number of adventurers produced per year
                 E = number of explorers produced per year
                 C = number of cruisers produced per year

      Maximize: Yearly profit = 7.5A + 15E + 30C (in 1000's)
        S.T. 60A + 100E + 200C ≤ 3000 worker-days/yr forming
            100A + 240E + 360C ≤ 6000 worker-days/yr wood trim
             80A + 100E + 160C ≤ 3000 worker-days/yr outfitting
                     A,E,C ≥   0   nonnegativity

Initial tableau

C_j	Prod. Mix	Qty.	7.5 A	15 E	30 C	0 S_1	0 S_2	0 S_3
0	S_1	300	6	10	20	1	0	0
0	S_2	600	10	24	36	0	1	0
0	S_3	300	8	10	16	0	0	1
	Z_j	0	0	0	0	0	0	0
	$C_j - Z_j$		7.5	15	30	0	0	0

We enter variable C in place of S_1:

Second tableau

C_j	Prod. Mix	Qty.	7.5 A	15 E	30 C	0 S_1	0 S_2	0 S_3
30	C	15	.3	.5	1	.05	0	0
0	S_2	60	−.8	.6	0	−1.8	1	0
0	S_3	60	3.2	2	0	−.8	0	1
	Z_j	$450	9	15	30	1.5	0	0
	$C_j - Z_j$		−1.5	0	0	−1.5	0	0

└──── alternative optimum

The solution is optimal. The company should produce 15
cruisers per year for an annual profit of $450,000. An
alternative optimal solution is to produce 10 explorers and
10 cruisers for the same profit. The second optimum can be
obtained by entering variable E in a third tableau in place
of variable S_2.

10-6   We define: X_{ij} = number of tons shipped from quarry i to
warehouse j.

Minimize: total cost = $5X_{11}$ + $1X_{12}$ + $6X_{13}$ + $3X_{14}$ + $1X_{15}$
$\qquad\qquad\qquad$ + $2X_{21}$ + $3X_{22}$ + $4X_{23}$ + $5X_{24}$ + $4X_{25}$
$\qquad\qquad\qquad$ + $4X_{31}$ + $2X_{32}$ + $3X_{33}$ + $2X_{34}$ + $3X_{35}$

S.T. X_{11} + X_{12} + X_{13} + X_{14} + X_{15} ≤ 200 tons from quar. 1
$\qquad$ X_{21} + X_{22} + X_{23} + X_{24} + X_{25} ≤ 100 tons from quar. 2
$\qquad$ X_{31} + X_{32} + X_{33} + X_{34} + X_{35} ≤ 150 tons from quar. 3
$\qquad\qquad$ X_{11} + X_{21} + X_{31} = 80 tons for warhse. 1
$\qquad\qquad$ X_{12} + X_{22} + X_{32} = 90 tons for warhse. 2
$\qquad\qquad$ X_{13} + X_{23} + X_{33} = 100 tons for warhse. 3
$\qquad\qquad$ X_{14} + X_{24} + X_{34} = 70 tons for warhse. 4
$\qquad\qquad$ X_{15} + X_{25} + X_{35} = 60 tons for warhse. 5
$\qquad\qquad$ all variables ≥ 0 nonnegativity

The optimal solution is: X_{12} = 90; X_{15} = 60; X_{21} = 80;
X_{23} = 20; X_{33} = 80; X_{34} = 70.
Total cost = Z = $770.

10-7   We define: T = barrels/day of Texas crude refined
               P = barrels/day of Penn. crude refined
               Θ = barrels/day of offshore crude refined

First we compute the revenue per barrel of each of the three types:

Texas: [(.35)(.91)+(.15)(.88)+(.25)(.95)+(.15)(.83)
                +(.10)(.78)] [42] = $37.401
Penn: [(.50)(.91)+(.15)(.88)+(.10)(.95)+(.20)(.83)
                +(.05)(.78)] [42] = $37.254
Offshore: [(.20)(.91)+(.25)(.88)+(.30)(.95)+(.15)(.83)
                +(.10)(.78)] [42] = $37.359

Subtracting costs, we obtain the contribution per barrel:

Texas: 37.401 - 16 - 4 = $17.401 per barrel
Penn: 37.254 - 11 - 4 = $22.254 per barrel
Offshore: 37.359 - 13 - 4 = $20.359 per barrel

Maximize: Daily contribution = 17.401T + 22.254P + 20.359Θ

Before formulating the constraints, we wish to obtain a measure of the difference in sulfur content of each type of crude compared to the allowable values. For example, let's assume we use only Texas crude:

Texas crude

	ounces/barrel	allowed oz/bbl	difference
Gasoline	.05	(.0009)(42)= .0376	-.0214 oz/bbl
Diesel	.05	(.0010)(42)= .0420	-.0080 oz/bbl
Fuel	.05	(.0008)(42)= .0336	-.0164 oz/bbl
Kerosene	.05	(.0009)(42)= .0376	-.0124 oz/bbl
Residual	.05	(.0008)(42)= .0336	-.0164 oz/bbl

A similar set of values may be obtained for both the Pennsylvania and offshore crudes. Using these differences, we may formulate the sulfur constraints using an overall target difference of zero as follows:

S.T. (.35)(-.0124)T +(.50)(.0076)P +(.20)(-.0024)$\Theta \geq$ 0 gas
      (.15)(-.0080)T +(.15)(.0120)P +(.25)(+.0020)$\Theta \geq$ 0 die.
      (.25)(-.0164)T +(.10)(.0036)P +(.30)(-.0064)$\Theta \geq$ 0 fuel
      (.15)(-.0124)T +(.20)(.0076)P +(.15)(-.0024)$\Theta \geq$ 0 ker.
      (.10)(-.0164)T +(.05)(.0036)P +(.10)(-.0064)$\Theta \geq$ 0 res.
                        T $\leq$ 12,000 bbl/day   Texas limit
                        P $\leq$ 18,000 bbl/day   Penn. limit
                        Θ $\leq$ 15,000 bbl/day   Offshore limit
      42T + 42P + 42Θ $\leq$ 150,000 gal/day   Refinery limit
             T,P,Θ $\geq$ 0   Nonnegativity

The optimal solution is: P = 3571.4287 barrels/day. The profit is Z = $79,478.57 per day.

10-8   We define: S = dollars in signature loans
                     I = dollars in installment loans
                     H = dollars in home improvement loans
                     M = dollars in misc. installment loans
                     U = dollars in government securities

Maximize: Ret. on inv. = .21S + .18I + .16H + .16M + .12U
S.T. .9S - .1I - .1H - .1M ≤ 0   sig. loans ≤ 10% total loan
           - .5I + .5H - .5M ≤ 0   home imp. ≤ 50% total sec.
                  1S - 1U ≤ 0   sig. loans ≤ gov't sec.
                       1U ≤ $10,000,000 limit gov't sec.
   1S + 1I + 1H + 1M + 1U = $25,000,000 investment limit
             S,I,H,M,U ≥ 0   nonnegativity

The optimal solution is: I = $25,000,000, which gives a return on investment of Z = $4,500,000 per year.

10-9   We define: AF = number of A cartons in the forward hold
                    AC = number of A cartons in the center hold
                    AA = number of A cartons in the aft hold
Similarly, BF, BC, BA, CF, CC, and CA are defined for the B and C type cartons.

Objective: maximize weight = 500AF + 500AC + 500AA + 700BF
                + 700BC + 700BA + 300CF + 300CC + 300CA
     S.T.   1AF +   1AC +   1AA ≤ 30 cartons Available A
            1BF +   1BC +   1BA ≤ 40 cartons Available B
            1CF +   1CC +   1CA ≤ 50 cartons Available C
          500AF + 700BF + 300CF ≤ 8000 lb for. wt. limit
          500AC + 700BC + 300CC ≤ 10000 lb cen. wt. limit
          500AA + 700BA + 300CA ≤ 6000 lb aft wt. limit
          200AF + 350BF + 100CF ≤ 3000 ft³ for. vol. limit
          200AC + 350BC + 100CC ≤ 4000 ft³ cen. vol. limit
          200AA + 350BA + 100CA ≤ 2500 ft³ aft vol. limit

The trim constraints are of the form:

$$\frac{500AF+700BF+300CF}{8000} = \frac{500AC+700BC+300CC}{10000} = \frac{500AA+700BA+300CA}{6000}$$

Only two trim constraint equations are necessary:

50AF + 70BF + 30CF - 40AC - 56BC - 24CC = 0 for. to cen.
30AF + 42BF + 18CF - 40AA - 56BA - 24CA = 0 for. to aft
                    all variables ≥ 0 nonnegativity

The optimal solution is: BF = 2.86; BC = 5.71; BA = 4.29; CF = 20; CC = 20; CA = 10 for a total weight = Z = 24,000 pounds. The solution is noninteger and must be rounded.

10-10   We define: A = pounds of 4-6-8 per pound of 10-13-10 mix
                   B = pounds of 5-10-10 per pound of 10-13-10 mix
                   C = pounds of 8-12-4 per pound of 10-13-10 mix
                   D = pounds of 20-20-20 per pound of 10-13-10 mix
                   E = pounds of filler per pound of 10-13-10 mix

The minimum and maximum percentage weight of the active
nutrients are:

Nutrient	Minimum weight (%)	Maximum weight (%)
Nitrogen	10	(10)(1.0025) = 10.0250
Phosphorus	13	(13)(1.0025) = 13.0325
Potash	10	(10)(1.0025) = 10.0250

Due to availabilities, the maximum pounds of each
ingredient in each pound of blend are:

Ingredient	Maximum lb/lb of 10-13-10 blend
4-8-6	30,000/100,000 = .3 lb
5-10-10	70,000/100,000 = .7 lb
8-12-4	80,000/100,000 = .8 lb
20-20-20	60,000/100,000 = .6 lb

Minimize: cost per lb of mix = 4A + 6B + 5C + 10D + 0.4E
    S.T. 4A + 5B + 8C + 20D $\geq$ 10   min. nitrogen
         4A + 5B + 8C + 20D $\leq$ 10.0250   max. nitrogen
         8A + 10B + 12C + 20D $\geq$ 13   min. phosphorus
         8A + 10B + 12C + 20D $\leq$ 13.0325   max. phosphorus
         6A + 10B + 4C + 20D $\geq$ 10   min. potash
         6A + 10B + 4C + 20D $\leq$ 10.0250   max. potash
         1A $\leq$ 0.3   avail. of 4-8-6
              1B $\leq$ 0.7   avail. of 5-10-10
                   1C $\leq$ 0.8   avail. of 8-12-4
                        1D $\leq$ 0.6   avail. of 20-20-20
         1A + 1B + 1C + 1D + 1E = 1   1 lb ingred. = 1 lb of mix
              all variables $\geq$ 0   nonnegativity

The optimal solution is: A = 0.26250; B = 0.13750;
    C = 0.309375; D = 0.290625; E = 0.
The cost for the 10-13-10 blend is Z = 6.328125 cents per
pound (cost per 100,000 lb = $6,328.125)
The resulting blend has the specifications: 10.025-13-10.

10-11   The primal problem is:

Maximize: Contribution = $6X_1$ + $6X_2$
    S.T. $2X_1$ + $1X_2$ $\leq$ 40 hours   Dept. A constraint
          $1X_1$ + $3X_2$ $\leq$ 40 hours   Dept. B constraint
              X_1 , X_2 $\geq$ 0   Nonnegativity

The corresponding dual is:

Minimize: 40A + 40B
  S.T. 2A + 1B $\geq$ 6
        1A + 3B $\geq$ 6
        A,B $\geq$ 0

Adding artificial and surplus variables, we have:

Min: 40A + 40B + MA_1 + $0S_1$ + MA_2 + $0S_2$
  S.T. 2A + 1B + $1A_1$ - $1S_1$ + $0A_2$ + $0S_2$ = 6
        1A + 3B + $0A_1$ + $0S_1$ + $1A_2$ - $1S_2$ = 6

Initial tableau

C_J	P.M.	Qty.	40 A	40 B	M A_1	0 S_1	M A_2	0 S_2
M	A_1	6	2	1	1	-1	0	0
M	A_2	6	1	3	0	0	1	-1
	Z_J	12M	3M	4M	M	-M	M	-M
	C_J-Z_J		40-3M	40-4M	0	M	0	M

We enter variable B in place of A_2:

Second tableau

C_J	P.M.	Qty.	40 A	40 B	M A_1	0 S_1	M A_2	0 S_2
M	A_1	4	5/3	0	1	-1	-1/3	1/3
40	B	2	1/3	1	0	0	1/3	-1/3
	Z_J	4M+80	5M/3+40/3	40	M	-M	40/3-M/3	M/3-40/3
	C_J-Z_J		80/3-5M/3	0	0	M	2M/3-40/3	40/3-M/3

We enter variable A in place of A_1:

Third tableau

C_J	P.M.	Qty.	40 A	40 B	M A_1	0 S_1	M A_2	0 S_2
40	A	12/5	1	0	3/5	-3/5	-1/5	1/5
40	B	6/5	0	1	-1/5	1/5	2/5	-2/5
	Z_J	144	40	40	16	-16	8	-8
	C_J-Z_J		0	0	M-16	16	M-8	8

The solution is optimal with A = 12/5 and B = 6/5 and the cost is $144. Therefore, another hour of productive capacity in Dept. A is worth $12/5, while another unit of capacity in Dept. B is worth $6/5.

184

10-12   The dual is:

Minimize: 5000A + 34B + 29C + 44D + 30E
  S.T. 60A + 1B ≥ 32
       74A + 1C ≥ 45
       46A + 1D ≥ 14
       52A + 1E ≥ 20
       A,B,C,D,E ≥ 0

The optimal solution is: A = 0.384615; B = 8.923077;
C = 16.538452; D = 0 and E = 0.   Cost = Z = 2706.0769.
Dual variable A is the increase in listener count due to an
increase of $1 allowable budget; dual variable B is the
increase in listener count for an additional ad with WFRA;
dual variable C is the increase in listener count for an
additional ad on WSMB.

10-13   The dual is:

Minimize: 200L + 140X + 110T + 240S + 320P + 120CΘ
  S.T. 5L + 2X + 1T + 4S + 10P + 10CΘ ≥ 200
       5L + 8X + 10T + 8S + 14P   ≥ 150
       2L + 1X +   16S + 8P + 8CΘ ≥ 150
       4L + 5X + 8T + 10S + 12P   ≥ 250

The optimal solution is: T = 29.891296; S = 1.086956;
and CΘ = 16.576080. Cost = Z = 5538.0430. Dual variable T
is the weekly contribution increase due to an extra hour in
the therapy area, while S and CΘ represent contribution
increases due to an extra hour in surgery and
cosmetic/ortho., respectively.

10-14   The dual is:

Minimize: 250BU + 1000R + 100A + 50B + 50C + 150D
  S.T. 1BU + 8R + 1A   ≥ 0.20
       1BU + 4R +   + 1B   ≥ 0.10
       1BU + 10R   + 1C   ≥ 0.15
       1BU   + 1D ≥ 0.10

The optimal solution is: BU = .10; R = .005; A = .06;
the cost for the solution is 36 thousand. Dual variable BU
is the increase in yield for each additional thousand
dollars invested; R is the yield increase due to a one unit
relaxation in the allowable risk, and A is the yield
increase due to a one unit increase in the limit invested
in plan A.

10-15   The dual is:

Minimize: 3000F + 6000W + 3000Θ
  S.T.   60F + 100W + 80Θ ≥ 7.5
        100F + 240W + 100Θ ≥ 15
        200F + 360W + 160Θ ≥ 30

The optimal solution is: F = 0.15 and Z = 450. Dual
variable F represents the profit increase due to an
additional worker-day in the forming department.

10-16   We define: C = bags of cocktail special produced
                     D = bags of deluxe mix produced
                     R = bags of royal mix produced
                     P = bags of party special produced

The cost of ingredients per 8-oz bag are:

Type	Cost of ingredients	
C	$(2/16)(2.56)+(2/16)(1.28)+(1/16)(2.08)$	
	$+(1/16)(3.20)+(1/16)(3.52)+(1/16)(2.72)$	= $1.20
D	$(3/16)(2.56)+(2/16)(2.08)+(2/16)(3.52)$	
	$+(1/16)(2.72)$	= $1.35
R	$(3/16)(2.56)+(2/16)(3.20)+(3/16)(3.52)$	= $1.54
P	$(4/16)(1.28)+(4/16)(3.52)$	= $1.20

Our LP problem is:
    Maximize profit = 1.80C + 2.15D + 2.46R + 2.30P
      S.T. 2C + 3D + 3R   ≤ 4800 oz cashews available
            1C + 2D   ≤ 1600 oz Brazils available
            1C   + 2R   ≤ 1200 oz filberts available
            1C + 2D + 3R + 4P   ≤ 3200 oz pecans available
            1C + 1D   ≤ 3200 oz almonds available
                      1R   ≤   20 bags limit on Royal mix
            1C   ≤   50 bags limit on Cocktail
                  C,D,R,P ≥   0   nonnegativity

If the objective is to maximize the number of bags sold, we
would have a new objective function as follows:

Maximize: bags sold = 1C + 1D + 1R + 1P

10-17 From the computer solution, we have the following (rounded off to even cents):

Var.	Description	Opt. value	C_j-Z_j value	C_j range
C	Cocktail	50	0	1.075 to inf.
D	Deluxe	775	0	1.150 to 3.60
R	Royal	20	0	1.725 to inf.
P	Party	385	0	0.000 to 3.28

Optimal Profit = Z = $2690.95

Const.	Description	Slack	C_j-Z_j value	RHS range
#1	Cashews	2315	0	2485 to inf.
#2	Brazils	0	0.50	50 to 3140
#3	Filberts	1110	0	90 to inf.
#4	Pecans	0	0.575	1660 to inf.
#5	Almonds	2375	0	825 to inf.
#6	R limit	0	0.735	0 to 533.33
#7	C limit	0	0.725	0 to 1160

Const.	Description	Change Vectors						
		C	D	R	P	S_1	S_3	S_5
#1	Cashews	0	0	0	0	1	0	0
#2	Brazils	0	.50	0	-.25	-1.50	0	-.50
#3	Filberts	0	0	0	0	0	1	0
#4	Pecans	0	0	0	.25	0	0	0
#5	Almonds	0	0	0	0	0	0	1
#6	R limit	0	0	1	-.75	-3	-2	0
#7	C limit	1	-.50	0	0	-.50	-1	-.50

a. For the Cocktail special mix, variable C, profit can drop to $1.075 (a price of $2.275). Any reduction below this value will change the product mix. Any increase in price will not change the product mix, because the maximum limit of 50 bags of C has already been reached.

b. We focus our attention on constraint #6 which limits the production of Royal mix to only 20 bags. The C_j-Z_j value for this constraint is .735, implying that a relaxation of the constraint to 21 bags would increase profit by $0.735. Consequently, by producing 21 bags, we can actually sell the added bag to our favored customer for the reduced price of $3.27 without reducing profit.

c. The constraint on pecans (constraint #6) has no slack. Any additional pecans purchased for less than $0.575 per ounce price increase will improve profits. At a price of $6.00 per pound which is an increase of $6.00 - $3.52 = $2.28 per pound or $0.155 per ounce, the offer is attractive. For each ounce purchased, profits will increase by $0.575 - $0.155 = $0.42. The upper limit of range on the pecan constraint is infinity--this is because product P which uses only ingredients of peanuts (supply unlimited) and pecans could be produced in unlimited numbers if pecans are unconstrained. To illustrate what happens, the students might be asked to solve the following problem (where CA, DA, RA, and PA are added Cocktail, Deluxe, Royal, and Party produced using additional pecans purchased at the $6.00 per pound price).

Max: $1.80C + 1.645CA + 2.15D + 1.84DA + 2.46R + 1.995RA + 2.30P + 1.68PA$

```
S.T. 2C + 2CA + 3D + 3DA + 3R + 3RA              ≤ 4800
     1C + 1CA + 2D + 2DA                          ≤ 1600
     1C + 1CA        + 2R + 2RA                    ≤ 1200
     1C        + 2D        + 3R        + 4P        ≤ 3200 old
         1CA         + 2DA       + 3RA       + 4PA ≤ 1000 new
     1C + 1CA + 1D + 1DA                           ≤ 3200
                          1R + 1RA                 ≤   20
     1C + 1CA                                      ≤   50
```

The addition of the constraint labeled "new" reflects an additional 1000 ounces of pecans purchased at the higher price.

The optimal solution is:

```
Cocktail special    C + CA = 50 + 0      =  50 bags
Deluxe mix          D + DA = 275 + 500    = 775 bags
Royal mix           R + RA = 20 + 0       =  20 bags
Party special       P + PA = 635 + 0      = 635 bags
```
Profit = Z = $3110.95, which is $420 more than the original solution or $0.42 improvement per ounce of additional pecans.

d. In the current solution, there are 1600 ounces of Brazil nuts from constraint #2. The RHS range on this constraint is 50 to 3140, so 1600 – 50 = 1550 ounces can be found to be rotten before the mix of the solution variables changes. The $c_j - z_j$ for Brazil nuts is 0.50, so profits are reduced by $0.50 for each ounce found rotten ($8.00 per pound). If 50 pounds are found rotten (800 ounces), we can use the change vector for constraint #2 to find the new optimal solution as follows:

188

Var.	Description	Old sol.	Change		New sol.	Obj.
C	Cocktail	50	(0)(800)=	0	50	90.00
D	Deluxe	775	(-.50)(800)=	-400	375	806.25
R	Royal	20	(0)(800)=	0	20	49.20
P	Party	385	(.25)(800)=	200	585	1345.50
S_1	Cashews	2315	(1.50)(800)=	1200	3515	0
S_3	Filberts	1110	(0)(800)=	0	1110	0
S_5	Almonds	2375	(.50)(800)=	400	2775	0
					Total =	$2290.95

e. For the new product, Snacker's Nosh, we have:

Resource	Coefficient	Shadow price	Total cost
Cashews	2	0	0
Brazils	2	0.50	1.00
Filberts	2	0	0
Pecans	2	0.575	1.15
			2.15

In order to realize a loss of $0.25, the selling price must be $2.15 - 0.25 = $1.90.

10-18   From the computer solution, we have the following (rounded off to even cents):

Var.	Description	Opt. value	$C_j - Z_j$ value	C_j range
C	Cocktail	50	0	.50 to inf.
D	Deluxe	775	0	.50 to 2
R	Royal	20	0	.75 to inf.
P	Party	385	0	0.00 to 1.33

Optimal Output = 1230 bags total

Const.	Description	Slack	$C_j - Z_j$ value	RHS range
#1	Cashews	2315	0	2485 to inf.
#2	Brazils	0	0.25	50 to 3140
#3	Filberts	1110	0	90 to inf.
#4	Pecans	0	0.25	1660 to inf.
#5	Almonds	2375	0	825 to inf.
#6	R limit	0	0.25	0 to 533.33
#7	C limit	0	0.50	0 to 1160

Const.	Description	Change Vectors						
		C	D	R	P	S_1	S_3	S_5
#1	Cashews	0	0	0	0	1	0	0
#2	Brazils	0	.50	0	-.25	-1.50	0	-.50
#3	Filberts	0	0	0	0	0	1	0
#4	Pecans	0	0	0	.25	0	0	0
#5	Almonds	0	0	0	0	0	0	1
#6	R limit	0	0	1	-.75	-3	-2	0
#7	C limit	1	-.50	0	0	-.50	-1	-.50

189

a. In order to produce 21 bags of Royal mix, the change vectors show us:

Var.	Description	Old sol.	Change		New sol.	Obj.
C	Cocktail	50	(0)(1)=	0	50	50.00
D	Deluxe	775	(0)(1)=	0	775	775.00
R	Royal	20	(1)(1)=	0	21	21.00
P	Party	385	(−.75)(1)=	−0.75	384.25	384.25
S_1	Cashews	2315	(−3)(1)=	−3.00	2312	0
S_3	Filberts	1110	(−2)(1)=	−2.0	1108	0
S_5	Almonds	2375	(0)(1)=	0	2375	0
					Total =	1230.25

By producing the additional bag of Royal mix, the total output has increased by 0.25 bags.

b. Since we have a maximization problem, we can drive variable C out of the basis by assigning it a coefficient in the objective function of a large negative value--say −1000. After doing this and resolving the problem, we obtain the solution:

C = 0; D = 800; R = 20; P = 385; and the number of bags produced = Z = 1205.

c. For the new product, Snacker's Nosh, we have:

Resource	Coefficient	Shadow price	Total cost
Cashews	2	0	0
Brazils	2	0.25	0.50
Filberts	2	0	0
Pecans	2	0.25	0.50
			1.00

By producing Snacker's Nosh, the cost is one bag of product lost, but this is offset by the additional bag of Snacker's Nosh produced. Consequently, there would be no change in total output.

For the new product Nosher's Snack, we have:

Resource	Coefficient	Shadow price	Total cost
Peanuts	2	0	0
Cashews	2	0	0
Brazils	2	0.25	0.50
Almonds	2	0	0.00
			0.50

In order to produce Nosher's Snack, only 0.50 bag of product is lost in order to produce. The net result is a gain of 0.50 bags total output.

190

d. Using the change vector for Brazil nuts, constraint #2, with an additional 50 pounds (800 ounces), we have:

Var.	Description	Old sol.	Change		New sol.	Obj.
C	Cocktail	50	(0)(800)=	0	50	50.00
D	Deluxe	775	(.50)(800)=	400	1175	1175.00
R	Royal	20	(0)(800)=	0	20	20.00
P	Party	385	(-.25)(800)=	-200	185	185.00
S_1	Cashews	2315	(-1.50)(800)=	-1200	1115	0
S_3	Filberts	1110	(0)(800)=	0	1110	0
S_5	Almonds	2375	(-.50)(800)=	-400	1975	0
					Total =	1430.00

With the additional 50 pounds of Brazil nuts, the optimal output increases by 1430 - 1230 = 200 bags.

10-19   a. The shadow prices ($C_j - Z_j$ values) for the three slack variables are:

Variable	Shadow price
S_1	$0.17
S_2	3.67
S_3	0

The first and second constraints are used to full capacity and profit improvements of $0.17 and $3.67, respectively, could be realized for each additional unit of available capacity.

b.

S_1		S_2		S_3	
$(8/3) \div (1/6)$	= 16	$(8/3) \div (-1/3)$ =	- 8	$(8/3) \div (0)$ =	inf.
$(56/3) \div (-1/12)$	= -224	$(56/3) \div (2/3)$ =	28	$(56/3) \div (0)$ =	inf.
$(44/3) \div (-1/3)$	= - 44	$(44/3) \div (-1/3)$ =	-44	$(44/3) \div (1)$ =	44/3

For S_1, we have   96 - 16   = 80
                      96 + 44   = 140

For S_2, we have   40 - 28   = 12
                      40 + 8   = 48

For S_3, we have   60 - 44/3 = 45 1/3
                      60 + inf. = no limit

c. For X_2 in the product mix, we have:

X_1	S_1	S_2
$(-19/3) \div (1/3) = -19$	$(-1/6) \div (1/6) = -1$	$(-11/3) \div (-1/3) = 11$

The range for X_2 is: 5 + 11 = 16
                        5 - 1 = 4

191

For X_3, we have:

X_1	S_1	S_2
$-(19/3) \div (5/6) = -38/5$	$(-1/6) \div (-1/12) = 2$	$(-11/3) \div (2/3) = -11/2$

The range for X_3 is: $8 + 2 = 10$

$8 - 11/2 = 2.5$

d. Each unit of X_1 produced would result in a reduction of profit of $19/3$. Therefore, the current contribution of \$2 per unit must increase by $19/3$ to become \$8.33. This value can also be read in the Z_j row (\$25/3 or \$8.33).

e. They tell the marketing department how much price flexibility it has.

10-20 a. We read the answers from the product mix and quantity columns as follows:

X_1 = 52 units per month

Contribution = Z = \$18,720 per month
Since X_2 is not in the product mix, we are not producing any product B at all.

b. The slack variable associated with machine P is S_2. Variable S_2 is in the product mix, and is equal to 144 hours per month. This means machine P is not used to full capacity; it is idle 144 hours/mo. Since the offer is to rent only 80 hours/mo., we would naturally accept it. The \$10 per hour revenue comes at no penalty in current output or profit.

c. We read the answer to this question in variable column X_2 in either the Z_j or $C_j - Z_j$ rows. The Z value of 432 indicates that to produce a unit of B, we forgo the production of \$432 worth of A. So to overcome this loss we must charge a price which is \$432 above variable cost (that is to receive a contribution of \$432 per unit). This is an increase in current price of \$432 - \$400, or \$32 per unit. The figure \$32 may also be read directly as the $C_j - Z_j$ value.

d. We read this as a substitution rate or change vestor: how much A is given up to produce a B? The product mix and X_2 columns are:

Product mix	X_2
X_1	6/5
S_2	-8/5

192

Therefore, to produce one unit of B, we must forgo the production of 6/5 units of A which results in an increase in slack time S_2 on machine P of 8/5 hours per month. So, to produce the 2 units of B, we must give up (2)(6/5) or 2.4 units of product A.

e. We compute the range of RHS values for machine L which has slack variable S_1.

$$(52) \div (1/5) = 260$$
$$(144) \div (-3/5) = -240$$

The range for S_1 is: 260 - 260 = 0
260 + 240 = 500

Therefore, the addition of 240 more hours per month will yield $72 additional contribution per hour.

f. For product mix variable X_1 (product A), we have:

X_2	S_1
$(-32) \div (6/5) = -80/3$	$(-72) \div (1/5) = -360$

The range for X_1 is: 360 - 80/3 = $333.33
360 + inf. = no limit

10-21 a. An optimum tableau for a maximization problem must contain all zeroes or negative figures in the $C_j - Z_j$ row. Therefore, the tableau is optimal.

b. We always find zero values of $C_j - Z_j$ in the columns for those variables which are in the product mix. In this case, X_1, S_2, and S_3 are in the mix, and zeroes appear in the $C_j - Z_j$ row for each of them. However, variable X_2, which is not in the product mix, also has a zero $C_j - Z_j$ value. This means we can enter X_2 in another iteration and still not change our optimal profit of $32 per day. In fact, whenever there exists another optimum solution, there are an infinite number of optimal solutions. The most X_2 we can enter is the least positive quotient of the three:

Quantity	X_2	Quotient
4	.75	5.33
4	.05	80
1.4	.175	8

Consequently, we can introduce any amount of X_2 in the continuous range of 0 to 5.33 units per day.

c. The objective function may be obtained from the C_j row.

Maximize: $8X_1 + 6X_2 + 0S_1 + 0S_2 + 0S_3$ ($32 per day).

d. Slack S_2, which is associated with machine B, is in the product mix, and S_2 = 4 hours per day of idleness. We can, therefore, take machine B down for maintenance for any time up to 4 hours without changing the output or affecting the optimum profit of $32 per day. Slack S_1, which is associated with machine A, is not in the product mix, however. This means there is no slack in machine A; it is used at full capacity. The shadow cost of S_1 is $20 per hour. To take the machine down for 1/2 hour results in a loss of profit of (1/2)($20) = $10.

e. The RHS range for S_1 whose current RHS is $(4) \div (2.5) = 1.6$:

$$(4) \div (2.5) = 1.6$$
$$(4) \div (-.5) = -8$$
$$(1.4) \div (-.75) = -1.87$$

S_1 range: $1.6 - 1.6 = 0$
$1.6 + 1.87 = 3.47$

f. In order to find the current RHS values of S_2 and S_3, we can enter variable S_1 in place of X_1 in order to give the initial tableau for the problem. This gives:

C_j	Product mix	Quantity	8 X_1	6 X_2	0 S_1	0 S_2	0 S_3
0	S_1	1.6	.4	.3	1	0	0
0	S_2	4.8	.2	.2	0	1	0
0	S_3	2.6	.3	.4	0	0	1
	Z_j	0	0	0	0	0	0
	$C_j - Z_j$		8	6	0	0	0

The current RHS values of S_2 and S_3 are 4.8 and 2.6, respectively.

For S_2, we have:

X_1	S_2	S_3
$(4) \div (0) = 0$	$(4) \div (1) = 4$	$(1.4) \div (0) = 0$

The range for S_2 is: 4.8 - 4 = 0.8
4.8 + inf. = inf.

For S_3, we have:

X_1	S_2	S_3
$(4) \div (0) = 0$	$(4) \div (0) = 0$	$(1.4) \div (1) = 1.4$

The range for S_3 is: 2.6 - 1.4 = 1.2
2.6 + inf. = inf.

10-22 For these calculations we ignore the noninteger nature of the problem. Final results must obviously be rounded.

a. With the current solution we have:

Number of WKYT slots used = 0 slots
Slack in WKYT constraint   = 44 slots
Reduced cost for WKYT   = 3.692 thousand

From the sensitivity analysis on objective coefficients:

LB	Current	UB
none	14	17.6923

Since the projected WKYT listener count is 25,000, which is above the upper bound (or an increase greater than 3.692 thousand), the slots should be purchased.

b. With the current solution we have:

Shadow price for budget = .385 thousand per dollar spent

This is above the .250 thousand per dollar minimum specified by Treasure Cove. We now find from the RHS ranges on the budget constraint:

LB	Current	UB
4186	5000	5746

Since $5500 is inside the budget range, the shadow price of .286 thousand per dollar is valid.

c. From the RHS change vectors:

Basic Variable	Old Solution	(Vector)(Change) =	New Solution
WLAW	15.6538	(.0192)(500) = 9.6	25.2538
WFRA	34.0000	(0)(500) = 0	34
WSMB	29.0000	(0)(500) = 0	29
max WKYT	44.0000	(0)(500) = 0	44
max WLAW	14.3462	(-.0192)(500)= -9.6	4.7462

The added $500 will be spent for 9.6 more slots on WLAW, bringing us to a total of 25.2538 slots and reducing the slack in WLAW ads to 4.7462 slots.

d. From the analysis on objective coefficients for WLAW we have:

LB	Current	UB
15.8261	20	27.7333

Since the new value of 17,000 is above the lower bound of 15,826, we would not change our advertising strategy.

10-23   a. The current solution has:

Slack in lab = 99.0580 hours/week
Slack in x-ray = 55.2536 hours/week
Shadow price for surgery = 1.087 dollars/hour/week

For the surgery constraint:

LB	Current	UB
170.5	240	377.5

Since the 40 hours per week lost in lab and x-ray are just a reduction in available slack; and since the added 80 hours per week in surgery, resulting in a final value of 320 hours/week, is within the RHS range for surgery hours, the shadow price of $1.087 per hour is valid.

(1.087 $/hr-week)(80 hr/week) = $86.96 per week added
profit

In order to offset the $2000 tuition cost, it will take 2000/86.96 = 23 weeks.

b.

Basic Variable	Old Solution	(Vector)(Change) =	New Solution
Lab slack	99.0580	(.1159)(80)=9.272	108.33-40=68.33
X-ray slack	55.2536	(.0072)(80)=0.576	55.83-40=15.83
Neurosurgery	12.7536	(.0072)(80)=.0576	13.3296
Orthopedic	5.0362	(.0725)(80)=5.800	10.8362
Physician slack	46.9565	(-0.870)(80)=-6.960	39.9965
Cosmetic	7.9710	(-.0580)(80)=-4.640	3.3310

c.   First, we note Henry's 30 hours loss from x-ray is no problem with 55 hours slack there anyway. Now we evaluate Brenda's 30-hour loss to surgery:

Basic Variable	Old Solution	(CV)(Change) =	New Solution
Lab slack	99.0580	(-.1159)(30)=-3.477	95.5810
X-ray slack	55.2536	(-.0072)(30)=-.0216	55.0376-30=25.0376
Neurosurgery	12.7536	(-.0072)(30)=-0.216	12.5376
Orthopedic	5.0362	(-.0725)(30)=-2.175	2.8612
Physician slack	46.9565	(+0.876)(30)= 2.610	49.5665
Cosmetic	7.9710	(+.0580)(30)= 1.740	9.7110

New contribution = 5538.0435 - (30)(1.087) = $5,505.4335

196

We see for the RHS for therapy:

LB	Current	UB	Blocking Var
0	110	143.7500	Physician slack

It appears we may be able to use 30 hours per week of Henry's time without exceeding the upper bound. We might also be able to use some of Brenda's time. We'll be able to use more than 33.7500 additional hours because the physician slack has increased from 46.9565 hours/week to 49.5665 hours/week due to the loss of Brenda's 30 hours/week from surgery. <u>Assuming</u> physician's slack will still be the blocking variable, we get:

$$49.5665/1.3913 = 35.6260 \text{ total increase (both Henry and Brenda).}$$

Basic Variable	Old Solution	(CV)(Change) =	New Solution
Lab slack	99.5810	(−.6449)(35.626) = −22.9752	95.5810
X-ray slack	25.0376	(−.6341)(35.626) = −22.5904	2.4472
Neurosurgery	12.5376	(+.1159)(35.626) = 4.1291	16.6666
Orthopedic	2.8612	(−.0906)(35.626) = −3.2277	−0.3665
Physician slack	46.5665	(−1.3913)(35.626) = −49.5665	0
Cosmetic	9.7110	(+.0725)(35.626) = 2.8289	12.2939

It is noted that the new solution results in negative orthopedic patients per week. Consequesntly, after making the surgery change for Brenda, the blocking variable for therapy hours is no longer physician time, but is instead orthopedic patients per week. The hours of time we can add to therapy is therefore:

$$2.8612/.0906 = 31.5806 \text{ hours/week (Henry and Brenda combined)}$$

Basic Variable	Old Solution	(CV)(Change) =	New Solution
Lab slack	95.5810	(−.6449)(31.5806) = −20.3663	75.2147
X-ray slack	25.0376	(−.6341)(31.5806) = −20.0253	5.0123
Neurosurgery	12.5376	(+.1159)(31.5806) = 3.6602	16.1978
Orthopedic	2.8612	(−.0906)(31.5806) = −2.8612	0
Physician slack	49.5665	(−1.3913)(31.5806) = −43.9381	5.6284
Cosmetic	9.7110	(+.0725)(31.5806) = 2.2896	12.0006

Therefore, we can use 30 hours of Henry's services but only 1.58 hours per week of Brenda's. The new contribution would be:

$$\$5,505.4335 + (31.5806)(29.891) = \$6,449.4092/\text{week}$$

10-24 a. Current Solution: E = 1.0625
                              N = 7.0000
                              A = 7.3750

(80)(1.0625) + (60)(7) + (40)(7.3750) = $800 per day budget
(10)(1.0625) + (6)(7) + (1)(7.3750) = 60 man-years

Rounded solution: E = 1   rounded down
                   N = 7
                   A = 7   rounded down

(80)(1) + (60)(7) + (40)(7) = $780 per day ($20 slack)
(10)(1) + (6)(7) + (1)(7) = 59 man-years (1 man-year
                                              violated)

The integer solution only violates the experience
requirement by 1 man-year and would probably be
satisfactory to both the union and present work force.

b. From the sensitivity analysis on objective
coefficients:

Type	Present output	Lower bound	Upper bound
Expert	20	none	20.44
Normal	16	15.75	none
Apprentice	12	10.00	12.67

The upper and lower bound values do not lend a great deal
of confidence in implementing the "optimal" solution.
Except for the LB-expert and UB-normal values, all others
are very close to the original estimates.

c. Coefficient x Shadow price = Cost

(70)(.313)	=	21.91	budget
(0)(0)	=	0	E available
(0)(.250)	=	0	N available
(0)(0)	=	0	A available
(8)(-500)	=	-4.00	Experience
		17.91	

Since the prospective machinist's output of 19 pieces per
day is greater then 17.91, she should be hired.

10-25 The profit for each of the arrangements is:
Economy 6.00 − (4)(.20)−(2)(.25)−(2)(.15)   =$4.40
Maytime 8.00 − (8)(.20)−(4)(.22)−(5)(.25)−(10)(.15) =$2.77
Spring 10.00 − (9)(.20)−(9)(.20)−(6)(.22)−(10)(.15) =$3.58
Deluxe 12.00 − (12)(.20)−(12)(.20)−(12)(.22)   =$4.56

We define X_1 as the number of arrangements of type i for i = 1,2,3,4.

Maximize profit = $4.40X_1 + 2.77X_2 + 3.58X_3 + 4.56X_4$
  S.T. $4X_1$ + $9X_3$ + $12X_4$ ≤ 800   red roses
        $2X_1$ + $5X_2$ ≤ 450   gardenias
        $2X_1$ + $10X_2$ + $10X_3$ ≤ 4000   carnations
              $8X_2$ + $9X_3$ + $12X_4$ ≤ 920   white roses
              $4X_2$ + $6X_3$ + $12X_4$ ≤ 420   yellow roses
             all variables ≥   0   nonnegativity

The optimal solution is: X_1 = 200 Economy; X_2 = 10 Maytime for a profit of $907.70. All of the red roses and the gardenias are used while there is slack with the other three flowers.

10-26 From the computer solution, we have the following (rounded off to even cents):

Var.	Description	Optimal value	$C_j - Z_j$ value	C_j range
X_1	Economy	200	0	2.70 to inf.
X_2	Maytime	10	0	0 to 7.02
X_3	Spring color	0	3.83	-inf. to 7.41
X_4	Deluxe rose	0	5.32	-inf. to 9.88

Const.	Description	Slack	$C_j - Z_j$ value	RHS range
#1	Red roses	0	.82	0 to 900
#2	Gardenias	0	.55	400 to 925
#3	Carnations	3500	0	500 to inf.
#4	White roses	840	0	80 to inf.
#5	Yellow roses	380	0	40 to inf.

		Change Vectors			
Const.	Description	X_1	X_2	S_3	S_4	S_5
#1	Red roses	.25	−.10	.50	.80	.40
#2	Gardenias	0	.20	−2.00	−1.60	−.80
#3	Carnations	0	0	1.00	0	0
#4	White roses	0	0	0	1.00	0
#5	Yellow roses	0	0	0	0	1.00

a. For the Economy arrangement, variable X_1, the current profit is $4.40 per unit, and the range on profit is $2.70 to infinity. Consequently, if profit drops by $1.70 implying a price drop from $6.00 to $4.30 then it will no longer be attractive to produce 200 arrangements. Fewer

199

Economy arrangements will be produced and Spring color arrangements will enter the solution.

b. For the Maytime arrangements, variable X_2, current profit is \$2.77 per unit, and the range on profit is \$0 to \$7.02. Consequently, if a \$4.25 increase in profit resulting in a new price of \$12.25 were to occur, then the number of Maytime arrangements will increase. This causes a decrease in the number of Economy arrangements produced and the introduction of a new product, the Spring color arrangements.

c. The range of C_j values for Deluxe arrangements is minus infinity to \$9.88. If profit rose above \$9.88, an increase of \$5.32, resulting in a price of \$17.32, it would become attractive to produce them.

d. Red roses are constrained by constraint #1 whose RHS is currently 800 roses. The shadow price for red roses is 0.82 and the RHS range is 0 to 900. Therefore, they could buy an additional 100 red roses at a top price of \$0.20 + 0.82 = \$1.02 per rose. If they can purchase them at the current price of \$0.20, then profits will increase by (.82)(100) = \$82.

e. With a shadow price of \$0.82, the loss of 100 red roses would result in a reduction in profit of (100)(.82) = \$82.

f. For the new product, Graduation Special, we have:

Resource	Coefficient	Shadow price	Total cost
Red roses	4	.82	3.28
Gardenias	6	.55	3.30
Carnations	6	0	0
White roses	0	0	0
Yellow roses	4	0	0
			6.58

In order to obtain a profit of \$2.25 per arrangement, the selling price must be \$6.58 + 2.25 = \$8.83.

g. The lowest price for the 30 gardenias sold must be equal to the shadow price of gardenias, \$0.55 per flower. If the other florist offers \$0.65 per flower, profits will increase by (.10)(30) = \$3.00.
Applying the change vector for constraint #2, with a reduction of 30 gardenias:

Var.	Description	Old sol.	Change		New sol.	Obj.
X_1	Economy	200	(0)(30)=	0	200	880.00
X_2	Maytime	10	(-.2)(30)=	-6	4	11.08
S_3	Carnations	3500	(2)(30)=	60	3560	0
S_4	White roses	840	(1.6)(30)=	48	888	0
S_5	Yellow roses	380	(.8)(30)=	24	404	0
					Total =	\$891.08

200

```
           Profit with 420 gardenias                = $891.08
           Revenue: sale of 30 gardenias  (30)(.65) =   19.50
                                          Total    = $910.58
```
Accounting for roundoff error in the shadow prices, this is about a $3 increase.

10-27 a. We compute the range on objective function coefficient for variable ECONOMY as follows:

Nonbasic Variable	$\dfrac{c_j - z_j}{c}$
SPRING	$(-3.827) \div (2.250) = -1.701$
DELUXE	$(-5.316) \div (3.000) = -1.772$
REDROSE	$(-0.823) \div (0.250) = -3.292$
GARDENIA	$(-0.554) \div (0.000) = -\text{inf.}$

The range of profit for ECONOMY is: $4.40 - 1.70 = $1.70
$4.40 + inf. = no limit
This corresponds to a range in price of $4.30 to no limit.

The least negative value of -1.701 is associated with the variable SPRING. Consequently, if profit drops below $1.70, SPRING will enter the solution and replace the variable with least positive quotient--ECONOMY.

b. We compute the range of the objective function coefficient for MAYTIME, as follows:

Nonbasic Variable	$\dfrac{c_j - z_j}{c}$
SPRING	$(-3.827) \div (-0.900) = 4.252$
DELUXE	$(-5.316) \div (-1.200) = 4.430$
REDROSE	$(-0.823) \div (-0.100) = 8.230$
GARDENIA	$(-0.554) \div (0.200) = -2.770$

The least positive value is $4.25 associated with SPRING, and the least negative value is -$2.77 associated with GARDENIA.

Range on MAYTIME   2.77 - 2.77 = $ 0
                      2.77 + 4.25 = $ 7.02

This corresponds to a price range of $5.23 to $12.25. At a price above $12.25, SPRING will enter the solution in place of ECONOMY, thus increasing the number of MAYTIME produced.

c. Adding the shadow price for DELUXE to its current profit, we find:

$$\$4.56 + 5.32 = \$9.88$$

Consequently, a profit above $9.88 (a price of $17.32) would be required before DELUXE would enter the solution.

d. The constraint REDROSE has the following RHS range:

Basic variable	Quantity ÷ REDROSE coefficient
ECONOMY	$(200) \div (0.250) = 800$
WHITEROSE	$(840) \div (0.800) = 1050$
YELLROSE	$(380) \div (0.400) = 950$
MAYTIME	$(10) \div (-0.100) = -100$
CARNATION	$(3500) \div (0.500) = 7000$

The least negative value is -100 associated with MAYTIME and the least positive value is 800 associated with ECONOMY.

The RHS range for REDROSE is: 800 - 800 = 0
800 + 100 = 900

A maximum of 100 red roses could be purchased at a top price of $0.20 + 0.823 = $1.02 per rose.

As the REDROSE constraint's RHS increases by one unit, the substitution rates in the REDROSE column tell us that ECONOMY increases by 0.250 arrangements while MAYTIME decreases by 0.100 units. By adding 100 more red roses, the number of ECONOMY = 200 + (100)(.250) = 225 while the number of MAYTIME = 10 - (100)(.100) = 0. The profit for the 225 ECONOMY is ($4.40)(225) = $990 (a $82.30 improvement). This can also be obtained by multiplying the shadow price for REDROSE by 100 new flowers:

$$(100)(.823) = \$82.30.$$

e. The shadow price for REDROSE indicates (.823)(100) or $82.30 profit will be lost. The new solution will be:
ECONOMY   200 - (0.250)(100) = 175
MAYTIME   10 + (0.100)(100) = 20
        Profit = (175)(4.40) +(20)(2.77) = $825.40.

f. For the new product, GRADUATION, we have:

Resource	Coefficient	Shadow price	Total cost
REDROSE	4	0.823	3.292
GARDENIA	6	0.554	3.324
CARNATION	6	0.000	0.000
WHITEROSE	0	0.000	0.000
YELLROSE	4	0.000	0.000
			6.616

In order to obtain a profit of $2.25 per arrangement, selling price must be $6.62 + 2.25 = $8.87.

g. The lowest price for the 30 gardenias must be $0.554 per flower. If 30 are sold at $0.10 above this value, profits will increase by (0.10)(30) = $3.00. Applying the substitution rates, we find the new solution:

Variable	Old sol.	Change			New sol.	Obj.
ECONOMY	200	(0)(30)	=	0	200	880.00
WHITEROSE	840	(1.600)(30)	=	48	888	0.00
YELLROSE	380	(0.800)(30)	=	24	400	0.00
MAYTIME	10	(-0.200)(30)	=	-6	4	11.08
CARNATION	3500	(2.000)(30)	=	60	3560	0.00
					Total =	$891.08

Profit with 420 Gardenias   = $891.08
Revenue: sale of 30 Gardenias (30)(.654) =   19.62
                                   Total = $910.70

10-28   The primal problem is:

Maximize: Contribution = $7X_1 + 5X_2$
   S.T. $3X_1 + 1X_2 \leq 48$ units of ingredient
          $2X_1 + 1X_2 \leq 40$ hours of labor
          $X_1, X_2 \geq 0$ nonnegativity

The corresponding dual is:

Minimize: $48I + 40L$
   S.T. $3I + 2L \geq 7$
         $1I + 1L \geq 5$
            $I, L \geq 0$

Adding artificial and surplus variables, we have:

Minimize: $48I + 40L + MA_1 + 0S_1 + MA_2 + 0S_2$
   S.T. $3I + 2L + 1A_1 - 1S_1 + 0A_2 + 0S_2 = 7$
        $1I + 1L + 0A_1 + 0S_1 + 1A_2 - 1S_2 = 5$
                          all variables ≥ 0

Initial tableau

C_J	Prod. Mix	Qty.	48 I	40 L	M A_1	0 S_1	M A_2	0 S_2
M	A_1	7	3	2	1	-1	0	0
M	A_2	5	1	1	0	0	1	-1
	Z_J	12M	4M	3M	M	-M	M	-M
	$C_J - Z_J$		48-4M	40-3M	0	M	0	M

We enter variable I in place of A_1:

203

Second tableau

C_j	Prod. Mix	Qty.	48 I	40 L	M A_1	0 S_1	M A_2	0 S_2
48	I	7/3	1	2/3	1/3	-1/3	0	0
M	A_2	8/3	0	1/3	-1/3	1/3	1	-1
	Z_j	8M/3+112	48	M/3+32	16-M/3	M/3-16	M	-M
	$C_j - Z_j$		0	8-M/3	2M/3-16	16-M/3	0	M

We enter variable L in place of I:

Third tableau

C_j	Prod. Mix	Qty.	48 I	40 L	M A_1	0 S_1	M A_2	0 S_2
40	L	7/2	3/2	1	1/2	-1/2	0	0
M	A_2	3/2	-1/2	0	-1/2	1/2	1	-1
	Z_j	140+3M/2	60-M/2	40	20-M/2	M/2-20	M	-M
	$C_j - Z_j$		M/2-12	0	M/2-20	20-M/2	0	M

Now we enter variable S_1 and remove A_2:

C_j	Prod. Mix	Qty.	48 I	40 L	M A_1	0 S_1	M A_2	0 S_2
40	L	5	1	1	0	0	1	-1
0	S_1	3	-1	0	-1	1	2	-2
	Z_j	200	40	40	0	0	40	-40
	$C_j - Z_j$		8	0	M	0	M-40	40

The solution is optimal with L = 5 and surplus variable
S_1 = 3 at a cost of $200. Therefore, another unit of labor
is worth $5, whereas the ingredient is not used to full
capacity.

10-29 a. The Plan C and D objective coefficient sensitivity
values are:

Plan	L.B.	Current	U.B.	New estimate
C	.100	.150	.225	.180
D	.067	.100	.150	.080

Plan C's new estimate of .180 is within the bounds of .100
to .225, and Plan D's new estimate of .080 is also within
its .067 and .150 limits. Therefore, no changes are
warranted.

b. The RHS sensitivity analysis on the budget constraint
is:

Block var	L.B.	Current	U.B.	Block var
Plan D	120	250	270	limit Plan D

The shadow price for the budget constraint is .10. The
implication of this is that as much as $20,000 more money
may be budgeted, bringing that total to $270,000 and the
added yield is .10 of the amount invested. The money would
be put in Plan D, because the blocking variable is the
limit on Plan D. In other words, the current solution had
$20,000 slack in the $150,000 limit for Plan D, and only
$20,000 more can be added to the current $130,000
expenditure for Plan D. No more than $20,000 can be added
to the budget, because the money would have to go to a plan
other than D, thus raising the risk about 1 million units.

We can also determine the same result using change vectors:

Basic Variable	Old Solution	(CV)(Change) =		New Solution
Plan D	130	(1.00)(20) =	20	150
Plan C	20	(0.00)(20) =	0	20
Plan A	100	(0.00)(20) =	0	100
limit B slack	50	(0.00)(20) =	0	50
limit C slack	30	(0.00)(20) =	0	30
limit D slack	20	(-1.00)(20) =	-20	0

c. The lower and upper bounds of the RHS of 1 million are
800 thousands and 1,300 thousands. So the 900 thousand
proposed level is within the limits. Consequently, the
shadow price of 0.005 thousand per 1 thousand change is a
valid number at the proposed level. The new annual yield
would be:

$$36 - (.005)(100) = \$35.5 \text{ thousand}$$

d. Using the change vectors for the risk constraint with a
change in the RHS of -100:

Basic Variable	Old Solution	(CV)(Change) =		New Solution
Plan D	130	(-.100)(-100) =	10	140
Plan C	20	(+.100)(-100) =	-10	10
Plan A	100	(0.00)(-100) =	0	100
limit B slack	50	(0.00)(-100) =	0	50
limit C slack	30	(-.100)(-100) =	10	40
limit D slack	20	(+.100)(-100) =	-10	10

Plan D's $130 thousand investment will be increased by $10 thousand, and the slack in the limit on Plan D's investment will decrease by the same amount. Plan C, on the other hand, will experience a $10 thousand drop from $20 thousand to $10 thousand, while its slack will increase to $40 thousand.

e. We find the minimum yield which Plan E would have to have in order to offset other investments which would have to be reduced in order to fund a new plan E.

Constraint	(Coefficient) x (Shadow price)	=	Cost
Budget	(1)(.100)	=	.10
Risk	(18)(.005)	=	.09
Limit A	(0)(.060)		
Limit B	(0)(0)		
Limit C	(0)(0)		
Limit D	(0)(0)		
			.19

Since Plan E only has a yield of .16 and as a minimum, a yield of .19 would be necessary, we should not consider Plan E. It is noted that if Plan E should have a degree of risk less than 12 units, it would be an attractive venture.

10-30 a. The shadow prices for the three slack variables are:

Variable	Shadow price
S_1	22/20 = $1.10
S_2	9/20 = $0.45
S_3	1/4 = $0.25

All three constraints are used to full capacity.

b.

S_1	S_2	S_3
$(1) \div (2/5) = 5/2$	$(1) \div (-1/5) = -5$	$(1) \div (0) = $ inf.
$(1) \div (-1/5) = -5$	$(1) \div (3/5) = 5/3$	$(1) \div (0) = $ inf.
$(1/2) \div (-1/10) = -5$	$(1/2) \div (1/20) = 10$	$(1/2) \div (1/4) = 2$

For S_1, we have: $4 - 5/2 = 1.5$
$\qquad\qquad\qquad\quad 4 + 5 = 9$

For S_2, we have: $3 - 5/3 = 4/3$
$\qquad\qquad\qquad\quad 3 + 5 = 8$

For S_3, we have: $3 - 2 = 1$
$\qquad\qquad\qquad\quad 3 + $ inf. $= $ inf.

c. We get for X_1:

Nonbasic Variable	$\frac{C_j - Z_j}{C}$
X_4	$(-7/20) \div (-1/5) = 7/4$
S_1	$(-22/20) \div (-1/5) = 11/2$
S_2	$(-9/20) \div (3/5) = -3/4$
S_3	$(-1/4) \div (0) = $ inf.

The range for X_1 is: 2 + 7/4 = \$3.75
                    2 - 3/4 = \$1.25

For X_2:

Nonbasic Variable	$\frac{C_j - Z_j}{C}$
X_4	$(-7/20) \div (2/5) = -7/8$
S_1	$(-22/20) \div (2/5) = -11/4$
S_2	$(-9/20) \div (-1/5) = 9/4$
S_3	$(-1/4) \div (0) = $ inf.

The range for X_2 is: 4 + 9/4 = \$6.25
                    4 - 7/8 = \$3.125

For X_3:

Product mix Variable	$\frac{C_j - Z_j}{X_1}$
X_4	$(-7/20) \div (3/20) = -7/3$
S_1	$(-22/20) \div (-1/10) = 11$
S_2	$(-9/20) \div (1/20) = -9$
S_3	$(-1/4) \div (1/4) = -1$

The range for X_3 is: 1 + 11 = \$12
                    1 - 1 = \$0

d. In order for X_4 to be in the solution, its $C_j - Z_j$ must be zero or more, and since $Z_j = 27/20$, then the C_j, or contribution per unit, must be 27/20 (or \$1.35). This is an increase of 7/20 or \$0.35 more than the current \$1 per unit contribution.

10-31 a. Cost = (.063281 \$/lb)(100,000 lb) = \$6,328.10

Ingredient	Percent x 10,000	Weight (lb)
4-8-6	(.2625)(100,000)	26,250
5-10-10	(.1375)(100,000)	13,750
8-12-4	(.3094)(100,000)	30,940
20-20-20	(.2906)(100,000)	29,060
filler	(0)(100,000)	0
		100,000

Ingredient	Nitrate	Phosphate	Potash
4-8-6	(.04)(26,250) = 1,050.0	(.08)(26,250) = 2,100.0	(.06)(26,250) = 1,575.0
5-10-10	(.05)(13,750) = 687.5	(.10)(13,750) = 1,375.0	(.10)(13,750) = 1,375.0
8-12-4	(.08)(30,940) = 2,475.2	(.12)(30,940) = 3,712.8	(.04)(30,940) = 1,237.6
20-20-20	(.20)(29,060) = 5,812.0	(.20)(29,060) = 5,812.0	(.20)(29,060) = 5,812.0
	10,024.7	12,999.8	9,999.6

Both the phosphate and potash are at lowest possible levels of 13% and 10% by weight. Nitrate, however, is at its highest level of 10.025%.

b. Since all the options involve changes that are within the corresponding RHS ranges, the shadow prices are valid. The data for the options are:

Option	Current Spec.	Alt. Spec.	Change	Shadow Price	Savings
1. Relax max. nit.	10.0250	10.1	0.0750	.375	.028125
2. Relax max. phos.	13.0325	14.9	1.8675	0	0
3. Relax min. pot	10.000	8.7	1.3000	.225	.2925
4. Relax max. pot.	10.0250	11.5	1.4750	0	0

The third option could reduce cost by 0.2925 cents per pound resulting in a cost of 6.3281 - .2925 = 6.0356 cents per pound; this is a profit of 0.9644 cent a pound. None of the other three options results in a larger savings than option 3.

c. Dropping from 10% to 8.7% with the minimum potash constraint is a change of -1.3. The new solution is:

Basic Variable	Old Solution	(CV)(Change) =	New Sol.	lb
8-12-4	.3094	(-.1250)(-1.3)= .1625	.4719	47,190
slack min. nit.	.0250	(0)(-1.3)= 0	.0250	
5-10-10	.1375	(.1000)(-1.3)=-.1300	.0075	750
surplus max. phos.	.0325	(0)(-1.3)= 0	.0325	
20-20-20	.2906	(.0250)(-1.3)=-.0325	.2581	25,810
surplus max. pot.	.0250	(-1.0000)(-1.3)=1.3000	1.3250	
slack avail. 4-8-6	.0375	(0)(-1.3)= 0	.0375	
slack avail. 5-10-10	.5625	(-.1000)(-1.3)= .1300	.6925	

(Continued)

```
slack avail. 8-12-4     .4906   (.1250)(-1.3)=-.1625   .3281
slack avail. 20-20-20 .3094   (-.0250)(-1.3)= .0325   .3419
4-8-6                    .2625      (0)(-1.3)=  0       .2625 26,250
                                              Total 100,000
```

The amount of 8-12-4 (costing 5 cents a pound) has
increased, while 5-10-10 (costing 6 cents) and 20-20-20
(costing 10 cents) have decreased. The amount of 4-8-6 has
remained the same.

10-32   a.   The optimum solution (rounded to even units) is:

Product	No. Unit 1	No. Unit 2	No. Unit 3	Total	Profit
Large	0	1800	0	1800	$ 360.00
Giant	4448	0	9411	13859	3326.16
Jumbo	292	10440	0	10732	3219.60
				Total	$6905.76

The program gives a profit for the noninteger solution of
690599.98062 cents or $6906. There are 2.55601 hours of
unused time on the milling machine, and all three packaging
machines are used to full capacity.

b.   For the variables L_3 and G_2 which give alternative
optima, the reduced costs are zero because by entering
either variable the optimum profit remains unchanged.

c.   If another hour of packaging time is available on
unit 3, we use the change vector:

Variable	Old sol.	Change			New sol.	Obj.
Largemax	400.00	(0)(1)	=	0	400.00	0.00
Giantmax	3080.00	(0)(1)	=	0	3080.00	0.00
Jumbomax	1918.00	(-66.67)(1)	=	-66.67	1851.33	0.00
L_2	1800.00	(0)(1)	=	0	1800.00	360.00
G_3	9411.76	(58.82)(1)	=	58.82	9470.58	2272.94
J_2	10440.00	(0)(1)	=	0	10440.00	3132.00
Milling	2.56	(-.80)(1)	=	-.80	1.76	0.00
G_1	4448.24	(-58.82)(1)	=	-58.82	4389.42	1053.46
Jumbomin	382.00	(66.67)(1)	=	66.67	448.67	0.00
J_1	292.00	(66.67)(1)	=	66.67	358.67	107.60
					Total =	$6926.00

This is a profit improvement of $20, which corresponds to
the output figure for shadow price on unit 3 given on the
printout as 2000 cents.

d.   An increase in output of large boxes from 2000 to 2100
boxes would require changing one constraint. The fourth
constraint previously read:
        $L_2 + L_3 \geq 1800$ (10% below 2000 box target)

With the new target of 2100 boxes, the constraint will read:

$$L_2 + L_3 \geq 1890 \quad (10\% \text{ below 2100 box target})$$

It is not necessary to change the constraint for 10% above target since there is currently a slack of 400 boxes in the optimal solution. Using the change vector for the LARGEMIN constraint we obtain the new solution as follows:

Variable	Old sol.	Change			New sol.	Obj.
Largemax	400.00	(-1.00)(90)	=	-90	310.00	0.00
Giantmax	3080.00	(0)(90)	=	0	3080.00	0.00
Jumbomax	1918.00	(.87)(90)	=	78.3	1996.30	0.00
L_2	1800.00	(1.00)(90)	=	90	1890.00	378.00
G_3	9411.76	(0)(90)	=	0	9411.76	2258.82
J_2	10440.00	(-.87)(90)	=	-78.3	10361.70	3108.51
Milling	2.56	(.001)(90)	=	.09	2.65	0.00
G_1	4448.24	(0)(90)	=	0	4448.24	1067.58
Jumbomin	382.00	(-.87)(90)	=	-78.3	303.70	0.00
J_1	292.00	(0)(90)	=	0	292.00	87.60
					Total =	$6900.51

This is a profit reduction of $6906 - 6900.51 = $5.49. The same result can be obtained by taking the shadow price for the LARGEMIN constraint of -6.00 cents and multiplying it by the increase in RHS of the LARGEMIN constraint of 90 boxes as follows:

$$(.06)(90) = \$5.40 \quad (\text{difference in roundoff})$$

e. Since the shadow price is 2000 cents on each of the three packaging units, we can determine the cost of introducing the new product, Family-size, as follows:

Resource	Coefficient	Shadow price	Total cost
Milling	0.010	0	0.00
Unit 1, 2, 3	0.016	2000	32.00
		Total =	32.00 cents

10-33 a. The optimum solution is:

Period	Number Report		Working 2nd 4 hr		Total	Cost
1	P_1 =	4	P_6 =	0	4	$ 384
2	P_2 =	3	P_1 =	4	7	264
3	P_3 =	17	P_2 =	3	20	1360
4	P_4 =	15	P_3 =	17	32	1260
5	P_5 =	15	P_4 =	15	30	1320
6	P_6 =	0	P_5 =	15	15	0
	Total =	54				$4588

The optimum solution provides for a total of 54 people working at a daily payroll cost of $4588. The minimum

210

numbers of people are on duty in each of the six 4-h blocks except period 4 (noon to 4PM) when 32 people are on duty (surplus of 20 people).

b. For variable P_6, the reduced cost is $2, so for a wage rate below $94 - 2 = $92 it would be beneficial for workers to report at 8 PM.

c. We wish to change the RHS of two constraints simultaneously. The constraint for period 1 will have a RHS of 6, and that of period 2 will have a RHS of 5. Using the periods 1 and 2 change vectors as well as the periods 1 and 2 shadow prices, we have:

Var.	Old sol.	Change Period #1	Change Period #2	New sol.	Obj.
P_1	4	(1)(2)= 2	(0)(-2)= 0	6	576
P_2	3	(-1)(2)=-2	(1)(-2)=-2	- 1	- 88
P_3	17	(1)(2)= 2	(-1)(-2)= 2	21	1680
P_4	15	(0)(2)= 0	(0)(-2)= 0	15	1260
P_5	15	(0)(2)= 0	(0)(-2)= 0	15	1320
P_6	0	(0)(2)= 0	(0)(-2)= 0	0	0
					$4748

Using the shadow prices for the periods 1 and 2 constraints we find the same cost of: 4588 + (2)(88) - (-2)(8) = $4748.

This solution, of course, is not feasible because variable P_2 is a negative value. The problem needs to be solved again. After doing so, we find the optimum solution: $P_1 = 5$; $P_2 = 0$; $P_3 = 20$; $P_4 = 16$; $P_5 = 14$; and $P_6 = 1$. The daily cost of the solution is $4570.

d. We introduce two new variables:
PT_1 = number of people reporting at the beginning of period 1 who work 12 hours, and:
PT_2 = number of people reporting at the beginning of period 2 who work 12 hours.
Our new formulation becomes:

Minimize: $96P_1 + 88P_2 + 80P_3 + 84P_4 + 88P_5 + 94P_6$
$+160PT_1 + 130PT_2$

$$
\begin{array}{l}
\text{S.T. } P_1 + P_2 + \qquad\qquad\qquad + PT_1 + PT_2 \geq 7 \\
\qquad\quad P_2 + P_3 \qquad\qquad\quad + PT_1 + PT_2 \geq 20 \\
\qquad\qquad\quad P_3 + P_4 \qquad\qquad\quad + PT_2 \geq 12 \\
\qquad\qquad\qquad\quad P_4 + P_5 \qquad\qquad\qquad \geq 30 \\
\qquad\qquad\qquad\qquad\quad P_5 + P_6 \qquad\qquad \geq 15 \\
\qquad P_1 \qquad\qquad\qquad\qquad\quad P_6 + PT_1 \geq 4 \\
\qquad\qquad\qquad\qquad\qquad\text{All variables} \geq 0
\end{array}
$$

211

The optimum solution is:

Per.	Report		Work 2nd 4 hr		Work 3rd 4 hr		Total	Cost
1	P_1 =	0	P_6 =	0				
	PT_1 =	4					4	$ 640
2	P_2 =	3	P_1 =	0				
	PT_2 =	0	PT_1 =	4			7	264
3	P_3 =	13	P_2 =	3	PT_1 =	4		
			PT_2 =	0			20	1040
4	P_4 =	15	P_3 =	13				
					PT_2 =	0	28	1260
5	P_5 =	15	P_4 =	15			30	1320
6	P_6 =	0	P_5 =	15			15	0
		50						$4524

All working periods provide the minimum number of people except for period 4 which has a surplus of 16 people.

e. Inspecting the sensitivity analysis on the objective function coefficients, we find for variable P_2 the range 86 to 176. If the cost for P_2 were to fall below 86, variable P_6 would enter the mix replacing variable P_1. On the other hand, if the cost for P_2 were to rise above 176, variable S_1 (surplus in period 1) would enter replacing variable P_2.

10-34 a. We read from the product mix and quantity columns:

P_2 = 3 people reporting for work at 4 AM
S_4 = 20 people surplus working in the noon to 4 PM period
P_3 = 17 people reporting for work at 8 AM
P_4 = 15 people reporting for work at noon
P_5 = 15 people reporting for work at 4 PM
P_1 = 4 people reporting for work at midnight

Daily cost = Z_j = $4588.

b. We read in the $C_j - Z_j$ row and P_6 column, the value 2, so for a wage rate below $94 - 2 = $92, it would be beneficial for workers to report at 8 PM.

c. Change vectors may be read from the tableau with reversed signs. For example, we can read down the S_1 column corresponding to the period 1 constraint, the values:

P_2	S_4	P_3	P_4	P_5	P_1
1	-1	-1	0	0	-1

These are commonly called substitution rates and are interpreted as changes in the given product mix variables with a **reduction** of one unit in the period 1 constraint.

The change vector for S_1 is interpreted as changes in the product mix variables given an **increase** of one unit. This gives rise to the change in sign for each value. As before, however, simulltaneously applying change vectors for two constraints yields an infeasible result. Consequently, the problem must be solved anew with both constraints changed.

d. To answer this question, one could reformulate the problem as described in the answer given for exercise 9-23 or qualitatively answer it as follows:

Reporting time	Periods worked	Shadow cost		
Midnight	1, 2, and 3	$S_1+S_2+S_3$ = 88+8+80	=	176
4 AM	2, 3, and 4	$S_2+S_3+S_4$ = 8+80+0	=	88

Since the wage rates are $160 and $130, respectively, and the $160 figure for 12-h shift workers reporting in period 1 is less than its shadow value, $176, a savings of $16 per worker can be realized. By inspecting the optimal solution given in exercise 9-23, we found that 4 people should be starting at midnight to work the 12-h shift with the resulting savings:

Original solution	=	$4588
Savings (4)(16)	=	- $64
New solution	=	$4524

e. We wish to obtain the range in objective function coefficient for the workers reporting at 4 AM, which is variable P_2.

Nonbasic Variable	$\dfrac{C_j - Z_j}{C}$
P_6	$(2) \div (-1) = -2$
S_2	$(8) \div (-1) = -8$
S_3	$(80) \div (0) = $ inf.
S_5	$(84) \div (0) = $ inf.
S_6	$(4) \div (0) = $ inf.
S_1	$(88) \div (1) = 88$
A_2	$(M) \div (1) = M$
A_3	$(M) \div (0) = $ inf.
A_4	$(M) \div (0) = $ inf.
A_5	$(M) \div (0) = $ inf.
A_6	$(M) \div (0) = $ inf.
A_1	$(M) \div (-1) = -M$

The least positive value is 88 and the least negative value is -2.

The range for P_2 is: 88 + 88 = 176
88 - 2 = 86

The value 88 is associated with variable S_1; so if the cost of P_2 rose above \$176, S_1 would enter the solution replacing P_2. The value of -2 is associated with variable P_6, so if the cost of P_2 fell below \$86, variable P_6 would enter the solution replacing P_1.

CHAPTER 11

SPECIALLY STRUCTURED

LINEAR PROGRAMS

11-1 (a) With $R_1 = 0$, we obtain:

$R_2 = -1$; $R_3 = 1$; $K_1 = 7$; $K_2 = 9$; $K_3 = 8$

For the unused squares.

Cell	Improvement index
R_1, C_3	$3 - 0 - 8 = -5$
R_2, C_1	$4 + 1 - 7 = -2$
R_3, C_1	$2 - 1 - 7 = -6$
R_3, C_2	$5 - 1 - 9 = -5$

(b) With $R_1 = 50$, we obtain:

$R_2 = 49$; $R_3 = 51$; $K_1 = -43$; $K_2 = -41$; $K_3 = -42$

Cell	Improvement index
R_1, C_3	$3 - 50 + 42 = -5$
R_2, C_1	$4 - 49 + 43 = -2$
R_3, C_1	$2 - 51 + 43 = -6$
R_3, C_2	$5 - 51 + 41 = -5$

(c) With $K_3 = 0$, we obtain:

$R_1 = 8$; $R_2 = 7$; $R_3 = 9$; $K_1 = -1$; $K_2 = 1$

Cell	Improvement index
R_1, C_3	$3 - 8 - 0 = -5$
R_2, C_1	$4 - 7 + 1 = -2$
R_3, C_1	$2 - 9 + 1 = -6$
R_3, C_2	$5 - 9 - 1 = -5$

(d) Comparing the three cases, we find that the R_1 and K_j values are not the same. However, the improvement indices are identical in all cases.

11-2   The Northwest corner allocation is:

To \ From	D	E	F	Supply
A	8 17	9 8	7	25
B	6	4 9	3	9
C	8	6	4 5	5
Demand	17	17	5	39 / 39

Used squares = total rim requirements - 1

$4 \neq 3 + 3 - 1 = 5 \longrightarrow$ degeneracy.

It may be observed that square C,F is dangling by itself
with no other stone square in row C or column F.
Therefore, the degeneracy can be resolved by making any
other square in row C or column F a zero stone square. It
would be fruitless to make unused square B,D a zero stone
square. Of all the unused squares which are candidates, it
is usually a good idea to select the one having least C_{ij}
cost to be selected as the zero stone square, because this
usually can save an iteration (i.e., in later loading some
unused square leading to an improved solution, no real
change is made except for moving the zero value to another
square). For this reason we would select square B,F to be
the zero stone square.

216

11-3

To From	A	B	C	Supply
W	5 120	4	9	120
X	4 20	3 140	5	160
Y	7	4 60	2 80	140
Demand	140	200	80	420 / 420

<u>Unused Square</u>   <u>Improvement Index</u>

W,B	+4 - 3 + 4 - 5 = 0 Alternative optimal
W,C	+9 - 2 + 4 - 3 + 4 - 5 = +7
X,C	+5 - 2 + 4 - 3 = +4
Y,A	+7 - 4 + 3 - 4 = +2

Cost = (120)(5) + (20)(4) + (140)(3) + (60)(4) + (80)(2)
     = $1500

11-4

To From	A	B	C	Supply
W	5 25	10 10	10	35
X	20 20	30	20 20	40
Y	5	8 40	12	40
Demand	45	50	20	115 / 115

217

Unused Square	Improvement Index
W,C	+10 - 20 + 20 - 5 = +5
X,B	+30 - 10 + 5 - 20 = +5
Y,A	+5 - 5 + 10 - 8 = +2
Y,C	+12 - 20 + 20 - 5 + 10 - 8 = +9

Cost = (25)(5) + (10)(10) + (20)(20) + (20)(20) + (40)(8)
    = $1345

11-5

R_i \ K_j		4 W	8 X	3 Y	Supply
0	A	12	8 170	5	170
7	B	11 30	15 30	10 190	250
-2	C	2 100	7	6	100
	Demand	130	200	190	520 / 520

Unused Square	Improvement Index
A,W	12 - 0 - 4 = +8
A,Y	5 - 0 - 3 = +2
C,X	7 + 2 - 8 = +1
C,Y	6 + 2 - 3 = +5

Cost = (170)(8) + (30)(11) + (30)(15) + (190)(10) +
    (100)(2) = $4240

Kj / Ri	To / From	K₁ =58 Assembly	K₂ =67 Machin- ing	K₃ =76 Packag- ing	K₄ =29 Inspec- tion	Avail- able
R₁ =0	App.	58 / 7	62	76 / 7	29 / 1	15
R₂ =27	Exp.	73	94 / 7	81	56 / 3	10
	Required	7	7	7	4	25 / 25

Unused Square	Cᵢⱼ − Rᵢ − Kⱼ	Improvement Index
12	62 − 0 − 67	−5
21	73 − 27 − 58	−12
23	81 − 27 − 76	−22

Total Productivity

Class	Department	Number	Productivity
Apprentice	Assembly	7	406
Apprentice	Packaging	7	532
Apprentice	Inspection	1	29
Experienced	Machining	7	658
Experienced	Inspection	3	168
		Total	1,793

11-7

K_j / R_i	To / From	K_1=460 Miami	K_2=420 Houston	K_3=420 New Orleans	Supply
R_1=0	Bananas	400	420 / 200	400	200
R_2=440	Avocados	900 / 300	860 / 50	850	350
R_3=-70	Oranges	100	300	350 / 210	210
R_4=-420	Dummy	0	0 / 50	0 / 550	600
	Limit	300	300	760	1360 / 1360

Unused Square	$C_{ij} - R_i - K_j$	Improvement Index
11	400 - 0 - 460	-60
13	400 - 0 - 420	-20
23	850 - 440 - 420	-10
31	100 - (-70) - 460	-290
32	300 - (-70) - 420	-50
41	0 - (-420) - 460	-40

Commodity	Port	Tons	Profit
Bananas	Houston	200	$ 84,000
Avocados	Miami	300	270,000
Avocados	Houston	50	43,000
Oranges	New Orleans	210	73,500
		Total profit	$470,500

220

K_j / R_i	To / From	A	B	C	D	Supply
		16	16	16	16	
0	W	16 / 20	18	19	17	20
-1	X	15 / 10	17	20	16	10
0	Y	17	16 / 20	18	18	20
2	Z	18 / 10	19	19	18 / 20	30
-16	Dum	0	0 / 10	0 / 20	0 / 0	30
	Demand	40	30	20	20	110 / 110

Unused Squares	Improvement Index
W,B	18 - 0 - 16 = +2
W,C	19 - 0 - 16 = +3
W,D	17 - 0 - 16 = +1
X,B	17 + 1 - 16 = +2
X,C	20 + 1 - 16 = +5
X,D	16 + 1 - 16 = +1
Y,A	17 - 0 - 16 = +1
Y,C	18 - 0 - 16 = +2
Y,D	18 - 0 - 16 = +2
Z,B	19 - 2 - 16 = +1
Z,C	19 - 2 - 16 = +1
Dum,A	0 + 16 - 16 = 0

The presence of the zero improvement index for unused square Dum,A would seem to indicate an alternative optimum solution. However, in loading Dum,A we would find that

Dum,A would only become a zero stone square in the degenerate solution instead of square Dum,D. No physical change in the lending arrangement would result. The solution is, therefore, a unique, but degenerate, optimal.

$$Cost = (20,000)(.16) + (10,000)(.15) + (20,000)(.16)$$
$$+ (10,000)(.18) + (20,000)(.18)$$
$$= \$13,300 \text{ annual interest}$$

11-9   Square X,A must be made an unused square. In order to do this we need to make some unused square in row X a basic or stone square. The candidates in row X are:

Unused square in row X	Improvement index
X,B	+2
X,C	+5
X,D	+1

Unused square X,D has the smallest improvement index. If we look for the closed path from X,D we find:

X,D(+) to Z,D(-) to Z,A(+) to X,A(-) and back to X,D

This path does provide a reduction in the prohibited stone square X,A and all 10 units can be shifted. Therefore, the change becomes:

Bank	Project	Loan(Previous)	Loan(Changed)
X	A	10	0
Z	A	10	20
Z	D	20	10
X	D	0	10

All other plans are unaffected. The increase in cost is $10,000 added to square X,D whose improvement index is +1.

$$Added\ cost = (10,000)(1) = \$10,000$$

11-10

R_i \ K_j	To / From	6	5	3	
		E	F	G	Supply
0	A	6 / 1	5 / 3	8 / 5	4
-3	B	3 / 3	4 /	9 /	3
0	C	6 / 1	10 /	3 / 5	6
0	D	9 /	7 /	3 / 1	1
	Demand	5	3	6	14 / 14

Unused Squares	Improvement Index
A,G	8 - 0 - 3 = +5
B,F	4 + 3 - 5 = +2
B,G	9 + 3 - 3 = +9
C,F	10 - 0 - 5 = +5
D,E	9 - 0 - 6 = +3
D,F	7 - 0 - 5 = +2

The solution is uniquely optimal.

Total miles = (1)(60) + (3)(50) + (3)(30) + (1)(60) + (5)(30) + (1)(30) = 540

11-11

K_J / R_i		56	11	-14	-4	-69	
	To / From	NY	A	H	LAS	Dum	Supply
0	RC	56 / 7250	120	145	110	0	7250
54	S	110 / 1450	65 / 5800	40 / 725	50 / 2175	0	10150
69	W	M	90	55 / 2175	M	0 / 2175	4350
	Demand	8700	5800	2900	2175	2175	21750 / 21750

Unused Square	Improvement Index
RC,A	$120 - 0 - 11 = +109$
RC,H	$145 - 0 + 14 = +159$
RC,LA	$110 - 0 + 4 = +114$
RC,Dum	$0 - 0 + 69 = +69$
S,Dum	$0 - 54 + 69 = +15$
W,NY	$M - 69 - 56 = M$
W,A	$90 - 69 - 11 = +10$
W,LA	$M - 69 + 4 = M$

The solution is uniquely optimal, and the cost is:

$$\text{Cost} = (7250)(5.60) + (1450)(11.0) + (5800)(6.5)$$
$$+ (725)(4) + (2175)(5) + (2175)(5.5)$$
$$= \$119,987.50$$

11-12 We use the symbols S = Seattle, A = Anchorage, R = regular time, O = overtime, J_p = Jan. production, J_s = Jan. sales, C = Chicken of the Ocean, and M = Moon Kist.

224

To / From	J_S C	J_S M	F_S C	F_S M	M_S C	M_S M	Dum	Sup.
J_P S_R	8	9	9	10	10	11	0	20
J_P S_O	11	12	12	13	13	14	0	5
J_P A_R	9	8	10	9	11	10	0	30
J_P A_O	10	9	11	10	12	11	0	10
F_P S_R	M	M	8	9	9	10	0	20
F_P S_O	M	M	11	12	12	13	0	5
F_P A_R	M	M	9	8	10	9	0	30
F_P A_O	M	M	10	9	11	10	0	10
M_P S_R	M	M	M	M	8	9	0	20
M_P S_O	M	M	M	M	11	12	0	5
M_P A_R	M	M	M	M	9	8	0	30
M_P A_O	M	M	M	M	10	9	0	10
Dmd	20	20	30	40	40	30	15	195

The C_{ij} value shown as a high cost M indicate infeasible routes (i.e., one cannot produce in March to meet January sales).

225

11-13 We define:

P_1 = Party production hours of demand in week 1
F_1 = Family production hours of demand in week 1
S_1 = Storage production hours of demand in week 1
R_1 = Regular production hours in week 1
O_1 = Overtime production hours in week 1

To / From	P_1	F_1	S_1	P_2	F_2	S_2	P_3	F_3	S_3	Dum	Supply
R_1	8 / 100	8 / 120	8 / 80	8	8	8 / 100	8	8	8	0	400
O_1	12	12	12	12	12	12	12	12	12	0 / 160	160
R_2	M	M	M	8 / 100	8 / 240	8 / 60	8 / 0	8	8	0	400
O_2	M	M	M	12	12	12	12	12	12	0 / 320	320
R_3	M	M	M	M	M	M	8 / 120	8 / 180	8 / 320	0 / 20	640
O_3	M	M	M	M	M	M	12	12	12	0 / 400	400
Demand	100	120	80	100	240	160	120	180	320	900	2320 / 2320

We omit the squares with costs of M and obtain:

Unused Squares	Improvement Index
Row R_1 and all columns except Dum	8 − 0 − 8 = 0
Row R_1, Col. Dum	0 − 0 − 0 = 0
Row O_1 and all columns	12 − 0 − 8 = +4
Row R_2, Cols. F_3 and S_3	8 − 0 − 8 = 0
Row R_2, Col. Dum	0 − 0 − 0 = 0
Row O_2 and all columns	12 − 0 − 8 = +4
Row O_3 and all columns	12 − 0 − 8 = +4

The solution is optimal. Since all production is on
regular time, the entire 1420 hours of production is at $8
per hour for a total cost of $11,360.

11-14 After row and column reductions, the opportunity costs are:

	Machine		
Job	X	Y	Z
A	0	1	3
B	0	0	1	line 2
C	0	3	0	line 3

line 1

The optimal allocation is:

Job	Machine	Cost
A	X	4
B	Y	3
C	Z	5
		$12

11-15 We may dominate machine Z because its cost is highest for
each job. After row and column reductions, the opportunity
costs are:

	Machine		
Job	W	X	Y
A	0	1	1
B	0	0	0	line 2
C	0	0	0	line 3

line 1

The optimal allocations are:

Job	Machine	Cost		Job	Machine	Cost
A	W	18		A	W	18
B	X	13		B	Y	17
C	Y	19		C	X	15
	Total =	$50			Total =	$50

11-16   The matrix of regret values are:

Individual	C	F	P	A	
A	~~150~~	~~100~~	~~0~~	~~150~~	line 2
B	50	0	150	100	
C	100	50	200	0	
D	~~0~~	~~0~~	~~150~~	~~50~~	line 3

Vehicle (header spanning C F P A)

line 1   line 4

The optimal assignment is:

Individual	Vehicle	Bid
Alice	Plymouth	1100
Bruce	Ford	1000
Charles	AMC	1050
Dora	Chevrolet	1150
	Revenue =	$4300

11-17   The matrix of regret values is:

Salesperson	Central	East	West	North	South	Lake
A	1	3	2	1	2	0
B	2	4	3	0	0	1
C	4	3	4	2	2	2
D	2	1	1	2	4	3
E	5	5	2	3	5	4
F	0	0	0	1	3	0

After row reduction:

Salesperson	Central	East	West	North	South	Lake	
A	1	3	2	1	2	0	
B	2	4	3	0	0	1	line 4
C	2	1	2	0	0	0	line 2
D	1	0	0	1	3	2	line 3
E	3	3	0	1	3	2	
F	0	0	0	1	3	0	line 1

line 5   line 6

Optimal assignment:

Salesperson	Area	Annual Sales
A	Lake	14
B	North	11
C	South	12
D	East	11
E	West	8
F	Central	14
	Total =	70 houses per year

228

11-18   After row and column reduction, we have:

	J	K	L	M	N	
A	8	2	10	21	0	
B	0	2	16	0	10	line 2
C	3	2	6	0	5	
D	15	4	0	1	5	line 3
E	10	0	5	5	2	

line 4   line 1 line 5

The optimum defensive assignment is:

Hoosier Player	Redmen Player	Expected Points
Allen	Nevers	14
Berg	Jones	16
Carl	Manion	10
Daniels	Layne	18
Evers	Kurtz	20
	Total	78 points

The Hoosiers need to score more than 78 points to win.

11-19   Min $Z = 22AJ + 18AK + 24AL + 35AM + 14AN$
$+ 16BJ + 20BK + 32BL + 16BM + 26BN$
$+ 13CJ + 14CK + 16CL + 10CM + 15CN$
$+ 33DJ + 24DK + 18DL + 19DM + 23DN$
$+ 28EJ + 20EK + 18EL + 23EM + 20EN$

$$AJ + AK + AL + AM + AN \geq 1$$
$$BJ + BK + BL + BM + BN \geq 1$$
$$CJ + CK + CL + CM + CN \geq 1$$
$$DJ + DK + DL + DM + DN \geq 1$$
$$EJ + EK + EL + EM + EN \geq 1$$
$$AJ + BJ + CJ + DJ + EJ \leq 1$$
$$AK + BK + CK + DK + EK \leq 1$$
$$AL + BL + CL + DL + EL \leq 1$$
$$AM + BM + CM + DM + EM \leq 1$$
$$AN + BN + CN + DN + EN \leq 1$$

The solution using the QAM disk matches the hand-computed solution as follows:

OBJECTIVE FUNCTION =   78.0000

BASIC STRUCTURAL VARIABLES
AN	1.0000
BJ	1.0000
BM	0.0000
CK	0.0000
CM	1.0000
DL	1.0000
EK	1.0000
EL	0.0000

11-20 Since each of the three tire sizes requires 300 units, we
       may use the dollars-per-tires figure without multiplying
       each figure by the constant--300 tires.

       After row and column reductions, we have:

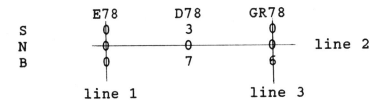

       The optimal assignment is:

Company	Tire Size	Cost
Billy's	E78 x 15	60 x 300 = $18,000
Southern	GR78 x 15	78 x 300 = $23,400
New Hope	D78 x 14	78 x 300 = $23,400
		Total = $64,800

11-21 We have four directors and only three grants so we add a
       dummy grant with a zero value of hours required for each of
       the four directors. After column reduction we have:

	Grant				
Director	1	2	3	Dum	
LG	34	0	24	0	line 2
AA	8	18	0	0	line 3
MA	0	14	18	0	line 4
NP	26	6	18	0	

                                              line 1

       Our optimal assignment is:

Director	Grant	Hours
LG	2	90
AA	3	30
MA	1	46
NP	none	none
	Total	166 hours

11-22 After reducing columns and rows, we have

Machines

Jobs	1	2	3	4	5	6	
A	5	2	0	5	3	3	
B	2	2	0	0	0	2	line 3
C	3	1	2	5	4	0	line 5
D	0	0	0	0	0	0	line 1
E	6	6	0	3	9	2	
F	0	0	0	5	8	12	line 3

line 2

We subtract 2 from all uncovered elements and add 2 to each element which is at an intersection of two lines. The revised table is:

Machines

Jobs	1	2	3	4	5	6	
A	3	0	0	3	1	1	
B	2	2	2	0	0	2	line 4
C	3	1	4	5	4	0	
D	0	0	2	0	0	0	line 1
E	4	4	0	1	7	0	
F	0	0	2	5	8	12	line 6

line 2   line 3   line 5

We can now make our optimal assignment:

Job	Machine	Time
C	6	6
B	4	5
D	5	1
F	1	12
A	2	6
E	3	10
	Total	40 hr

There are other optimal solutions to this problem besides the one shown.

11-23 To solve this as an assignment problem we need to create a dummy salesperson; all assignment problems must be n by n, or 5 by 5 in this case. Any value may be assigned to the dummy as long as it is an identical value for all sales districts; let us arbitrarily select a value of 70, which is lower than all others in the table.

The regret matrix is:

Salesperson	District 1	2	3	4	5
A	0	4	2	0	10
B	8	6	0	9	12
C	2	4	3	5	0
D	14	0	7	7	5
Dummy	92	94	96	91	93

After row reductions we have:

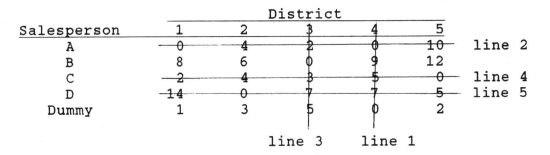

Salesperson	District 1	2	3	4	5	
A	0	4	2	0	10	line 2
B	8	6	0	9	12	
C	2	4	3	5	0	line 4
D	14	0	7	7	5	line 5
Dummy	1	3	5	0	2	

line 3   line 1

The optimal assignment is:

Salesperson	District	Rating
A	1	92
B	3	96
C	5	93
D	2	94
Dummy	4	-- (not covered)
	Total =	375

232

11-24 Demand is greater than supply. Consequently, at least one project will not be able to meet demand. We create a dummy supplier and find the minimum cost solution.

R_1 K_1	To / From	2 / A	3 / B	3 / C	Supply
0	W	4	8	3 / 45	45
4	X	6 / 50	7 / 10	9	60
-1	Y	8	2 / 60	5	60
-3	Dum	0	0 / 5	0 / 5	10
	Demand	50	75	50	175 / 175

Unused Square	Improvement Index
W,A	4 − 0 − 2 = +2
W,B	8 − 0 − 3 = +5
X,C	9 − 4 − 3 = +2
Y,A	8 + 1 − 2 = +7
Y,C	5 + 1 − 3 = +3
Dum,A	0 + 3 − 2 = +1

Cost = (45)(3) + (50)(6) + (10)(7) + (60)(2) = $625

11-25 The problem formulation (with a dummy plant, D, added) becomes:

Min Z = 4WA + 8WB + 3WC + 6XA + 7XB + 9XC
+ 8YA + 2YB + 5YC + 0DA + 0DB + 0DC

$$
\begin{array}{llllll}
\text{S.T.} & \text{WA} + \text{XA} + \text{YA} + \text{DA} & \geq & 50 \\
& \text{WB} + \text{XB} + \text{YB} + \text{DB} & \geq & 75 \\
& \text{WC} + \text{XC} + \text{YC} + \text{DC} & \geq & 50 \\
& \text{WA} + \text{WB} + \text{WC} & \leq & 45 \\
& \text{XA} + \text{XB} + \text{XC} & \leq & 60 \\
& \text{YA} + \text{YB} + \text{YC} & \leq & 60 \\
& \text{DA} + \text{DB} + \text{DC} & \leq & 10 \\
\end{array}
$$

The computer produced optimal solution matches up with the solution we obtained using the transportation method as follows:

WC = 45   XA = 50   XB = 10   YB = 60   DB = 5   DC = 5

Cost = $625

11-26

K_j R_i		29	28	26	0	
	To From	A	B	C	Dum	Supply
0	X	29 3	30	26 3	0 0	6
0	Y	31	28 2	29	0 3	5
0	Z	30	29	29	0 3	3
	Demand	3	2	3	6	14 14

Unused square	Improvement index
X,B	30 - 0 - 28 = +2
Y,A	31 - 0 - 29 = +2
Y,C	29 - 0 - 26 = +3
Z,A	30 - 0 - 29 = +1
Z,B	29 - 0 - 28 = +1
Z,C	29 - 0 - 26 = +3

The solution is a uniquely optimal, degenerate solution.

$$\text{Cost} = (3)(290) + (3)(260) + (2)(280) = \$2,210$$

11-27   a.   The lowest improvement indices are +1 ($10 per 1000
feet) in unused squares ZA and ZB.   The closed path to ZA
is ZA+, XA-, XDum+, and ZDum-.   This includes XA, a
shipment of type A pipe from Manufacturer X.   So XA can be
reduced by 1000 feet of pipe and costs will only increase
by $10.   The 1000 feet of type A pipe not supplied by X
will be ordered from Manufacturer Z.

b.   Unused square ZC has an improvement index of +3 ($30
per 1000 feet).   Therefore, Maunfacturer Z's price for type
C pipe must drop from $290 to less than $260 per 1000 feet
before you would purchase any.   At $275 per 1000 feet, it
is not a good buy.

c.   Usused square ZB has the closed path ZB+, YB-, YDum+,
and ZDum-.   The improvement index for ZB is +1 ($10 per
1000 feet).   Consequently, if the cost of square YB
increases from 28 to 30, it is no longer optimal to
purchase type B pipe from Y and it will be purchased from
Manufacturer Z.

11-28   After row and column reductions, we have:

Co.	Subcontract					
	V	W	X	Y	Z	
A	5	30	45	35	0	
B	0	15	0	25	5	line 3
C	10	30	40	35	0	
D	0	0	40	0	5	line 1
E	25	0	40	25	10	line 4

line 2

We cannot make an optimal statement as yet, so we subtract
5 from all uncovered numbers and add 5 to all
intersectional numbers to obtain:

Co.	Subcontract					
	V	W	X	Y	Z	
A	0	25	40	30	0	line 4
B	0	15	0	25	10	line 3
C	2	25	35	30	0	
D	0	0	40	0	10	line 1
E	25	0	40	25	15	line 5

line 2

235

The optimal assignment is:

Co.	Subcontract	Cost
A	V	45
B	X	40
C	Z	40
D	Y	55
E	W	25
	Total =	$205,000

11-29   Since each company can receive up to two subcontracts, we
solve the problem as a transportation problem. The
companies are called suppliers and each is given a total
supply of 2. The subcontracts are taken as demand centers
and each has a total demand of 1. The optimal solution is:

Company	Subcontract(s)	Cost
A	Z	$30,000
B	X	40,000
C	none	
D	V and Y	85,000
E	W	25,000
		$180,000

The savings over the solution of Exercise 11-28 is
205,000 - 180,000 = $25,000

K_j R_i	To From	18 A	21 B	22 S	Supply
0	B	18 / 1	21 / 1	22 / 9	11
0	F	18 / 14	25	24	14
-1	S	22	22	21 / 12	12
-5	SC	19	16 / 8	20	8
	Demand	15	9	21	45 / 45

Unused Squares	Improvement Index
F,B	25 − 0 − 21 = +4
F,S	24 − 0 − 22 = +2
S,A	22 + 1 − 18 = +5
S,B	22 + 1 − 21 = +2
SC,A	19 + 5 − 18 = +6
SC,S	20 + 5 − 22 = +3

The solution is uniquely optimal.

$$\text{Cost} = (1)(180) + (1)(210) + (9)(220) + (14)(180)$$
$$+ (12)(210) + (8)(160) = \$8690$$

11-31 (a) We examine the improvement indices of the unused cells F,B and S,B which are possible routes to Buford and find that S,B has an improvement index of only +2. Therefore, we use the stepping stone method to load cell S,B. The change is:

Old schedule				New Schedule		
B to B	1 unit			B to B	none	
B to S	9 units			B to S	10 units	
S to B	none			S to B	1 unit	
S to S	12 units			S to S	11 units	

All other routes remain unchanged and costs increase by (1)(20) = $20. The new total cost is $8710.

(b) The new improvement index for square SC,S is now: 16 + 5 - 22 = -1. Therefore, you would load square SC,S using the stepping stone method. The new solution is:

K_j / R_i		18	21	22	
	To / From	A	B	S	Supply
0	B	18 / 1	21 / 9	22 / 1	11
0	F	18 / 14	25	24	14
-1	S	22	22	21 / 12	12
-6	SC	19	16 / 0	16 / 8	8
	Demand	15	9	21	45 / 45

Unused Squares	Improvement Index
F,B	25 - 0 - 21 = +4
F,S	24 - 0 - 22 = +2
S,A	22 + 1 - 18 = +5
S,B	22 + 1 - 21 = +2
SC,A	19 + 6 - 18 = +5
SC,B	16 + 6 - 21 = +1

Costs are reduced by $80. The new total cost is $8610.

11-32 Since demand is greater than supply, one or more of the lots will be short by a total of 60 cars or 12 truck loads. Rim requirements in the following table are stated in the truck loads of 5 cars each.

238

K_J		75	50	50	60	
R_1	To / From	M	B	OS	P	Supply
0	G	75 / 6	50 / 22	50 / 22	150	50
15	BM	90 / 7	120	140	75 / 33	40
-75	Dum	0 / 12	0	0	0	12
	Demand	25	22	22	33	102 / 102

Unused Square	Improvement Index
G,P	150 − 0 − 60 = +90
BM,B	120 − 15 − 50 = +55
BM,OS	140 − 15 − 50 = +75
Dum,B	0 + 75 − 50 = +25
Dum,OS	0 + 75 − 50 = +25
Dum,P	0 + 75 − 60 = +15

$$\text{Cost} = (6)(75) + (22)(50) + (22)(50) + (7)(90) + (33)(75) = \$5755$$

11-33 a. The twelve truckloads now in the square for Mobile and Dummy must be reduced from 12 truckloads to 5 truckloads. The 7 truckloads reduction will be picked up by Biloxi, Ocean Springs, and/or Pensacola. The lowest improvement index in any unused square in the dummy row is +15 in square Pensacola and Dummy. The closed path into Dum,P is: Dum,P+; Dum,M−; BM,M+ and BM,P−. Therefore, 7 more truckloads will be shipped to Mobile from Bay Minette while 7 less will be shipped from Bay Minette to Pensacola. Costs will increase by (15)(7) = $105.

b. The improvement index for unused square BM,OS is +75. It would, therefore, require at least a $75 per truckload reduction in cost before this route would be considered.

c. Currently, the optimal solution calls for 33 truckloads to be shipped from Bay Minette to Pensacola. If there is any reduction from the 33, it would be necessary to move into either unused square G,P or Dum,P. The improvement indices for these are +90 and +15, respectively. Consequently, a $10 per truckload increase in BM,P will not cause the solution to change.

11-34

Company	Bids				
	V	W	X	Y	Z
A	45	60	75	100	30
B	50	55	40	100	45
C	60	70	80	110	40
D	30	20	60	55	25
E	60	25	65	185	35

Using the greedy heuristic, we find the smallest cost of any unassigned company/project.

	Cost
1. Assign company D to project W	20
2. Assign company A to project Z	30
3. Assign company B to project X	40
4. Assign company E to project V (tied with C/V)	60
5. Assign company C to project Y	110
Total =	$260

Using the VAM heuristic:

Company/Project	2nd smallest	Smallest	Opp. cost
A	45	30	15
B	45	40	5
C	60	40	20
D	25	20	5
E	35	25	10
V	45	30	15
W	25	20	5
X	60	40	20
Y	100	55	45--largest
Z	30	25	5

We assign company D to project Y, and update the opportunity costs with D and Y eliminated:

Company/Project	2nd smallest	Smallest	Opp. cost
A	45	30	15
B	45	40	5
C	60	40	20
E	35	25	10
V	50	45	5

(Continued)

240

	2nd smallest	Smallest	Opp. cost
W	55	25	30--largest
X	65	40	25
Z	35	30	5

We assign company E to project W, and update the
opportunity costs with E and W eliminated:

Company/Project	2nd smallest	Smallest	Opp. cost
A	45	30	15
B	45	40	5
C	60	40	20
V	50	45	5
X	75	40	35--largest
Z	40	30	10

We assign company B to project X, and update the
opportunity costs with B and X eliminated:

Company/Project	2nd smallest	Smallest	Opp. cost
A	45	30	15
C	60	40	20--largest
V	60	45	15
Z	40	30	10

After assigning company C to project Z, we have only A and
V left to assign.

The heuristic assignment is:

Company	Project	Cost
D	Y	55
E	W	25
B	X	40
C	Z	40
A	V	45
	Total =	$205

(optimum by VAM)

11-35

To From	W	X	Y	Supply
A	12	8	5 / 170	170
B	11 / 30	15 / 200	10 / 20	250
C	2 / 100	7	6	100
Demand	130	200	190 / 520	520

Using the greedy heuristic, we find the lowest cost of $2 per unit is in cell CW, so we ship 100 units from C to W. Excluding the row C costs, the next lowest cost is $5 per unit in cell AY, so we ship 170 units from A to Y. Excluding row C and row A costs, we have only row B remaining as a possible supplier. Therefore, 30 units are assigned to BW, 200 units are assigned to BX, and 20 units are assigned to BY, thus completing the greedy solution. The cost of the solution is $4580, which is $340 greater than the optimum solution.

Using the Vogel Approximation Method:

Row or Column	Lowest	Second lowest	Opportunity cost
Row A	5	8	3
Row B	10	11	1
Row C	2	6	4
Col W	2	11	9--highest
Col X	7	8	1
Col Y	5	6	1

The highest opportunity cost, associated with column W, is selected and 100 units are assigned to its lowest cost cell (cell CW).

Row or Column	Lowest	Second lowest	Opportunity cost
Row A	5	8	3
Row B	10	11	1
Col W	11	12	1
Col X	8	15	7--highest
Col Y	5	10	5

We assign 170 units to cell AX. With both rows A and C satisfied, the remaining shipments are all assigned to supplier B. The heuristic solution is:

To From	W		X		Y		Supply
A		12	170	8		5	170
B	30	11	30	15	190	10	250
C	100	2		7		6	100
Demand	130		200		190		520 / 520

The cost of the Vogel solution is $4240, which is optimum.

11-36 Using the VAM heuristic:

Row or Column	Highest	Second highest	Opportunity cost
B	420	400	20
A	900	860	40
O	350	300	50
D	0	0	0
M	900	400	500--highest
H	860	420	440
N	850	400	450

We load 300 units into cell AM and eliminate Column M.

Row or Column	Highest	Second highest	Opportunity cost
B	420	400	20
A	860	850	10
O	350	300	50
D	0	0	0
H	860	420	440
N	850	400	450--highest

We load 50 units into cell AN and eliminate row A.

Row or Column	Highest	Second highest	Opportunity cost
B	420	400	20
O	350	300	50
D	0	0	0
H	420	300	120--highest
N	400	350	50

We load 200 units into cell BH and eliminate row B.

Row or Column	Highest	Second highest	Opportunity cost
O	350	300	50
D	0	0	0
H	300	0	300
N	350	0	350--highest

We load 210 units into cell ON and eliminate row O. The only remaining row is the dummy row which must pick up all other requirements. Our solution is:

To From	Miami	Houston	New Orleans	Supply
Bananas	400	420 200	400	200
Avocados	900 300	860	850 50	350
Oranges	100	300	350 210	210
Dummy	0	0 100	0 500	600
Limit	300	300	760	1360 / 1360

Profit = (200)(420) + (300)(900) + (50)(850) + (210)(350)
       = $470,000

This solution is $500 less than the optimum.

11-37 Using the VAM heuristic:

Row or Column	Highest	Second highest	Opportunity cost
A	14	13	1
B	14	13	1
C	12	12	0
D	12	11	1
E	10	9	1
F	14	14	0
C	14	13	1
E	12	11	1
W	10	9	1
N	11	10	1
S	14	12	2--highest
L	14	14	0

We assign salesperson B to the South area. Eliminating Row
B and Column S, we have:

Row or Column		Highest	Second highest	Opportunity cost
A		14	13	1
C		12	10	2--highest
D		12	11	1
E		10	9	1
F		14	14	0
	C	14	13	1
	E	12	11	1
	W	10	9	1
	N	10	10	0
	L	14	14	0

We assign salesperson C to the Lake area. Eliminating Row
C and Column L, we have:

Row or Column		Highest	Second highest	Opportunity cost
A		13	10	3--highest
D		12	11	1
E		9	8	1
F		14	12	2
	C	14	13	1
	E	12	11	1
	W	10	9	1
	N	10	10	0

We assign salesperson A to the Central area. Eliminating
Row A and Column C, we have:

Row or Column		Highest	Second highest	Opportunity cost
D		11	9	2--highest
E		8	8	0
F		12	10	2--highest
	E	12	11	1
	W	10	9	1
	N	10	9	1

The tie in opportunity cost is broken in favor of F
(highest sales of 12) rather than D (highest sales
of 11). We assign salesperson F to the East area.
Eliminating row F and Column E, we have:

Row or Column		Highest	Second highest	Opportunity cost
D		9	9	0
E		8	8	0
	W	9	8	1--highest
	N	9	8	1--highest

We can now assign salesperson D to the West area and
salesperson E to the North area or vice versa. Our
solution is:

Salesperson	Area	Annual sales
A	Central	13
B	South	14
C	Lake	12
D	West	9
E	North	8
F	East	12

Total = 68 houses per year

Our heuristic solution is 2 units less than the optimum.

CHAPTER 12

NETWORKS

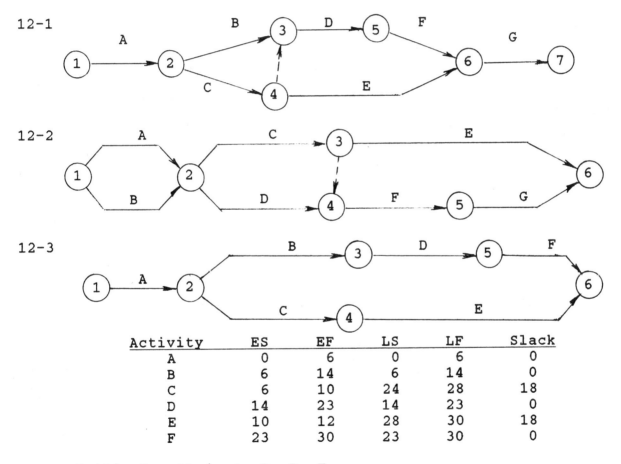

12-1

12-2

12-3

Activity	ES	EF	LS	LF	Slack
A	0	6	0	6	0
B	6	14	6	14	0
C	6	10	24	28	18
D	14	23	14	23	0
E	10	12	28	30	18
F	23	30	23	30	0

Critical path is A, B, D, F.

12-4

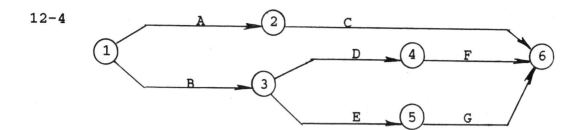

Activity	ES	EF	LS	LF	Slack
A	0	4	14	18	14
B	0	9	0	9	0
C	4	7	18	21	14
D	9	17	11	19	2
E	9	16	9	16	0
F	17	19	19	21	2
G	16	21	16	21	0

The critical path is B, E, and G.

12-5

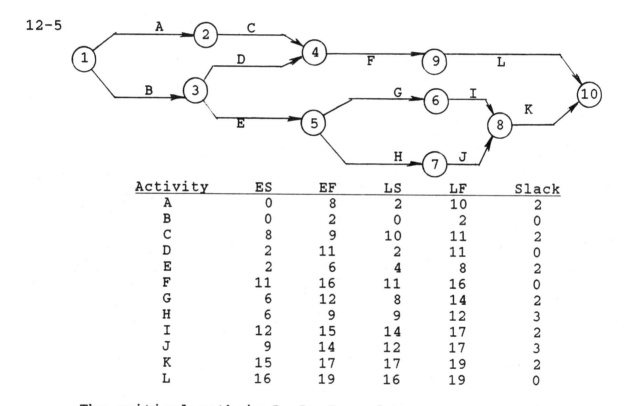

Activity	ES	EF	LS	LF	Slack
A	0	8	2	10	2
B	0	2	0	2	0
C	8	9	10	11	2
D	2	11	2	11	0
E	2	6	4	8	2
F	11	16	11	16	0
G	6	12	8	14	2
H	6	9	9	12	3
I	12	15	14	17	2
J	9	14	12	17	3
K	15	17	17	19	2
L	16	19	16	19	0

The critical path is B, D, F, and L.

12-6   The remainder of the project with F, I, and J all starting
        at 12 is:

Activity	ES	EF	LS	LF	Slack
F	12	17	11	16	-1
I	12	15	14	17	2
J	12	17	12	17	0
K	17	19	17	19	0
L	17	20	16	19	-1

Either F or L must be crashed by one week depending upon
which can be crashed at least cost. If resources are taken
from another activity, then this must be activity I which
is the only one having a slack greater than zero.

12-7

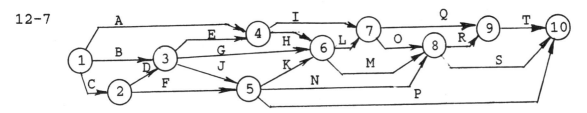

Activity	ES	EF	LS	LF	Slack
A	0	8	10	18	10
B	0	2	10	12	10
C	0	3	0	3	0
D	3	12	3	12	0
E	12	16	14	18	2
F	3	9	9	15	6
G	12	19	12	19	0
H	16	17	18	19	2
I	16	18	23	25	7
J	12	15	12	15	0
K	15	19	15	19	0
L	19	25	19	25	0
M	19	27	21	29	2
N	15	20	24	29	9
O	25	29	25	29	0
P	15	19	33	37	18
Q	25	28	28	31	3
R	29	31	29	31	0
S	29	30	36	37	7
T	31	37	31	37	0

There are two critical paths:

Path 1:   C, D, G, L, O, R, and T
Path 2:   C, D, J, K, L, O, R, and T

12-8 Of the two activities in progress, G is on the critical
      path while N is not. Activity G should be completed by the
      end of week 23, resulting in a negative slack for milestone
      6 of minus 4 weeks. Consequently, the slack for the
      unscheduled activities are:

Activity	Slack (weeks)
L	0 - 4 = -4
M	2 - 4 = -2
O	0 - 4 = -4
Q	3 - 4 = -1
R	0 - 4 = -4
S	7 - 4 = +3
T	0 - 4 = -4

Possible courses of action:
1. Divert manpower from activity N to activity G.
Activity N has 3 weeks remaining (scheduled completion
at the end of week 24) and its current slack is 5
weeks. If activity G can finish in only one week
instead of 2 weeks this will result in activities L, O,
R, and T having only -3 weeks slack while activity M's
slack would be -1 and Q's slack would be zero.

2. Divert manpower from activity N to activity L.
Activity N could still have positive slack even when
activity G is completed.

3. Divert manpower from activity S, which currently has +3
weeks slack, to either activity R or T or both.

4. Crash any of the remaining activities with negative
slack with emphasis of course placed on those with -4
weeks slack.

12-9

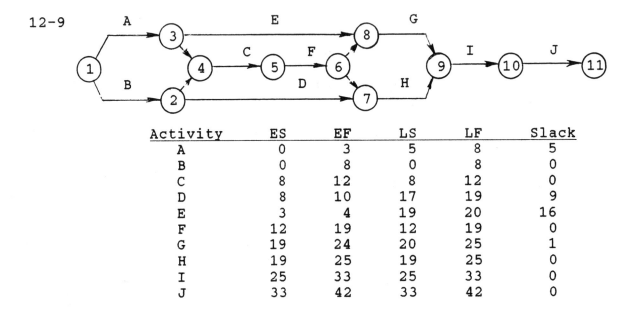

Activity	ES	EF	LS	LF	Slack
A	0	3	5	8	5
B	0	8	0	8	0
C	8	12	8	12	0
D	8	10	17	19	9
E	3	4	19	20	16
F	12	19	12	19	0
G	19	24	20	25	1
H	19	25	19	25	0
I	25	33	25	33	0
J	33	42	33	42	0

250

The critical path is: B, C, F, H, I, and J.

12-10 Activity C can now be started, but it is 2 weeks late.
Since C is critical the current slacks of the activities
not started are:

Activity	Slack (weeks)
C	0 - 2 = -2
D	9 - 2 = +7
F	0 - 2 = -2
G	1 - 2 = -1
H	0 - 2 = -2
I	0 - 2 = -2
J	0 - 2 = -2

Possible courses of action:
1. Divert manpower from D to either C or F. Activity D is
the only activity remaining in the project with
positive slack.

2. Crash any of the critical path activities C or F.
These should take the top priority over any of the
other critical path activities which follow them.

12-11

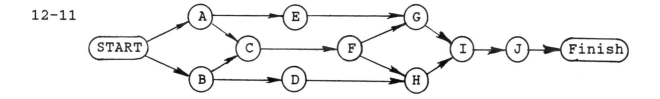

12-12

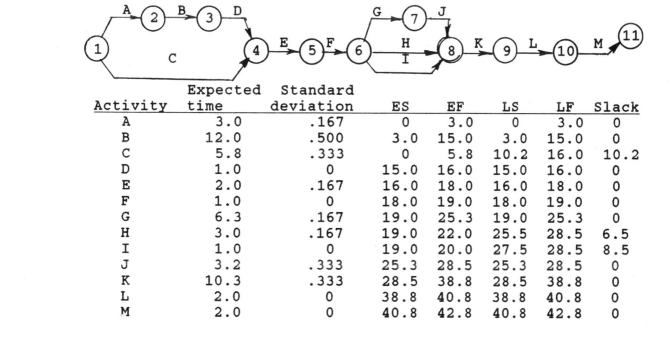

Activity	Expected time	Standard deviation	ES	EF	LS	LF	Slack
A	3.0	.167	0	3.0	0	3.0	0
B	12.0	.500	3.0	15.0	3.0	15.0	0
C	5.8	.333	0	5.8	10.2	16.0	10.2
D	1.0	0	15.0	16.0	15.0	16.0	0
E	2.0	.167	16.0	18.0	16.0	18.0	0
F	1.0	0	18.0	19.0	18.0	19.0	0
G	6.3	.167	19.0	25.3	19.0	25.3	0
H	3.0	.167	19.0	22.0	25.5	28.5	6.5
I	1.0	0	19.0	20.0	27.5	28.5	8.5
J	3.2	.333	25.3	28.5	25.3	28.5	0
K	10.3	.333	28.5	38.8	28.5	38.8	0
L	2.0	0	38.8	40.8	38.8	40.8	0
M	2.0	0	40.8	42.8	40.8	42.8	0

The critical path is: A, B, D, E, F, G, J, K, L, and M.

Project mean completion = 42.8 weeks
Project variance = .028 + .25 + .028 + .028 + .111 + .111
                 = .556
Project standard deviation = .746 weeks

a. From Appendix 1 at 90% area z = 1.28
    Bid quote = 42.8 + (1.28)(.746) = 43.8 weeks

b. 41 weeks is $\dfrac{42.8 - 41}{.746}$ = 2.41 standard deviations
    to the left of the mean.
    From Appendix 1 at z = 2.41 the probability is .99202
    Probability of completion by 41 weeks = 1 - .99202
    or about 1%

c. The probability of completion by 44 weeks ($10,000 penalty) is:

    $z = \dfrac{44 - 42.8}{.746}$ = 1.61 std. dev. to the right of the mean

    Probability of not completing = 1 - .94630
                                  = .0537 or about 5.4%

    The probability of completion by 45 weeks ($20,000 penalty) is:

    $z = \dfrac{45 - 42.8}{.746}$ = 2.95

    Probability of not completing = 1 - .99841
                                  = .00159 or about 0.2%

12-13 We compute first the expected time and standard deviation
       for each activity using equations 12-1 and 12-2.

Activity	Expected time	Standard deviation
A	6	1
B	5	1
C	4	2/3
D	4	4/3
E	4	5/3
F	6	2/3
G	6	7/3

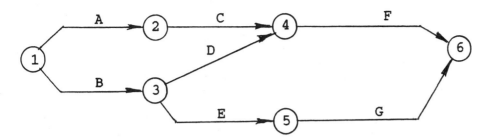

	Activity	ES	EF	LS	LF	Slack
A	0	6	0	6	0	
B	0	5	1	6	1	
C	6	10	6	10	0	
D	5	9	6	10	1	
E	5	9	6	10	1	
F	10	16	10	16	0	
G	9	15	10	16	1	

The critical path is A, C, and F.

Std. dev. (A, C, F) = $(1)^2 + (2/3)^2 + (2/3)^2$ = 1.37

The prob. of completing in 18 weeks = $P(Z \leq \frac{18-16}{1.37}$

$$= P(Z \leq 1.46) = .928$$

For noncritical path B, E, and G:

Std. dev. (B, E, G) = $(1)^2 + (5/3)^2 + (7/3)^2$ = 3.04

The prob. of completing in 18 weeks = $P(Z \leq \frac{18-15}{3.04}$

$$= P(Z \leq .99) = .839$$

The probability of completing the noncritical path in 18 weeks is less than the probability of completing the critical path in 18 weeks.

12-14 The slacks for a normal time schedule are:

Activity	ES	EF	LS	LF	Slack
A	0	3	0	3	0
B	3	9	6	12	3
C	3	8	8	13	5
D	3	11	3	11	0
E	11	13	11	13	0
F	9	20	12	23	3
G	13	23	13	23	0
H	11	16	21	26	10
I	23	26	23	26	0

(Continued)

J	11	20	24	33	13
K	11	15	32	36	21
L	20	23	33	36	13
M	26	34	26	34	0
N	34	36	34	36	0
O	23	34	23	34	0

There are two critical paths: Path 1 is A, D, E, G, I, M, N
Path 2 is A, D, E, G, O, N

The crash costs in dollars/week for the critical path
activities are:

Activity	Crashing cost/week
A	6000/2 = 3000
D	24000/6 = 4000
E	5000/1 = 5000
G	4500/3 = 1500
I	3500/1 = 3500
M	4000/5 = 800
N	6000/1 = 6000
O	4200/7 = 600

We follow these steps:

		Cost	New length
1)	Crash O to 5 weeks (path I to M cannot be crashed below 5 weeks)	$3600	36 weeks
2)	Crash M to 3 weeks	$4000	31 weeks
3)	Crash I to 2 weeks	$3500	30 weeks
4)	Crash G to 7 weeks	$4500	27 weeks
5)	Crash A to 1 weeks	$6000	25 weeks
6)	Crash D to 2 weeks	$24000	25 weeks
7)	Crash C to 4 weeks	$2000	25 weeks
8)	Crash F to 5 weeks	$3000	19 weeks
9)	Crash N to 1 week	$6000	18 weeks
		$56,600	

Cost = Σ normal costs + $56,600 = 121,000 + 56,600
    = $177,600

An alternate method for solving this problem is to compute
the slack for all activities assuming everything is done
according to a crash time. Then, those activities with
slack can be increased in time with a resultant savings
below crash cost.

Activity	ES	EF	LS	LF	Slack
A	0	1	0	1	0
B	1	4	6	9	5
C	1	5	1	5	0
D	1	3	2	4	1
E	3	4	4	5	1

(Continued)

F	4	7	9	12	5
G	5	12	5	12	0
H	3	4	13	14	10
I	12	14	12	14	0
J	3	7	12	16	9
K	3	4	17	18	14
L	7	9	16	18	9
M	14	17	14	17	0
N	17	18	17	18	0
O	12	16	13	17	1

The critical path is A, C, G, I, M, and N. These activities must remain at their crash times in order to finish in 18 weeks.

The steps are:

		Savings
1)	Increase K to 4 weeks	$ 900
2)	Increase H to 5 weeks	$10000
3)	Increase J to 9 weeks	$ 2000
4)	Increase L to 3 weeks	$ 7000
5)	Increase O to 5 weeks	$ 600
6)	Increase B to 6 weeks	$ 3000
7)	Increase F to 5 weeks	$ 1000
8)	Increase E to 2 weeks	$ 5000
	Savings =	$29,500

Cost = 207,100 - 29,500 = $177,600

12-15 We define X_i = time event i will occur.
Y_j = number of weeks we reduce the normal time of activity j.

Minimize: 3000YA + 1000YB + 2000YC + 4000YD + 5000YE
+ 500YF + 1500YG + 2500YH + 3500YI + 400YJ
+ 300YK + 7000YL + 800YM + 6000YN + 600YO

S.T.   X2 + YA ≥ 3   YA ≤ 2
       X3 - X2 + YB ≥ 6   YB ≤ 3
       X4 - X2 + YC ≥ 5   YC ≤ 1
       X5 - X2 + YD ≥ 8   YD ≤ 6
       X4 - X5 + YE ≥ 2   YE ≤ 1
       X6 - X3 + YF ≥ 11   YF ≤ 8
       X6 - X4 + YG ≥ 10   YG ≤ 3
       X7 - X5 + YH ≥ 5   YH ≤ 4
       X7 - X6 + YI ≥ 3   YI ≤ 1
       X9 - X5 + YJ ≥ 9   YJ ≤ 5
      X10 - X5 + YK ≥ 4   YK ≤ 3
      X10 - X9 + YL ≥ 3   YL ≤ 1
       X8 - X7 + YM ≥ 8   YM ≤ 5
      X10 - X8 + YN ≥ 2   YN ≤ 1
       X8 - X6 + YO ≥ 11   YO ≤ 7
              X10 ≤ 18

From the computer solution:

Cost = $56,600

YA = 2	X2 = 1
YC = 1	X3 = 7
YD = 6	X4 = 5
YF = 6	X5 = 3
YG = 3	X6 = 12
YI = 1	X7 = 14
YM = 5	X8 = 17
YN = 1	X9 = 12
YO = 6	X10 = 18

12-16   The total of indirect costs and utility costs per week
after the 25 weeks is $2000 + $7000 per week. We found
from problem 12-25 that the cost to crash the project from
30 weeks to 25 weeks is 3600 + 4000 + 3500 + 4500 + 6000
= $21,600 or $4,320 per week. Since this is less than the
utility and indirect costs of $7000 per week, the contract
should be crashed to at least 25 weeks. We would further
reduce the project to less than 25 weeks if the crash costs
are less than the indirect costs of $2000 per week. But,
to do this, we must crash either E or D as well as F or B.
However, the costs of crashing either E or D are well in
excess of the $2000 savings which would result. It is the
most cost effective strategy to pursue the policy of
finishing in 25 weeks.

12-17   The CPM network is:

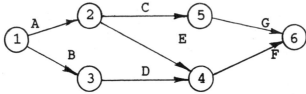

There are three paths in this network with normal path
lengths as follows:

Path	Activities	Normal length, wk
1	A-C-G	8 + 5 + 4 = 17
2	A-E-F	8 + 3 + 5 = 16
3	B-D-F	7 + 4 + 5 = 16

The critical path is path 1 at 17 weeks. We wish to remove
one week from this path as a first move. To remove more
than one week may make one or more other paths more
critical. We see there is a tie between:
Activity A at $1000/wk crash cost
Activity G at $1000/wk crash cost

256

We select activity A in preference to G since it lies on two paths (1 and 2).

Now we have:

Path	Activities	Length, wk
1	A-C-G	7 + 5 + 4 = 16
2	A-E-F	7 + 3 + 5 = 15
3	B-D-F	7 + 4 + 5 = 16

Now we see we must remove another week from path 1 as well as from path 3. There are no activities in common on these two paths, and so one activity from each path must be crashed. On path 1 we select A for the same reason as before (it places some slack in path 2). On path 3 we have a tie for least crash cost between:
    Activity D at $800/wk crash cost
    Activity F at $800/wk crash cost

Since F is on two paths, we select this to crash. In doing so we place 2 weeks of slack in activity E, thus allowing greater flexibility in the schedule. In summary, we have:

Activity	Crash, wk	Crash cost	Time, wk
A	2	$2000	6
B			7
C			5
D			4
E			3
F	1	800	4
G			4
		Total $2800	

	Activity	ES	EF	LS	LF	Months in progress (Late schedule)
12-18	A	0	3	3	6	4,5,6
	B	0	1	0	1	1
	C	1	6	1	6	2,3,4,5,6
	D	6	10	6	10	7,8,9,10
	E	1	7	4	10	5,6,7,8,9,10
	F	10	16	13	19	14,15,16,17,18,19
	G	10	17	10	17	11,12,13,14,15,16,17
	H	10	14	15	19	16,17,18,19
	I	17	19	17	19	18,19
	J	19	20	19	20	20
	K	17	18	19	20	20
	L	14	17	19	22	20,21,22
	M	20	22	20	22	21,22

257

Costs are in 1000's

Act.	1	2	3	4	5	6	7	8	9	10	11	12	13	14	15	16	17	18	19	20	21	22
A				20	20	20																
B	10																					
C		4	4	4	4	4																
D							10	10	10	10												
E					20	20	20	20	20	20												
F														30	30	30	30	30	30			
G											5	5	5	5	5	5	5					
H																20	20	20	20			
I																		15	15			
J																				5		
K																				40		
L																				30	30	30
M																					9	9
Tot.	10	4	4	24	44	44	30	30	30	30	5	5	5	35	35	55	55	65	65	75	39	39

Total funds committed = $728,000
Total months = 22

Average commitment per month = $33,091
Average commitment over project life = $364,000

12-19

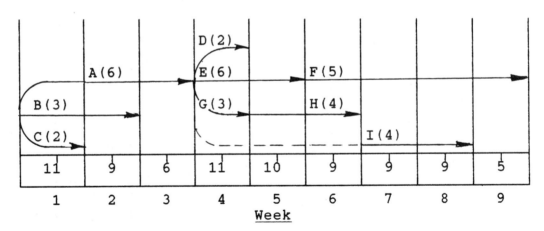

Relaxing the manpower constraint to 11 men per week does
not appear to advance the completion of the project. The
fact that activities D, E, G, and I cannot begin until
activity A is completed does not allow us to use the slack
manpower time available in the second and third weeks.
Further, since activities E and F must be done in
succession, their combined time of 6 weeks, together with
A's time of 3 weeks, makes it impossible to reduce the
project time below 9 weeks total.

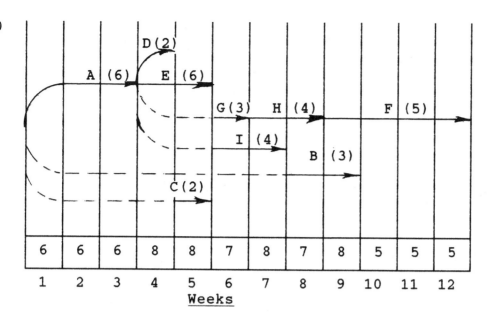

It does not appear possible to design a schedule that used 7 or 8 men each week; it would appear that the nearest one can come is a schedule that meets the 7 or 8 men constraint in all weeks but the first three and last three. The sample solution proposed above is realistic in the sense that it does not use _more_ men than are available; it is true however that there is an idle man for the first three weeks and two idle men for the last three weeks if we _must_ employ 7 men on the project.

12-21

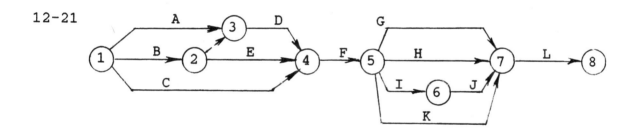

Activity	ES	EF	LS	LF	Slack
A	0	10	9	19	9
B	0	15	0	15	0
C	0	12	11	23	11
D	15	19	19	23	4
E	15	23	15	23	0
F	23	43	23	43	0
G	43	73	51	81	8
H	43	58	66	81	23
I	43	63	43	63	0
J	63	81	63	81	0
K	43	49	75	81	32
L	81	101	81	101	0

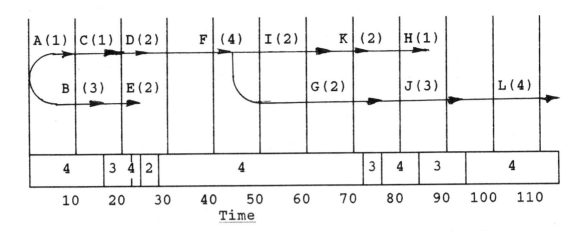

The above schedule (not unique) shows the number of technicians scheduled and provides for all tests to be accomplished in 114 minutes.

12-22   Step 1:   Path P-1-S: Min. flow 40
                Step 2:   Path P-2-4-S: Min. flow 30
                Step 3:   Path P-3-5-2-4-S: Min. flow 15
                Step 4:   Path P-3-5-S: Min. flow 25
                Step 5:   Path P-3-6-S: Min. flow 5

Flow assigned to each branch:

					Branches						
P-1	P-2	P-3	1-4	1-S	2-4	3-5	3-6	4-S	5-2	5-S	6-S
40				40							
	30				30			30			
		15			15	15		15	15		
		25				25				25	
		5					5				5
40	30	45		40	45	40	5	45	15	25	5

Total flow = 40 + 45 + 25 + 5 = 115 thousand

Note: There are other optimal solutions.

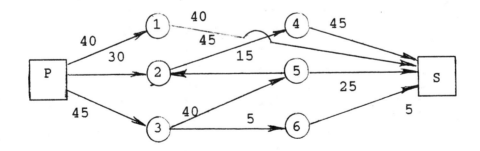

260

12-23 Step 1: Path A - 1 - 4 - D: Min. flow 6,000
       Step 2: Path A - 2 - 4 - D: Min. flow 10,000
       Step 3: Path A - 3 - D: Min. flow 5,000
       Step 4: Path A - 3 - 2 - 4 - D: Min. flow 1,000
       Step 5: Path A - 3 - 1 - 4 - D: Min. flow 1,000

Flow assigned to each branch

A-1	A-2	A-3	1-3	1-4	2-3	2-4	3-2	3-1	3-D	4-1	4-2	4-D
6				6								6
	10					10						10
		5							5			
		1				1	1					1
		1		1				1				1
6	10	7		7		11	1	1	5			18

Total flow = 5 + 18 = 23 thousand men.

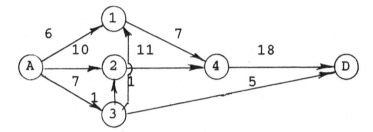

12-24 Step 1: Path D - L   Min. flow 150
       Step 2: Path D - 6 - 7 - L   Min. flow 10
       Step 3: Path D - 6 - 8 - L   Min. flow 10
       Step 4: Path D - 1 - 2 - 4 - L   Min. flow 10
       Step 5: Path D - 1 - 3 - 4 - L   Min. flow 20
       Step 6: Path D - 1 - 3 - 5 - L   Min. flow 10

Flow assigned to each branch:

D-1	D-6	D-L	1-2	1-3	2-4	3-4	3-5	4-5	4-L	5-L	6-7	6-8	7-L	8-L
		150												
	10										10		10	
	10											10		10
10			10		10				10					
20				20		20			20					
10				10			10			10				
40	20	150	10	30	10	20	10		30	10	10	10	10	10

261

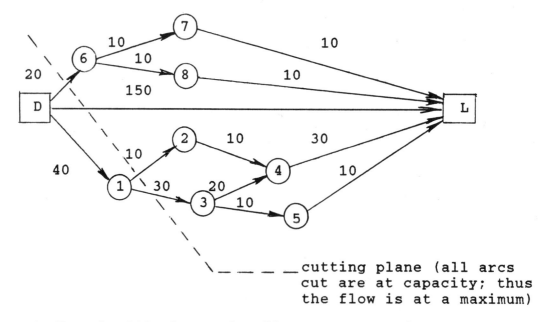

cutting plane (all arcs
cut are at capacity; thus
the flow is at a maximum)

Total flow is 210 thousand gallons per second.

12-25 Flow must be increased only on arcs which are cut (see answer to Exercise 12-24 above). Therefore, Projects 1 and 2 can be eliminated. Projects 3 and 4 are in the cut, but Project 4 falls short of the needed 20 thousand gallons per second. Therefore, Project 3 should be adopted at a cost of $70,000.

12-26 Step 1: Distances between nodes

From node	To node									
	SO	YS	YC	D	P	S	L	W		K
SO	0	40	85	80	M	M	M	M		M
YS	40	0	90	M	110	M	M	M	M	M
YC	85	90	0	70	120	90	M	M	M	M
D	80	M	70	0	M	50	65	M	M	M
P	M	110	120	M	0	40	M	50	M	M
S	M	M	90	50	40	0	80	M	60	M
L	M	M	M	65	M	80	0	M	M	100
W	M	M	M	M	50	M	M	0	90	175
B	M	M	M	M	M	60	M	90	0	80
K	M	M	M	M	M	M	100	175	80	0

Step 2: Select node SO and mark row SO with an X and delete column SO.
Step 3: Circle the value 40 in row SO; column YS.
Step 4: Mark row YS with an X and delete column YS.
Step 3: Circle the value 80 in row SO; column D.
Step 4: Mark row D with an X and delete column D.
Step 3: Circle the value 50 in row X and delete column S.
Step 4: Mark row S with an X and delete column S.

262

Our reduced problem now appears as:

From node	SO	YS	YC	D	P	S	L	W	B	K
X SO		(40)	85	(80)	M		M	M	M	M
X YS			90		110		M	M	M	M
YC			0		120		M	M	M	M
X D			70		M	(50)	65	M	M	M
P			120		0		M	50	M	M
X S			90		40	80		M	60	M
L			M				0	M	M	100
W			M			50	M	0	90	175
B			M			M	M	90	0	80
K			M			M	M	100	175	80	0

Step 3: Circle the value 40 in row S; column P.
Step 4: Mark row P with an X and delete column P.
Step 3: Circle the value 50 in row P; column W.
Step 4: Mark row W with an X and delete column W.
Step 3: Circle the value 60 in row S; column B.
Step 4: Mark row B with an X and delete column B.

Our reduced problem now appears as:

From node	SO	YS	YC	D	P	S	L	W	B	K
X SO		(40)	85	(80)			M			M
X YS			90					M		
	M									
YC			0				M			M
X D			70			(50)	65			M
X P			120				M	(50)		M
X S			90		(40)	80			(60)	M
L			M				0			100
X W			M				M			175
X B			M				M			80
K			M				100			0

Step 3: Circle the value 65 in row D; column L.
Step 4: Mark row L with an X and delete column L.
Step 3: Circle the value 70 in row D; column YC.
Step 4: Mark row YC with an X and delete column YC.
Step 3: Circle the value 80 in row B; column K.
Step 4: Mark row K with an X and delete column K.

The solution is now complete as follows:

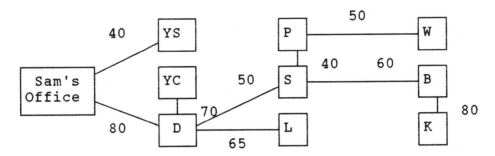

12-27   Step 1:   Distances between nodes

From	To node										
node	1	2	3	4	5	6	7	8	9	10	11
1	0	70	25	M	150	M	M	M	M	M	M
2	70	0	M	M	90	M	M	M	M	M	M
3	25	M	0	50	M	150	M	M	M	M	M
4	M	M	50	0	M	120	M	M	M	M	M
5	M	90	M	M	0	M	300	250	M	M	M
6	M	M	150	120	M	0	M	M	300	M	M
7	M	M	M	M	300	M	0	100	M	250	M
8	M	M	M	M	250	M	100	0	120	M	400
9	M	M	M	M	M	300	M	120	0	M	300
10	M	M	M	M	M	M	250	M	M	0	50
11	M	M	M	M	M	M	M	400	300	50	0

Step 2:   Select node 1 and mark row 1 with an X and delete
          column 1.
Step 3:   Circle the value 25 in row 1 and column 3.
Step 4:   Mark row 3 with an X and delete column 3.
Step 3:   Circle the value 50 in row 3 and column 4.
Step 4:   Mark row 4 with an X and delete column 4.
Step 3:   Circle the value 70 in row 1 and column 2.
Step 4:   Mark row 2 with an X and delete column 2.
Step 3:   Circle the value 90 in row 2 and column 5.
Step 4:   Mark row 5 with an X and delete column 5.
Step 3:   Circle the value 120 in row 4 and column 6.
Step 4:   Mark row 6 with an X and delete column 6.
Step 3:   Circle the value 250 in row 5 and column 8.
Step 4:   Mark row 8 with an X and delete column 8.
Step 3:   Circle the value 100 in row 8 and column 7.
Step 4:   Mark row 7 with an X and delete column 7.
Step 3:   Circle the value 120 in row 8 and column 9.
Step 4:   Mark row 9 with an X and delete column 9.
Step 3:   Circle the value 250 in row 7 and column 10.
Step 4:   Mark row 10 with an X and delete column 10.
Step 3:   Circle the value 50 in row 10 and column 11.
Step 4:   Mark row 11 with an X and delete column 11.

Our solution should now read:

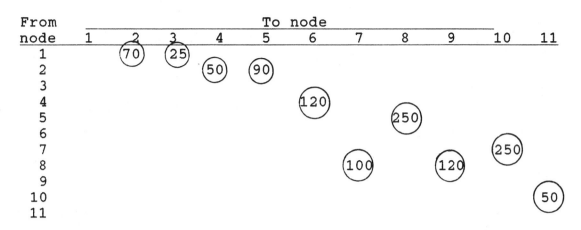

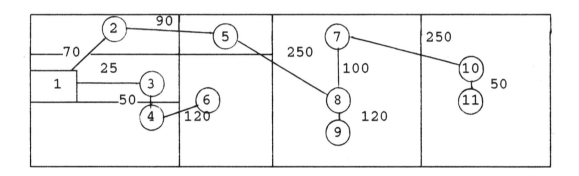

12-28

From node	To node								
	R	E	F	S	M	W	G	B	D
R	0	(50)	80	(60)	M	M	M	M	M
E	50	0	70	M	100	M	M	M	M
F	80	70	0	60	M	80	(40)	M	M
S	60	M	(60)	0	M	(70)	M	M	M
M	M	100	M	M	0	M	20	(40)	M
W	M	M	80	70	M	0	80	M	100
G	M	M	40	M	(20)	80	0	60	M
B	M	M	M	M	40	M	60	0	(50)
D	M	M	M	M	M	100	M	50	0

Step 2: Select node R and mark row R with an X and delete column R
Step 3: Circle the value 50 in row R and column E
Step 4: Mark row E with an X and delete column E
Step 3: Circle the value 60 in row R and column S
Step 4: Mark row S with an X and delete column S
Step 3: Circle the value 60 in row S and column F
Step 4: Mark row F with an X and delete column F
Step 3: Circle the value 40 in row F and column G
Step 4: Mark row G with an X and delete column G

```
Step 3:  Circle the value 20 in row G and column M
Step 4:  Mark row M with an X and delete column M
Step 3:  Circle the value 40 in row M and column B
Step 4:  Mark row B with an X and delete column B
Step 3:  Circle the value 50 in row B and column D
Step 4:  Mark row D with an X and delete column D
Step 3:  Circle the value 70 in row S and column W
Step 4:  Mark row W with an X and delete column W
```

Our solution is:

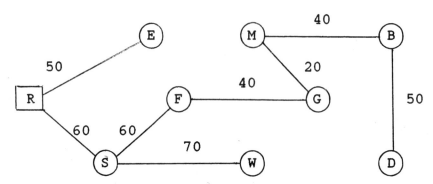

Total cost is $390,000.

12-29   Branches leading out of each node.

A	B	C	D	E	F	G
AB-33	BC-12	CB-12	DE-43	EB-23	FD-70	
AC-47	BG-120	CE-70	DF-70	EC-70	FG-33	
AD-52	BE-23			ED-43		
				EG-20		

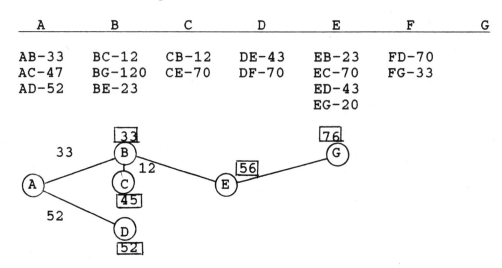

The summary of steps are:

```
Step 1--place 33 at node B
Step 2--place 45 at node C
Step 3--place 52 at node D
Step 4--place 56 at node E
Step 5--place 76 at node G
```

The optimal route is from A to B to E to G at 76 feet distance.

266

12-30 Branches leading out of each node.

A	B	C	D	E	F	G	H	I
AB-40	BC-12	CB-12	DC-10	EB-20	FC-28	GC-17	HD-39	
AC-85	BE-20	CD-10	DH-39	EF-25	FE-25	GI-60	HI-40	
AD-50		CF-28			FI-30			
		CG-17						

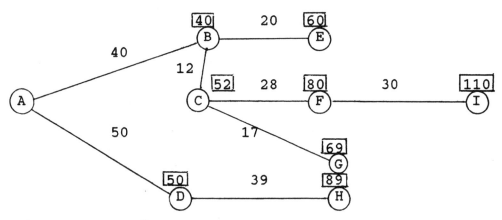

The summary of steps are:

        Step 1--place 40 at node B
        Step 2--place 50 at node D
        Step 3--place 52 at node C
        Step 4--place 60 at node E
        Step 5--place 69 at node G
        Step 6--place 80 at node F
        Step 7--place 89 at node H
        Step 8--place 110 at node I

The optimal route is from A to B to C to F to I at 110 feet
distance.

12-31 For convenience, we designate G1 as mill 1 in Georgia, N3
       as mill 3 in North Carolina, etc.

Stage 1

Input nodes	Output nodes	Shortest distance to home	
N1	Home	900	<--
N2	Home	800	<--
N3	Home	200	<--

Stage 2

Input nodes	Output nodes	Shortest distance to home	
S1	N1	600 + 900 = 1500	
S1	N2	700 + 800 = 1500	
S1	N3	600 + 200 = 800	<--
S2	N1	300 + 900 = 1200	
S2	N2	900 + 800 = 1700	
S2	N3	800 + 200 = 1000	<--

Stage 3

Input nodes	Output nodes	Shortest distance to home	
G1	S1	400 + 800 = 1200	<--
G1	S2	600 + 1000 = 1600	
G2	S1	200 + 800 = 1000	<--
G2	S2	500 + 1000 = 1500	

Stage 4

Input nodes	Output nodes	Shortest distance to home	
A1	G1	600 + 1200 = 1800	
A1	G2	700 + 1000 = 1700	<--

The optimal route is from A1 to G2 to S1 to N3 to home for a total distance of 1700 air miles.

12-32 We define n as a stage, where n = 1 is Abbot County, n = 2 is Babson County, and n = 3 is Clark County. Further, we define X_n as the number of salespeople as yet unassigned at stage n, and d_n is the decision made at stage n.

If we work backwards from stage 3, we find that we could have X_1 = 1, 2,..., 8 salespeople yet unassigned at stage 1, Abbot County. Our first tableau, then, represents stage 1.

X_1 \ d_1	0	1	2	3	4	5	6 or more	Best payoff	Best decision(s)
0	0							0	0
1	0	45						45	1
2	0	45	90					90	2
3	0	45	90	135				135	3
4	0	45	90	135	180			180	4
5	0	45	90	135	180	180		180	4,5
6 or more	0	45	90	135	180	180	180	180	4,5,6

268

The second tableau is for stage 2--Babson County.

X_2 \\ d_2	0	1	2	3	4	5	≥6	Best Pay	Dec
0	0							0	0
1	0+45 =45	15+0 =15						45	0
2	0+90 =90	15+45 =60	30+0 =30					90	0
3	0+135 =135	15+90 =105	30+45 =75	60+0 =60				135	0
4	0+180 =180	15+135 =150	30+90 =120	60+45 =105	120+0 =120			180	0
5	0+180 =180	15+180 =195	30+135 =165	60+90 =150	120+45 =165	150+0 =150		195	1
6 or more	0+180 =180	15+180 =195	30+180 =210	60+135 =195	120+90 =210	150+45 =195	150+0 =150	210	2,4

At the stage 3 level--Clark County--we know we have eight salespeople available. This tableau is therefore the single state, $X_3 = 8$.

X_3 \\ d_3	0	1	2	3	4	5	≥6
8	0+210 =210	30+210 =240	60+210 =270	90+195 =285	120+180 =300	150+135 =285	180+90 =270

The best payoff is decision $d_3 = 4$ for a payoff of 300. We now work backward through the tableaux to find our solution.

Stage, n	State, X_n	Best Decision, d_n*	Profit
3	8	4	$120
2	4	0	0
1	4	4	180
			$300

12-33   In this problem we will have n = 6 stages with each stage representing one of the six projects. Working backwards from project 6, we develop the stage 1 tableau where the states X_n represent available unassigned funds and the decisions d_n represent either funding the project or not.

Stage 1-- Route 6 considered (cost of 4; importance 8)

X_1 \\ d_1	Don't fund 0	Fund 1	Best payoff 0	Best decision(s) 0
0-3	0		0	0
4 or more	0	8	8	1

Stage 2-- Route 5 considered (cost of 8; importance 3)

X_2	d_2		Best payoff	Best decision(s)
	0	1		
0-3	0 + 0 = 0		0	0
4-7	0 + 8 = 8		8	0
8-11	0 + 8 = 8	3 + 0 = 3	8	0
12 or more	0 + 8 = 8	3 + 8 = 11	11	1

Stage 3-- Route 4 considered (cost of 6; importance 7)

X_3	d_3		Best payoff	Best decision(s)
	0	1		
0-3	0		0	0
4-9	0 + 8 = 8	7 + 0 = 7	8	0
10-17	0 + 8 = 8	7 + 8 = 15	15	1
18 or more	0 + 11 = 11	7 + 11 = 18	18	1

Stage 4-- Route 3 considered (cost of 5; importance of 4)

X_4	d_4		Best payoff	Best decision(s)
	0	1		
0-3	0		0	0
4	0 + 8 = 8		8	0
5-8	0 + 8 = 8	4 + 0 = 4	8	0
9	0 + 8 = 8	4 + 8 = 12	12	1
10-14	0 + 15 = 15	4 + 8 = 12	15	0
15-17	0 + 15 = 15	4 + 15 = 19	19	1
18-22	0 + 18 = 18	4 + 15 = 19	19	1
23-24	0 + 18 = 18	4 + 18 = 22	22	1

In summary, this tableau says that when Route 3 is to be considered (with Route 4, 5, and 6 still undecided upon), and there are as yet 0 to 8 million or 10 to 14 million unassigned, Route 3 should not be budgeted. However, if 9 million are unassigned or anything between 15 to 24 million are unassigned, Route 3 should be funded.

Stage 5-- Route 2 considered (cost of 7; importance 6)

X_2	d_2		Best payoff	Best decision(s)
	0	1		
0-3	0		0	0
4	0 + 8 = 8		8	0
5	0 + 8 = 8		8	0
6	0 + 8 = 8		8	0
7	0 + 8 = 8	6 + 0 = 6	8	0
8	0 + 8 = 8	6 + 0 = 6	8	0

(Continued)

	0	1	Best payoff	Best decision(s)
9	0 + 12 = 12	6 + 0 = 6	12	0
10	0 + 15 = 15	6 + 0 = 6	15	0
11	0 + 15 = 15	6 + 8 = 14	15	0
12	0 + 15 = 15	6 + 8 = 14	15	0
13	0 + 15 = 15	6 + 8 = 14	15	0
14	0 + 15 = 15	6 + 8 = 14	15	0
15	0 + 19 = 19	6 + 8 = 14	19	0
16	0 + 19 = 19	6 + 12 = 18	19	0
17	0 + 19 = 19	6 + 15 = 21	21	1
18	0 + 19 = 19	6 + 15 = 21	21	1
19	0 + 19 = 19	6 + 15 = 21	21	1
20	0 + 19 = 19	6 + 15 = 21	21	1
21	0 + 19 = 19	6 + 15 = 21	21	1
22	0 + 19 = 19	6 + 19 = 25	25	1
23	0 + 22 = 22	6 + 19 = 25	25	1
24	0 + 22 = 22	6 + 19 = 25	25	1

Now we come to the last stage where route 1 is considered. At this stage all 24 million are available.

Stage 6-- Route 1 considered (cost of 4; importance 5)

X_6	d_6 0	1	Best payoff	Best decision(s)
24	0 + 25 = 25	5 + 21 = 26	26	1

Now, we go back through the tableaux as follows:

Stage, n	X_n	Best payoff	Decision	Million remaining
6	24	26	Fund route 1	24 - 4 = 20
5	20	21	Fund route 2	20 - 7 = 13
4	13	15		13 - 0 = 13
3	13	15	Fund route 4	13 - 6 = 7
2	7	8		7 - 0 = 7
1	7	8	Fund route 6	7 - 4 = 3

The optimal decision is to fund routes 1, 2, 4, and 6 for a total cost of 24 million and a total importance of 26.

12-34 Let X_k denote the earliest completion for event k.

Objective: Minimize X_6

	Name
S.T. $X_6 \geq 5 + X_4$	X4 to X6
$X_6 \geq 6 + X_5$	X5 to X6
$X_5 \geq 2 + X_3$	X3 to X5

(Continued)

271

$$X_4 \geq 4 + X_2 \qquad \text{X2 to X4}$$
$$X_4 \geq 1 + X_3 \qquad \text{X3 to X4}$$
$$X_3 \geq 8 \qquad\qquad \text{origin to X3}$$
$$X_2 \geq 2 \qquad\qquad \text{origin to X2}$$
$$X_k \geq 0, \text{ all } k$$

12-35 The constraints are named as shown above with Exercise 12-34.

a. The objective function value is 16 which is the earliest project completion time.

b. The values of the basic structural variables are earliest finish times as follows:

$$X2 = 2, \quad X3 = 8, \quad X4 = 9, \quad X5 = 10, \quad X6 = 16$$

c. Those constraints having no slack will be critical path arcs. These are easily identified by the shadow prices. Critical arcs have a shadow price of 1 as follows:

X5 to X6
X3 to X5
origin to X3

The critical path goes from origin to X3 to X5 to X6.

d. There are two basic surplus variables as follows:

Variable	Constraint	Value
Surplus	X4 to X6	2
Surplus	X2 to X4	3

These variables take on values equal to the independent slack on these arcs. We may develop the slack for each activity as follows:

Act.	Arc	Independent slack	Follower with least slack	Follower slack	Total slack
G	X5 to X6		---	---	0
F	X4 to X6	2	---	---	2
E	X3 to X5		X5 to X6	0	0 + 0 = 0
D	X3 to X4		X4 to X6	2	0 + 2 = 2
C	X2 to X4	3	X4 to X6	2	3 + 2 = 5
B	origin to X3		X3 to X5	0	0 + 0 = 0
A	origin to X2		X2 to X4	5	0 + 5 = 5

The activities shown as having zero slack, namely activities G, E, and B, represent the critical path.

12-36 Using equations 12-1 and 12-2, we compute the expected time
       (mean) and standard deviation for each activity.

Activity	Expected time	Standard deviation
A	1.1	0.3
B	2.0	0.3
C	3.0	0.7
D	4.0	0.3
E	3.0	0.3
F	5.0	0.7
G	5.0	0.3
H	7.0	0.3
I	4.0	0.7
J	6.2	0.5
K	2.0	0.3
L	5.0	0.7

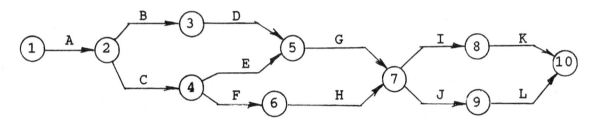

Activity	ES	EF	LS	LF	Slack	Std. Dev.
A	0	1.1	0	1.1	0	.3
B	1.1	3.1	5.1	7.1	4	
C	1.1	4.1	1.1	4.1	0	.7
D	3.1	7.1	7.1	11.1	4	
E	4.1	7.1	8.1	11.1	4	
F	4.1	9.1	4.1	9.1	0	.7
G	7.1	12.1	11.1	16.1	4	
H	9.1	16.1	9.1	16.1	0	.3
I	16.1	20.1	21.3	25.3	5.2	
J	16.1	22.3	16.1	22.3	0	.5
K	20.1	22.1	25.3	27.3	5.2	
L	22.3	27.3	22.3	27.3	0	.7

The critical path is A, C, F, H, J, and L.

The standard deviation of project completion time is
computed using equation 12-6.

$$\text{Project std. dev.} = \sqrt{(.3)^2 + (.7)^2 + (.7)^2 + (.3)^2 + (.5)^2 + (.7)^2}$$
$$= 1.38$$

At a completion time of 30 weeks, we find the number of
standard deviations to the right of the mean (27.3 weeks):

$$Z = \frac{30 - 27.3}{1.38} = 1.97 \text{ standard deviations}$$

273

From Appendix Table 1, we find that the probability of
completing the project by 30 weeks is about 98%.

12-37

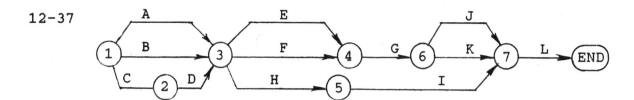

Activity	ES	EF	LS	LF	Slack
A	0	4	1	5	1
B	0	3	2	5	2
C	0	3	0	3	0
D	3	5	3	5	0
E	5	6	6	7	1
F	5	7	5	7	0
G	7	10	7	10	0
H	5	8	6	9	1
I	8	13	9	14	1
J	10	12	12	14	2
K	10	14	10	14	0
L	14	16	14	16	0

The critical path is: C, D, F, G, K, and L.

a. 1. This will not help. There is already a week's slack
       in frame design.
    2. This will not help. Wheel design is not critical
       with 2 week's slack.
    3. This would help shorten the project. The designers
       could be reassigned from wheel design where there
       are 2 week's slack.
    4. This will not help. Activity J has 2 week's slack
       and does not constrain the completion of event 7.
    5. This would help shorten the project. Activity K is
       critical and is currently constraining event 7.
b. 1. This would not help. The performance test is
       critical but its completion time of 10 weeks occurs
       before week 12 and is not on the same path as
       activity I which would still be completed at the end
       of 13 weeks.
    2. This would help. If activity H, an immediate
       predecessor to I, is completed one week early, then
       activity I would also be completed one week early at
       the end of week 12.
    3. This will not help because activity G, the
       performance test, is not on the same path as
       activity I. In fact this could jeopardize shipment
       to the dealers, because if the performance test is
       done by Lenny in week 13, activities J and K would
       start after week 13 instead of week 10, thus
creating   at least a 3 week delay.

12-38   <u>Stage 1</u>

Input nodes	Output nodes	Shortest distance to Downtown
4	Downtown	6 <--
5	Downtown	5 <--
6	Downtown	2 <--

<u>Stage 2</u>

Input nodes	Output nodes	Shortest distance to Downtown
1	4	3 + 6 = 9 <--
1	5	6 + 5 = 11
2	4	8 + 6 = 14
2	5	7 + 5 = 12
2	6	2 + 2 = 4 <--
3	5	5 + 5 = 10 <--
3	6	10 + 2 = 12

<u>Stage 3</u>

Input nodes	Output nodes	Shortest distance to Downtown
Westvale	1	6 + 9 = 15
Westvale	2	4 + 4 = 8 <--
Westvale	3	9 + 10 = 19

The optimal solution is to travel from Westvale to node 2,
then to node 6, then to Downtown for a total of 8 minutes.

12-39   Branches leading out of each node:

W	1	2	3	4	5	6	D
W1-6	12-1	21-1	35-5	41-3	51-6	62-2	
W2-4	14-3	24-8	36-10	42-8	52-7	63-10	
W3-9	15-6	25-7		4D-6	53-5	6D-2	
		26-2			5D-5		

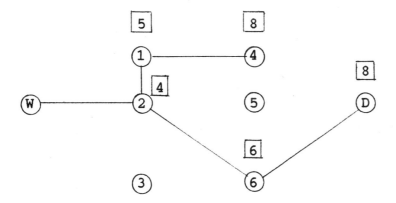

275

The summary of steps are:

Step 1:   place 4 at node 2
Step 2:   place 5 at node 1
Step 3:   place 6 at node 6
Step 4:   place 8 at node 4, or place 8 at node D

The shortest route is W to 2 to 6 to D at 8 minutes.

12-40   Let X_1 = time of event 1
        X_2 = time of event 2
        X_3 = time of event 3
        X_4 = time of event 4
        X_5 = time of event 5
        X_6 = time of event 6
        Y_A = weeks A is crashed
        Y_B = weeks B is crashed
        Y_C = weeks C is crashed
        Y_D = weeks D is crashed
        Y_E = weeks E is crashed
        Y_F = weeks F is crashed
        Y_G = weeks G is crashed

        Our objective function is:
        Minimize: $Z = 1000Y_A + 1200Y_B + 1500Y_C + 800Y_D + 600Y_E + 800Y_F + 1000Y_G$

        Subject to: $X_2 \geq 8 - Y_A + 0$ event 2 constraint
                      $X_3 \geq 7 - Y_B + 0$ event 3 constraint
                      $X_4 \geq 3 - Y_E + X_2$ event 4 constraint
                      $X_4 \geq 4 - Y_D + X_3$ event 4 constraint
                      $X_5 \geq 5 - Y_C + X_2$ event 5 constraint
                      $X_6 \geq 4 - Y_G + X_5$ event 6 constraint
                      $X_6 \geq 5 - Y_F + X_4$ event 6 constraint
                      $Y_A \leq 2$
                      $Y_B \leq 2$
                      $Y_C \leq 1$
                      $Y_D \leq 1$
                      $Y_E \leq 1$
                      $Y_F \leq 2$
                      $Y_G \leq 1$
                      $X_6 \leq 15$ Project completion constraint

12-41   a. We look for the shadow price for the last constraint
        which read $X_6 \leq 15$. This shadow price is given as $1800,
        so to lower the RHS from 15 to 14 would increase costs by
        $1800.

        b. The reduced cost for variable Y_C is $500, so if Y_C's
        objective coefficient (currently $1500) is reduced by $500

to a crash cost of $1000 per week we would be indifferent in our choice between activities A, C, and G. But since the given reduction from $8,500 to $7,900 is $600, crashing activity C is more attractive than crashing A or G, so we would definitely reevaluate our crashing plan.

c. An increase in crash cost for activity B will not affect our crashing plan. In fact the reduced cost for Y_B of $400 indicates that activity B's $1200 per week crash cost would have to drop below $800 per week before it would be cost effective to crash B.

12-42 First we compute the earliest and latest start time schedules:

Activity	ES	EF	LS	LF	Slack
A	0	1	1	2	1
B	0	3	0	3	0
C	1	4	2	5	1
D	3	5	3	5	0
E	3	4	5	6	2
F	5	7	7	9	2
G	5	7	5	7	0
H	4	5	6	7	2
I	7	8	9	10	2
J	7	10	7	10	0
K	7	9	9	11	2
L	10	12	10	12	0
M	9	10	11	12	2

We see that the critical path length is 12 months, which is the contract project length. Therefore, the critical path activities cannot be delayed from their established yearly schedule. The other activities are placed into the schedule heuristically in order of least slack so that we do not exceed the target figures established for cumulative costs at each quarter. The schedule is developed as follows:

Month

Activity	1	2	3	4	5	6	7	8	9	10	11	12
A	10											
B	20	20	20									
C			30	30	30							
D				25	25							
E				40								
F							35	35				
G						10	10					
H							15					
I										10		
J								15	15	15		
K										20	20	
L											20	20
M												25
Total	30	20	50	95	55	10	60	50	15	45	40	45
Cum.	30	50	100	195	250	260	320	370	385	430	470	515
Maximum			133			262			391			515

The above schedule translates into the following start and finish times and slacks:

Activity	Start time	Finish time	Slack
A	0	1	1
B	0	3	0
C	2	5	0
D	3	5	0
E	3	4	2
F	6	8	1
G	5	7	0
H	6	7	0
I	9	10	0
J	7	10	0
K	9	11	0
L	10	12	0
M	11	12	0

With this schedule we have kept cumulative costs below our target figures and have also maintained some slack in three of the activities.

12-43 An early start schedule is use to develop the schedule graph:

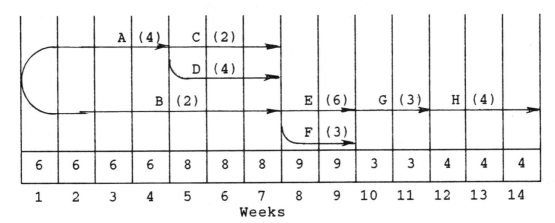

Our first step is to shift activity C all the way to the right since it is the only activity which may run parallel with activity H during weeks 12, 13, and 14 when resource utilization is low. At this point we have a constant 6 workers required for all weeks except weeks 8 and 9 (9 workers) and weeks 10 and 11 (only 3 workers). By shifting activity F to the right by 2 weeks, we can achieve a perfectly balanced loading of workers as follows:

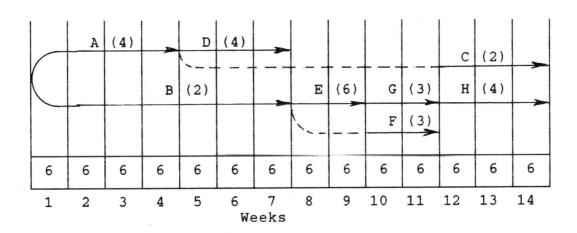

12-44 The production costs are:

Production (aircraft/mo.)	Cost (thousands)
1	100
2	200
3	300
4	400
5	500
6	650
7	800

279

Each month is a stage and the state variable is the number of aircraft on hand at the beginning of the month. The decision variable is how many to produce.

Stage 1 (month 3) Demand = 8 aircraft

In this stage, we must have at least 1 aircraft in inventory, because demand is for 8 aircraft and we can produce at most 7 of them. The maximum number we could have in inventory is 4, because if we produce the maximum in the first two months (14 aircraft) and meet the first two months' demand of 10 aircraft, we would have only 4 at most.

X_1 \ d_1	4	5	6	7	Best payoff	Best decision
1				800+10 810	810	7
2			650+20 670		670	6
3		500+30 530			530	5
4	400+40 440				440	4

cost of prod.   holding cost

Stage 2 (month 2) Demand = 6
    Min inventory at beginning = 0
    Max inventory at beginning = 3

X_2 \ d_2	4	5	6	7	Best dec.	Best pay
0				800+810 =1610	7	1610
1			650+10+810 =1470	800+10+670 =1480	6	1470
2		500+20+810 =1330	650+20+670 =1340	800+20+530 =1350	5	1330
3	400+30+810 =1240	500+30+670 =1200	650+30+530 =1210	800+30+440 =1270	5	1200

280

Stage 3 (month 1) Demand = 4
        Beginning inventory = 0

X₃ \ d₃	4	5	6	7	Best dec.	Best pay
0	400+1610 =2010	500+1470 =1970	650+1330 =1980	800+1200 =2000	5	1970

The optimal solution is:

Month	Decision	Ending Inv.	Production	Holding	Total Cost
1	5	1	500		500
2	6	1	650	10	660
3	7		800	10	810
					$1,970 thousand

CHAPTER 13

EXTENSIONS OF
LINEAR PROGRAMMING

13-1 (a) We let: W = Wood doors produced next week
                   A = Aluminum doors produced next week
                   P = Plastic doors produced next week
                   C = Composite doors produced next week
                  IW = 0-1 variable for wood door setup
                  IA = 0-1 variable for aluminum door setup
                  IP = 0-1 variable for plastic door setup
                  IC = 0-1 variable for composite door setup

Max: 3W + 6A + 5P + 10C - 5IW - 6IA - 5IP - 10IC

Subject to:

1W	+4A	+3P	+1C				≤48 Cutting
3W	+1A	+1P	+3C				≤42 Assembly
1W	+1A	+2P	+3C				≤27 Finishing
1W				-14W			≤0 W setup
	1A				-12IA		≤0 A setup
		1P				-13IP	≤0 P setup
			1C			-9IC	≤0 C setup

W, A, P, C ≥ 0, and integer
IW, IA, IP, IC binary

(b) To ensure no more than two types of doors are
produced, the following constraint is added:

1IW + 1IA + 1IP + 1IC ≤ 2

13-2 (a) We are interested in ensuring that installment loans
(variable I in exercise 10-8), is either 0 or it is at
least $1 million. We introduce a binary 0-1 integer

variable, II. The coefficient for this variable in the objective function is 0; it's coefficient is also 0 for all canstraints given in the exercise 10-8 formulation. We now need to add to this formulation just two additional constraints as follows:

$1I - 25,000,000II \leq 0$ if I > 0, then II = 1
$-1I + 1,000,000II \leq 0$ if II = 1, then I ≥ $1 million

(b) We introduce a new binary 0-1 integer variable for signature loan called IS. Now two new constraints may be added as follows:

$1S - 2,500,000IS \leq 0$ if S > 0, then IS = 2
$1II + 1IS \leq 1$ cannot have both I > 0 and S > 0

13-3   We define a matrix where "1" indicates the prospective site which is within 1 mile of the competitor's current location as follows:

	Wiener Max Outlet			
	1	2	3	4
Site 1			1	
Site 2	1	1		
Site 3	1	1		1
Site 4		1		1
Site 5			1	

We let X1, X2, X3, X4, and X5 be defined as binary, 0-1 integer variables. If site i is used to locate a restaurant, then X_1 = 1; if not, then X_1 = 0.

Min: 15X1 + 22X2 + 29X3 + 16X4 + 12X5

S.T.

X2 + X3	≥ 1	Region 1
X2 + X3 + X4	≥ 1	Region 2
X1 + X5	≥ 1	Region 3
X3 + X4	≥ 1	Region 4

All variables are 0-1 binary integers.

13-4   We define a 0-1 integer variable for each course and each module.

if   A = 0, course A is not developed
     A = 1, course A is developed

if   P = 0, module P is not developed
     P = 1, module P is developed

Similar variables are defined for all other courses and modules.

Max: $13A + 17B + 19C + 12D + 20E + 15F - 11P - 11Q - 11R$
$- 11S - 11T - 11U - 11V - 11W$

S.T. $A + B + C - 3P \leq 0$ if A, B and/or C = 1, then P = 1
$A + D + E - 3Q \leq 0$ if A, D and/or E = 1, then Q = 1
$B + E \quad\quad - 2R \leq 0$ if B and/or E = 1, then R = 1
$B + C \quad\quad - 2S \leq 0$ if B and/or C = 1, then S = 1
$D + F \quad\quad - 2T \leq 0$ if D and/or F = 1, then T = 1
$E \quad\quad\quad - 1U \leq 0$ if E = 1, then U = 1
$C + F \quad\quad - 2V \leq 0$ if C and/or F = 1, then V = 1
$E \quad\quad\quad - 1W \leq 0$ if E = 1, then W = 1
$A + B + C + D + E + F \geq 4$ at least 4 courses

13-5 (a) We define 0-1 integer variables, X_{ij}, where:

$X_{ij} = 1$ if client i is serviced by truck j
$X_{ij} = 0$ if client i is not serviced by truck j

In addition, we define four additional 0-1 integer variables, F_j, where:

$F_j = 1$ if any $X_{ij} = 1$ (i.e., truck j is used by at least one client)

$F_j = 0$ if all $X_{ij} = 0$ (i.e., truck j is not used by any client)

Min: $450F_1 + 500F_2 + 550F_3 + 600F_4$

S.T. $X_{11} + X_{12} + X_{13} + X_{14} = 1$ Client 1 must be assigned a truck
$X_{21} + X_{22} + X_{23} + X_{24} = 1$ Client 2 must be assigned a truck
$X_{31} + X_{32} + X_{33} + X_{34} = 1$ Client 3 must be assigned a truck
$X_{41} + X_{42} + X_{43} + X_{44} = 1$ Client 4 must be assigned a truck
$X_{51} + X_{52} + X_{53} + X_{54} = 1$ Client 5 must be assigned a truck

$X_{11} + X_{21} + X_{31} + X_{41} + X_{51} - 5F_1 \leq 0$ $F_1 = 1$ if truck 1 used
$X_{12} + X_{22} + X_{32} + X_{42} + X_{52} - 5F_2 \leq 0$ $F_2 = 1$ if truck 2 used
$X_{13} + X_{23} + X_{33} + X_{43} + X_{53} - 5F_3 \leq 0$ $F_3 = 1$ if truck 3 used
$X_{14} + X_{24} + X_{34} + X_{44} + X_{54} - 5F_4 \leq 0$ $F_4 = 1$ if truck 4 used

$1500\, X_{11} + 2000X_{21} + 3000X_{31} + 3500\, X_{41} + 5000\, X_{51} \leq 5000$ truck 1 cap
$1500\, X_{12} + 2000X_{22} + 3000X_{32} + 3500\, X_{42} + 5000\, X_{52} \leq 6000$ truck 2 cap
$1500\, X_{13} + 2000X_{23} + 3000X_{33} + 3500\, X_{43} + 5000\, X_{53} \leq 7000$ truck 3 cap
$1500\, X_{14} + 2000X_{24} + 3000X_{34} + 3500\, X_{44} + 5000\, X_{54} \leq 11000$ truck 4 cap

All variables 0-1 binary integer

(b) If truck 4 is not used, the most weight which can be
carried is:

Truck 1	5000
Truck 2	6000
Truck 3	7000
	18,000 pounds

Since the total weight which must be carried is 15,000
pounds, none of the three trucks can be deleted.

(c) The optimal solution is:

$$X_{11} = X_{22} = X_{32} = X_{41} = X_{53} = F_1 = F_2 = F_3 = 1$$

All other variables are zero.

Cost = $1500

Truck	Client	Weight	Total
1	1	1500	
1	4	3500	5000
2	2	2000	
2	3	3000	5000
3	5	5000	5000

13-6 (a) We define all variables as 0-1 binary integers. For
example:

    B1 = 0 if project B1 is not funded
    B1 = 1 if project B1 is funded

With an objective of maximizing net present value with up
to $10 million (or $100 in $100,000's):

Max: 22B1 + 46B2 + 40B3 + 23E1 + 31E2 + 43M1 + 29M2
      + 37M3 + 19S1 + 23S2 + 54W1 + 32W2

S.T. 13B1 + 27B2 + 19B3 + 11E1 + 18E2 + 25M1 + 14M2
      + 23M3 + 9S1 + 13S2 + 26W1 + 17W2 ≤ 100 budget limit

All variables 0-1 binary integers

(b) 1: No more than 4.5 million in electronics:
11E1 + 18E2 + 25M1 + 14M2 + 23M3 ≤ 45 electronics limit

    2: At least two biotechnology funded:
        B1 + B2 + B3 ≥ 2

    3: At most one waste management funded:
        W1 + W2 ≤ 1

    4: S1 not funded unless M1 is also funded:
        -M1 + S1 ≤ 0

13-7　We define:　S = number of scooters produced
　　　　　　　　　M = number of metros produced
　　　　　　　　　D = number of delivery specials produced

Obj.　Maximize profit = $270S + 300M + 450D$
　S.T.　$1S + 3M + 4D + 1S_1 + 0S_2 = 100$ batteries
　　　　$2S + 3M + 5D + 0S_1 + 1S_2 = 127$ generators
　　　　　　　　　　　　　$S, M, D \geq 0$　nonnegativity

Initial tableau

C_j	Mix	Qty.	270 S	300 M	450 D	0 S_1	0 S_2
0	S_1	100	1	3	4	1	0
0	S_2	127	2	3	5	0	1
	Z_j	0	0	0	0	0	0
	$C_j - Z_j$		270	300	450	0	0

We enter variable D and remove S_1:

Second tableau

C_j	Mix	Qty.	270 S	300 M	450 D	0 S_1	0 S_2
450	D	25	1/4	3/4	1	1/4	0
0	S_2	2	3/5	-3/4	0	-5/4	1
	Z_j	11250	225/2	675/2	450	225/2	0
	$C_j - Z_j$		315/2	225/2	0	-225/2	0

We enter variable S and remove S_2.

C_j	Mix	Qty.	270 S	300 M	450 D	0 S_1	0 S_2
450	D	73/3	0	1	1	2/3	-1/3
270	S	8/3	1	-1	0	-5/3	4/3
	Z_j	35010/3	270	180	450	-150	210
	$C_j - Z_j$		0	120	0	150	-210

We enter variable S_1 and remove D:

C_j	Mix	Qty.	270 S	300 M	450 D	0 S_1	0 S_2
0	S_1	73/2	0	3/2	3/2	1	-1/2
270	S	127/2	1	3/2	5/2	0	1/2
	Z_j	17145	270	405	675	0	135
	$C_j - Z_j$		0	-105	-225	0	-135

The solution is a noninteger optimal.　We may introduce a
cut constraint by arbitrarily selecting variable S.　We
write the values in the S row as the sum of an integer and
a nonnegative fraction.

$(1+0)S + (1+1/2)M + (2+1/2)D + (0+1/2)S_2 = (63+1/2)$

Taking the integer coefficients to the right:

$1/2M + 1/2D + 1/2S_2 = 1/2 + (63 - 1S - 1M - 2D)$

This gives the relationship:

$1/2M + 1/2D + 1/2S_2 \geq 1/2$

We can get the cut constraint by multiplying by -2.

$-M - D - S_2 \leq -1$

To yield: $-M - D - S_2 + S_3 = -1$

First tableau for integer solution

			270	300	450	0	0	0
C_j	Mix	Qty.	S	M	D	S_1	S_2	S_3
0	S_1	73/2	0	3/2	3/2	1	-1/2	0
270	S	127/2	1	3/2	5/2	0	1/2	0
0	S_3	-1	0	-1	-1	0	-1	1
	Z_j	17145	270	405	675	0	135	0
	$C_j - Z_j$		0	-105	-225	0	-135	0

We wish to remove the infeasibility ($S_3 = -1$) by entering the smallest of:

```
-105/-1 = 105  variable M--smallest
-225/-1 = 225  variable D
-135/-1 = 135  variable S₂
```

We enter variable M and remove S_3

Second tableau for integer solution

			270	300	450	0	0	0
C_j	Mix	Qty.	S	M	D	S_1	S_2	S_3
0	S_1	35	0	0	0	1	-2	3/2
270	S	62	1	0	1	0	-1	3/2
300	M	1	0	1	1	0	1	-1
	Z_j	17040	270	300	570	0	30	105
	$C_j - Z_j$		0	0	-120	0	-30	-105

This is the optimum integer solution. We produce 62 Scooters and 1 Metro for a profit of $17,040.

13-8   Initial tableau

			6	4	0	0
C_j	Mix	Qty.	L	H	S_1	S_2
0	S_1	105300	40	42	1	0
0	S_2	92400	26	32	0	1
	Z_j	0	0	0	0	0
	$C_j - Z_j$		6	4	0	0

We enter variable L and remove S_1.

Second tableau

	C_j	Mix	Qty.	6 L	4 H	0 S_1	0 S_2
6		L	2632.5	1	1.05	.025	0
0		S_2	23955	0	4.70	−.650	1
		Z_j	15795	6	6.30	.150	0
		$C_j - Z_j$		0	−2.30	−.150	0

This is an optimum noninteger solution. To make the cut, we select variable L; row L becomes:

$$(1+0)L + (1+.05)H + (0+.025)S_1 = (2632+.5)$$

Taking the integer coefficients to the right:

$$.05H + .025S_1 = .5 + (2632 - 1L - 1H)$$

Giving: $.05H + .025S_1 \geq .5$

Multiplying through by −2, we obtain the cut constraint:

$-.1H - .05S_1 \leq -1$, which when augmented becomes:

$$-.1H - .05S_1 + S_3 = -1$$

First tableau for integer solution

	C_j	Mix	Qty.	6 L	4 H	0 S_1	0 S_2	0 S_3
6		L	2632.5	1	1.05	.025	0	0
0		S_2	23955	0	4.70	−.650	1	0
0		S_3	−1	0	−.10	−.050	0	1
		Z_j	15795	6	6.30	.150	0	0
		$C_j - Z_j$		0	−2.30	−.150	0	0

We now enter the smaller of:

    −2.3/−.10 = 23   variable H
    −.15/−.05 = 3   variable S_1 --smaller

Second tableau for integer solution

	C_j	Mix	Qty.	6 L	4 H	0 S_1	0 S_2	0 S_3
6		L	2632	1	1	0	0	.5
0		S_2	23968	0	6	0	1	−13
0		S_1	20	0	2	1	0	−20
		Z_j	15792	6	6	0	0	3
		$C_j - Z_j$		0	−2	0	0	−3

This is an optimum integer solution. We produce 2632 limousines and accept 23,968 slack hours in interior labor as well as 20 slack hours in bodywork labor.

13-9 We define: A = number of apprentices hired
                     J = number of journeymen hired

Objective: Maximize profits = $5A + 9J$
  S.T. $64A + 90J \leq 500$ dollars per day
       $8A + 5J \leq 16$ hours of supervision
       $A, J \geq 0$ nonnegativity and integer

Initial tableau

C_j	Mix	Qty.	5 A	9 J	0 S_1	0 S_2
0	S_1	500	64	90	1	0
0	S_2	16	8	5	0	1
	Z_j	0	0	0	0	0
	$C_j - Z_j$		5	9	0	0

We enter variable J and remove S_2 :

Second tableau

C_j	Mix	Qty.	5 A	9 J	0 S_1	0 S_2
0	S_1	212	-80	0	1	-18
9	J	3.2	1.6	1	0	.2
	Z_j	28.8	14.4	9	0	1.8
	$C_j - Z_j$		-9.4	0	0	-1.8

The solution is a noninteger optimal. We make the cut by selecting variable J, and row J becomes:

$(1+.6)A + (1+0)J + (0+.2)S_2 = (3+.2)$

Taking the integer coefficients to the right:

$.6A + .2S_2 = .2 + (3 - 1A - 1J)$

Yielding: $.6A + .2S_2 \geq .2$

Multiplying through by -5, we obtain the cut constraint:

$-3A - 1S_2 \leq -1$, which becomes: $-3A - 1S_2 + S_3 = -1$

289

First tableau for integer solution

C_j	Mix	Qty.	5 A	9 J	0 S_1	0 S_2	0 S_3
0	S_1	212	-80	0	1	-18	0
9	J	3.2	1.6	1	0	.2	0
0	S_3	-1	-3	0	0	-1	1
	Z_j	28.8	14.4	9	0	1.8	0
	C_j-Z_j		-9.4	0	0	-1.8	0

Now we enter the smaller of:

$-9.4/-3 = 3.133$ variable A
$-1.8/-1 = 1.8$ variable S_2 --smaller

Second tableau for integer solution

C_j	Mix	Qty.	5 A	9 J	0 S_1	0 S_2	0 S_3
0	S_1	230	-26	0	1	0	-18
9	J	3	1	1	0	0	.2
0	S_2	1	3	0	0	1	-1
	Z_j	27	9	9	0	0	1.8
	C_j-Z_j		-4	0	0	0	-1.8

This is the optimum integer solution. We hire 3 new
journeymen electricians for a profit of $27 per day. We
add 500 - 230 = $270 to payroll costs and require
16 - 1 = 15 hours of supervision.

13-10   We define: G = number of Grandfather clocks per day
                     M = number of Mantle clocks per day
                     W = number of Wall clocks per day
                     C = number of Chime clocks per day

Objective: Maximize 5G + 6.5M + 5W + 5.5C
    S.T.   5G + 5M + 3.75W + 6.25C ≤ 300 pounds/day brass
           5G + 6.25M + 5W + 3.75C ≤ 375 ft² daily storage
           G/3.75 + M/7.5 + W/2.5 + C/3.75 ≤ 8 hr/day time
                            G,M,W,C ≥ 0 and integer

First we attempt to reduce the complexity of the problem
by examining the constraints to see if any are redundant.
If we multiply the third constraint by 37.5 to yield a RHS
value of 300, we obtain:

   10G + 5M + 15W + 10C ≤ 300

Since each coefficient in this constraint is greater than
or equal to the corresponding coefficient in the first
constraint, we may eliminate the first constraint. Now if
we multiply the third constraint by 46.875 to obtain a RHS
value of 375, we obtain:

$$12.5G + 6.25M + 18.75W + 12.5C \leq 375$$

Each coefficient in the revised third constraint is greater than or equal to the corresponding coefficient in the second constraint. Consequently, the second constraint is redundant and may be eliminated. We now reformulate the third constraint in terms of minutes required per face:

$$16G + 8M + 24W + 16C \leq 480 \text{ minutes/day available}$$

Initial tableau

C_j	Mix	Qty.	5 G	6.5 M	5 W	5.5 C	0 S_1
0	S_1	480	16	8	24	16	1
	Z_j	0	0	0	0	0	0
	$C_j - Z_j$		5	6.5	5	5.5	0

We enter variable M in place of S_1.

C_j	Mix	Qty.	5 G	6.5 M	5 W	5.5 C	0 S_1
6.5	M	60	2	1	3	2	1/8
	Z_j	390	13	6.5	19.5	13	13/16
	$C_j - Z_j$		-8	0	-14.5	-7.5	-13/16

We have an optimum integer solution. We produce 60 Mantle clocks per day for a profit of $390 per day.

13-11 Since variable S_2 is already integer, we select variable X_1 to develop our cut constraint. We obtain from row X_1:

$$(1+0)X_1 + (1+1/3)X_2 + (0+1/6)S_1 = 6 + 1/3$$

Taking integers to the right:

$$1/3X_2 + 1/6S_1 = 1/3 + (6 - 1X_1 - 1X_2)$$

Giving: $1/3X_2 + 1/6S_1 \geq 1/3$

Multiplying through by -3 and augmenting, we obtain:

$$-1X_2 - 1/2S_1 + 1S_3 = -1$$

291

First tableau for integer solution

C_j	Mix	Qty.	1 X_1	1 X_2	0 S_1	0 S_2	0 S_3
1	X_1	19/3	1	4/3	1/6	0	0
0	S_2	5	0	4	-1	1	0
0	S_3	-1	0	-1	-1/2	0	1
	Z_j	19/3	1	4/3	1/6	0	0
	C_j-Z_j		0	-1/3	-1/6	0	0

We now enter the smaller of:

$$-1/3 \div -1 = 1/3 \quad \text{variable } X_2$$
$$-1/6 \div -1/2 = 1/3 \quad \text{variable } S_1$$

We arbitrarily select X_2 to enter in place of S_3.

Second tableau for integer solution

C_j	Mix	Qty.	1 X_1	1 X_2	0 S_1	0 S_2	0 S_3
1	X_1	5	1	0	-1/2	0	4/3
0	S_2	1	0	0	-3	1	4
1	X_2	1	0	1	1/2	0	-1
	Z_j	6	1	1	0	0	1/3
	C_j-Z_j		0	0	0	0	-1/3

This is an optimum integer solution. It may be noted that
an alternative optimum is indicated by the presence of a
zero valued C_j-Z_j for nonbasic variable S_1. If we had
entered S_1 instead of X_2 in going to the second tableau
above, we would have arrived at the solution $X_1 = 6$ and
$X_2 = 0$ for the same profit of 6.

13-12   We find the cut constraint by selecting variable X_2, and
row X_2 becomes:

$$(0+1/2)X_1 + (1+0)X_2 + (0+1/12)S_2 = 3+1/2$$

Regrouping:

$$1/2X_1 + 1/12S_2 = 1/2 + (3-1X_2) \quad \text{which gives:}$$

$$1/2X_1 + 1/12S_2 \geq 1/2$$

Multiplying through by -2 and augmenting, we obtain:

$$-1X_1 - 1/6S_2 + 1S_3 = -1$$

First tableau for integer solution

C_J	Mix	Qty.	6 X_1	14 X_2	0 S_1	0 S_2	0 S_3
0	S_1	10	2	0	1	-2/3	0
14	X_2	3.5	1/2	1	0	1/12	0
0	S_3	-1	-1	0	0	-1/6	1
	Z_J	49	7	14	0	7/6	0
	$C_J - Z_J$		-1	0	0	-7/6	0

We now enter the smaller of:

$$-1 \div -1 = 1 \quad \text{variable } X_1 \text{ --smaller}$$
$$-7/6 \div -1/6 = 7 \quad \text{variable } S_2$$

Second tableau for integer solution

C_J	Mix	Qty.	6 X_1	14 X_2	0 S_1	0 S_2	0 S_3
0	S_1	8	0	0	1	-1	2
14	X_2	3	0	1	0	0	1/2
6	X_1	1	1	0	0	1/6	-1
	Z_J	48	6	14	0	1	1
	$C_J - Z_J$		0	0	0	-1	-1

This is an optimum integer solution.

13-13 This problem is known as the classical traveling salesman
problem. At each node, we can compute a lower bound
similar to that used when solving the assignment problem.
Our initial node (node 1) has a lower bound:

M-S	1
J-M	2
W-P or S	1
P-W	2
H-P	2
S-J, W or P	2
	10 miles

As we branch from node 1, we fix the leg from Marcel's
office to each of the five jobs.

Node	Assignment fixed	Lower bound	Feasible?
2	M-J	4+3+1+2+2+2 = 14	no
3	M-W	3+2+1+3+2+2 = 13	no
4	M-P	6+2+1+2+3+2 = 16	no
5	M-H	2+2+1+2+2+2 = 11	yes
6	M-S	1+2+1+2+2+2 = 10	no

Node 5 is feasible because it is a complete tour from
M-H-P-W-S-J-M. Its distance, 11 miles, becomes our
incumbent current upper bound. Only node 6 has a lower
bound less than 11, so we prune all other nodes except
node 6. Branching from node 6, we create four new nodes
where we continue from M-S and fix the leg from S, the
Stuart job.

Node	Assignment fixed	Lower bound	Feasible?
7	M-S-J	1+2+3+1+2+2 = 11	no
8	M-S-W	1+2+2+1+3+2 = 11	no
9	M-S-P	1+2+2+2+2+3 = 12	no
10	M-S-H	1+5+2+1+2+2 = 13	no

At this point our problem is solved. Node 5's upper
bound, valued at 11 miles, is not larger than the lower
bound of any other node. Our solution is:

   M-H-W-S-J-M = 11 miles.

13-14 One common approach in branch-and-bound is to start off
with a lower bound to our maximization problem using a
heuristic solution as a lower bound. Let's do this using
Vogel's method as follows:

Row or Column	Largest	Second Largest	Opportunity Cost	
G	6	5	1	
H	6	5	1	
I	6	5	1	
J	6	5	1	
K	6	5	1	
L	6	5	1	
A	4	4	0	
B	6	6	0	
C	6	5	1	<--
D	6	6	0	
E	5	5	0	
F	5	5	0	

We break the tie in opportunity cost by biasing our
selection to the only column in the tied set.

Step 1: Assign G to C   Payoff 6

Row or Column		Largest	Second Largest	Opportunity Cost	
H		6	5	1	
I		6	5	1	
J		6	5	1	
K		6	4	2	<--
L		6	5	1	
	A	4	4	0	
	B	6	6	0	
	D	6	6	0	
	E	5	5	0	
	F	5	5	0	

Step 2: Assign K to B   Payoff 6

Row or Column		Largest	Second Largest	Opportunity Cost	
H		5	4	1	
I		6	5	1	<--
J		6	5	1	
L		5	4	1	
	A	4	4	0	
	D	6	6	0	
	E	5	5	0	
	F	5	5	0	

We break the tie by selecting the largest number in LARGEST column. Since there are two (I and J rows) tied with 6's, we further break the tie arbitrarily.

Step 3: Assign I to D   Payoff 6

Row or Column		Largest	Second Largest	Opportunity Cost	
H		5	4	1	<--
J		5	4	1	
L		5	4	1	
	A	4	3	1	
	E	5	4	1	
	F	5	5	0	

Here we have very little to distinguish among the rows/columns tied with highest opportunity cost. We arbitratily break the tie again.

Step 4: Assign H to E   Payoff 5

Row or Column	Largest	Second Largest	Opportunity Cost	
J	5	4	1	
L	5	3	2	<--
A	4	3	1	
F	5	5	0	

Step 5: Assign L to F   Payoff 5
Step 6: This leaves J to A   Payoff 4

The total payoff for the Vogel heuristic solution is 32.

We now start the branch-and-bound procedure with a lower bound of 32 (LB = 32).

Node 1 is an assignment of each person to his/her highest valued shift. Since it is unlikely that this solution will be optimal, node 1 will serve to provide an upper bound to the value of the optimal solution.

```
G - C    6
H - B    6
I - D    6
J - D    6
K - B    6
L - B    6
        ──
        36   (upper bound for node 1)
```

Since the solution is not feasible, we branch to nodes 2 through 7 fixing each person to shift A.

Node	Assignment fixed	Upper bound	Feasible?	LB=32 Pruned?
2	G-A	1+6+6+6+6=31	No	Yes
3	H-A	2+6+6+6+6=32	No	Yes
4	I-A	4+6+6+6+6=34	No	No
5	J-A	4+6+6+6+6=34	No	No
6	K-A	1+6+6+6+6=31	No	Yes
7	L-A	3+6+6+6+6=33	No	No

Only nodes 4, 5, and 7 are open. The largest upper bound is 34 so we select one of those with UB = 34 for the next branch.

Branching from Node 4 fixing shift B

Node	Assignment fixed	Upper bound	Feasible?	LB=32 Pruned?
8	I-A; G-B	4+4+5+6+5=5=29	Yes	Yes
9	I-A; H-B	4+6+6+6+5+5=32	No	Yes
10	I-A; J-B	4+3+6+5+5+5=28	No	Yes
11	I-A; K-B	4+6+6+5+6+5=32	Yes	Yes
12	I-A; L-B	4+6+6+5+6+5=32	No	Yes

Node 11 is, at best, an alternative optimal solution. Only nodes 5 and 7 remain open. We branch from node 5.

Branching from Node 5 fixing shift B

Node	Assignment fixed	Upper bound	Feasible?	LB=32 Pruned?
13	J-A; G-B	4+4+5+6+5=5=29	Yes	Yes
14	J-A; H-B	4+6+6+6+5+5=32	No	Yes
15	J-A; I-B	4+1+6+5+5+5=25	No	Yes
16	J-A; K-B	4+6+6+5+6+5=32	Yes	Yes
17	J-A; L-B	4+6+6+5+6+5=32	No	Yes

It is noted that node 16 could have been eliminated because it is the lower bound solution we got from the Vogel heuristic, and are using it to conduct our pruning. Now we branch from our only open node-- node 7.

Branching from Node 7 fixing shift B

Node	Assignment fixed	Upper bound	Feasible?	LB=32 Pruned?
18	L-A; G-B	3+4+5+6+6=5=29	No	Yes
19	L-A; H-B	3+6+6+6+6+5=32	No	Yes
20	L-A; I-B	3+1+6+5+6+5=26	No	Yes
21	L-A; J-B	3+3+6+5+6+5=28	No	Yes
22	L-A; L-B	3+6+6+5+6+6=32	No	Yes

The heuristic solution we got using the Vogel method is optimal. Node 11 is an alternative optimal solution.

Vogel Solution			Node 11		
George	- Shift C	6	George	- Shift C	6
Hilda	- Shift E	5	Hilda	- Shift E	5
Issac	- Shift D	6	Issac	- Shift A	4
James	- Shift A	4	James	- Shift D	6
Karen	- Shift B	6	Karen	- Shift B	6
Lauren	- Shift F	5	Lauren	- Shift F	5
		32			32

13-15 Our initial node (node 1) is an assignment of each of the
       five autos to its lowest cost mechanic:

```
       V - B   6
       M - H   6
       F - H   5
       S - A   6
       D - B,A 5
              28
```

Since the solution is not feasible, we make a branching
with each of the five cars assigned to Ham.

Node	Assignment fixed	Lower bound	Feasible?
2	V-H	8+9+6+6+5 = 34	yes
3	M-H	6+6+6+6+5 = 29	no
4	F-H	5+6+9+6+5 = 31	no
5	S-H	8+6+9+6+5 = 34	yes
6	D-H	9+6+9+6+6 = 36	yes

We keep node 2 (or node 5) as our current upper bound
valued at 34. Nodes 5 and 6 with lower bounds equal to or
greater than the incumbent upper bound are pruned. Of the
two remaining open nodes (3 and 4), node 3 has the least
lower bound so we branch from node 3 (where M-H is fixed)
and create four new nodes with V, F, S and D fixed to
Lacy.

Node	Assignment fixed	Lower bound	Feasible?
7	M-H & V-L	6+7+6+6+5 = 30	yes
8	M-H & F-L	6+7+6+6+5 = 30	no
9	M-H & S-L	6+9+6+6+5 = 32	yes
10	M-H & D-L	6+8+6+6+6 = 32	yes

We keep node 7 as our current upper bound of 30 and all
other nodes whose lower bounds are ≥ 30 are pruned making
node 7 our optimum solution as follows:

M-H; V-L; F-T; S-A; D-B at a cost of 30 total hours.

13-16 Our initial node (node 1) in the tree is an assignment of
       each plant to its minimum cost quarry.

```
       T - L   11
       K - S   20
       C - S   32
       R - L   27
              90    (lower bound for node 1)
```

Since the solution is not feasible, we branch to four
nodes with each plant assigned to the Linwood quarry.

298

Node	Assignment fixed	Lower bound	Feasible?
2	T - L	11+20+32+32 = 95	no
3	K - L	27+24+32+32 = 115	no
4	C - L	43+24+20+32 = 119	no
5	R - L	27+24+20+32 = 103	no

We select node 2 which has the least lower bound, and
branch to all assignments for K, C, and R fixed to the
Sherrard quarry.

Node	Assignment fixed	Lower bound	Feasible?
6	T - L & K - S	11+20+32+41 = 104	no
7	T - L & C - S	11+35+55+41 = 142	yes
8	T - L & R - S	11+32+55+32 = 132	yes

Our current upper bound, or best feasible solution, is 132
at node 8. We can prune away node 7.

We now select node 5 whose LB = 103 is the least of all
lower bounds for the open nodes. In branching from node 5
we fix T, K, and C to Sherrard.

Node	Assignment fixed	Lower bound	Feasible?
9	R - L & T - S	27+35+55+32 = 149	yes
10	R - L & K - S	27+20+24+32 = 103	no
11	R - L & C - S	27+35+24+55 = 141	yes

We prune nodes 9 and 11 whose lower bounds are equal to or
greater than the current upper bound of 132. The open,
unpruned nodes are now nodes 3, 4, 6, and 10, and our tree
appears as follows:

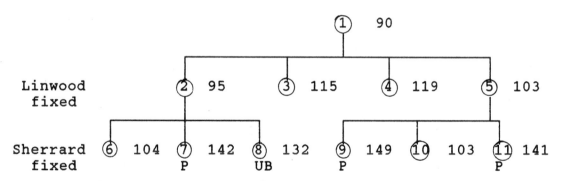

P   indicates a pruned node
UB indicates the current upper bound

We now branch from node 10 which has least lower bound of
all open nodes. Since R - L and K - S are fixed our
branching to two new nodes are to fix T and C to the
Johnsville quarry.

Node	Assignment fixed	Lower bound	Feasible?
12	R-L & K-S & T-J	27+20+44+32 = 123	yes
13	R-L & K-S & C-J	27+20+59+24 = 130	yes

Node 12 is a feasible solution whose value of 123 is the best feasible solution obtained so far. We now set our current upper bound to 123 and prune nodes 8 and 13. Our open nodes are 3, 4, and 6. We branch from node 6 to two new nodes fixing C and R to the Johnsville quarry.

Node	Assignment fixed	Lower bound	Feasible?
14	T-L & K-S & C-J	11+20+59+41 = 131	yes
15	T-L & K-S & R-J	11+20+44+32 = 107	yes

Now we may set our upper bound to 107 (node 15), which is the best feasible solution yet obtained. We can now prune nodes 3, 4, 12, and 14. We now have an optimum solution represented by node 15 as follows:

T - L; K - S; R - J; C - A at a cost of $107,000.

13-17 In the initial node (node 1) each of the concessions is assigned to the most profitable location:

R-N 12
B-N 11
T-N 14
C-N <u>12</u>
    49

The initial node has an upper bound of $49 thousand, but since all concessions are assigned to the North location, it is not feasible.

In the first branch, we select the North location as the decision, because this will force unassigned concessions to select less profitable locations in the upper bound assignments, thus strengthening the upper bound. This is a heuristic branching decision rule (branch into the strength of the bound).

Node	Assignment fixed	Upper bound	Feasible?
2	R-N	12+9+12+11 = 44	yes
3	B-N	11+9+12+11 = 43	yes
4	T-N	14+9+9+11 = 43	no
5	C-N	12+9+9+12 = 42	yes

Node 2 is a feasible solution with a profit of $44 thousand. Our current lower bound is set to 44. Since the upper bound of each of the other nodes is less than 44, they are all pruned. Our optimum solution is:

Concession stand	Location	Profit
Ring toss	North	12
Basketball	South	9
Target	West	12
Cotton candy	East	11
	Total profit	$44,000

13-18   In computing the lower bound, we select for each color as
a predecessor, another color for follower which requires
least setup time. For our initial lower bound (node 1),
where none of the colors are fixed in sequence, the lower
bound is:

Predecessor	Least costly follower	Cost
Blue	Black	3
White	Any color	1
Red	Black	2
Black	Blue	4
		10

The lower bound solution is not feasible because it does
not constitute a complete tour (Black is the least costly
follower for more than one predecessor).

In our first branch, we may select any color and fix each
of the other three colors to follow it. Selecting Blue as
the first color, we develop the nodes:

Node 2   Blue-Black fixed in sequence

Predecessor	Cheapest follower	Cost	
Blue	Black	3	(fixed)
White	Red or Blue	1	(cannot precede Black)
Red	Blue	3	(cannot precede Black)
Black	Red	6	(cannot precede Blue)
	Lower bound =	13	(not feasible)

Node 3   Blue-White fixed in sequence

Predecessor	Cheapest follower	Cost	
Blue	White	9	(fixed)
White	Red or Black	1	(cannot precede Blue)
Red	Black	2	(cannot precede White)
Black	Blue	4	(cannot precede White)
	Lower bound =	16	(feasible)

Node 4   Blue-Red fixed in sequence

Predecessor	Cheapest follower	Cost	
Blue	Red	6	(fixed)
White	Blue or Black	1	(cannot precede Red)
Red	Black	2	(cannot precede Blue)
Black	Blue	4	(cannot precede Red)
	Lower bound =	13	(not feasible)

Node 3 becomes our initial upper bound with the feasible sequence Blue-White-Red-Black-Blue at a cost of 16 hours.

We now branch from node 2 where Blue-Black has already been fixed and fix a follower to Black:

Node 5 The fixed sequence is Blue-Black-Red. White is the only unfixed color, so it must be inserted between Red and Blue giving the sequence Blue-Black-Red-White-Blue at a cost of 20.

Node 6 The fixed sequence is Blue-Black-White. With only Red remaining, the only feasible sequence, at a cost of 21, is Blue-Black-White-Red-Blue.

Since nodes 5 and 6 have lower bounds which are greater than the current upper bound of 16, both are pruned leaving only node 4. Branching from node 4:

Node 7 The fixed sequence is Blue-Red-White and the only feasible sequence is Blue-Red-White-Black-Blue at a cost of 21.

Node 8 The fixed sequence is Blue-Red-Black and the only feasible sequence is Blue-Red-Black-White-Blue at a cost of 23.

Nodes 7 and 8 are pruned and only node 3, the current upper bound, remains in the tree. Node 3 is our optimum solution.

13-19   Since each machine must process exactly three jobs, we can find a minimum completion time on either machine by adding the three shortest process times. At node 1, the initial node, where none of the jobs have been fixed to a particular machine, we have:

Machine	Three shortest jobs	Minimum completion time
A	4, 1, 2	10 + 12 + 13 = 35
B	2, 1, 4	8 + 9 + 9 = 26

The earliest time all jobs can be completed is the larger of the times 35 or 26. Therefore, the lower bound on node 1 is 35 hours. The lower bound solution is not feasible because the shortest jobs on machine A (1, 2, and 4) are not uniquely different from the three shortest jobs on machine B (same three).

Our first branching focuses on job 1. We branch to node 2 where job 1 is fixed to machine A's schedule and to node 3 where job 1 is fixed to machine B's schedule.

Node 2

Machine	Jobs fixed	Remaining Shortest	Minimum time
A	1	4, 2	12 + 10 + 13 = 35
B	none	2, 4, 3	8 + 9 + 10 = 27

(Lower bound = 35; not feasible)

Node 3

Machine	Jobs fixed	Remaining Shortest	Minimum time
A	none	4, 2, 3	10 + 13 + 15 = 38
B	1	2, 4	9 + 8 + 9 = 26

(Lower bound = 38; not feasible)

Since node 2 has a smaller lower bound, we make a branching operation from node 2 and fix job 2.

Node 4

Machine	Jobs fixed	Remaining Shortest	Minimum time
A	1, 2	4	12 + 13 + 10 = 35
B	none	4, 3, 5	9 + 10 + 10 = 29

(Lower bound = 35; not feasible)

Node 5

Machine	Jobs fixed	Remaining Shortest	Minimum time
A	1	4, 3	12 + 10 + 15 = 37
B	2	4, 3 or 5	8 + 9 + 10 = 27

(Lower bound = 37; not feasible)

We now branch from node 4 where our decision is to fix job 3.

Node 6

Machine	Jobs fixed	Remaining Shortest	Minimum time
A	1, 2, 3		12 + 13 + 15 = 40
B	none	4, 5, 6	9 + 10 + 19 = 38

(Lower bound = 40; feasible)

Node 7

Machine	Jobs fixed	Remaining Shortest	Minimum time
A	1, 2	4	12 + 13 + 10 = 35
B	3	4, 5	10 + 9 + 10 = 29

(Lower bound = 35; not feasible)

Node 6 is a feasible solution with a scheduled completion time of 40 hours. Node 6 becomes our first upper bound.

Our tree now has three open nodes (nodes 3, 5, and 7) and appears as follows:

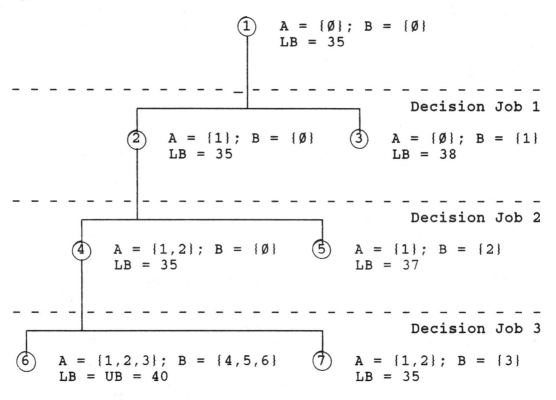

We now branch from node 7 where our decision is to fix job 4 to either machine A or B.

Node 8

Machine	Jobs fixed	Remaining Shortest	Minimum time
A	1, 2, 4		12 + 13 + 10 = 35
B	3	5, 6	10 + 10 + 19 = 39

(Lower bound = 39; feasible)

Node 9

Machine	Jobs fixed	Remaining Shortest	Minimum time
A	1, 2	5	12 + 13 + 16 = 41
B	3, 4	5	10 + 9 + 10 = 29

(Lower bound = 41; not feasible)

Node 8 is a feasible solution valued at 39. Therefore we set our current best upper bound to 39 and prune away all nodes whose lower bounds are equal to or greater then 39. This allows us to prune nodes 6 and 9. The only open nodes now in the tree are 3 and 5.

We now branch from node 5 where our branching decision is on job 3.

304

Node 10

Machine	Jobs fixed	Remaining Shortest	Minimum time
A	1, 3	4	12 + 15 + 10 = 37
B	2	4, 5	8 + 9 + 10 = 27

(Lower bound = 37; not feasible)

Node 11

Machine	Jobs fixed	Remaining Shortest	Minimum time
A	1	4, 5	12 + 10 + 16 = 38
B	2, 3	4	8 + 10 + 9 = 27

(Lower bound = 38; not feasible)

Our open nodes are now:

Node	Fixed jobs	Lower bound
3	A = {∅}; B = {1}	38
10	A = {1,3}; B = {2}	37
11	A = {1}; B = {2,3}	38

Our next branch is from node 10 where our decision involves the fixing of job 4.

Node 12

Machine	Jobs fixed	Remaining Shortest	Minimum time
A	1, 3, 4		12 + 15 + 10 = 37
B	2	5, 6	8 + 10 + 19 = 37

(Lower bound = 37; feasible)

Node 13

Machine	Jobs fixed	Remaining Shortest	Minimum time
A	1, 3	5	12 + 15 + 16 = 43
B	2, 4	5	8 + 9 + 10 = 27

(Lower bound = 43; not feasible)

Node 12 is a feasible solution whose solution is superior to the previous best solution. Node 12 then becomes our incumbent upper bound, and with all other open nodes having a lower bound greater than 37 hours, all of them are pruned. Node 12 is the optimum solution as follows:

    Machine A schedule--Jobs 1, 3, and 4 for 37 hours
    Machine B schedule--Jobs 2, 5, and 6 for 37 hours.

13-20 An effective heuristic measure for problems of this type
       is a ratio of objective function coefficient to constraint
       coefficient. For example, let's assume in our problem
       that the objective function is a payoff in dollars per
       unit, and the constraint is given in total pounds with
       each variable's coefficient being pounds per unit. This
       approach gives us:

Variable	Obj. function coef. ($/unit)	÷	Constraint coef. (lb/unit)	=	Measure $/lb
A	36		22		1.6363
B	21		13		1.6154
C	5		3		1.6667
D	13		8		1.6250
E	7		5		1.4000

Using the greedy approach, we pick variable C whose
measure of 1.6667 is the highest of the 5. Since C can be
any integer (in some knapsack type problems C would have
to be either 0 or 1), we set C equal to its largest
possible integer value of 10. Since no other variable can
be a nonzero integer, our greedy solution is:

        C = 10 units
        Obj. function = 50

This, of course, is not optimal; we can readily see that
with C = 10, only (3)(10) = 30 pounds are loaded in the
knapsack which can hold 32 pounds. Consequently, we could
substitute one unit of E for one C giving us a better
solution: C = 9 units; E = 1 unit.

This results in a payoff of:

        Obj. function = (9)(5) + (7)(1) = 52
        Weight = (3)(9) + (5)(1) = 32 pounds

This is a better solution, so our greedy heuristic is not
optimal.

13-21 Using standard U.S. coins, change for 77¢ using the greedy
       heuristic is:

                        1 half-dollar
                        1 quarter
                        2 pennies
                        4 coins total

This is an optimal solution.

Using a system where 30¢ pieces are used instead of half-dollars, the greedy heuristic gives:

2 30¢ pieces
1 dime
1 nickel
2 pennies
6 coins total

This is not optimal, a better solution is:

3 quarters
2 pennies
5 coins total

13-22 Starting with the optimal tableau given in Table 13-9, we enter variable D_{op} and remove S_A:

C_j.	Mix	Qty.	T	C	S_A	S_F	D_{up}	D_{op}	D_{ut}	D_{ot}
0	D_{ot}	5	0	1/2	1/4	0	0	0	-1	1
0	T	15	1	1/2	1/4	0	0	0	0	0
0	D_{op}	20	0	-2	2	0	-1	1	0	0
0	S_F	18	0	3	-1/8	1	0	0	0	0
	Z_j	0	0	0	0	0	0	0	0	0
	$C_j - Z_j$		0	0	0	0	1	0	1	0

With this solution, both the goals are exceeded. The production of tables (T=15) is exceeded by D_{ot} = 5 units and profit (8)(15) = $120 is exceeded by D_{op} = $20. All slack has been removed on the now-capacitated assembly constraint (S_A = 0) and the slack on the finishing constraint is reduced to S_F = 18 hours.

13-23 X_{11} = number of X-79 motors produced on regular time
      X_{12} = number of X-79 motors produced on overtime
      X_{13} = number of X-79 motors produced with temporary labor
      X_{14} = number of X-79 motors produced by subcontract
      X_{21} = number of X-85 motors produced on regular time
      X_{22} = number of X-85 motors produced on overtime
      X_{23} = number of X-85 motors produced with temporary labor
      X_{24} = number of X-85 motors produced by subcontract
      D_u = underachievement of demand (loss of goodwill) X-79
      D_o = overachievement of demand (inventory costs) X-79
      C_u = underachievement of target cost
      F_u = underachievement of demand (loss of goodwill) X-85
      F_o = overachievement of demand (inventory costs) X-85

Objective: Minimize $2D_u + 1D_o + 2F_u + 1F_o + 1C_o$

S.T. $X_{11} + X_{12} + X_{13} + X_{14} + D_u - D_o = 1000$ X-79 goal
$X_{21} + X_{22} + X_{23} + X_{24} + F_u - F_o = 1500$ X-85 goal
$6X_{11} + 7.5X_{21} \leq 12000$ worker-hours regular time
$6X_{12} + 7.5X_{22} \leq 3000$ worker-hours overtime
$7.5X_{13} + 9.5X_{23} \leq 2500$ worker-hours temporary labor
$90X_{11} + 138X_{12} + 105X_{13} + 165X_{14} + 112.5X_{21}$
$\qquad + 172.5X_{22} + 133X_{23} + 209X_{24} + C_u - C_o = \$250,000$
$\qquad\qquad$ target cost goal
all variables ≥ 0 nonnegativity

The optimum solution is:

$X_{11} = 666.67$ motors on regular time; $X_{13} = 333.33$ motors
using temporary labor; $X_{21} = 1066.67$ motors on regular
time; $X_{22} = 202.90$ motors produced on overtime.
$F_u = 230.43$ underachievement of X-85 motor demand. With
the exception of the X-85 demand not being met, all other
over- and underachievement goals are met. The value of
the objective function is $Z = 460.87$ reflecting $(2)(F_u)$.

13-24 We define: D = number of desk lamps produced/month
$\qquad\qquad$ B = number of bedside lamps produced/month
$\qquad\qquad$ F = number of floor lamps produced/month
$\qquad\qquad F_u$ = underachievement of finishing goal, hr/mo.
$\qquad\qquad P_u$ = underachievement of profit goal, \$/mo.
$\qquad\qquad P_o$ = overachievement of profit goal, \$/mo.

Objective: Minimize $1F_u + 1P_u$

S.T. $35D + 40B + 65F + P_u - P_o = 20,000$ profit goal
$1.5D + 1.5B + 4F + F_u = 1000$ hr/mo. finishing goal
$1D + 3B + 1.5F \leq 2000$ hr/mo. turning constraint
$4D + 3B + 6F \leq 3000$ lb/mo. brass constraint
all variables ≥ 0 nonnegativity

The optimum solution by computer is B = 240; F = 160;
D = 0; P_o = 0; P_u = 0; and F_u = 0 (both goals satisfied so
the objective function value, Z = 0). There will be 1040
idle hours per month in turning labor and 1320 pounds per
month of unused brass.

13-25 We define the following variables, all of which are in millions of cruzeiros per year:

C = amount loaned for commercial purposes
A = amount loaned for agricultural purposes
D_{ue} = amount the earnings goal is underachieved
D_{oe} = amount the earnings goal is overachieved
D_{ua} = amount the agricultural loans goal is underachieved
D_{oa} = amount the agricultural loans goal is overachieved

Objective: Minimize $D_{ue} + D_{ua}$
S.T. $.08C - .02A + D_{ue} - D_{oe} = 1$ earnings goal
      $1A + D_{ua} - D_{oa} = 150$ agricultural loans goal
      $1C + 1A \leq 300$ loans constraint

After adding a slack variable to the loans constraint, we arrive at the first tableau:

C_j	Mix	Qty.	0 C	0 A	1 D_{ue}	0 D_{oe}	1 D_{ua}	0 D_{oa}	0 S_1
1	D_{ue}	1	.08	−.02	1	−1	0	0	0
1	D_{ua}	150	0	1	0	0	1	−1	0
0	S_1	300	1	1	0	0	0	0	1
	Z_j	151	.08	.98	1	−1	1	−1	0
	$C_j - Z_j$		−.08	−.98	0	1	0	1	0

We enter variable A and remove D_{ua}:

Second tableau

C_j	Mix	Qty.	0 C	0 A	1 D_{ue}	0 D_{oe}	1 D_{ua}	0 D_{oa}	0 S_1
1	D_{ue}	4	.08	0	1	−1	.02	−.02	0
0	A	150	0	1	0	0	1	−1	0
0	S_1	150	1	0	0	0	−1	1	1
	Z_j	4	.08	0	1	−1	.02	−.02	0
	$C_j - Z_j$		−.08	0	0	1	.98	.02	0

We now enter variable C and remove D_{ue}:

Third tableau

C_j	Mix	Qty.	0 C	0 A	1 D_{ue}	0 D_{oe}	1 D_{ua}	0 D_{oa}	0 S_1
0	C	50	1	0	12.5	−12.5	.25	−.25	0
0	A	150	0	1	0	0	1	−1	0
0	S_1	100	0	0	−12.5	12.5	−1.25	1.25	1
	Z_j	0	0	0	0	0	0	0	0
	$C_j - Z_j$		0	0	1	0	1	0	0

We can meet both goals with our funding level of 300 million cruzeiros. In fact, these goals can be met with only 200 million cruzeiros (S_1 = 100 million slack).

13-26   (a)   The optimal solution meets both goals with 50 million in commercial loans and 150 million in agricultural loans. There is available another 100 million cruzeiros which is not loaned to either and instead shows up as slack in the maximum loans contraint.

(b)   When the coefficient for D_{oe} = -1 in the objective function of our minimization problem, variable D_{oe} will be driven into the basis assuming both goals are met (i.e., D_{ue} and D_{ua} are both zero). This gives the optimal solution of loaning 150 million to commercial and 150 million to agriculture. The earnings goal is overachieved by 8 million.

(c)   When the coefficient for D_{oa} = -1 in the objective function of our minimization problem, the solution provides for 70 million in commercial loans and 230 million in agriculture loans (again using all the available 300 million). In this case, however, as the added funds increase for agricultural loans, they also increase for the commercial loans as well. Observe that $1 needs to be invested in commercial loans for every $4 invested in agriculture loans. This ensures that the 2% loss in agriculture loans is properly compensated by the 8% gain in commercial loans, thus preserving our attainment of the 1 million earnings goal.

13-27   We define: A = Allenwood stop
                  B = Bristo stop
                  C = Cedarwood stop
                  D = Dryden stop
                  E = Eustis stop
                  F = Farnsworth stop
                  G = Gardenville stop
                  H = Harrow stop
        D_{un} = underachievement of 5 stop goal
        D_{on} = overachievement of 5 stop goal
        D_{uc} = amount below cost goal
        D_{oc} = amount above cost goal
        D_{ud} = underachievement of Dryden goal

Objective: Minimize $P_1 D_{un}$ + $P_2 D_{oc}$ + $P_3 D_{ud}$
    S.T.   A + B + C + D + E + F + G + H + D_{un} - D_{on} = 5 stops
        3600A + 3400B + 3800C + 4000D + 3200E + 3900F
            + 4100G + 3900H + D_{uc} - D_{oc} = $19000 cost
        D + D_{ud} = 1 Dryden goal
        all variables $\geq$ 0   nonnegativity

Initial tableau

C_j	Mix	Qty.	0 A	0 B	0 C	0 D	0 E	0 F	0 G	0 H	P_1 D_{un}	0 D_{on}	0 D_{uc}	P_2 D_{oc}	P_3 D_{ud}
P_1	D_{un}	5	1	1	1	1	1	1	1	1	1	-1	0	0	0
0	D_{uc}	190	36	34	38	40	32	34	41	39	0	0	1	-1	0
P_3	D_{ud}	1	0	0	0	1	0	0	0	0	0	0	0	0	1
	Z_j	1	0	0	0	1	0	0	0	0	0	0	0	0	1
	$C_j - Z_j$		0	0	0	-1	0	0	0	0	0	0	0	0	0
	Z_j	0	0	0	0	0	0	0	0	0	0	0	0	0	0
	$C_j - Z_j$		0	0	0	0	0	0	0	0	0	0	0	1	0
	Z_j	5	1	1	1	1	1	1	1	1	1	-1	0	0	0
	$C_j - Z_j$		-1	-1	-1	-1	-1	-1	-1	-1	0	1	0	0	0

13-28 We define: S = number of sport fishermen produced
T = number of twin cabin cruisers produced
F = number of flying bridges produced
B_u, B_o = under- and overachievement of boat goal
L_u = underachievement of lumber goal
F_u, F_o = under- and overachievement of finishing
P_u, P_o = under- and overachievement of profit goal

Objective: Minimize $P_1 B_u + P_2 L_u + P_3 F_u + P_4 P_u$

S.T.
$1S + 1T + 1F + 1B_u - 1B_o = 4$ boats goal
$5S + 8T + 9.5F + 1L_u = 19$ K-board-ft lumber goal
$9S + 11.5T + 13F + 1F_u - 1F_o = 20$ 100-hr finish
$1F_o \leq 20$ 100-hrs finish constraint
$3S + 5T + 6F + 1P_u - 1P_o = 10$ K-dollars profit goal
$1.8S + 2.3T + 3F \leq 8$ K-hr assembly constraint
All variables ≥ 0 nonnegativity

After adding slack variables S_F and S_A to the finishing and assembly constraints, we have:

C_j	Mix	Qty.	0 S	0 T	0 F	P_1 B_u	0 B_o	P_2 L_u	P_3 F_u	0 F_o	P_4 P_u	0 P_o	0 S_F	0 S_A
P_1	B_u	4	1	1	1	1	-1	0	0	0	0	0	0	0
P_2	L_u	19	5	8	9.5	0	0	1	0	0	0	0	0	0
P_3	F_u	20	9	11.5	13	0	0	0	1	-1	0	0	0	0
0	S_F	20	0	0	0	0	0	0	0	1	0	0	1	0
P_4	P_u	10	3	5	6	0	0	0	0	0	1	-1	0	0
0	S_A	8	1.8	2.3	3	0	0	0	0	0	0	0	0	1
	Z_j	10	3	5	6	0	0	0	0	0	1	-1	0	0
	$C_j - Z_j$		-3	-5	-6	0	0	0	0	0	0	1	0	0
	Z_j	20	9	11.5	13	0	0	0	1	-1	0	0	0	0
	$C_j - Z_j$		-9	-11.5	-13	0	0	0	0	1	0	0	0	0
	Z_j	19	5	8	9.5	0	0	1	0	0	0	0	0	0
	$C_j - Z_j$		-5	-8	-9.5	0	0	0	0	0	0	0	0	0
	Z_j	4	1	1	1	1	-1	0	0	0	0	0	0	0
	$C_j - Z_j$		-1	-1	-1	0	1	0	0	0	0	0	0	0

13-29 We define the following variables:

M = number of Monet prints produced per month
R = number of Renoir prints produced per month
D = number of Degas prints produced per month
D_{up} = amount the profit goal is underachieved
D_{op} = amount the profit goal is overachieved
D_{ud} = amount the Degas goal is underachieved
D_{od} = amount the Degas goal is overachieved
S_1 = slack in the manpower constraint; also the amount the manpower goal is underachieved

Objective: Minimize $P_1 D_{up} + P_2 D_{ud} + P_3 S_1$

S.T. $26M + 22R + 28D + D_{up} - D_{op} = 300{,}000$ profit goal
$1D + D_{ud} - D_{od} = 1500$ Degas goal
$6.1M + 5.2R + 5.3D + S_1 = 60{,}000$ labor constraint

Note that the slack term in the labor constraint is S_1. This variable, representing unused labor man-hours per month, also is a goal value in the objective function. We could have expressed some variable, D_{um}, as the amount we underachieved the manpower goal (we can never overachieve the goal of zero idle man-hours per month). The goal constraint with D_{um} would then be:

$D_{um} - S_1 = 0$

In effect, this constraint only specifies $D_{um} = S_1$. Thus to add a constraint of this type adds an unnecessary constraint and an unnecessary variable.

The first tableau becomes:

			0	0	0	P_3	P_1	0	P_2	0
C_j	Mix	Qty.	M	R	D	S_1	D_{up}	D_{op}	D_{ud}	D_{od}
P_1	D_{up}	300,000	26	22	28	0	1	-1	0	0
P_2	D_{ud}	1,500	0	0	1	0	0	0	1	-1
P_3	S_1	60,000	6.1	5.2	5.3	1	0	0	0	0
	Z_j	60,000	6.1	5.2	5.3	1	0	0	0	0
	$C_j - Z_j$		-6.1	-5.2	-5.3	-1	0	0	0	0
	Z_j	1,500	0	0	1	0	0	0	1	-1
	$C_j - Z_j$		0	0	-1	0	0	0	0	1
	Z_j	300,000	26	22	28	0	1	-1	0	0
	$C_j - Z_j$		-26	-22	-28	0	0	1	0	0

13-30 Let X_1 = thousands funded for Agriculture
       X_2 = thousands funded for Housing
       X_3 = thousands funded for Education
       X_4 = thousands funded for Interior
       X_5 = thousands funded for Environment
       D_{UD} = thousands district goal underachieved
       D_{OD} = thousands district goal overachieved
       D_{UN} = thousands Native American goal underachieved
       D_{ON} = thousands Native American goal overachieved
       D_{UF} = thousands farmers goal underachieved
       D_{OF} = thousands farmers goal overachieved

Objective: Min $Z = 1 D_{UD} + 1 D_{UN} + 1 D_{UF}$

Subject to:

$.12X_1 + .03X_2 + .03X_3 + .04X_4 + .01X_5 + 1D_{UD} - 1D_{OD} = 160$
district goal
$.06X_1 + .04X_2 + .20X_3 + .45X_4 + .20X_5 + 1D_{UN} - 1D_{ON} = 600$
Native American goal
$.89X_1 + .15X_2 + .08X_3 + 0 X_4 + .16X_5 + 1D_{UF} - 1D_{OF} = 1200$
farmers goal
$1X_1 + 1X_2 + 1X_3 + 1X_4 + 1X_5 \leq 2210$
budget constraint
$X_1 \leq 1287$
max. Ag.
$X_2 \leq 1873$
max. Ho.
$X_3 \leq 964$
max. Ed.
$X_4 \leq 775$
max. In.
$X_5 \leq 1053$
max. En.

all variables ≥ 0 nonnegativity

13-31 (a) According to the optimal solution:

Program	Funding (thousands of $)
Agriculture- Line 17	1,287
Housing- Line 263	0
Education- Line 37	0
Interior- Line 22	775
Environment- Line 272	148

Goals	Thousands	Met?	Shortfall (thousands of $)
District	160	Yes	------
N. Amer.	600	No	144.43
Farmers	1,200	No	30.89

The district goal is overachieved by $26.92 thousand, while the other two goals are not achieved.

(b) The shadow price for the total budget constraint indicates $0.36 improvement in the goals objective per $1 increase in the budget. The range over which the .36 shadow price is valid is:

Lower bound	Current	Upper bound
2062	2210	2403

The $100 proposed increase is within the bounds, so the $.36 figure is valid, and Olympia should fight for the budget increase.

(c) Using the change vectors for a $100 thousand increase in budget:

Basic Variable	Old Solution	(CV)(Change) =		New Solution
X_4	775.00	(0)(100) =	0	775.00
$D_{U\,N}$	144.43	(−.20)(100) =	−20	124.43
$D_{U\,F}$	30.89	(−.16)(100) =	−16	14.89
X_5	148.00	(1)(100) =	100	248.00
X_1	1287.00	(0)(100) =	0	1287.00
X2 slack	1873.00	(0)(100) =	0	1873.00
X3 slack	964.00	(0)(100) =	0	964.00
$D_{O\,D}$	26.92	(.01)(100) =	1	27.92
X5 slack	905.00	(−1)(100) =	−100	805.00

With the additional $100 thousand, neither Agriculture-Line 17 (X_1) nor Interior-Line 22 (X_4) will change funding levels-- both are at their limits. The entire $100 thousand will go to increase Environment- Line 272 (X_5) from $148 thousand to $248 thousand. As far as goals are concerned, the change vectors give us the following:

Goal	Old solution Underach.	Overach.	New solution Underach.	Overach.
District		26.92		27.92
N. Amer.	144.43		124.43	
Farmers	30.89		14.89	
	175.32	26.92	139.32	27.92

(d) From the reduced costs for X_2, housing, we find an additional dollar funded for the Housing program would result in a 17 cent increase in the total amount of goal underachievement. An additional dollar given up to X_3, education, results in only an 8-cents degradation in goals.

CHAPTER 14

WAITING LINES

14-1 Using equation 14-4 to find the time waiting in line:

$$W_q = \frac{\lambda}{\mu(\mu - \lambda)} = \frac{30}{40(40 - 30)} = .075 \text{ hrs.} = 4.5 \text{ minutes}$$

Therefore, on the average she can complete lunch within the 30 minute lunch hour.

14-2 With the proposed new policy we find the mean time in the system which represents unproductive time of the repair people:

$$W_s = \frac{1}{\mu - \lambda} = \frac{1}{90 - 40} = .02 \text{ day per arrival.}$$

Cost($/day) = (.02 day/arr.)(40 arr./day)($90/day) + $70/day
            = $142 per day

With current pilferage losses running at $160 per day, it is more cost-effective to adopt the new service desk policy.

14-3 We use equation 14-10 to find the percent of time spent scheduling conference rooms.

With the manual system:

$$P_w = \frac{12}{16} = .75$$

so 25% of the time or (.25)(8) = 2 hours/day are available for other productive work.

With the computerized system:

$$P_w = \frac{12}{26} = .46$$

so 54% of the time or (.54)(8) = 4.3 hours/day are available for other productive work.

Use of the computerized system frees up over 2 hours/day of additional productive time.

14-4 Assuming the fast worker, we compute the mean out of service time as:

$$W_s = \frac{1}{\mu - \lambda} = \frac{1}{5 - 3} = .5 \text{ hours per lathe}$$

Expenses ($/hr) = (3 lathes/hr)(.5 hr/lathe)($80/hr) + $18/hr
= $138 per hour

With the slower worker, the computed mean out of service time is:

$$W_s = \frac{1}{4 - 3} = 1 \text{ hour per lathe}$$

Expenses ($/hr) = (3)(1)(80) + 10 = $250 per hour

With both hired assumed to be a team of one:

$$\mu = 5 + 4 = 9 \text{ repairs per hour}$$

$$W_s = \frac{1}{9 - 3} = .16667 \text{ hours per lathe}$$

Expenses ($/hr) = (3)(.16667)(80) + 18 + 10 = $68/hr

Both workers should be hired.

14-5 With this problem we use equation 14-4 to compute μ, given W_q is 4 hours.

$$W_q = \frac{\lambda}{\mu(\mu-\lambda)}; \quad 4 = \frac{7}{\mu(\mu-7)}$$

$$4\mu^2 - 28\mu - 7 = 0$$

Using the quadratic equation:

$$\mu = \frac{28 + \sqrt{784 + 112}}{8} = 7.242 \text{ trucks per hour}$$

14-6   Assuming that the conditions of Poisson arrivals and
       exponential service times are satisfied, we have a single-
       channel queuing model:

Given: λ = 25 jobs/hr
         μ = (1/2)(60) = 30 jobs/hr

If we let μ^* be the service rate of the faster machine:

       μ^* = 60 jobs/hr

Using the equation for the single-channel model, we have:

	Present machine	Faster machine
Mean length of system	5 typists	.71 typist
Mean length of queue	4.17 typists	.30 typist
Mean time waiting in system	.200 hr	.029 hr
Mean time waiting in queue	.167 hr	.012 hr

COST EVALUATION, $/DAY:

	Typist cost	Rental cost	Total cost
Present	(5)($6/hr)(8 hr/day) =$240	$ 6	$246
Faster	(.71)($6/hr)(8 hr/day) =$ 34	$60	$ 94

Obviously Beth is much better off renting the faster
machine. She can reduce the average number of typists at
the duplicating center by 5 - .71 = 4.29 people.
Therefore, it is not necessary to hire new typists.

14-7   With a normally distributed service time, we have:

$$\mu = \frac{60}{1.5} = 40 \text{ per hour}$$

$$\sigma = \frac{.2}{60} = .00333 \text{ hr}$$

$$\sigma^2 = .00001111$$

Using equations 14-6 through 14-9, we have:

$$L_q = \frac{(30)^2(.00001111) + (30/40)^2}{2(1 - 30/40)} = \frac{.01 + .5625}{.5} = 1.145$$

$L_s = 1.145 + .75 = 1.895$

$W_q = 1.895/30 = .06317$ hr $= 3.79$ minutes

$W_s = .06317 + .025 = .08817$ hr $= 5.29$ minutes

The expense is $(.08817)(12) = \$1.06$ per truck.

14-8   We use equations 14-6 through 14-9 for a single channel model with any service time distribution.

$\sigma^2 = (2/8)^2 = .0625$ days^2

$L_q = \dfrac{(10)^2(.0625) + (10/11)^2}{2(1 - 10/11)} = \dfrac{7.0764}{.181818} = 38.92$ claims

$L_s = 38.92 + 10/11 = 39.83$ claims

$W_q = 38.92/10 = 3.89$ days

$W_s = 3.89 + 1/11 = 3.98$ days average time in system.

14-9   Equations 14-6 through 14-10 apply to this system assuming arrivals are distributed Poisson.

$P_w = \dfrac{\lambda}{\mu} = .80$ where $\mu = 2$ per hour

$\lambda = (.80)(2) = 1.6$ arrivals per hour

$\sigma^2 = (10/60)^2 = .02778$ hr^2

$L_q = \dfrac{(1.6)^2(.02778) + (.8)^2}{2(1 - .8)} = 1.7778$

$L_s = 1.7778 + .80 = 2.5778$

$W_q = \dfrac{1.7778}{1.6} = 1.1111$ hr $= 66.67$ minutes

$W_s = 1.1111 + \tfrac{1}{2} = 1.6111$ hr $= 96.67$ minutes at her
workstation

14-10   We wish to compute M such that $P_M = .05$ or less.

Given $\lambda = 20$ arrivals per hour and $\mu = 60/2.5 = 24$ customers per hour.

We now use a trial and error approach using equations 14-11 and 14-13.

318

M	P_0	P_M
5	.2506	.1007
7	.2172	.0606
8	.2067	.0481

Therefore, the restaurant should allow for 8 spaces including the service area space.

14-11 Since 6 cars can wait, the maximum number in the system includes 6 plus one auto being serviced: M = 7. We use equations 14-11 through 14-13.

$$P_0 = \frac{1 - (10/12)}{1 - (10/12)^8} = .2172$$

$$P_w = 1 - .2172 = .7828 \text{ or about 78.3\% busy working inspections}$$

$$P_m = (10/12)^7 (.2172) = .061 \text{ or a bit over 6\% of the customers lost.}$$

14-12 Using equations 14-11 and 14-13:

We can solve by trial and error using different values of M:

M	P_0	P_m
5	.3041	.0722
6	.2885	.0513
7	.2778	.0371

She needs a rotary system with seven incoming lines in order to ensure less than 5% lost calls.

14-13 We use the limited queue model, equations 14-11 and 14-13:
At 8 arrivals/hour and M=4:

$$P_0 = \frac{1 - (8/9)}{1 - (8/9)^5} = \frac{.1111}{.4451} = .2496$$

$$P_m = (8/9)^4 (.2496) = .1558$$

At 5 arrivals/hour and M=4:

$$P_0 = \frac{1 - (5/9)}{1 - (5/9)^5} = \frac{.4444}{.9471} = .4692$$

$$P_m = (5/9)^4 (.4692) = .0447$$

Lost profit at 8 arrivals per hour = (.1558)(8)(4 hr)($20)
= $99.71 per day

Lost profit at 5 arrivals per hour = (.0447)(5)(4 hr)($20)
= $1.88 per day

He would be willing to spend up to 99.71 − 1.88 = $97.83 per day.

14-14 With one attendant, the mean waiting time is:

$$W_s = \frac{1}{\mu - \lambda} = \frac{1}{50 - 45} = .2 \text{ hr/arrival}$$

Expenses ($/hr) = (45)(.2)(15) + 10 = $145 per hour

With two attendants where $P_0 = .379375$ (interpolated).

$$L_s = \frac{(45)(50)(45/50)^2}{(1)!(100-45)^2} (.379375) + \frac{45}{50} = 1.1286$$

$$W_s = \frac{L_s}{\lambda} = \frac{1.1286}{45} = .0251 \text{ hr/arrival}$$

Expenses ($/hr) = (.0251)(45)(15) + 20 = $36.94 hour

With three attendants where $P_0 = .40346$:

$$L_s = \frac{(45)(50)(45/40)^3}{(2)!(150-45)^3} (.40346) + \frac{45}{50} = .93$$

$$W_s = \frac{L_s}{\lambda} = \frac{.93}{45} = .0207 \text{ hr/arrival}$$

Expenses ($/hr) = (.0207)(45)(15) + 30 = $43.97/hour

The optimal number of attendants is two.

14-15 In order to ensure the arrivals can be handled, at least 500/60 = 8.3333 clerks must be provided. So for a first attempt, we try 9 clerks.

$$P_0 = .00012$$

$$L_s = \frac{(500)(60)(500/60)^9}{(8)!(540-500)^2} (.00012) + \frac{500}{60} = 19.15$$

$$W_s = \frac{19.15}{500} = .0383 \text{ hours/student} = 2.3 \text{ minutes/student}$$

Consequently, 9 clerks are adequate.

14-16 With 2 servers the mean length of the queue, L_q, is:

$$L_q = \frac{(30)(20)(30/20)^2}{(1)!(40-30)^2}(.1429) = 1.9292$$

If he expands to 3 servers, where $P_0 = .21053$:

$$L_q = \frac{(30)(20)(30/20)^2}{(2)!(60-30)^2}(.21053) = .2368$$

This is a reduction in mean line length which is more than 50%. Therefore, three washers is adequate.

14-17 At least 60/40 = 1.5 nurses are needed. We try first k = 2 nurses.

$$P_0 = .1429$$

$$L_s = \frac{(60)(40)(60/40)^2}{(1)!(80-60)^2}(.1429) + \frac{60}{40} = 3.4292$$

$$W_s = \frac{L_s}{\lambda} = \frac{3.4292}{40} = .08573 \text{ hr/pat.} = 5.1437 \text{ min/patient}$$

The average total time required to receive the shots is less than 15 minutes. Therefore 2 nurses are adequate.

14-18 a) $P_0 = \frac{1-(\lambda/\mu)}{1-(\lambda/\mu)^{m+1}} = \frac{1-(30/40)}{1-(30/40)^5} = .328$

b) $P_w = 1-P_0 = .672$

c) $P_m = (\lambda/\mu)^m P_0 = (30/40)^4(.328) = .104$

$$L_s = \frac{P_w - M(\lambda/\mu)P_m}{1-(\lambda/\mu)} = \frac{.672-(4)(.75)(.104)}{1-.75} = 1.44 \text{ members}$$

$$W_s = \frac{L_s}{\lambda(1-P_m)} = \frac{1.44}{(30)(1-.104)} = .0536 \text{ hours} = 3.21 \text{ min}$$

d) From part c, P_m = .104 is the proportion of customers lost. In eight hours (30)(8)(.104) = 25 customers per 8-hour day.

14-19 The current profit per hour is (500)(1) = $500. With one more machine and 750 customers per hour, profit becomes (750)(.80) = $600 per hour. Adding 2 more machines gives a profit of (750)(.60) = $450 per hour. Therefore, we investigate the option of adding one more machine giving a total of 2 machines.

At k = 2, λ = 750 and μ = 600, P_0 = .23081

$$L_s = \frac{(750)(600)(750/600)^2}{(1)!(1200-750)^2}(.23081) + \frac{750}{600} = 2.051$$

W_s = L_s/750 = .0027 hours << 4 hours

The second machine should be added.

14-20 Given: λ = 20 students/hr
μ = 7 students/hr
k = 4 physicians

The mean length of the system, L_s is:

$$L_s = \frac{\lambda\mu(\lambda/\mu)^k}{(k-1)!(k\mu-\lambda)^2} \; P_0 + \frac{\lambda}{\mu}$$

and from Appendix Table 5, P_0 = .04645. Thus,

$$L_s = \frac{(20)(7)(20/7)^4}{(4-1)!(28-20)^2}(.04645) + \frac{20}{7}$$

$$= \frac{9329.45}{(6)(64)}(.04645) + \frac{20}{7}$$

$$= 3.99 \text{ students}$$

(a) The average time spent in the clinic is:

$$W_s = \frac{L_s}{\lambda} = \frac{3.99}{20}$$

$$= 0.19928 \text{ hr, or 12 minutes}$$

(b) The average number of students in the waiting room is:

$$W_q = \frac{L_q}{\lambda} = \frac{L_s - \lambda/\mu}{\lambda}$$

$$= \frac{3.99 - 20/7}{20}$$

$$= .057 \text{ student}$$

(c) The clinic's utilization factor is:

$$P_w = \frac{1}{k!}\left(\frac{\lambda}{\mu}\right)^k \frac{k\mu}{k\mu-\lambda} P_0$$

$$= \frac{1}{4!}\left(\frac{20}{7}\right)^4 \left(\frac{28}{28-20}\right) (.04645)$$

$$= .4510$$

14-21 This is a multiple channel model. Therefore, we use the equations for this model to compute the following values:

	Number of clerks		
	2	3	4
Mean no. of machinists in the system	4.72	0.78	0.68
Mean no. of machinists in the queue	4.05	0.11	0.01
Mean time spent in system by machinist	0.118	0.020	0.017
Mean time spent in queue by machinist	0.101	0.003	0.003

The total costs for each option are:

Machinists' cost/day	Clerk's cost/day

2 clerks (4.72)(8 hr)($14/hr) = $528.64 (2)(8 hr)($10/hr)=$160
      Total = $688.64

3 clerks (.78)(8 hr)($14/hr) = $ 87.36 (3)(8 hr)($10/hr)=$240
      Total = $327.36

4 clerks (.68)(8 hr)($14/hr) = $ 76.16 (4)(8 hr)($10/hr)=$320
      Total = $396.16

The most cost-effective alternative is to hire 1 more clerk, bringing the total number of clerks to 3.

14-22   This is a multiple-channel queuing system with
λ = 400 people/hr
μ = 100 people/hr
W_s = ≤ 1 hr
K = ?

We will solve the problem with trial and error, starting with k = 5 (when k=4, kμ = 400 = λ, which is not feasible), and compute W_s. When we arrive at a value for k such as W_s ≤ 1 hour, we have a minimum number of technicians required. First, try k = 5:

P_0 = .0130   from Appendix Table 5

$$L_s = \frac{\lambda \mu (\lambda/\mu)^k}{(k-1)!(k\mu-\lambda)^2} P_0 + \frac{\lambda}{\mu}$$

$$= \frac{(400)(100)(400/100)^5}{(4)!(500-400)^2}(.0130) + \frac{400}{100}$$

= 6.22 persons

W_s = L_s /λ

= 6.22/400

= .016 hr

Therefore, 5 medical technicians can easily handle the job.

14-23   The solution to this problem uses the table of random numbers found in Appendix Table 6.

Since 2 is the expected number of arrivals in any 10-minute period, we have arbitrarily let the appearance of either 3 or 6 represent an arrival.

We begin the simulation using row #1 of the table of random numbers, and continue it through a simulated 3-hour period, using each row in turn.

10 Minute Period Number	Number of Arrivals
1	2
2	1
3	2
4	2
5	3
6	0
7	0
8	2
9	1

(Continued)

10	3
11	1
12	3
13	2
14	2
15	2
16	1
17	1
18	2

Concerning the point within the 10-minute interval at which each arrival takes place, we have defined the following conventions for this solution:

a. If there be one arrival, it shall be assumed to arrive at the beginning of the first minute.
b. If there be two arrivals, one shall be assumed to arrive at the beginning of the first minute, the other at the beginning of the sixth minute.
c. If there be three arrivals, one shall be assumed to arrive at the beginning of the first minute, one at the beginning of the fourth minute, and one at the beginning of the seventh minute.

Results summary:

1 attendant:

```
        Total waiting time in 3 hours = 604 minutes
        Total time per 8-hour shift = 1611 minutes
                                    = 26.8 hours
                                    x $8.00/hour
            Waiting time cost =$214.40
         Attendant's wage/day =  40.00
            Total daily cost =$254.40
```

2 attendants:

```
        Total waiting time in 3 hours = 5½ minutes
        Total waiting time per 8-hour shift = 14.7 minutes
                                            = .245 hours
                                            x $8.00/hour
            Waiting time cost =$ 1.96
       2 attendant's wages/day = 80.00
            Total daily cost =$81.96
```

Further simulation with respect to three attendants is not necessary because even if three attendants did remove all of the waiting time, their combined wages per day would be $120, which, of course, is higher than the total cost obtained with the optimum alternative (e.g., 2 attendants).

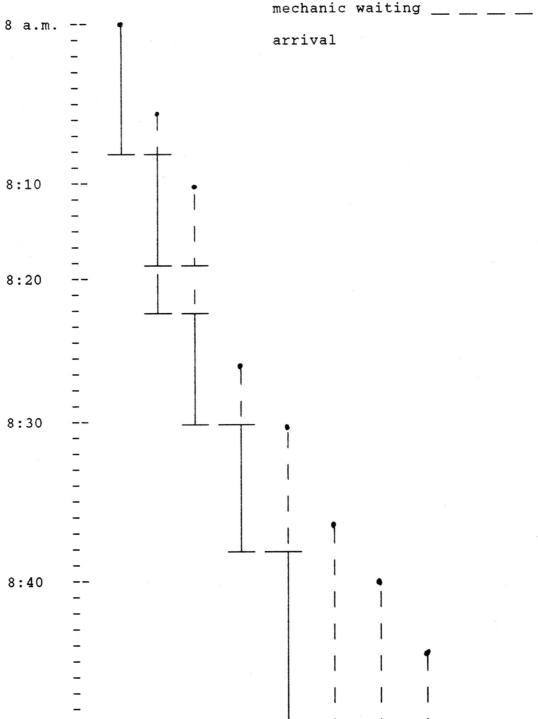

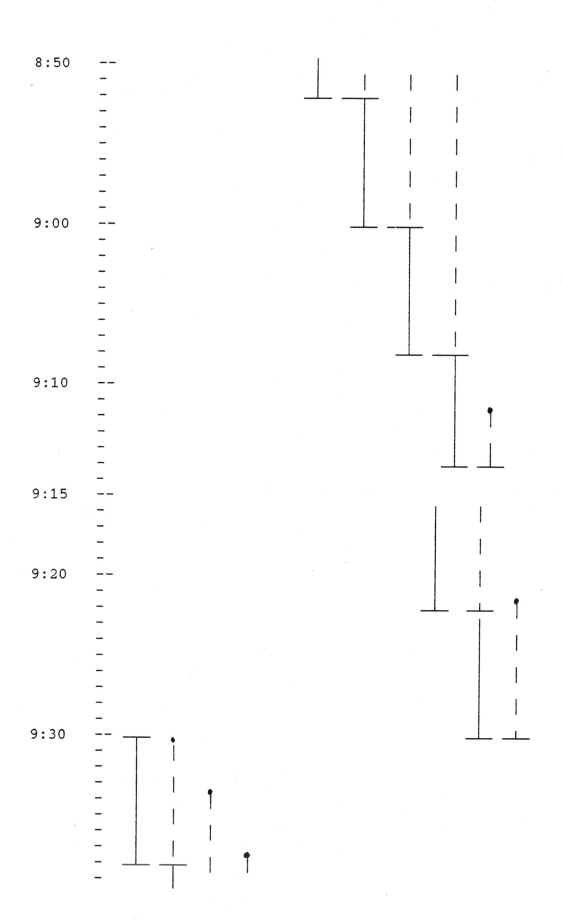

327

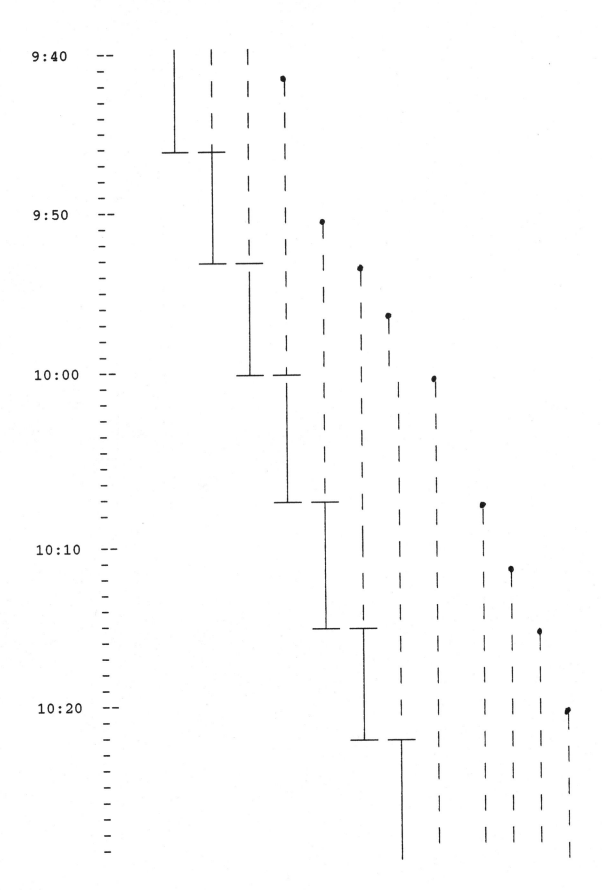

9:40

9:50

10:00

10:10

10:20

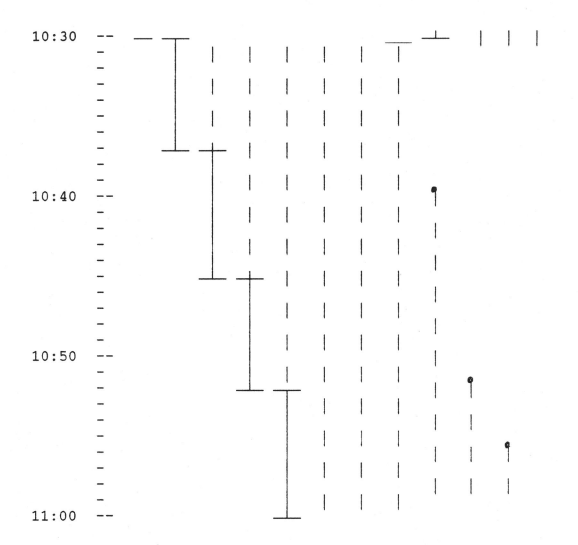

SIMULATION WITH TWO ATTENDANTS:

329

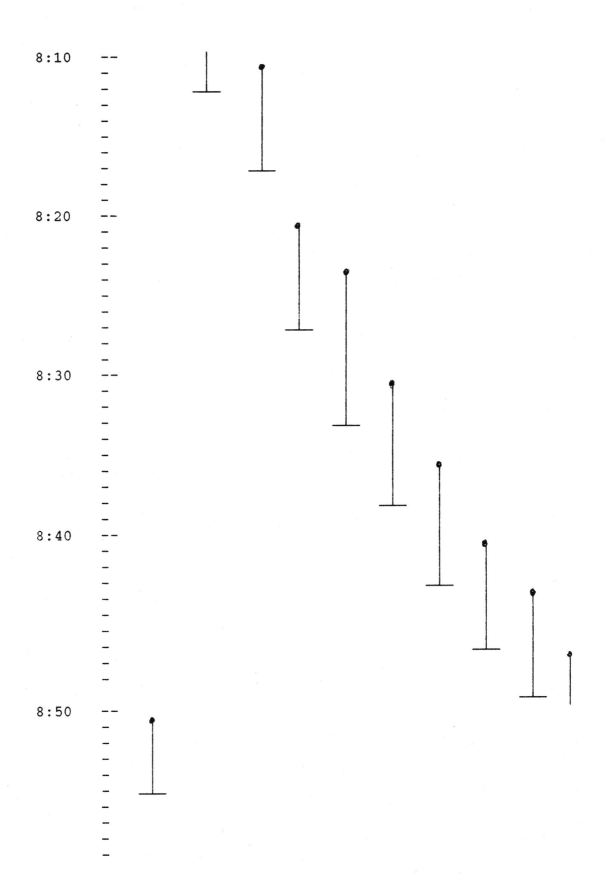

8:10

8:20

8:30

8:40

8:50

330

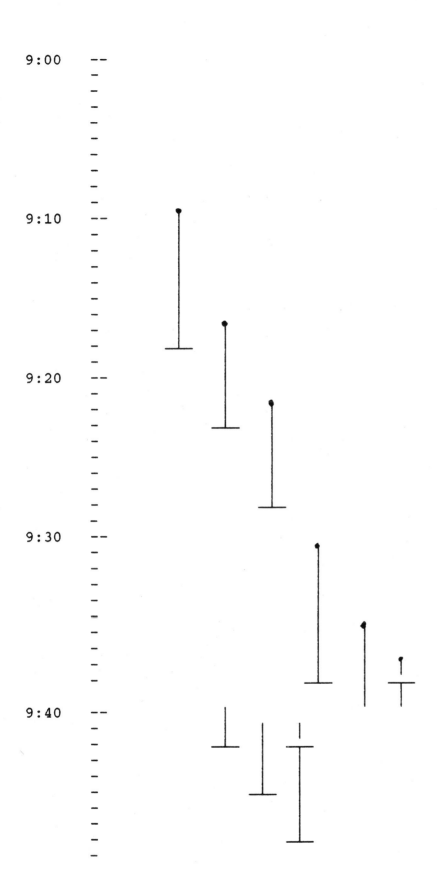

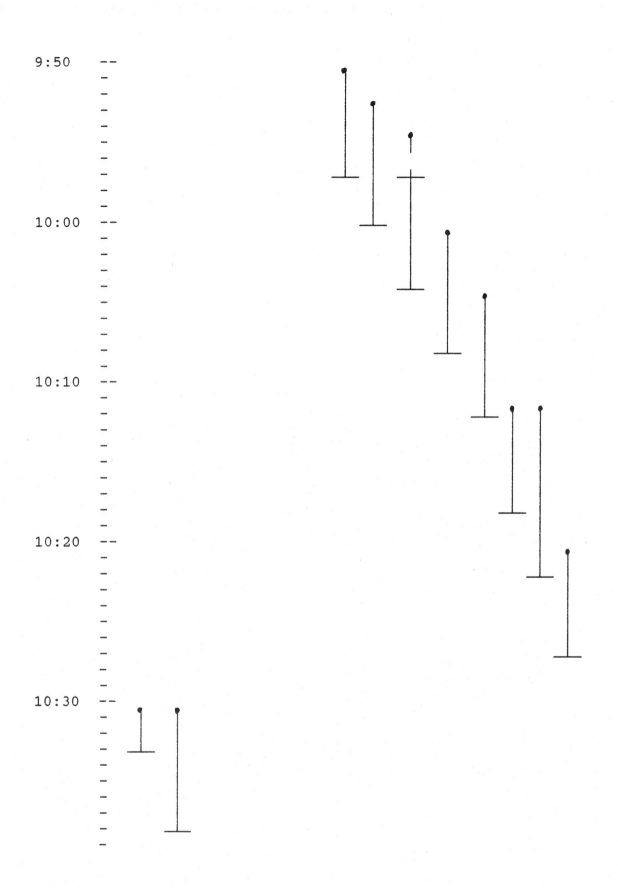

332

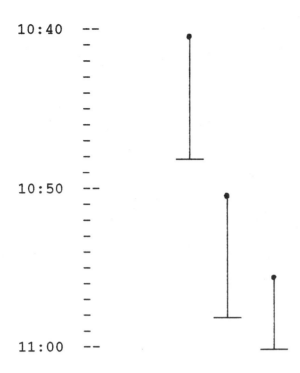

```
10:40  --
        -
        -
        -
        -
        -
        -
        -
        -
        -
10:50  --
        -
        -
        -
        -
        -
        -
        -
        -
        -
11:00  --
```

14-24   The assigned random numbers for arrival deviation are:

Simulated event	RN range
No show	00 - 09
On time	10 - 69
½ hr early	70 - 84
½ hr late	85 - 99

We will use the normal distribution table given in exercise 11 of chapter 15 to simulate the normally distributed service times. The two leftmost random numbers will be drawn down column 4 of Appendix Table 6 for arrivals and the four leftmost numbers from column 5 for service times.

Assuming the first patient is scheduled for an 8 a.m. appointment, and assuming the doctor is always available to serve an early arrival, we have:

Patient	RN	Actual Arrival	RN	Service Time	Start	Finish	Waiting
1	83	7:30	4637	29	7:30	7:59	
2	70	8:00	6472	34	8:00	8:34	
3	06	no show	0933	17			
4	12	9:30	4890	30	9:30	10:00	
5	59	10:00	9776	50	10:00	10:50	
6	46	10:30	2229	22	10:50	11:12	20
7	54	11:00	2966	25	11:12	11:37	12
8	04	no show	0140	8			

(Continued)

Patient	RN	Actual Arrival	RN	Service Time	Start:Finish		Waiting
9	51	12:00	4011	27	12:00	12:27	
10	99	1:00	7544	37	1:00	1:37	
11	84	12:30	1074	18	12:30	12:48	
12	81	1:00	0927	17	1:37	1:54	37
13	15	2:00	7016	35	2:00	2:35	
14	36	2:30	4141	28	2:35	3:03	5
15	12	3:00	4020	28	3:03	3:31	3
16	54	3:30	3768	27	3:31	3:58	1
							78

The average waiting time is 78/14 = 5.57 minutes.
The doctor is idle for 1 hour and 41 minutes during the simulated day.

14-25 The current waiting time is obtained using equation 14-3, which gives mean waiting in the system.

$$W_s = \frac{1}{\mu - \lambda} = \frac{1}{6 - 3} = .3333 \text{ hours/customers}$$

With two bays we use equations 14-6 and 14-8. From Appendix Table 5, $P_0 = .6$ (estimated)

$$L_s = \frac{\lambda \mu (\lambda/\mu)^k}{(k-1)!(k\mu-\lambda)^2} P_0 + \frac{\lambda}{\mu} = \frac{(3)(6)(3/6)^2}{(1)(12-3)^2}(.6) + \frac{3}{6}$$

$$L_s = .5333$$

$$W_s = \frac{L_s}{\lambda} = \frac{.5333}{3} = .1778 \text{ hours/customer}$$

The waiting time is reduced by slightly more than half. Therefore, the second bay should be added.

14-26 For one crew working with exponentially distributed service time:

$$L_s = \frac{3}{4 - 3} = 3 \text{ skidders}$$

Cost ($/hr) = (60)(3) + (5)(8.50) = $222.50 per hour
skidder wait plus crew cost.

With the offloader option, normally distributed:

$\mu = 7$ skidders per hour

$\sigma^2 = (2/60)^2 = .001111$

334

Using equations 14-6 and 14-7:

$$L_q = \frac{(3)^2 (.001111) + (3/7)^2}{2 (1 - 3/7)} = \frac{.19367}{1.14286} = .16946 \text{ skidders}$$

$$L_s = .16946 + .42857 = .59803 \text{ skidders}$$

$$\begin{aligned} \text{Cost (\$/hr)} &= (60)(.59803) + (2)(5)(8.50) \\ &= \$120.88 \text{ per hour skidder wait plus} \\ &\quad \text{offloader cost} \end{aligned}$$

With two crews $P_0 = .45461$

$$L_s = \frac{(3)(4)(3/4)^2}{(1)!(8-3)^2} (.45461) + \frac{3}{4} = .8727 \text{ skidders}$$

$$\begin{aligned} \text{Cost (\$/hr)} &= (.8727)(60) + 14 + (2)(5)(8.50) \\ &= \$151.36 \text{ per hour skidder wait plus} \\ &\quad \text{two crews} \end{aligned}$$

The most effective option is to use the offloader.

14-27

$$P_0 = \frac{1 - (\lambda/\mu)}{1 - (\lambda/\mu)^{m+1}}$$

at m = 5   at m = 7

$$P_0 = \frac{1 - (20/40)}{1 - (20/40)^6} = \frac{.5}{.9844} \qquad P_0 = \frac{1 - (20/40)}{1 - (20/40)^8} = \frac{.5}{.9961}$$

$$P_0 = .508 \qquad\qquad\qquad\qquad P_0 = .502$$

$$P_m = (\lambda/\mu)^m P_0$$

at m = 5

$$P_m = (.5)^5 (.508) \qquad\qquad P_m = (.5)^7 (.502)$$
$$P_m = .0159 \qquad\qquad\qquad P_m = .0039$$

The proportion of lost customers is so low with 4 waiting spaces that very little is gained by adding two or more slots.

14-28 Assuming exponential service time and using equation 14-1:

$$L_q = \frac{\lambda^2}{\mu(\mu-\lambda)} = \frac{6^2}{(10)(10-6)} = 0.9 \text{ jobs in queue}$$

Assuming any service distribution and using equation 14-6:

$$L_q = \frac{\lambda^2 \sigma^2 + (\lambda/\mu)^2}{2(1-\lambda/\mu)} \qquad \text{where } \sigma^2 = (5/60)^2 = .00694 \text{ hr}^2$$

$$L_q = \frac{(6)^2(.00694) + (.6)^2}{2(1-.6)} = \frac{.25 + .36}{.80} = .7625 \text{ jobs in queue}$$

The queue length is slightly longer assuming the exponential distribution.

14-29   The assumptions are:

a. Poisson arrivals
b. Exponential service times
c. No line switching
d. The lines are selected randomly by the arrivals which gives X single-channel servers and:
$\lambda = 110/X$ during peak hours
$\lambda = 60/X$ during normal hours
$\lambda = 30/X$ during low hours

A. During peak periods: where $\mu = 60/5 = 12$ per hour and desired $W_q = 15$ minutes $= .25$ hours:

$$W_q = .25 = \frac{110/X}{\mu(\mu - 110/X)} = \frac{110}{12(12X - 110)}$$

$$12X - 110 = \frac{110}{(12)(.25)}$$

$$X = 12.22$$

So, 13 counters must be open to ensure the average waiting time does not exceed 15 minutes.

B. During normal periods:

$$W_q = .167 = \frac{60}{12(12X - 60)}$$

$$12X - 60 = \frac{60}{(12)(.167)}$$

$$X = 7,500, \text{ so 8 counters must be open.}$$

C. During low periods:

$$W_q = .083 = \frac{30}{12(12X - 30)}$$

$$12X - 30 = \frac{30}{(12)(.083)}$$

$$X = 5, \text{ so } 5 \text{ counters must be open.}$$

14-30 Using equation 14-5 to find μ:

$$\mu = \frac{\lambda}{P_w} = \frac{20}{.80} = 25 \text{ customers/hour}$$

From equation 14-3:

$$W_q = \frac{\lambda}{\mu(\mu-\lambda)} = \frac{20}{(25)(5)} = 0.16 \text{ hour} = 9.6 \text{ minutes}$$

14-31 R = number of parents each hour who wish to buy prints.

Say, for example, the 6 sets of parents arrive at 10:00, then we assume:

if R = 1 they wish to buy at 10:00
   R = 2 they wish to buy at 10:00 and 10:30
   R = 3 they wish to buy at 10:00, 10:20, 10:40
   R = 4 they wish to buy at 10:00, 10:15, 10:30, 10:45
   R = 5 they wish to buy at 10:00, 10:12, 10:24, 10:36, 10:48
   R = 6 they wish to buy at 10:00. 10:10, 10:20, 10:30, 10:40, 10:50

From Appendix Table 2 in the text:

at R = .50, N = 6:

Event	Range of Random Numbers
R = 0	.9999 - .9844
R = 1	.9844 - .8906
R = 2	.8906 - .6563
R = 3	.6563 - .3438
R = 4	.3438 - .1094
R = 5	.1094 - .0156
R = 6	.0156 - .0000

The service times:

Time	Random number
10	0
15	1,2
20	3,4,5,6,7
25	8
30	9

We will draw random numbers from Appendix Table 6 drawing a five-digit sequence from Column 3 to designate number of buyers each hour, and drawing a single number beginning in Column 4 to designate service times of the buyers.

The summary is as follows (beginning at 9 a.m.):

		Service Times (minutes)										
		No. of	Buyer #1		Buyer #2		Buyer #3		Buyer #4		...
Time		Buyers	RN	Time	RN	Time	RN	Time	RN	Time	
9:00	82621	2	8	25	3	20					
10:00	30892	4	7	20	4	20	8	25	5	20	
11:00	95861	1	6	20							
12:00	11652	4	0	10	4	20	9	30	7	20	
1:00	18824	4	0	10	5	20	5	20	5	20	
2:00	12963	4	0	10	8	25	7	20	6	20	
3:00	96708	1	7	20							
4:00	52913	3	0	10	6	20	8	25			

Designating the 23 prospective buyers as 1 to 23, their assumed time of wishing to see a representative is:

No.	Time	No.	Time	No.	Time	No.	Time
1	9:00	7	11:00	13	1:15	19	2:45
2	9:30	8	12:00	14	1:30	20	3:00
3	10:00	9	12:15	15	1:45	21	4:00
4	10:15	10	12:30	16	2:00	22	4:20
5	10:30	11	12:45	17	2:15	23	4:40
6	10:45	12	1:00	18	2:30		

The event summary is as follows for two servers:

Time		Event	Server A	Server B	Waiting	Lost Customers
9:00	1	arrives	1	---	---	---
9:25	1	departs	---	---	---	---
9:30	2	arrives	2	---	---	---
9:50	2	departs	---	---	---	---
10:00	3	arrives	3	---	---	---
10:15	4	arrives	3	4	---	---
10:20	3	departs	---	4	---	---
10:30	5	arrives	5	4	---	---
10:35	4	departs	5	---	---	---
10:45	6	arrives	5	6	---	---
10:55	5	departs	---	6	---	---
11:00	7	arrives	7	6	---	---
11:05	6	departs	7	---	---	---
11:20	7	departs	---	---	---	---
12:00	8	arrives	8	---	---	---
12:10	8	departs	---	---	---	---
12:15	9	arrives	9	---	---	---
12:30	10	arrives	9	10	---	---
12:35	9	departs	---	10	---	---
12:45	11	arrives	11	10	---	---
1:00	10	departs				
	12	arrives	11	12	---	---
1:05	11	departs	---	12	---	---
1:10	12	departs	---	---	---	---
1:15	13	arrives	13	---	---	---
1:30	14	arrives	13	14	---	---
1:35	13	departs	---	14	---	---
1:45	15	arrives	15	14	---	---
1:50	14	departs	15	---	---	---
2:00	16	arrives	15	16	---	---
2:05	15	departs	---	16	---	---
2:10	16	departs	---	---	---	---
2:15	17	arrives	17	---	---	---
2:30	18	arrives	17	18	---	---
2:40	17	departs	---	18	---	---
2:45	19	arrives	19	18	---	---
2:50	18	departs	19	---	---	---
3:00	20	arrives	19	20	---	---
3:05	19	departs	---	20	---	---
3:20	20	departs	---	---	---	---
4:00	21	arrives	21	---	---	---
4:10	21	departs	---	---	---	---
4:20	22	arrives	22	---	---	---
4:40	22	departs				
	23	arrives	23	---	---	---
5:05	23	departs	---	---	---	---

The event summary is as follows for <u>one server</u>:

Time		Event	Server	Waiting	Lost Customers
9:00	1	arrives	1	---	---
9:25	1	departs	---	---	---
9:30	2	arrives	2	---	---
9:50	2	departs	---	---	---
10:00	3	arrives	3	---	---
10:15	4	arrives	3	4	---
10:20	3	departs	4	---	---
10:30	5	arrives	4	5	---
10:40	4	departs	5	---	---
10:45	6	arrives	5	6	---
11:00	7	arrives	6	6 , 7	---
11:05	5	departs	6	7	---
11:25	6	departs	7	---	---
11:45	7	departs	---	---	---
12:00	8	arrives	8	---	---
12:10	8	departs	---	---	---
12:15	9	arrives	9	---	---
12:30	10	arrives	9	10	---
12:35	9	departs	10	---	---
12:45	11	arrives	10	11	---
1:00	12	arrives	10	11 , 12	---
1:05	10	departs	11	12	---
1:15	13	arrives	11	12 , 13	---
1:25	11	departs	12	13	---
1:30	11	arrives	12	13 , 14	---
1:35	12	departs	13	14	---
1:45	15	arrives	13	14 , 15	---
1:55	13	departs	14	15	---
2:00	16	arrives	14	15 , 16	---
2:15	14	departs			
	17	arrives	15	16 , 17	---
2:30	18	arrives	15	16 , 17	18
2:35	15	departs	16	17	---
2:45	16	departs	17		
	19	arrives	17	19	---
3:00	20	arrives	17	19 , 20	---
3:10	17	departs	19	20	---
3:30	19	departs	20	---	---
3:50	20	departs	---	---	---
4:00	21	arrives	21	---	---
4:10	21	departs	---	---	---
4:20	22	arrives	22	---	---
4:40	22	departs			
	23	arrives	23	---	---
5:05	23	departs	---	---	---

On the basis of this limited simulation, one server should be used. Only one customer is lost ($20 profit loss), but the $40 cost of a second server is saved.

340

14-32   Sam rationalized that the English department, by only
        having 1 faculty member on duty, viewed a single server as
        its least-cost position. To have 2 or more servers would
        increase its total costs. Sam wasn't sure how much these
        costs would rise, and so in order to give the English
        department the benefit of the doubt, he assumed that the
        1-server and 2-server cases were at identical total cost.
        Where T.C. stands for total cost and X is the value of a
        freshman's time, these costs are:

        1 server: T.C. = (1 server)($8/hr) + (55 students)($X/hr)
        2 servers: T.C. = (2 servers)($8/hr)+ (10 students)($X/hr)

        X is found by setting the two expressions to an equality:

$$(1)(8) + 55X = (2)(8) + 10X$$
$$45X = 8$$
$$X = \$0.18/hr$$

        After reading Frieda's claims in the campus paper, the
        English department scheduled 3 faculty members to assist in
        registering students for English 102 in the spring
        semester.

14-33   Using equations 14-11 and 14-13:

$$P_0 = \frac{1 - (30/45)}{1 - (30/45)^6} = \frac{.33333}{.91221} = .36541$$

        $P_m = (30/45)^5(.36541) = .0481198$ or slightly less than 5%.

14-34   Using equations 14-6, 14-8, and 14-9:

$$\sigma^2 = (1.2/60)^2 = .0004 \ hr^2$$

        $\mu = 60/2 = 30$ customers/hour

$$L_q = \frac{(24)^2(.0004) + (24/30)^2}{2(1 - 24/30)} = \frac{.2304 + .64}{.4} = 2.176$$

        $W_q = 2.176/24 = .09067$

        $W_s = .09067 + 1/30 = .124 \ hr = 7.44$ minutes in the system
        waiting and being served.

CHAPTER 15

SIMULATION

Notes (1) It should be emphasized to the students that
the purpose of these exercises is illustrative.
With such small sample sizes (length of the
simulation run) conclusive inferences cannot be
made.

(2) It is sometimes helpful in class discussions
to compare "answers." If comparable results
to the exercises are desired, the students
should be advised to use designated random
numbers as noted in each of the exercises.

15-1 We define L = late and N = not late. The possible
outcomes, probabilities, and random numbers assigned to
the outcomes are:

Outcome				Cum.	Ran. No.
Proj. 1	Proj. 2	Proj. 3	Probability	Prob.	Assigned
N	N	N	(.7)(.7)(.7)=.343	.343	000-342
L	N	N	(.3)(.7)(.7)=.147	.490	343-489
N	L	N	(.7)(.3)(.7)=.147	.637	490-636
N	N	L	(.7)(.7)(.3)=.147	.784	637-783
L	L	N	(.3)(.3)(.7)=.063	.847	784-846
L	N	L	(.3)(.7)(.3)=.063	.910	847-909
N	L	L	(.7)(.3)(.3)=.063	.973	910-972
L	L	L	(.3)(.3)(.3)=.027	1.000	973-999

15-2 In this exercise, the students can compute the probability
values of 0, 1, ..., 14 arrivals in an hourly period using
the Poisson formula given in the text as equation 2-10.
Alternatively, the students can use cumulative Poisson
distribution tables taken from a statistics text. The
values are as follows:

X(arr. per hour)	Prob(X)	Cum. Prob.	Assigned RN
0	.0183	.0183	0000-0182
1	.0733	.0916	0183-0915
2	.1465	.2381	0916-2380
3	.1954	.4335	2381-4334
4	.1954	.6289	4335-6288
5	.1563	.7852	6289-7851
6	.1042	.8894	7852-8893
7	.0595	.9489	8894-9488
8	.0298	.9787	9489-9786
9	.0132	.9919	9787-9918
10	.0053	.9972	9919-9971
11	.0019	.9991	9972-9990
12	.0006	.9997	9991-9996
13	.0002	.9999	9997-9998
14	.0001	1.0000	9999

Reading down the first column of Appendix Table 6, we find the following random numbers, and using the RN assignments given above, we simulate the following arrivals:

Hour	RN	Number of arrivals
1	1581	2
2	0928	2
3	4112	3
4	7457	5

15-3 (a) EV= (10)(.02)+(11)(.09)+(12)(.15)+(13)(.24)+(14)(.19)
+(15)(.12)+(16)(.07)+(17)(.05)+(18)(.04)+(19)(.03)
EV= 13.83

(b) The RN assignements are:

Value	Cum. Prob.	RN Range
10	.02	00 - 01
11	.11	02 - 10
12	.26	11 - 25
13	.50	26 - 49
14	.69	50 - 68
15	.81	69 - 80
16	.88	81 - 87
17	.93	88 - 92
18	.97	93 - 96
19	1.00	97 - 99

(c) We draw random numbers from Appendix 6 by reading the first two digits down column 1. Then we go to column 2 reading again only the first two digits. Finally, we read the first two digits down the third column until 100 numbers have been drawn.

(d) The value, 14, appeared nineteen times. This is 19% of the total, as expected.

1st Sample			2nd Sample			3rd Sample			4th Sample		
#	RN	Value	#	RN	Value	#	RN	Value	#	RN	Value
1	15	12	1	41	13	1	29	13	1	55	14
2	09	11	2	96	18	2	78	15	2	49	13
3	41	13	3	20	12	3	70	15	3	18	12
4	74	15	4	45	13	4	06	11	4	70	15
5	00	10	5	38	13	5	78	15	5	35	13
6	72	15	6	01	10	6	76	15	6	20	12
7	67	14	7	67	14	7	47	13	7	72	15
8	55	14	8	63	14	8	46	13	8	34	13
9	71	15	9	39	13	9	93	18	9	54	14
10	35	13	10	55	14	10	12	12	10	30	13
		132			134			140			134

5th Sample			6th Sample			7th Sample			8th Sample		
#	RN	Value	#	RN	Value	#	RN	Value	#	RN	Value
1	22	12	1	48	13	1	47	13	1	82	16
2	48	13	2	55	14	2	36	13	2	95	18
3	74	15	3	91	17	3	57	14	3	18	12
4	76	15	4	40	13	4	04	11	4	96	18
5	02	11	5	93	18	5	79	15	5	20	12
6	07	11	6	01	10	6	55	14	6	84	16
7	64	14	7	83	16	7	10	11	7	56	14
8	95	18	8	63	14	8	13	12	8	11	12
9	23	12	9	47	13	9	57	14	9	52	14
10	91	17	10	52	14	10	09	11	10	03	11
		138			142			128			143

9th Sample			10th Sample			OVERALL SUMMARY		
#	RN	Value	#	RN	Value	Sample number	Sum of values	Mean
1	51	14	1	76	15	1	132	13.2
2	40	13	2	18	12	2	134	13.4
3	34	13	3	33	13	3	140	14.0
4	38	13	4	81	16	4	134	13.4
5	72	15	5	35	13	5	138	13.8
6	11	12	6	96	18	6	142	14.2
7	50	14	7	84	16	7	128	12.8
8	55	14	8	87	16	8	143	14.3
9	08	11	9	87	16	9	131	13.1
10	11	12	10	95	18	10	153	15.3
		131			153			

Total 1375

Mean of the means 13.75

344

Sample	Mean	Sample	Mean
1	13.2	6	14.2
2	13.4	7	12.8
3	14.0	8	14.3
4	13.4	9	13.1
5	13.8	10	15.3

Overall mean = 13.75
E.V. = 13.83

15-4 We assign the following:

Yield	Prob.	Cum. Prob.	RN Assignment
120	.18	.18	00-17
140	.26	.44	18-43
160	.44	.88	44-87
180	.12	1.00	88-99

For the 10-year sample, we draw the first two digits from column 2 of Appendix Table 6.

Year	RN	Simulated yield
1	20	140
2	72	160
3	34	140
4	54	160
5	30	140
6	22	140
7	48	160
8	74	160
9	76	160
10	02	120

15-5 The assignment of random numbers are:

Price	Prob.	Cum. Prob.	RN Assigned
$2.00	.05	.05	00-04
2.10	.15	.20	05-19
2.20	.30	.50	20-49
2.30	.25	.75	50-74
2.40	.15	.90	75-89
2.50	.10	1.00	90-99

The simulated prices are developed using the first two digits reading down column 3 of Appendix Table 6. The simulated yields are taken from Exercise 15-3.

Year	RN	Price	Yield	Revenue/Acre
1	82	$2.40	140	$336
2	95	2.50	160	400
3	18	2.10	140	294
4	96	2.50	160	400
5	20	2.20	140	308
6	84	2.40	140	336
7	56	2.30	160	368
8	11	2.10	160	336
9	52	2.30	160	368
10	03	2.00	120	240

15-6 The assignment of random numbers is:

Interarrival time	Prob.	Cum. Prob.	RN Assigned
1	.17	.17	00-16
2	.25	.42	17-41
3	.25	.67	42-66
4	.20	.87	67-86
5	.13	1.00	87-99

Service time	Prob.	Cum. Prob.	RN Assigned
1	.10	.10	00-09
2	.30	.40	10-39
3	.40	.80	40-79
4	.20	1.00	80-99

Reading down column 5 of Appendix Table 6, we select the first two digits for interarrivals and the last two digits for service time.

Scheduled Events

Customer number	RN	Interarrival time	RN	Service time	Time of arrival
1	46	3	88	4	3
2	64	3	34	2	6
3	09	1	14	2	7
4	48	3	05	1	10
5	97	5	01	1	15
6	22	2	83	4	17
7	29	2	80	4	19
8	01	1	98	4	20
9	40	2	63	3	22
10	75	4	52	3	26
11	10	1	31	2	27
12	09	1	37	2	28
13	70	4	39	2	32
14	41	2	18	2	34

(Continued)

15	40	2	57	3	36
16	37	2	78	3	38
17	21	2	96	4	40
18	38	2	86	4	42
19	14	1	97	4	43
20	32	2	51	3	45

Simulated current events

Time	Event	In service	Customers waiting	Lost	Waiting time
3	1 arr.	1(4)			0
6	2 arr.	1(1)	2		1
7	1 dep.	2(2)			
	3 arr.		3		
9	2 dep.	3(2)			2
10	4 arr.	3(1)	4		
11	3 dep.	4(1)			1
12	4 dep.				
15	5 arr.	5(1)			0
16	5 dep.				
17	6 arr.	6(4)			0
19	7 arr.	6(2)	7		
20	8 arr.	6(1)	7, 8		
21	6 dep.	7(4)	8		2
22	9 arr.	7(3)	8, 9		
25	7 dep.	8(4)	9		5
26	10 arr.	8(3)	9, 10		
27	11 arr. & dep.	8(2)	9, 10	11	
28	12 arr. & dep.	8(1)		12	
29	8 dep.	9(3)	10		7
32	9 dep.	10(3)			6
	13 arr.		13		
34	14 arr.	10(1)	13, 14		
35	10 dep.	13(2)	14		3
36	15 arr.	13(1)	14, 15		
37	13 dep.	14(2)	15		3
38	16 arr.	14(1)	15, 16		
39	14 dep.	15(3)	16		3
40	17 arr.	15(2)	16, 17		
42	15 dep.	16(3)			4
	18 arr.		17, 18		
43	19 arr. & dep.	16(2)	17, 18	19	
45	16 dep.	17(4)			5
	20 arr.		18, 20		
49	17 dep.	18(4)	20		7
53	18 dep.	20(3)			8
56	20 dep.				

Total waiting time = $\overline{57}$

Note: The entries under In service are coded to show
transaction number and time to go. For example, the entry

347

15(2) at a clock time of 40 indicates that customer 15 is being served and 2 minutes of service time remain before its service will be completed.

$$\text{Mean waiting time} = \frac{57}{17} = 3.35 \text{ minutes}$$

Total lost customers = 3.

15-7 Using expected values:

Mean interarrival rate = (1)(.17) + (2)(.25)
                        + (3)(.25) + (4)(.20) + (5)(.13)
                        = 2.87 minutes

$$\text{Mean arrival rate} = \frac{1}{\text{mean interarrival rate}} = \frac{1 \text{ arrival}}{2.87 \text{ min}}$$
$$= .3484 \text{ arrivals/min}$$

Mean service time = (1)(.10) + (2)(.30) + (3)(.40)
                     + (4)(.20)
                     = 2.7 min/customer

$$\mu = \frac{1 \text{ customers}}{2.7 \text{ min}} = .3704 \text{ customers/min}$$

Using these values, $\lambda = .3484$ and $\mu = .3704$, equations 14-11 through 14-17 give:

$$P_0 = \frac{1 - (.3484/.3704)}{1 - (.3484/.3704)^4} = \frac{.059353}{.2172401}$$

$$P_0 = .2734$$

$$P_w = 1 - .2734 = .7266$$

$$P_M = (.3484/.3704)^3 (.2734) = .2275$$

$$L_s = \frac{.7266 - (3)(.9406047)(.2275)}{.0593953} = 1.4240$$

$$W_s = \frac{1.4240}{(.3484)(1-.2275)} = 5.2909 \text{ minutes}$$

$$W_q = 5.2909 - (1/.3704) = 2.5911 \text{ minutes}$$

This result is somewhat different from the mean waiting time value of 3.35 minutes obtained in simulation exercise 15-5. This difference can be attributed to the facts:
    a. The simulation was not in steady state (i.e., the warm-up period is reflected in the statistics).

b. Equations 14-11 through 14-17 assume Poisson arrivals and an exponentially distributed service time.

15-8 We assign the following random numbers to the event times:

Time	Station 1	Station 2	Station 3
4	00-24	00-09	00-04
5	25-49	10-39	05-29
6	50-74	40-79	30-54
7	75-99	80-99	55-99

Using the first two digits in columns one, two and three of Appendix Table 6, respectively, the set of simulated service times are:

	Station 1		Station 2		Station 3	
Item	RN	Time	RN	Time	RN	Time
1	15	4	20	5	82	7
2	09	4	72	6	95	7
3	41	5	34	5	18	5
4	74	6	54	6	96	7
5	00	4	30	5	20	5
6	72	6	22	5	84	7
7	67	6	48	6	56	7
8	55	6	74	6	11	5
9	71	6	76	6	52	6
10	35	5	02	4	03	4

Simulated current events

	Station 1		Station 2		Station 3	
Item	Start	Finish	Start	Finish	Start	Finish
1	0	4	4	9	9	16
2	4	8	9	15	16	23
3	9	14	16	21	23	28
4	16	22	23	29	29	36
5	23	27	29	34	36	41
6	29	35	36	41	41	48
7	36	42	42	48	48	55
8	42	48	48	54	55	60
9	48	54	55	61	61	67
10	55	60	61	65	67	71

During the simulation, which takes 71 minutes, 10 units of output were produced giving an output rate of 10/71 = .14 units per minute or 8.45 units per hour. This figure is somewhat distorted, of course, because the simulation starts with stations 2 and 3 systematically idle. If a computer simulation were to be conducted for the problem, the system should be "warmed up" before statistical data is collected:

15-9 We draw random numbers for arrivals as the first digit
      down column 3 of Appendix 6. We use the first digit
      reading down column 4 for service time.

	Interarrivals			Service times	
Time	Cum. Prob.	RN Range	Time	Cum. Prob.	RN Range
5	.2	0-1	4	.2	0-1
6	.4	2-3	5	.4	2-3
7	.6	4-5	6	.6	4-5
8	.8	6-7	7	.8	6-7
9	1.0	8-9	8	1.0	8-9

We schedule the 5 warm-up and 20 data samples:

Number	RN	Interarrival	Arrival clock	RN	Service
1W	8	9	9	8	8
2W	9	9	18	7	7
3W	1	5	23	0	4
4W	9	9	32	1	4
5W	2	6	38	5	6
1	8	9	47	4	6
2	5	7	54	5	6
3	1	5	59	0	4
4	5	7	66	5	6
5	0	5	71	9	8
6	5	7	78	8	8
7	4	7	85	8	8
8	3	6	91	1	4
9	3	6	97	3	5
10	7	8	105	1	4
11	1	5	110	5	6
12	5	7	117	9	8
13	5	7	124	0	4
14	0	5	129	4	6
15	1	5	134	4	6
16	7	8	142	1	4
17	1	5	147	2	5
18	3	6	153	4	6
19	8	9	162	5	6
20	3	6	168	2	5

We now record the simulation results ensuring we record
idle time of the server.

Time	Event	Transaction being served (time to go)	Waiting	Idle time
9	1W arr.	1W (8)		warm-up
17	1W dep.	idle		warm-up
18	2W arr.	2W (7)		warm-up

(Continued)

```
23      3W arr.          2W (2)              3W        warm-up
25      2W dep.          3W (4)                        warm-up
29      3W dep.          idle                          warm-up
32      4W arr.          4W (4)                        warm-up
36      4W dep.          idle                          warm-up
38      5W arr.          5W (6)                        warm-up
44      5W dep.          idle           Sim starts  clock=44
47       1 arr.           1 (6)                           3
53       1 dep.          idle
54       2 arr.           2 (6)                           1
59       3 arr.           2 (1)              3
60       2 dep.           3 (4)
64       3 dep.          idle
66       4 arr.           4 (6)                           2
71       5 arr.           4 (1)              5
72       4 dep.           5 (8)
78       6 arr.           5 (2)              6
80       5 dep.           6 (8)
85       7 arr.           6 (3)              7
88       6 dep.           7 (8)
91       8 arr.           7 (5)              8
96       7 dep.           8 (4)
97       9 arr.           8 (3)              9
100      8 dep.           9 (5)
105    10 arr.;  9 dep.  10 (4)
109     10 dep.          idle
110     11 arr.          11 (6)                           1
116     11 dep.          idle
117     12 arr.          12 (8)                           1
124     13 arr.          12 (1)             13
125     12 dep.          13 (4)
129    14 arr.;13 dep.   14 (6)
134     15 arr.          14 (1)             15
135     14 dep.          15 (6)
141     15 dep.          idle
142     16 arr.          16 (4)                           1
146     16 dep.          idle
147     17 arr.          17 (5)                           1
152     17 dep.          idle
153     18 arr.          18 (6)                           1
159     18 dep.          idle
162     19 arr.          19 (6)                           3
168    20 arr.;19 dep.   20 (5)
173     20 dep.       Simulation ends; Clock = 173

        Total idleness = 14
        Total run time = 173 - 44 = 129
```

$$\text{Utilization} = \frac{129 - 14}{129} = .8915$$

351

Using means, or midpoints, of the uniform distributions:

Theoretical utilization = 6/7 = .8571

15-10   We develop joint probabilities for the various development
         time and sales volume outcomes:

Development time	Sales volume (millions)	Strategy 1 probability	Strategy 2 probability
6	1	(.2)(.2)=.04	(.4)(.2)=.08
9	1	(.3)(.4)=.12	(.4)(.4)=.16
12	1	(.5)(.5)=.25	(.2)(.5)=.10
6	1.5	(.2)(.8)=.16	(.4)(.8)=.32
9	1.5	(.3)(.6)=.18	(.4)(.6)=.24
12	1.5	(.5)(.5)=.25	(.2)(.5)=.10
		1.00	1.00

Prob(sales of 1 mil.|strategy 1) = .04 + .12 + .25 = .41
Prob(sales of 1 mil.|strategy 2) = .08 + .16 + .10 = .34
Prob(sales of 1.5 mil.|strategy 1) = .16 + .18 + .25 = .59
Prob(sales of 1.5 mil.|strategy 2) = .32 + .24 + .10 = .66

We now compute profits (in millions) for the various
outcomes:

Sales	Strategy 1	Strategy 2
1 mil.	(2.5)(1)-.6 = $1.90	(3.25)(1)-1.5 = $1.750
1.5 mil.	(2.5)(1.5)-.6 = $3.15	(3.25)(1.5)-1.5 = $3.375

The assignment of random numbers is:

Strategy 1		Strategy 2	
RN	Profits	RN	Profits
00-40	$1.900 mil.	00-33	$1.750 mil.
41-99	$3.150 mil.	34-99	$3.375 mil.

We draw the first two random digits going down column 1 of
Appendix Table 6 for strategy 1 and the first two digits
going down column 2 for strategy 2.

Trial	Strategy 1		Strategy 2	
	RN	Simulated Profit	RN	Simulated Profit
1	15	1.900	20	1.750
2	09	1.900	72	3.375
3	41	3.150	34	3.375
4	74	3.150	54	3.375
5	00	1.900	30	1.750
6	72	3.150	22	1.750
7	67	3.150	48	3.375

(Continued)

8	55	3.150	74	3.375
9	71	3.150	76	3.375
10	35	1.900	02	1.750
		Mean = $2.650		Mean = $2.725

Using expected value:

E.P. | Strategy 1 = (.41)(1.9) + (.59)(3.15) = $2.6375
E.P. | Strategy 2 = (.34)(1.75) + (.66)(3.375) = $2.8225

15-11 Random number assignments for each activity are as follows:

		Random Number		
Days	A	B	C	D
1				00-09
2				10-19
3				20-39
4			00-29	40-69
5		00-19	30-79	70-79
6	00-39	20-69	80-99	80-89
7	40-49	70-99		90-99
8	50-59			
9	60-69			
10	70-79			
11	80-89			
12	90-99			

We read the random digits as the first two numbers from column 4 of Appendix Table 6.

		First simulated completion		
Activity	RN	Duration	Date started	Date completed
A	83	11	0	11
B	70	7	11	18
C	06	4	11	15
D	12	2	18	20

Days late = 20 - 15 = 5   Penalty = $10,000 x 5 = $50,000

		Second simulated completion		
Activity	RN	Duration	Date started	Date completed
A	59	8	0	8
B	46	6	8	14
C	54	5	8	13
D	04	1	14	15

Days late = 15 - 15 = 0   Penalty = none

			Third simulated completion	
Activity	RN	Duration	Date started	Date completed
A	51	8	0	8
B	99	7	8	15
C	84	6	8	14
D	81	6	15	21

Days late = 21 - 15 = 6   Penalty = $10,000 x 6 = $60,000

15-12 For this exercise, we draw the first four random digits reading down column one of Appendix Table 6 to simulate the daily demand. The first four random digits reading down column 2 are used to simulate reorder lead time.

Day	Beginning inventory	RN	Demand	Lost sales	Receipts	Ending inv.	RN	Lead time
1	180	1581	15			165	2068	5
2	165	0928	14			151		
3	151	4112	19			132		
4	132	7457	24			108		
5	108	0099	9			99		
6	99	7245	23		100	176	7295	7
7	176	6749	23			153		
8	153	5503	21			132		
9	132	7164	23			109		
10	109	3593	18			91		
11	91	4192	19			72		
12	72	9697	30			142		
13	42	2007	16		100	126	3440	6
14	126	4584	20			106		
15	106	3840	19			87		
16	87	0190	10			77		
17	77	6766	23			54		
18	54	6315	22			132		
19	32	3908	18		100	114		
20	114	5570	21			93	5435	6
						2119		

Average weekly lost sales = 0
Average on-hand stock = 2119/20 = 105.95 units

15-13 Using the same demand figures, we have:

Day	Begin. on-hand	Dmd	Lost sales	Receipts	Ending on-hand	Ending on-hand plus on-order	RN	Lead time
1	180	15			165	165	2068	5
2	165	14			151	251		
3	151	19			132	232		
4	132	24			108	208		

(Continued)

5	108	9		99	199		
6	99	23	100	176	176	7295	7
7	176	23		153	253		
8	153	21		132	232		
9	132	23		109	209		
10	109	18		91	191		
11	91	19		72	172	3440	6
12	72	30		42	242		
13	42	16	100	126	226		
14	126	20		106	206		
15	106	19		87	187		
16	87	10		77	177	5435	6
17	77	23	100	154	254		
18	154	22		132	232		
19	132	18		114	214		
20	114	21		93	193		
				2319			

Average weekly lost sales = 0
Average on-hand stock = 2319/20 = 115.95

For these simulations, the average on-hand stock increased when ordering is based on on-hand plus on-order levels. This is to be expected. The simulations did not point out any differences in lost sales. However, if a computer simulation were run on these problems over a much larger sample of several thousand days of simulated operations, the on-hand plus on-order rule would be expected to result in lower levels of average weekly lost sales.

15-14 We draw the first four random digits in column 4 of Appendix Table 6 to determine simulated receipts and the first four random digits of column 5 for disbursements.

Day	RN	Cash Receipts	RN	Cash Disbursements	Cash on hand	Cumulative loans
1	8374	62000	4637	47700	14300	
2	7055	56000	6472	49200	21100	
3	0684	32000	0933	44100	9000	
4	1291	36800	4890	48000		2200
5	5973	52400	9776	54000		3800
6	4676	50000	2229	45600	600	
7	5432	51200	2966	46500	5300	
8	0414	29600	0140	41400		6500
9	5133	50000	4011	47100		3600
10	9999	86000	7544	50100	32300	
11	8408	62000	1074	41700	52600	
12	8123	60800	0927	40800	72600	
13	1531	38000	7016	49500	61100	
14	3643	46400	4141	47400	60100	
15	1267	36800	4020	47400	49500	

The maximum loan accumulated during the 15 simulated days of operation is $6500.

15-15 The failure history of 15 bearings of each type is included for reference. The first four random digits are drawn from columns 2 and 3 of Appendix Table 6 for the two bearing types.

Trial	RN	Life	RN	Life
1	2068	70.4	8262	118
2	7295	87.2	9586	134
3	3440	75.2	1882	82
4	5435	81.2	9670	136
5	3090	74.0	2039	84
6	2275	71.6	8416	120
7	4832	80.0	5670	104
8	7413	88.4	1198	76
9	7666	88.4	5263	102
10	0272	57.2	0385	64
11	0700	62.0	5169	100
12	6488	84.8	4031	96
13	9564	100.4	3457	92
14	2389	71.6	3859	94
15	9120	96.8	7228	112

For 1000 simulated hours of operation, the bearings would be replaced as follows (on a replace only-when-failed basis).

Number	Replacement Hours (Bearing 1)	Replacement Hours (Bearing 2)
1	70.4	118
2	157.6	252
3	232.8	334
4	314.0	470
5	388.0	554
6	459.6	674
7	539.6	778
8	628.0	854
9	716.4	956
10	773.6	
11	835.6	
12	920.4	

The associated costs are:

Labor   (12 + 9)(90) = $1890
Bearing 1 (12)(80)   =   960
Bearing 2 (9)(50)   =   450
                         $3300

If both bearings are replaced when either fails, we have:

Replacement	Bearing failing	Failed after	Time replaced
1	1	70.4	70.4
2	1	87.2	157.6
3	1	75.2	232.8
4	1	81.2	314.0
5	1	74.0	388.0
6	1	71.6	459.6
7	1	80.0	539.6
8	2	76.0	615.6
9	1	88.4	704.0
10	1	57.2	716.2
11	1	62.0	823.2
12	1	84.8	908.0
13	2	92.0	1000.0

The associated costs are:

Labor	(13)(110)	=	$1430
Bearing 1	(13)(80)	=	1040
Bearing 2	(13)(50)	=	650
			$3120

The policy of replacing both bearings together when either fails is less costly according to these simulation results.

15-16   Two digit random numbers are drawn from column 1 of Appendix Table 6 for arrivals and from column 2 for service times.
The random number assignments are:

Interarrival times   Service times

Hours	RN		Hours	RN	
0.0- 6	00-09		12-16	00-99	uniform
6.1-12	10-19				
12.1-18	20-89				
18.1-24	90-99				

Ship Number	RN	Prescheduled events Interarr. time	Arrival time	RN	Service time
1	N/A	N/A	0	N/A	7.0
2	N/A	N/A	3	20	12.8
3	15	9.4	12.4	72	14.9
4	09	6.0	18.4	34	13.4
5	41	13.9	32.3	54	14.2
6	74	16.7	49.0	30	13.2
7	00	0.0	49.0	22	12.9
8	72	16.5	65.5	48	13.9
9	67	16.1	81.6	74	15.0
10	55	15.1	96.7	76	15.1

| | | Simulated events | | |
Ship Number	Time of arrival	Time service begins	Time service ends	Waiting time
1	0	0	7	--
2	3	7	19.8	4
3	12.4	19.8	34.7	7.4
4	18.4	34.7	48.1	16.3
5	32.3	48.1	62.3	15.8
6	49.0	62.3	75.5	13.3
7	49.0	75.5	88.4	26.5
8	65.5	88.4	102.3	22.9
9	81.6	102.3	117.3	20.7
10	96.7	117.3	132.4	20.6
				147.5

The mean waiting time for the nine ships is 147.5/9 or
16.39 hours.

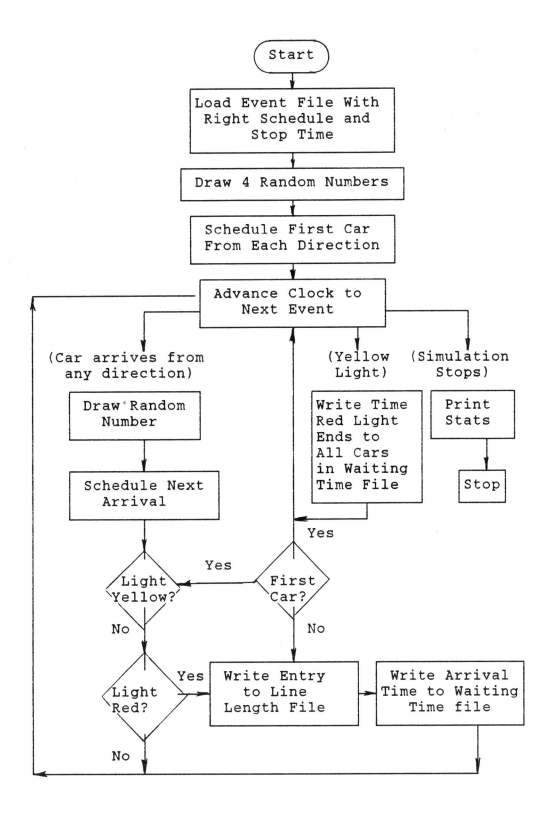

15-18 First we assign ranges of random numbers for which each of the discrete interarrival and service times is to be simulated.

Time between arrivals	Probability	Cumulative Probability	Range of random numbers
0	.15	.15	00-14
5	.10	.25	15-24
10	.12	.37	25-36
15	.14	.51	37-50
20	.17	.68	51-67
30	.26	.94	68-93
40	.06	1.00	94-99

Service time	Probability	Cumulative Probability	Range of random numbers
14	.05	.05	00-04
16	.50	.55	05-54
18	.20	.75	55-74
20	.20	.95	75-94
22	.05	1.00	95-99

Next we determine the simulated times for the 15 customers using the random numbers in column 1 of Appendix Table 6 for arrivals and column 2 for service times.

FUTURE EVENTS LIST

Customer Number	RN for Arrival	Interarrival Time	Arrival Clock	RN for Service	Service Time
1	15	5	8:05	20	16
2	09	0	8:05	72	18
3	41	15	8:20	34	16
4	74	30	8:50	54	16
5	00	0	8:50	30	16
6	72	30	9:20	22	16
7	67	20	9:40	48	16
8	55	20	10:00	74	18
9	71	30	10:30	76	20
10	35	10	10:40	02	14
11	41	15	10:55	07	16
12	96	40	11:35	64	18
13	20	5	11:40	96	22
14	45	15	11:55	23	16
15	38	15	12:10	91	20

Now that we have all the customers on a "future" event list, we tabulate the status of the shop, keeping track of who is in Beth's chair, who is waiting, etc. In order to make it easier to determine when the system changes state, we will use a convention as the following example describes:

Time	Service	Wait 1	Wait 2	Cumulative Idle Time	Lost Customers
10:15	9(10)	11	12	40	10

This means that our simulator clock is now at 10:15 A.M. The figures 9(10) under Service mean that customer 9 is in the chair having her hair cut and set and it will take another 10 minutes before she is finished. Two people are waiting--customers 11 and 12--with customer 11 being next in line. The beautician has accumulated 40 minutes of idle time as of 10:15. Finally, we use the last column to log in a customer who is lost because two people were waiting when she arrived. We will increment our clock in the event log when either a customer arrives or a customer is finished.

EVENT LOG

Time	Service	Wait 1	Wait 2	Cumulative Idle Time	Lost Customers
8:05	1(16)			5	
8:05	1(16)	2			
8:20	1(1)	2	3		
8:21	2(18)	3			
8:39	3(16)				
8:50	3(5)	4			
8:50	3(5)	4	5		
8:55	4(16)	5			
9:11	5(16)				
9:20	5(7)	6			
9:27	6(16)				
9:40	6(3)	7			
9:43	7(16)				
9:59	Idle				
10:00	8(18)			6	
10:18	Idle				
10:30	9(20)				18
10:40	9(10)	10			
10:50	10(14)				
10:55	10(9)	11			
11:04	11(16)				
11:20	Idle				
11:35	12(18)				33
11:40	12(13)	13			
11:53	13(22)				
11:55	13(20)	14			
12:10	13(5)	14	15		
12:15	14(16)	15			
12:31	15(20)				
12:51	Simulation ends				

During the simulation, Beth was idle a total of 33 minutes. No customers were lost.

15-19 There is no bias in the selections, so each show has equal
       probability as follows:

Show	Probability	Cum. Prob.	RN Range
Nature Hour	.3333	.3333	0000-3332
Whodunit?	.3333	.6667	3333-6666
Guess My Name	.3333	1.0000	6667-9999

We will draw sequentially for the products in turn until
one of the three programs has been assigned two of the
products. The first 4 digits of column 4 of Appendix
Table 6 are used.

Product	RN	Show assigned
Bran Cereal	8374	Guess My Name
Fruit Snack	7055	Guess My Name

Guess My Name is now satisfied with two programs assigned
so we update probabilities for the other two:

Show	Probability	Cum. Prob.	RN Range
Nature Hour	.5000	.5000	0000-4999
Whodunit?	.5000	1.0000	5000-9999

Continuing to draw, we have:

Product	RN	Show assigned
Nut Bar	0684	Nature Hour
Fresh Fibre	1291	Nature Hour

The last two products are now assigned to Whodunit?

Our heuristic solution is:

Product	Show	Revenue increase
Bran Cereal	Guess My Name	60
Fruit Snack	Guess My Name	75
Nut Bar	Nature Hour	75
Fresh Fibre	Nature Hour	60
Happy Mix	Whodunit?	65
Camper Delight	Whodunit?	40
		Total = 375

The second heuristic solution:

Product	RN	Show assigned
Bran Cereal	5973	Whodunit?
Fruit Snack	4676	Whodunit?

Whodunit? is now satisfied with two programs assigned so
we update probabilities for the other two:

Show	Probability	Cum. Prob.	RN Range
Nature Hour	.5000	.5000	0000-4999
Guess My Name	.5000	1.0000	5000-9999

Continuing to draw, we have:

Product	RN	Show assigned
Nut Bar	5432	Guess My Name
Fresh Fibre	0414	Nature Hour
Happy Mix	5133	Guess My Name

The last product--Camper Delight--is assigned to Nature Hour, and our second heuristic solution is:

Product	Show	Revenue increase
Bran Cereal	Whodunit?	40
Fruit Snack	Whodunit?	80
Nut Bar	Guess My Name	65
Fresh Fibre	Nature Hour	60
Happy Mix	Guess My Name	75
Camper Delight	Nature Hour	85
	Total =	405

15-20   We select first a show to assign to Bran Cereal. For this product, we have increased revenue values of 50, 40, and 60 for the three shows or a total of 50+40+60 = 150. We therefore can bias according to proportion of the total as follows:

For Bran Cereal:

Show	Probability	Cum. Prob.	RN range
Nature Hour	50/150 = .3333	.3333	0000-3332
Whodunit?	40/150 = .2667	.6000	3333-5999
Guess My Name	60/150 = .4000	1.0000	6000-9999

With our first RN draw of 8374, we assign Bran Cereal to Guess My Name.

For Fruit Snack:

Show	Probability	Cum. Prob.	RN range
Nature Hour	70/225 = .3111	.3111	0000-3110
Whodunit?	80/225 = .3556	.6667	3111-6666
Guess My Name	75/225 = .3333	1.0000	6667-9999

With our second RN draw of 7055, we assign Fruit Snack to Guess My Name. Now only Nature Hour and Whodunit? remain unassigned:

For Nut Bar:

Show	Probability	Cum. Prob.	RN range
Nature Hour	75/145 = .5172	.5172	0000-5171
Whodunit?	70/145 = .4828	1.0000	5172-9999

Our third RN draw is 0684, so we assign Nut Bar to Nature Hour.

For Fresh Fibre:

Show	Probability	Cum. Prob.	RN range
Nature Hour	60/105 = .5714	.5714	0000-5713
Whodunit?	45/105 = .4286	1.0000	5714-9999

Our fourth RN draw is 1291, so we assign Fresh Fibre to Nature Hour.

Our heuristic solution is:

Product	Show	Revenue increase
Bran Cereal	Guess My Name	60
Fruit Snack	Guess My Name	75
Nut Bar	Nature Hour	75
Fresh Fibre	Nature Hour	60
Happy Mix	Whodunit?	65
Camper Delight	Whodunit?	40
		Total = 375

15-21 The random number ranges for simulated events are:

Time-to-failure	Prob.	Cum. Prob.	RN Range
180	.20	.20	00-19
190	.30	.50	20-49
200	.25	.75	50-74
210	.12	.87	75-86
220	.08	.95	87-94
230	.05	1.00	95-99

Repair Time	Prob.	Cum. Prob.	RN Range
50	.50	.50	00-49
60	.36	.86	50-85
70	.08	.94	86-93
80	.04	.98	94-97
90	.02	1.00	98-99

We begin by placing all times-to-failure and repair times on a future events list:

FUTURE EVENTS LIST

Machine A		Machine B		Machine C		Repair Tool	
RN	Time	RN	Time	RN	Time	RN	Time
15	180	20	190	82	210	83	60
09	180	72	200	95	230	70	60
41	190	34	190	18	180	06	50
74	200	54	200	96	230	12	50
						59	60
						46	50
						54	60
						04	50
						51	60
						99	90

On the events log, we will use a code by machine. For example, say it is clock time 920, and we have recorded N(50) under the machine A column, R(20) under machine B, and W under machine C. This means machine A is in normal operation, with its next breakdown due to occur 50 minutes later, at a clock time of 970. Machine B is being repaired, with the repair being completed 20 minutes later at clock time 990. Machine C is in a state of breakdown, waiting until the repair tool is released before starting its repair. Our events log is as follows:

EVENTS LOG

Clock Time	Machine A	Machine B	Machine C	Idled Waiting for tool
0	N(180)	N(190)	R(60)	
60	N(120)	N(130)	N(210)	
180	R(60)	N(10)	N(90)	
190	R(50)	W	N(80)	
240	N(180)	R(50)	N(30)	50
270	N(150)	R(20)	W	
290	N(130)	N(200)	R(50)	20
340	N(80)	N(150)	N(230)	
420	R(60)	N(70)	N(150)	
480	N(190)	N(10)	N(90)	
490	N(180)	R(50)	N(80)	
540	N(130)	N(190)	N(30)	
570	N(100)	N(160)	R(60)	
630	N(40)	N(100)	N(180)	
670	R(50)	N(60)	N(140)	
720	N(200)	N(10)	N(90)	
			Total =	70

During the 720 minutes time, 70 worker-minutes of idleness were recorded while the operators were waiting for the repair tool.

15-22 With no bias we assign equal probabilities for selecting either an apprentice or a journeyman. Therefore, if the two-digit random number drawn is 49 or less, we add an apprentice. If the random number is greater, we add a journeyman.

First Solution

Random Number	Selection	Money Used	Hours Used	Money Remaining	Hours Remaining
--	initialize	--	--	500	16
15	apprentice	64	8	436	8
09	apprentice	64	8	372	0

Profit = (5)(2) + (9)(0) = $10 per day

Second Solution

Random Number	Selection	Money Used	Hours Used	Money Remaining	Hours Remaining
--	initialize	--	--	500	16
41	apprentice	64	8	436	8
74	journeyman	90	5	346	3

Profit = (5)(1) + (9)(1) = $14 per day

Third Solution

Random Number	Selection	Money Used	Hours Used	Money Remaining	Hours Remaining
--	initialize	--	--	500	16
00	apprentice	64	8	436	8
72	journeyman	90	5	346	3

Profit = (5)(1) + (9)(1) = $14 per day

Fourth Solution

Random Number	Selection	Money Used	Hours Used	Money Remaining	Hours Remaining
--	initialize	--	--	500	16
67	journeyman	90	5	410	11
55	journeyman	90	5	320	6
71	journeyman	90	5	230	1

Profit = (5)(0) + (9)(3) = $27 per day (optimum)

Fifth Solution

Random Number	Selection	Money Used	Hours Used	Money Remaining	Hours Remaining
--	initialize	--	--	500	16
35	apprentice	64	8	436	8
55	apprentice	64	8	372	0

Profit = (5)(2) + (9)(0) = $10 per day

15-23 For our first selection, all six projects are available
       and we have $24 million unassigned.

| | | | | Random Number |
Project	Importance	Probability	Cum. Prob.	Range
Route 1	5	5/33=.1516	.1516	0000-1515
Route 2	6	6/33=.1818	.3334	1516-3333
Route 3	4	4/33=.1212	.4546	3334-4545
Route 4	7	7/33=.2121	.6667	4546-6666
Route 5	3	3/33=.0909	.7576	6667-7575
Route 6	8	8/33=.2424	1.0000	7576-9999
Total =	33			

Our first random number draw is 2068, so we select first
the route 2 project leaving 24-7 = $17 million unassigned.

For the next selection, the probabilities become:

Project	Importance	Probability	Cum. Prob.	Range
Route 1	5	5/27=.1852	.1852	0000-1851
Route 3	4	4/27=.1481	.3333	1852-3332
Route 4	7	7/27=.2593	.5926	3333-5925
Route 5	3	3/27=.1111	.7037	5926-7036
Route 6	8	8/27=.2963	1.0000	7037-9999
Total =	27			

Our second random number draw is 7295, so we select the
route 6 project leaving 17-4 = $13 million unassigned.

Project	Importance	Probability	Cum. Prob.	Range
Route 1	5	5/19=.2632	.2632	0000-2631
Route 3	4	4/19=.2105	.4737	2632-4736
Route 4	7	7/19=.3684	.8421	4737-8420
Route 5	3	3/19=.1579	1.0000	8421-9999
Total =	19			

Our third random number draw is 3440, so we select the
route 3 project leaving 13-5 = $8 million unassigned.

Project	Importance	Probability	Cum. Prob.	Range
Route 1	5	5/15=.3333	.3333	0000-3332
Route 4	7	7/15=.4667	.8000	3333-7999
Route 5	3	3/15=.2000	1.0000	8000-9999
Total =	15			

Our fourth random number draw is 5435, so we select the
route 4 project leaving 8-6 = $2 million unassigned.
Since the two remaining projects, routes 1 and 5, each
require more than $2 million, our solution is complete.
This solution is to fund projects 2,3,4 and 6 for a total
importance level of 6 + 4 + 7 + 8 = 25, which is one unit
below the optimum solution of 26.

15-24

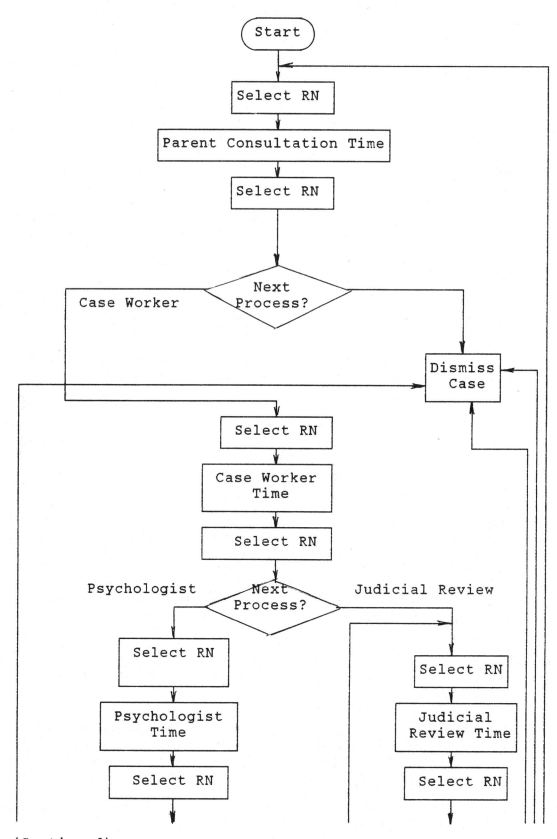

(Continued)

368

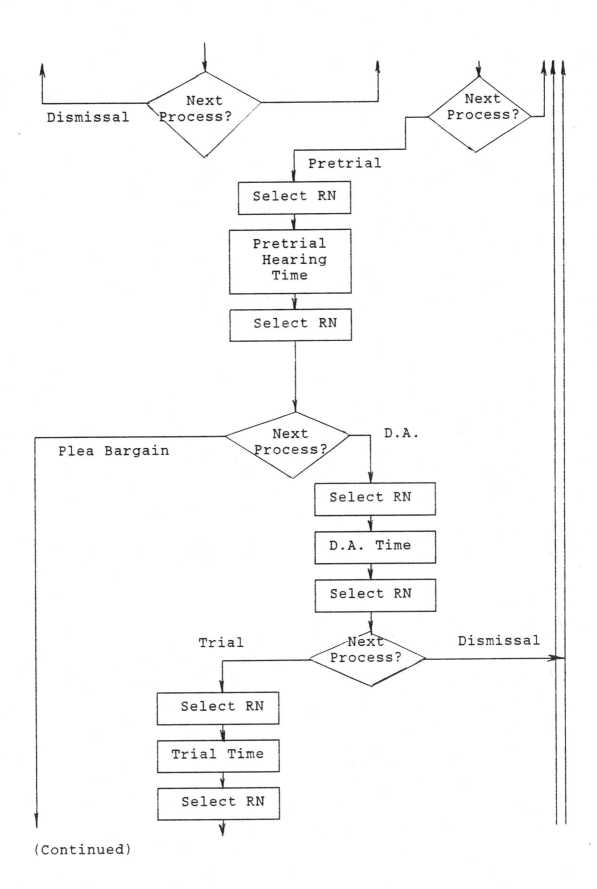

(Continued)

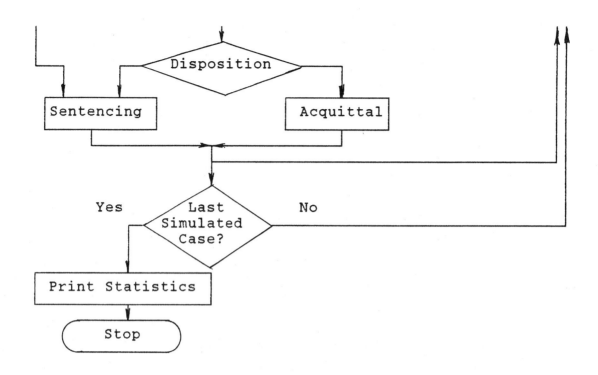

15-25 First we assign random number ranges for determining the
time taken at each stage in the process as well as random
number ranges for determining the next stage to take in
the process.

Parent Consultation Stage

Time	RN range		Next stage	RN range
1	00-19		Case Worker	00-74
2	20-69		Dismissal	75-99
3	70-99			

Case Worker Stage

Time	RN range		Next stage	RN range
9	00-19		Psychologist	00-39
10	20-39		Judicial Review	40-99
11	40-69			
12	70-99			

Psychologist Stage

Time	RN range		Next stage	RN range
12	00-39		Judicial Review	00-79
13	40-89		Dismissal	80-99
14	90-99			

370

Judicial Review Stage

Time	RN range	Next stage	RN range
15	00-29	Pretrial Hearing	00-89
16	30-59	Dismissal	90-99
17	60-99		

Pretrial Hearing Stage

Time	RN range	Next stage	RN range
2	00-49	Plea Bargain	00-29
3	50-99	District Attorney	30-99

Plea Bargaining Stage

Time	RN range	Next stage	RN range
3	00-19	Sentencing	NR
4	20-59		
5	60-99		

District Attorney Stage

Time	RN range	Next stage	RN range
30	00-29	Trial	00-89
35	30-69	Dismissal	90-99
40	70-99		

Trial Stage

Time	RN range	Next stage	RN range
8	00-49	Sentencing	00-79
9	50-89	Acquittal	80-99
10	90-99		

First Simulated Case

Day Started	Event time or Disposition	RN	Outcome
0	Parent Consultation	15	1 day
1	Next Stage	09	Case Worker
1	Case Worker	41	11 days
12	Next Stage	74	Judicial Review
12	Judicial Review	00	15 days
27	Next Stage	72	Pretrial Hearing
27	Pretrial Hearing	67	3 days
30	Next Stage	55	District Attorney
30	District Attorney	71	40 days
70	Next Stage	35	Trial
70	Trial	41	8 days
78	Disposition	96	Acquittal

371

Second Simulated Case

Day Started	Event time or Disposition	RN	Outcome
0	Parent Consultation	20	2 days
2	Next Stage	45	Case Worker
2	Case Worker	38	10 days
12	Next Stage	01	Psychologist
12	Psychologist	67	13 days
25	Next Stage	63	Judicial Review
25	Judicial Review	39	16 days
41	Next Stage	55	Pretrial Hearing
41	Pretrial Hearing	29	2 days
43	Next Stage	78	District Attorney
43	District Attorney	70	40 days
83	Next Stage	06	Trial
83	Trial	78	9 days
92	Disposition	76	Sentencing

Third Simulated Case

Day Started	Event time or Disposition	RN	Outcome
0	Parent Consultation	47	2 days
2	Next Stage	46	Case Worker
2	Case Worker	93	12 days
14	Next Stage	12	Psychologist
14	Psychologist	55	13 days
27	Next Stage	49	Judicial Review
27	Judicial Review	18	15 days
42	Next Stage	70	Pretrial Hearing
42	Pretrial Hearing	35	2 days
44	Next Stage	97	District Attorney
44	District Attorney	55	35 days
79	Next Stage	46	Trial
79	Trial	84	9 days
88	Disposition	18	Sentencing

For the three simulated cases, all three went to trial. One of the three was acquitted, while the other two were sentenced. On average, it took (78+92+88)/3 = 86 days to process a case.

15-26 The range of random numbers assigned to the possible events for a day which follows either a price increase or no change in price are:

Price change	Probability	Cum. Prob.	RN range
-4	.05	.05	00-04
-2	.10	.15	05-14
NC	.20	.35	15-34
+2	.25	.60	35-59
+4	.30	.90	60-89
+6	.10	1.00	90-99

A second range of random numbers are assigned to the events which are possible on a day following a drop in price as follows:

Price change	Probability	Cum. Prob.	RN range
-6	.10	.10	00-09
-4	.30	.40	10-39
-2	.25	.65	40-64
NC	.15	.80	65-79
+2	.20	1.00	80-99

Simulated Events

Day	Ounces owned	Previous day	RN	Price change	Ending price	Action
1	1000	incr.	82	+4	304	
2	1000	incr.	95	+6	310	
3	1000	incr.	18	NC	310	sell at 310
4	900	NC	96	+6	316	sell at 316
5	800	incr.	20	NC	316	sell at 316
6	700	NC	84	+4	320	sell at 320
7	600	incr.	56	+2	322	sell at 322
8	500	incr.	11	-2	320	
9	500	decr.	52	-2	318	
10	500	decr.	03	-6	312	buy at 312
11	600	decr.	51	-2	310	buy at 310
12	700	decr.	40	-2	308	buy at 308
13	800	decr.	34	-4	304	buy at 304
14	900	decr.	38	-4	300	buy at 300
15	1000	decr.	72	NC	300	
16	1000	NC	11	-2	298	
17	1000	decr.	50	-2	296	
18	1000	decr.	55	-2	294	buy at 294
19	1100	decr.	08	-6	288	buy at 288
20	1200	decr.	11	-4	284	buy at 284

Cash inflow from sales is:
(100)(310)+(200)(316)+(100)(320)+(100)(322) = $158,400

Cash outflow from purchases is:
(100)(312)+(100)(310)+(100)(308)+(100)(304)+(100)(300)
        +(100)(294)+(100)(288)+(100)(284) = $240,000

The net cash outflow is $81,600, so Marty's position is:

```
Ending book value      = (1200)(284) = $340,800
Net cash outflow                     = -81,600
Beginning book value   = (1000)(300) = -300,000
                         Net change in wealth = -$40,800
```

15-27 We draw random numbers from column 5. We use the first 2 digits of each random number.

Since all counties have equal probability (i.e., no bias), the assigned RN ranges are:

```
        Abbott    00-32
        Babson    33-65
        Clark     66-99
```

| Heuristic solution #1 | | | | Heuristic solution #2 | | |
Salesperson	RN	County		Salesperson	RN	County
1	46	B		1	40	B
2	64	B		2	75	C
3	09	A		3	10	A
4	48	B		4	09	A
5	97	C		5	70	C
6	22	A		6	41	B
7	29	A		7	40	B
8	01	A		8	37	B

County	People	Profit		County	People	Profit
Abbott	4	180		Abbott	2	90
Babson	3	60		Babson	4	120
Clark	1	30		Clark	2	60
		$270				$270

The optimal profit is $300.

15-28 We again draw the same set of random numbers as in Exercise 15-27.

First heuristic solution

		A	B	C
1st Salesperson	current	0	0	0
	next	45	15	30
	increase	45	15	30

374

County	Prob.	Cum. prob.	RN range
A	45/90 = .50	.50	00-49
B	15/90 = .17	.67	50-66
C	30/90 = .33	1.00	67-99

RN draw is 46 so person 1 assigned to Abbott.

2nd Salesperson		A	B	C
	current	45	0	0
	next	90	15	30
	increase	45	15	30
	RN range	00-49	50-66	67-99

RN draw is 64 so person 2 is assigned to Babson.

3rd Salesperson		A	B	C
	current	45	15	0
	next	90	30	30
	increase	45	15	30
	RN range	00-49	50-66	67-99

RN draw is 09 so person 3 is assigned to Abbott.

4th Salesperson		A	B	C
	current	90	15	0
	next	135	30	30
	increase	45	15	30
	RN range	00-49	50-66	67-99

RN draw is 48 so person 4 is assigned to Abbott.

5th Salesperson		A	B	C
	current	135	15	0
	next	180	30	30
	increase	45	15	30
	RN range	00-49	50-66	67-99

RN draw is 97 so person 5 is assigned to Clark.

6th Salesperson		A	B	C
	current	135	15	30
	next	180	30	60
	increase	45	15	30
	RN range	00-49	50-66	67-99

RN draw is 22 so person 6 is assigned to Abbott.

7th Salesperson		A	B	C
	current	180	15	30
	next	180	30	60
	increase	0	15	30
	RN range	----	00-32	33-99

RN draw is 29 so person 7 is assigned to Babson.

8th Salesperson		A	B	C
	current	180	30	30
	next	180	60	60
	increase	0	30	30
	RN range	----	00-49	50-99

RN draw is 01 so person 8 is assigned to Babson.

Biased Sampling Solution #1

County	People	Profit
Abbott	4	180
Babson	3	60
Clark	1	30
		$270

Second heuristic solution

1st Salesperson		A	B	C
	current	0	0	0
	next	45	15	30
	increase	45	15	30
	RN range	00-49	50-66	67-99

RN draw is 40 so person 1 assigned to Abbott.

2nd Salesperson		A	B	C
	current	45	0	0
	next	90	15	30
	increase	45	15	30
	RN range	00-49	50-66	67-99

RN draw is 75 so person 2 is assigned to Clark.

3rd Salesperson		A	B	C
	current	45	0	30
	next	90	15	60
	increase	45	15	30
	RN range	00-49	50-66	67-99

RN draw is 10 so person 3 is assigned to Abbott.

			A	B	C
4th Salesperson		current	90	0	30
		next	135	15	60
		increase	45	15	30
		RN range	00-49	50-66	67-99

RN draw is 09 so person 4 is assigned to Abbott.

			A	B	C
5th Salesperson		current	135	0	30
		next	180	15	60
		increase	45	15	30
		RN range	00-49	50-66	67-99

RN draw is 70 so person 5 is assigned to Clark.

			A	B	C
6th Salesperson		current	135	0	60
		next	180	15	90
		increase	45	15	30
		RN range	00-49	50-66	67-99

RN draw is 41 so person 6 is assigned to Abbott.

			A	B	C
7th Salesperson		current	180	0	60
		next	180	15	90
		increase	0	15	30
		RN range	----	00-32	33-99

RN draw is 40 so person 7 is assigned to Clark.

			A	B	C
8th Salesperson		current	180	0	90
		next	180	15	120
		increase	0	15	30
		RN range	----	00-32	33-99

RN draw is 37 so person 8 is assigned to Clark.

Biased Sampling Solution #2

County	People	Profit
Abbott	4	180
Babson	0	0
Clark	4	120
		$300

This is the optimal solution we obtained in Exercise 12-32 using dynamic programming.

15-29 We do not use a bias, so for our first selection, we have each person having a 1/6 probability of being selected.

Person	Cum. Prob.	RN range
A	.1667	0000-1666
B	.3333	1667-3332
C	.5000	3333-4999
D	.6667	5000-6666
E	.8333	6667-8332
F	1.0000	8333-9999

Our first RN is 4637, so we select Casey to be processed first. Each of the remaining 5 persons has a 1/5 probability of being selected second.

Person	Cum. Prob.	RN range
A	.2000	0000-1999
B	.4000	2000-3999
D	.6000	4000-5999
E	.8000	6000-7999
F	1.0000	8000-9999

Our second RN is 6472, so Edgars is selected second.

Person	Cum. Prob.	RN range
A	.2500	0000-2499
B	.5000	2500-4999
D	.7500	5000-7499
F	1.0000	7500-9999

Our third RN is 0933, so Ames is selected third.

Person	Cum. Prob.	RN range
B	.3333	0000-3332
D	.6667	3333-6666
F	1.0000	6667-9999

Our fourth RN is 4890, so Danvers is selected fourth.

Person	Cum. Prob.	RN range
B	.5000	0000-4999
F	1.0000	5000-9999

Our fifth RN is 9776, so Flutie is selected fifth leaving Booth to be processed sixth.

Our solution with this processing sequence is:

| | Station 1 | | Station 2 | |
Person	Start	Finish	Start	Finish
Casey	0	20	20	45
Edgars	20	45	45	80
Ames	45	80	80	120
Danvers	80	110	120	180
Flutie	110	160	180	210
Booth	160	200	210	255

With this trial solution it takes 255 minutes to complete processing of all six people.

15-30

Person	Probability	Cum. Prob.	RN range
C	.2857	.2857	0000-2856
E	.2381	.5238	2857-5237
D	.1905	.7143	5238-7142
A	.1429	.8572	7143-8571
B	.0952	.9524	8572-9523
F	.0476	1.0000	9524-9999

Our first RN draw is 4637, so we select Edgars first.

Person	Probability		Cum. Prob.	RN range
C	5/15 =	.3333	.3333	0000-3332
D	4/15 =	.2667	.6000	3333-5999
A	3/15 =	.2000	.8000	6000-7999
B	2/15 =	.1333	.9333	8000-9332
F	1/15 =	.0667	1.0000	9333-9999

Our second RN draw is 6472, so we select Ames second.

Person	Probability		Cum. Prob.	RN range
C	4/10 =	.4000	.4000	0000-3999
D	3/10 =	.3000	.7000	4000-6999
B	2/10 =	.2000	.9000	7000-8999
F	1/10 =	.1000	1.0000	9000-9999

Our third RN draw is 0933, so we select Casey third.

Person	Probability		Cum. Prob.	RN range
D	3/6 =	.5000	.5000	0000-4999
B	2/6 =	.3333	.8333	5000-8332
F	1/6 =	.1667	1.0000	8333-9999

Our fourth RN draw is 4890, so we select Danvers fourth.

Person	Probability		Cum. Prob.	RN range
B	2/3 =	.6667	.6667	0000-6666
F	1/3 =	.3333	1.0000	6667-9999

Our fifth RN draw is 9776, so we select Flutie fifth leaving Booth as the sixth in sequence.

Our trial solution is:

Person	Station 1 Start	Station 1 Finish	Station 2 Start	Station 2 Finish
Edgars	0	25	25	60
Ames	25	60	60	100
Casey	60	80	100	125
Danvers	80	110	125	185
Flutie	110	160	185	215
Booth	160	200	215	260

With this trial solution it takes 260 minutes to complete processing of all six people.

CHAPTER 16

MARKOV ANALYSIS

16-1   a. $\begin{pmatrix} 3 & 2 \\ 9 & 4 \end{pmatrix} - \begin{pmatrix} 9 & -3 \\ -4 & 0 \end{pmatrix} = \begin{pmatrix} -6 & 5 \\ 13 & 4 \end{pmatrix}$

    b. $\begin{pmatrix} 3 & 2 \\ 9 & 4 \end{pmatrix} \times \begin{pmatrix} 3 & 2 \\ 9 & 4 \end{pmatrix} = \begin{pmatrix} 27 & 14 \\ 63 & 34 \end{pmatrix}$

    c. $\begin{pmatrix} 3 & 2 \\ 9 & 4 \end{pmatrix} \times \begin{pmatrix} 9 & -3 \\ -4 & 0 \end{pmatrix} = \begin{pmatrix} 19 & -9 \\ 65 & -27 \end{pmatrix}$

    d. $\begin{pmatrix} 9 & -3 \\ -4 & 0 \end{pmatrix} \times \begin{pmatrix} 3 & 2 \\ 9 & 4 \end{pmatrix} = \begin{pmatrix} 0 & 6 \\ -12 & -8 \end{pmatrix}$

16-2   a. $\begin{pmatrix} 9 & 3 & -7 \\ 4 & 6 & 2 \end{pmatrix} \times \begin{pmatrix} 3 & 7 \\ 0 & 3 \\ -2 & -6 \end{pmatrix} = \begin{pmatrix} 41 & 114 \\ 8 & 34 \end{pmatrix}$

    b. $\begin{pmatrix} 3 & 7 \\ 0 & 3 \\ -2 & -6 \end{pmatrix} \times \begin{pmatrix} 9 & 3 & -7 \\ 4 & 6 & 2 \end{pmatrix} = \begin{pmatrix} 55 & 51 & -7 \\ 12 & 18 & 6 \\ -42 & -42 & 2 \end{pmatrix}$

16-3 $\begin{pmatrix} 3 & -2 \\ 4 & -3 \end{pmatrix} \begin{pmatrix} 1 & 0 \\ 0 & 1 \end{pmatrix}$

    $\begin{pmatrix} 1 & -2/3 \\ 4 & -3 \end{pmatrix} \begin{pmatrix} 1/3 & 0 \\ 0 & 1 \end{pmatrix}$ Mult. row 1 by 1/3.

    $\begin{pmatrix} 1 & -2/3 \\ 0 & -1/3 \end{pmatrix} \begin{pmatrix} 1/3 & 0 \\ -4/3 & 1 \end{pmatrix}$ Mult. row 1 by 4 and subtract
                                                    it from row 2.

$$\begin{pmatrix} 1 & -2/3 \\ 0 & 1 \end{pmatrix} \begin{pmatrix} 1/3 & 0 \\ 4 & -3 \end{pmatrix}$$ Mult. row 2 by -3.

$$\begin{pmatrix} 1 & 0 \\ 0 & 1 \end{pmatrix} \begin{pmatrix} 3 & -2 \\ 4 & -3 \end{pmatrix}$$ Mult. row 2 by -2/3 and subtract it from row 1.

The inverse is $\begin{pmatrix} 3 & -2 \\ 4 & -3 \end{pmatrix}$

16-4 (a)

$$A - B = \begin{bmatrix} 2 & -6 & 0 \\ 1 & -3 & 5 \\ -2 & 4 & 2 \end{bmatrix}$$

(b)

$$A + B = \begin{bmatrix} 2 & 0 & 0 \\ 13 & 3 & -9 \\ -6 & 2 & 10 \end{bmatrix}$$

(c)

$$A \times B = \begin{bmatrix} -18 & -3 & 21 \\ 4 & 23 & -8 \\ 6 & -9 & 3 \end{bmatrix}$$

(d)

$$B \times A = \begin{bmatrix} 21 & 0 & -6 \\ 61 & -39 & -48 \\ -27 & 18 & 26 \end{bmatrix}$$

16-5

$$\begin{pmatrix} 3 & -4 \\ 0 & -6 \end{pmatrix} \begin{pmatrix} 1 & 0 \\ 0 & 1 \end{pmatrix}$$

$$\begin{pmatrix} 1 & -4/3 \\ 0 & -6 \end{pmatrix} \begin{pmatrix} 1/3 & 0 \\ 0 & 1 \end{pmatrix}$$ Multiply row 1 by 1/3

$$\begin{pmatrix} 1 & -4/3 \\ 0 & 1 \end{pmatrix} \begin{pmatrix} 1/3 & 0 \\ 0 & -1/6 \end{pmatrix}$$ Multiply row 2 by -1/6

$$\begin{pmatrix} 1 & 0 \\ 0 & 1 \end{pmatrix} \begin{pmatrix} 1/3 & -2/9 \\ 0 & -1/6 \end{pmatrix}$$ Multiply row 2 by -4/3 and subtract from row 1

The inverse is: $\begin{pmatrix} 1/3 & -2/9 \\ 0 & -1/6 \end{pmatrix}$

16-6 The matrix of transition probabilities is:

$$
\begin{array}{c}
\quad\quad A \quad\quad J \quad\quad \phi \\
\begin{array}{c} A \\ J \\ \phi \end{array}
\left(
\begin{array}{ccc}
.80 & .08 & .12 \\
.06 & .85 & .09 \\
.07 & .07 & .86
\end{array}
\right)
\end{array}
$$

The equations at equilibrium are:

$$A = .80A + .06J + .07\phi$$
$$J = .08A + .85J + .07\phi$$
$$\phi = .12A + .09J + .86\phi$$
$$1 = A + J + \phi$$

Dropping the third equation and regrouping we have:

$$0 = -.20A + .06J + .07\phi$$
$$0 = .08A - .15J + .07\phi$$
$$1 = A + J + \phi$$

Solving simultaneously, we obtain:

$$J = .329$$
$$A = .247$$
$$\phi = .424$$

16-7 (a)

$$
(1/3 \quad 1/3 \quad 1/3)
\left(
\begin{array}{ccc}
.80 & .16 & .04 \\
.18 & .76 & .06 \\
.12 & .04 & .84
\end{array}
\right)
= (.367 \quad .320 \quad .313)
$$

(b) The equilibrium equations are:

$$0 = -.2F + .18B + .12C$$
$$0 = .16F - .24B + .04C$$
$$1 = F + B + C$$

Solving simultaneously, we find the equilibrium shares:

$$F = .437$$
$$B = .330$$
$$C = .233$$

16-8 The matrix of transition probabilities is:

$$
\begin{array}{c}
\quad\quad\quad P \quad\quad\quad\quad D \quad\quad\quad\quad B \\
\begin{array}{c} P \\ D \\ B \end{array}
\left(
\begin{array}{ccc}
285/300 & 10/300 & 5/300 \\
20/750 & 700/750 & 30/750 \\
10/450 & 50/450 & 390/450
\end{array}
\right) =
\end{array}
$$

$$
\begin{array}{c}
\quad\quad\ \ P \quad\quad\ \ D \quad\quad\ \ B \\
\begin{array}{c} P \\ D \\ B \end{array}
\begin{pmatrix}
.950 & .033 & .017 \\
.027 & .933 & .040 \\
.022 & .111 & .867
\end{pmatrix}
\end{array}
$$

$$
\text{Feb. 1} = (300 \quad 750 \quad 450)
\begin{pmatrix}
.950 & .033 & .017 \\
.027 & .933 & .040 \\
.022 & .111 & .867
\end{pmatrix}
= (315 \quad 760 \quad 425)
$$

$$
\text{Mar. 1} = (315 \quad 760 \quad 425)
\begin{pmatrix}
.950 & .033 & .017 \\
.027 & .933 & .040 \\
.022 & .111 & .867
\end{pmatrix}
= (329 \quad 767 \quad 404)
$$

$$
\text{Apr. 1} = (329 \quad 767 \quad 404)
\begin{pmatrix}
.950 & .033 & .017 \\
.027 & .933 & .040 \\
.022 & .111 & .867
\end{pmatrix}
= (342 \quad 771 \quad 387)
$$

16-9 The matrix of transition probabilities for a 3-month period is:

$$
\begin{array}{c}
\quad\quad\ \ 1 \quad\quad\ \ 2 \quad\quad\ \ 3 \\
\begin{array}{c} 1 \\ 2 \\ 3 \end{array}
\begin{pmatrix}
.900 & .067 & .033 \\
.050 & .950 & 0 \\
.100 & .100 & .800
\end{pmatrix}
\end{array}
$$

In another 3-month period (to December) we predict:

$$
(34 \quad 63 \quad 33)
\begin{pmatrix}
.900 & .067 & .033 \\
.050 & .950 & 0 \\
.100 & .100 & .800
\end{pmatrix}
= (37 \quad 65 \quad 28)
$$

16-10 (a) Next year's predicted market percentages are:

$$
(1/3 \quad 1/3 \quad 1/3)
\begin{pmatrix}
.80 & .05 & .15 \\
.10 & .90 & 0 \\
.20 & .20 & .60
\end{pmatrix}^2
= (.382 \quad .413 \quad .205)
$$

(b) The equilibrium equations are:

$$
0 = -.2A + .10B + .2C
$$
$$
0 = .05A - .10B + .2C
$$
$$
1 = A + B + C
$$

Solving simultaneously, we find the equilibrium shares:

$$
A = .381
$$
$$
B = .476
$$
$$
C = .143
$$

16-11   We define: A = age 0 to 20
                     B = age 20 to 40
                     C = age 40 to 60
                     D = age 60 to 80
                     E = age 80 to 100
                     F = age 100 to 120

The matrix of transition probabilities is:

	A	B	C	D	E	F
A	.05	.95	0	0	0	0
B	.15	0	.85	0	0	0
C	.25	0	0	.75	0	0
D	.60	0	0	0	.40	0
E	.96	0	0	0	0	.04
F	1	0	0	0	0	0

The equilibrium equations are:

$$A = .05A + .15B + .25C + .60D + .96E + F$$
$$B = .95A$$
$$C = .85C$$
$$D = .75C$$
$$E = .40D$$
$$F = .04E$$
$$1 = A + B + C + D + E + F$$

Solving simultaneously, we obtain the equilibrium states:

A = .277   D = .168
B = .263   E = .069
C = .224   F = .003

With 100 births each year, in a 20-year period there are
(100)(20) = 2000 births. Therefore, (.277)(Population) =
2000 and Population = 2000/.277 = 7220 persons.

16-12   In one year the population will be:

$$(.50 \quad .40 \quad .10) \begin{pmatrix} .60 & .30 & .10 \\ .15 & .70 & .15 \\ .20 & .10 & .70 \end{pmatrix} = (.38 \quad .44 \quad .18)$$

After two years, the population distribution is predicted
to be:

$$(.38 \quad .44 \quad .18) \begin{pmatrix} .60 & .30 & .10 \\ .15 & .70 & .15 \\ .20 & .10 & .70 \end{pmatrix} = (.33 \quad .44 \quad .23)$$

16-13
$$\begin{array}{c c} & \begin{array}{cccc} N & \quad I & \quad A & \quad P \end{array} \\ \begin{array}{c} N \\ I \\ A \\ P \end{array} & \left(\begin{array}{cccc} .8 & .2 & 0 & 0 \\ .3 & .4 & .3 & 0 \\ 0 & .1 & .8 & .1 \\ .4 & 0 & .3 & .3 \end{array}\right) \end{array}$$

The equilibrium equations are:

N = .8N + .3I + .4P	0 = -.2N + .3I + .4P eq 1
I = .2N + .4I + .1A	0 = .2N - .6I + .1A eq 2
A = .3I + .8A + .3P	0 = .3I - .2A + .3P eq 3
P = .1A + .3P	0 = .1A - .7P eq 4
1 = N + I + A + P	1 = N + I + A + P eq 5

Solving simultaneously, we get:

N = .39130
I = .19130
A = .36522
P = .05217

So out of 60 enrollees (.05217)(60) = 3.1302 are the expected number of professionals.

Camp revenue = (3.1302)(.10)(200,000) = $62,604 per year.

16-14   The equilibrium equations are:

0 = -.5$\emptyset$ + .2B + .3D
0 = .3$\emptyset$ - .4B + .2D
1 = $\emptyset$ + B + D

Solving simultaneously, we find the equilibrium states:

$\emptyset$ = .3265
B = .3877
D = .2857

16-15   The equilibrium equations are:

0 = -.4M + .1F + .15K + .2$\emptyset$
0 = .1M - .3F + .1K + .1$\emptyset$
0 = .05M + 0F - .4K + .1$\emptyset$
1 = M + F + K + $\emptyset$

Solving simultaneously, we find the equilibrium shares:

        M = .2815
        F = .2500
        K = .1219
        ∅ = .3466

With a shrinking market, the company should not expect antitrust action.

16-16 The matrix of transition probabilities is:

                    N   R   PD   PY

        N   ⎛ .85   .15   0   0 ⎞
        R   ⎜ .15   .70   .15   0 ⎟
        PD   ⎜ .10   0   .75   .15 ⎟
        PY   ⎝ .30   0   0   .70 ⎠

The condition next year is found to be:

                        ⎛ .85 .15   0   0 ⎞
                        ⎜ .15 .70   .15   0 ⎟
(190 130 120 75)   ⎜ .10   0   .75   .15 ⎟ = (215.5 119.5 109.5 70.5)
                        ⎝ .30   0   0   .70 ⎠

16-17 We define: H = healthy
                   A = First month in hospital
                   B = Second month in hospital

                    H   A   B

        H   ⎛ .999   .001   0   ⎞
        A   ⎜ .6 + .2   0   .20 ⎟
        B   ⎝ .9 + .1   0   0   ⎠

The equilibrium equations are:

        0 = -.001H + .8A + 1B
        0 = .001H - 1A
        1 = H + A + B

Solving simultaneously, we obtain:

        H = .9988
        A = .0010
        B = .0002

So, out of a population of 100,000, 100 persons are in the hospital during the first month and 20 are in the hospital during their second month.

$$(.2)(100) + (.1)(20) = 22 \text{ persons die each month.}$$

16-18   The matrix of transition probabilities is:

$$\begin{array}{c}\ \\ A \\ B \\ C \\ D\end{array}\begin{array}{cccc} A & B & C & D \\ \left(\begin{array}{cccc} .95 & 0 & 0 & .05 \\ .20 & .70 & 0 & .10 \\ 0 & .20 & .65 & .15 \\ 0 & 0 & .20 & .80 \end{array}\right)\end{array}$$

After one year the state of the system will be:

$$(50 \ \ 100 \ \ 150 \ \ 200) \left(\begin{array}{cccc} .95 & 0 & 0 & .05 \\ .20 & .70 & 0 & .10 \\ 0 & .20 & .65 & .15 \\ 0 & 0 & .20 & .80 \end{array}\right) = (67.5 \ \ 100 \ \ 137.5 \ \ 195)$$

16-19   With current trends:

$$(2500 \ \ 3000 \ \ 3500) \times \left(\begin{array}{ccc} .80 & .10 & .10 \\ .05 & .80 & .15 \\ .08 & .12 & .80 \end{array}\right) = (2430 \ \ 3070 \ \ 3500)$$

Annual profit = 2430(300-50) - 250,000 = \$350,000 per year

With the pool addition:

$$(2500 \ \ 3000 \ \ 3500) \times \left(\begin{array}{ccc} .90 & .03 & .07 \\ .15 & .75 & .10 \\ .20 & .10 & .70 \end{array}\right) = (3400 \ \ 2675 \ \ 2925)$$

Annual profit = 3400(300-50) - 250,000 = \$600,000 per year

The increase in annual profit next year = 600,000 - 350,000 = \$250,000. They should build the pool.

16-20   Next year's market shares would be:

$$(.2 \ \ .4 \ \ .4) \left(\begin{array}{ccc} .85 & .10 & .05 \\ .08 & .85 & .07 \\ .07 & .03 & .90 \end{array}\right) = (.230 \ \ .372 \ \ .398)$$

The additional \$100,000 expenditure would result in a gain in market share for company A from 20% to 23%. The added net income is $(.05)(.03)(\$100,000) = \$150,000$ which is greater than the $100,000,000 expenditure. Company A, should, therefore, adopt the selling plan.

16-21 Under Policy 1, all bearings will be replaced at each inspection, but none will wear out, so cost/truck/inspection is $50.

Under Policy 2: N = New, A = State 2 (states 3 and 4 go immediately to state N).

$$
\begin{array}{cc}
 & \begin{array}{cc} N & A \end{array} \\
\begin{array}{c} N \\ A \end{array} & \left(\begin{array}{cc} .1 & .9 \\ .3+.1 & .6 \end{array} \right)
\end{array}
\qquad
\begin{array}{l}
N = .1N + .4A \\
A = .9N + .6A \\
N + A = 1
\end{array}
\qquad
\begin{array}{l}
\text{Solving gives:} \\
N = 4/13, \\
A = 9/13
\end{array}
$$

Thus at the next inspection $(4/13)(1/10) + (9/13)(3/10) = 31/130$ is the fraction needing replacement because it is in state 3, and $(9/13)(1/10) = 9/130$ is the fraction worn out. So we have:

Cost/truck/inspection = $31/130(50) + 9/130(250) = \$29.23$

Policy 2 should be used.

16-22 Solving the pre-1986 equilibrium conditions we have:

$$
\begin{array}{llll}
D = .70D + .03W + .04B & \quad 0 = -.30D + .03W + .04B & \text{eq. 1} \\
W = .15D + .85W + .06B & \quad 0 = .15D - .15W + .06B & \text{eq. 2} \\
B = .15D + .12W + .90B & \quad 0 = .15D + .12W - .10B & \text{eq. 3} \\
1 = D + W + B & \quad 1 = D + W + B & \text{eq. 4}
\end{array}
$$

Solving simultaneously, we have the equilibrium market shares:

D = .10788
W = .33195
B = .56017

Performing identical calculations to obtain the post-1986 conditions, we have the following equilibrium market shares:

D = .16667
W = .27778
B = .55555

The advertising campaign for Devlon was quite successful, because their equilibrium market share has risen about 6 percentage points yielding about a 50% sales increase for them. It is apparent that in directing advertising toward the middle-age, middle-income group, Devlon penetrated Williams Sportsgear's market, but had very little impact on Bounceright's market.

16-23 The market shares next year are projected to be:

$$(.25 \quad .40 \quad .35) \begin{pmatrix} .80 & .15 & .05 \\ .15 & .80 & .05 \\ .05 & .05 & .90 \end{pmatrix} = (.2775 \quad .3750 \quad .3475)$$

With an increase from .25 to .2775 market share, the profit gained is (.06)(.0275)($1,000,000) = $1,650. Since this is greater than the $1,500 cost, Pedal Power should adopt the plan.

16-24 Step 1: Partitioning the matrix in 4 submatrices I, O, R, and Q:

$$\begin{array}{c} \\ \text{Paid} \\ \text{Bad debt} \\ \text{Current} \\ \text{Late} \end{array} \begin{pmatrix} \overbrace{}^{I} & & \overbrace{}^{O} & \\ 1 & 0 & 0 & 0 \\ \underline{0} & \underline{1} & \underline{0} & \underline{0} \\ .7 & 0 & .2 & .1 \\ .4 & .2 & .3 & .1 \\ \underbrace{}_{R} & & \underbrace{}_{Q} & \end{pmatrix}$$

Step 2: $N = I - Q = \begin{pmatrix} .8 & -.1 \\ -.3 & .9 \end{pmatrix}$

Step 3: Find N^{-1}

$\begin{pmatrix} .8 & -.1 \\ -.3 & .9 \end{pmatrix} \begin{pmatrix} 1 & 0 \\ 0 & 1 \end{pmatrix}$ Multiply row 1 by 10/8

$\begin{pmatrix} 1 & -.125 \\ -.3 & .9 \end{pmatrix} \begin{pmatrix} 1.25 & 0 \\ 0 & 1 \end{pmatrix}$ Multiply row 1 by .3 and add to row 2

$\begin{pmatrix} 1 & -.125 \\ 0 & .8625 \end{pmatrix} \begin{pmatrix} 1.25 & 0 \\ .375 & 1 \end{pmatrix}$ Divide row 2 by .8625

$\begin{pmatrix} 1 & -.125 \\ 0 & 1 \end{pmatrix} \begin{pmatrix} 1.25 & 0 \\ .43478 & 1.15942 \end{pmatrix}$ Multiply row 2 by .125 and add to row 1

$\begin{pmatrix} 1 & 0 \\ 0 & 1 \end{pmatrix} \begin{pmatrix} 1.30435 & .14493 \\ .43478 & 1.15942 \end{pmatrix}$

Check: Find N x N⁻¹

$$\begin{pmatrix} .8 & -.1 \\ -.3 & .9 \end{pmatrix} \begin{pmatrix} 1.30435 & .14493 \\ .43478 & 1.15942 \end{pmatrix} = \begin{pmatrix} 1 & 0 \\ 0 & 1 \end{pmatrix}$$

Step 4:

$$N^{-1}R = \begin{pmatrix} 1.30435 & .14493 \\ .43478 & 1.15942 \end{pmatrix} \begin{pmatrix} .7 & 0 \\ .4 & .2 \end{pmatrix} = \begin{pmatrix} .97102 & .02899 \\ .76811 & .23188 \end{pmatrix}$$

$$(68,000 \quad 26,000) \begin{pmatrix} .97102 & .02899 \\ .76811 & .23188 \end{pmatrix} = (86,000 \quad 8,000)$$

Expected to be paid = $86,000
Expected bad debt = $ 8,000.

16-25 Step 1: Partition the matrix into 4 submatrices (I, Θ, R, and Q)

$$\begin{array}{cc} & \text{I} \qquad\qquad\quad \Theta \\ \begin{matrix} \text{Paid} \\ \text{Bad debt} \\ \text{Current} \\ \text{Overdue} \end{matrix} & \left(\begin{array}{cc|cc} 1 & 0 & 0 & 0 \\ 0 & 1 & 0 & 0 \\ \hline .4 & 0 & .3 & .3 \\ .5 & .1 & .2 & .2 \end{array}\right) \\ & \quad\ \text{R} \qquad\qquad \text{Q} \end{array}$$

Step 2:

$$N = I - Q = \begin{pmatrix} .7 & -.3 \\ -.2 & .8 \end{pmatrix}$$

Step 3:

Find N⁻¹: $\begin{pmatrix} .7 & -.3 \\ -.2 & .8 \end{pmatrix}$ $\begin{pmatrix} 1 & 0 \\ 0 & 1 \end{pmatrix}$ Multiply row 1 by 10/7

$\begin{pmatrix} 1 & -3/7 \\ -1/5 & 4/5 \end{pmatrix}\begin{pmatrix} 10/7 & 0 \\ 0 & 1 \end{pmatrix}$ Multiply row 1 by 1/5 and add to row 2

$\begin{pmatrix} 1 & -3/7 \\ 0 & 5/7 \end{pmatrix}\begin{pmatrix} 10/7 & 0 \\ 2/7 & 1 \end{pmatrix}$ Multiply row 2 by 7/5

$\begin{pmatrix} 1 & -3/7 \\ 0 & 1 \end{pmatrix}\begin{pmatrix} 10/7 & 0 \\ 2/5 & 7/5 \end{pmatrix}$ Multiply row 2 by 3/7 and add to row 1

$\begin{pmatrix} 1 & 0 \\ 0 & 1 \end{pmatrix} \begin{pmatrix} 8/5 & 3/5 \\ 2/5 & 7/5 \end{pmatrix}$

Step 4:

$$N^{-1}R = \begin{pmatrix} 8/5 & 3/5 \\ 2/5 & 7/5 \end{pmatrix}\begin{pmatrix} 4/10 & 0 \\ 5/10 & 1/10 \end{pmatrix} = \begin{pmatrix} .94 & .06 \\ .86 & .14 \end{pmatrix}$$

Expected paid = .94(20,000) + .86(14,000) = 18,800 + 12,040
                = $30,840
Exp. bad debt = .06(20,000) + .14(14,000) = 1,200 + 1,960
                = $ 3,160

16-26 For the present situation the equilibrium equations are:

        A = .7A + .4J + .3M   0 = -.3A + .4J + .3M   eq. 1
        J = .3A + .4J + 0M   0 = .3A - .6J + 0M   eq. 2
        M = 0A + .2J + .7M   0 =   0A + .2J + .3M   eq. 3
        1 = A + J + M   1 = A + J + M

Solving simultaneously, we have the equilibrium values:

        J = .27   No. of J = (.27)(20) = 5.4
        M = .18   No. of M = (.18)(20) = 3.6
        A = .55   No. of A = (.54)(20) = 11.0

For the proposal pay scale, we perform similar calculations
to obtain the equilibrium values:

        J = .27   No. of J = (.27)(20) = 5.4
        M = .40   No. of M = (.40)(20) = 8.0
        A = .33   No. of A = (.33)(20) = 6.6

With the old pay scale, the detected defects per day are:

        Defects detected = (3)(11.0)(+ (5)(5.4) + (8)(3.6)
                         = 88.8 defects per day.

With the new pay scale, we have:

        Defects detected = (3)(6.6) + (5)(5.4) + (8)(8)
                         = 110.8 defects per day.

Cost savings for detecting defects = (110.8 - 88.8)($100)
                                   = $2,200 per day.

New payroll costs =(6.6)(60)+(5.4)(78)+(8.0)(98) =$1,601.20
Old payroll costs =(11.0)(48)+(5.4)(56)+(3.6)(74)=$1,096.80
                                   increase in payroll = $ 504.40

Since the cost savings in undetected defects is greater
than the added payroll cost, there is a convincing argument
for raising the wage rate.

16-27 We multiply the population in each state at the beginning
       of the first week in June by the matrix of transition
       probabilities to obtain our predicted state for the second
       week in June.

392

$$(30 \quad 70 \quad 100 \quad 300 \quad 99{,}500) \times \begin{pmatrix} .05 & .60 & .15 & 0 & .20 \\ .20 & .20 & .30 & .30 & 0 \\ 0 & .10 & .10 & .80 & 0 \\ 0 & 0 & .10 & 0 & .90 \\ .001 & .001 & .003 & 0 & .995 \end{pmatrix}$$

$$= (115 \quad 141.5 \quad 364 \quad 101 \quad 99{,}278.5)$$

The predicted state of next week's hospital system is:

Critical:	115 people
Poor:	142 people
Fair:	364 people
Good:	101 people
Total =	722 people

16-28 Step 1: partition

$$I = \begin{pmatrix} 1 & 0 \\ 0 & 1 \end{pmatrix} \qquad O = \begin{pmatrix} 0 & 0 \\ 0 & 0 \end{pmatrix}$$

$$R = \begin{pmatrix} .2 & .4 \\ .9 & .1 \end{pmatrix} \qquad Q = \begin{pmatrix} 0 & .4 \\ 0 & 0 \end{pmatrix}$$

Step 2: Find $N = I - Q$:

$$N = \begin{pmatrix} 1 & 0 \\ 0 & 1 \end{pmatrix} - \begin{pmatrix} 0 & .4 \\ 0 & 0 \end{pmatrix} = \begin{pmatrix} 1 & -.4 \\ 0 & 1 \end{pmatrix}$$

Step 3: Find the inverse of N:

$$\begin{pmatrix} 1 & -.4 \\ 0 & 1 \end{pmatrix} \begin{pmatrix} 1 & 0 \\ 0 & 1 \end{pmatrix} \qquad \begin{array}{l} \text{Multiply row 2 by .4 and} \\ \text{add to row 1} \end{array}$$

$$\begin{pmatrix} 1 & 0 \\ 0 & 1 \end{pmatrix} \begin{pmatrix} 1 & .4 \\ 0 & 1 \end{pmatrix}$$

$$N^{-1} = \begin{pmatrix} 1 & .4 \\ 0 & 1 \end{pmatrix}$$

check $$\begin{pmatrix} 1 & -.4 \\ 0 & 1 \end{pmatrix} \times \begin{pmatrix} 1 & .4 \\ 0 & 1 \end{pmatrix} = \begin{pmatrix} 1 & 0 \\ 0 & 1 \end{pmatrix}$$

Step 4: Find $N^{-1} \times R$:

$$\begin{pmatrix} 1 & .4 \\ 0 & 1 \end{pmatrix} \times \begin{pmatrix} .2 & .4 \\ .9 & .1 \end{pmatrix} = \begin{pmatrix} .56 & .44 \\ .90 & .10 \end{pmatrix}$$

With all 30 officers being in state F at the beginning and none being in state S, we have:

$$(30 \quad 0) \quad X \quad \begin{pmatrix} .56 & .44 \\ .90 & .10 \end{pmatrix} = \quad (16.8 \quad 13.2)$$

Consequently, the expected number reaching retirement is 16.8 officers with the remaining 13.2 being the expected number to quit the police force.

16-29   We first need to adjust the recorded June movements for the vehicles not rented. At Allenville, for example, the following vehicles arrived in June:

30	arrived from B
60	arrived from C
50	arrived from D
140	arrived

The following vehicles left Allenville:

40	departed for B
80	departed for C
60	departed for D
180	departed

Therefore, the inventory on hand in Allenville on the first of June was

Old inventory + arrivals - departures = new inventory

150	now on hand (new inventory)
-140	arrived
+180	departed
190	were on hand June 1

Thus, we find that 190-180 = 10 vehicles remained in Allenville through the month (5 of the 10 were rented and returned to Allenville, while the other 5 were not rented).

The retention at Allenville is 10. Performing these same calculations for the other cities, we get:

From	A	B	C	D	June 1 inventory total across row
A	10	40	80	60	190 vehicles
B	30	10	50	40	130 vehicles
C	60	60	10	10	140 vehicles
D	50	50	20	30	150 vehicles
					620 vehicles

Our matrix of transition probabilities is:

Retention and loss

	A	B	C	D	
A	.053	.200	.421	.316	Retention
B	.231	.077	.385	.308	and gain
C	.429	.429	.071	.071	
D	.333	.333	.133	.200	

We now develop our predicted inventory position for August 1:

$$(150 \quad 160 \quad 160 \quad 150) \times \begin{pmatrix} .053 & .211 & .421 & .316 \\ .231 & .077 & .385 & .308 \\ .429 & .429 & .071 & .071 \\ .333 & .333 & .133 & .200 \end{pmatrix} = \begin{pmatrix} 163.50 \\ 162.56 \\ 156.06 \\ 138.04 \end{pmatrix}$$

<u>Beginning Inventory for August</u>
Allenville	163 vehicles
Bakertown	163 vehicles
Charlesburg	156 vehicles
Delta City	<u>138 vehicles</u>
	620 vehicles

Since we have more than the minimum of 135 vehicles in each of the cities, we anticipate no redistributions going into August. Now we develop our predicted inventory for the first of September:

$$(163 \quad 163 \quad 156 \quad 138) \times \begin{pmatrix} .053 & .211 & .421 & .316 \\ .231 & .077 & .385 & .308 \\ .429 & .429 & .071 & .071 \\ .333 & .333 & .133 & .200 \end{pmatrix} = \begin{pmatrix} 159.16 \\ 159.81 \\ 160.81 \\ 140.39 \end{pmatrix}$$

<u>Beginning Inventory for September</u>
Allenville	159 vehicles
Bakertown	160 vehicles
Charlesburg	161 vehicles
Delta City	<u>140 vehicles</u>
	620 vehicles

Again, we are above the 135-vehicle minimum, and no redistribution is forecast to be required going into September.

16-30 Let B_1 = fraction of blood up to 1 period old
  B_2 = fraction of blood up to 2 periods old
  B_3 = fraction of blood up to 3 periods old
  B_4 = fraction of blood up to 4 periods old
  B_5 = fraction of blood thrown away

With the old policy the transition matrix is:

$$
\begin{array}{c c}
 & \begin{array}{c c c c c} B_1 & B_2 & B_3 & B_4 & B_5 \end{array} \\
\begin{array}{c} B_1 \\ B_2 \\ B_3 \\ B_4 \\ B_5 \end{array} &
\left(\begin{array}{c c c c c}
.3 & .7 & 0 & 0 & 0 \\
.3 & 0 & .7 & 0 & 0 \\
.3 & 0 & 0 & .7 & 0 \\
.3 & 0 & 0 & 0 & .7 \\
1.0 & 0 & 0 & 0 & 0
\end{array}\right)
\end{array}
$$

Solving for equilibrium:

$$B_1 = .3B_1 + .3B_2 + .3B_3 + .3B_4 + B_5$$
$$B_2 = .7B_1$$
$$B_3 = .7B_2$$
$$B_4 = .7B_3$$
$$B_5 = .7B_4$$
$$1 = B_1 + B_2 + B_3 + B_4 + B_5$$

$$B_1 = .3606$$
$$B_2 = .2524$$
$$B_3 = .1767$$
$$B_4 = .1237$$
$$B_5 = .0866$$

So: $(.0866)(200) = 17$ pints are thrown away each period.

Number of donors $= (.3)(200) + 17 = 77$ donors each period.

used   thrown
         away

With the new policy, at equilibrium, it is intuitive that all blood will be used (i.e., none thrown away). We know that $(.3)(200) = 60$ pints are used each period, and at an inventory level of 200 pints, then:

$$200/60 = 3 \tfrac{1}{3} \text{ periods}$$

of inventory are on hand. The blood is good for 4 periods, however, so none need be wasted. All blood in state B_4 will be used in each period and X% of the blood in B_3 will be used. The translation matrix is:

$$
\begin{array}{c c}
 & \begin{array}{c c c c} B_1 & B_2 & B_3 & B_4 \end{array} \\
\begin{array}{c} B_1 \\ B_2 \\ B_3 \\ B_4 \end{array} &
\left(\begin{array}{c c c c}
0 & 1 & 0 & 0 \\
0 & 0 & 1 & 0 \\
X & 0 & 0 & 1-X \\
1 & 0 & 0 & 0
\end{array}\right)
\end{array}
$$

At equilibrium:

$$B_1 = XB_3 + B_4$$
$$B_2 = B_1$$
$$B_3 = B_2 = B_1$$
$$B_4 = (1-X)B_3 = (1-X)B_1$$
$$1 = B_1 + B_2 + B_3 + B_4$$

In order to solve this we introduce B_1', B_2', B_3', and B_4' where B_1' is the number of pints (rather than fraction). The last equilibrium can then be written:

$$200 = B_1' + B_2' + B_3' + B_4' \quad \text{where } B_1' = 60 \text{ pints}$$

Therefore: $B_1' = 60$ pints
$B_2' = 60$ pints
$B_3' = 60$ pints
$B_4' = 20$ pints

$$B_4' = (1 - X)B_1' \qquad 1 - X = 20/60 = 1/3 \qquad X = 2/3$$

Yielding:

| | Retention and loss | | | |
	B_1	B_2	B_3	B_4
Retention B_1	0	1	0	0
and B_2	0	0	1	0
gain B_3	2/3	0	0	1/3
B_4	1	0	0	0

$B_1 = .3$
$B_2 = .3$
$B_3 = .3$
$B_4 = .1$

Therefore: 17 fewer donors are required with the new policy or a total of 60 donors are required. Two-thirds of the blood taken from the inventory will be 2 to 3 months old and 1/3 will be 3 to 4 months old.

16-31 We take our matrix of transition probabilities:

	A	B	C	D
A	.50	.20	.20	.10
B	.20	.40	.20	.20
C	.10	.20	.60	.10
D	.10	.20	.20	.50

397

Now we solve for the equilibrium values of A, B, C, and D:

```
A = .5A + .2B + .1C + .1D
B = .2A + .4B + .2C + .2D
C = .2A + .2B + .6C + .2D
1 = A + B + C + D
```

Regrouping and eliminating one equation, we have:

```
0 = -.5A + .2B + .1C + .1D     (1)
0 = -.2A - .6B + .2C + .2D     (2)
0 =  .2A + .2B - .4C + .2D     (3)
1 = A + B + C + D              (4)
```

Solving these equations simultaneously, we obtain the fraction of workers who would be holding each of the jobs at equilibrium.

```
A = .2083
B = .2500
C = .3333
D = .2083
```

16-32 The transition matrix is:

$$
\begin{array}{c c}
 & \begin{array}{ccc} \Theta & F & N \end{array} \\
\begin{array}{c} \Theta \\ F \\ N \end{array} &
\left(\begin{array}{ccc}
.92 & .05 & .03 \\
.06 & .92 & .02 \\
.06 & .04 & .90
\end{array}\right)
\end{array}
$$

The equilibrium equations are:

```
0 = -.08Θ + .06F + .06N
0 =  .05Θ - .08F + .04N
1 =    Θ +    F +    N
```

Solving simultaneously we get:

```
Θ = .4286
F = .3690
N = .2024
```

16-33 With the policy of replacing piston rings that are state 3 or worse, our matrix of transition probabilities is:

Retention and loss

$$
\begin{array}{c c}
 & \begin{array}{cccc} S_1 & S_2 & S_3 & S_4 \end{array} \\
\begin{array}{c} S_1 \\ S_2 \\ S_3 \\ S_4 \end{array} &
\left(\begin{array}{cccc}
0 & .8 & .2 & 0 \\
0 & .5 & .4 & .1 \\
1 & 0 & 0 & 0 \\
1 & 0 & 0 & 0
\end{array}\right)
\end{array}
$$

Retention and gain

The equilibrium equations are:

$$S_1 = 0S_1 + 0S_2 + 1S_3 + 1S_4 \qquad (1)$$
$$S_2 = .8S_1 + .5S_2 + 0S_3 + 0S_4 \qquad (2)$$
$$S_3 = .2S_1 + .4S_2 + 0S_3 + 0S_4 \qquad (3)$$
$$S_4 = 0S_1 + 1S_2 + 0S_3 + 0S_4 \qquad (4)$$
$$1 = S_1 + S_2 + S_3 + S_4 \qquad (5)$$

Solving simultaneously, we get:

$$S_1 = .278$$
$$S_2 = .444$$
$$S_3 = .233$$
$$S_4 = .044$$

The expected cost per period per piston ring is:

$$Cost = (.044)(\$800) + (.233)(\$100)$$
$$= \$58.50$$

Now we consider the case where all rings in state 2 or worse are replaced. Since state 4 can never be reached, our matrix of transition probabilities is:

Retention and loss

	S_1	S_2	S_3	
S_1	0	.8	.2	Retention and gain
S_2	1	0	0	
S_3	1	0	0	

This yields the equilibrium equations:

$$S_1 = 0S_1 + 1S_2 + 1S_3$$
$$S_2 = .8S_1 + 0S_2 + 0S_3$$
$$S_3 = .2S_1 + 0S_2 + 0S_3$$
$$1 = S_1 + S_2 + S_3$$

Which gives us the values:

$$S_1 = .500$$
$$S_2 = .400$$
$$S_3 = .100$$

The expected average cost per piston ring for this case is:

$$Cost = (.100)(\$100) + (.400)(\$100)$$
$$= \$50$$

The least-cost alternative is to replace the rings when they are state 2 or worse.

16-34 $N = I - Q = \begin{pmatrix} 1 & 0 \\ 0 & 1 \end{pmatrix} - \begin{pmatrix} .12 & .08 \\ .30 & .25 \end{pmatrix} = \begin{pmatrix} .88 & -08 \\ -.30 & .75 \end{pmatrix}$

Finding N^{-1}:

$\begin{pmatrix} .88 & -08 \\ -.30 & .75 \end{pmatrix} \begin{pmatrix} 1 & 0 \\ 0 & 1 \end{pmatrix}$ Divide row 1 by .88

$\begin{pmatrix} 1 & -.0909 \\ -.3 & .75 \end{pmatrix} \begin{pmatrix} 1.1364 & 0 \\ 0 & 1 \end{pmatrix}$ Multiply row 1 by .3 and add to row 2

$\begin{pmatrix} 1 & -.0909 \\ 0 & .7227 \end{pmatrix} \begin{pmatrix} 1.1364 & 0 \\ .3409 & 1 \end{pmatrix}$ Divide row 2 by .7227

$\begin{pmatrix} 1 & -.0909 \\ 0 & 1 \end{pmatrix} \begin{pmatrix} 1.1364 & 0 \\ .4717 & 1.3837 \end{pmatrix}$ Multiply row 2 by .0909 and add to row 1

$\begin{pmatrix} 1 & 0 \\ 0 & 1 \end{pmatrix} \begin{pmatrix} 1.1793 & .1258 \\ .4717 & 1.3837 \end{pmatrix}$

$N^{-1} = \begin{pmatrix} 1.1793 & .1258 \\ .4717 & 1.3837 \end{pmatrix}$

$N^{-1}R = \begin{pmatrix} 1.1793 & .1258 \\ .4717 & 1.3837 \end{pmatrix} \begin{pmatrix} .8 & 0 \\ .2 & .25 \end{pmatrix} = \begin{pmatrix} .9686 & .0315 \\ .6541 & .3459 \end{pmatrix}$

$(6,000,000 \quad 500,000) \begin{pmatrix} .9686 & .0315 \\ .6541 & .3459 \end{pmatrix} = (6,138,650 \quad 361,950)$

Consequently, the bank can expect to foreclose on $361,950 of the currently outstanding debt. This will involve foreclosure proceedings on 361,950/50,000 = 7.239 farms.

16-35 The eqilibrium equations are:

$$0 = -.02P + .15M1 + .20M2 + .83M3$$
$$0 = .02P - .90M1 + .06M2 + 0M3$$
$$0 = 0P + .70M1 - .92M2 + .05M3$$
$$1 = P + M1 + M2 + M3$$

Solving simultaneously we get:

$$P = .9456$$
$$M1 = .0222$$
$$M2 = .0177$$
$$M3 = .0145$$

Since the element in row P and column M1 of the matrix of transitional probabilities is given as .02 and this is also given as 100 new members per month, the total number in state P must be P = 100/.02 = 5000.

Since these 5000 members of P constitute .9456 of the total number in the system, we have:

$$.9456N = 5000$$
$$N = 5000/.9456 = 5288$$

Total steady state members = N - P = 288 members

Steady state profit = (288)($50) = $14,400 per month

16-36 The equlibrium equations are:

$$0 = -.02P + .15M1 + .34M2 + .96M3$$
$$0 = .02P - .96M1 + 0M2 + 0M3$$
$$0 = 0P + .68M1 - .97M2 + 0M3$$
$$1 = P + M1 + M2 + M3$$

Solving simultaneously we get:

$$P = .9543$$
$$M1 = .0199$$
$$M2 = .0139$$
$$M3 = .0119$$

We assume N remains constant at 5288.

Total steady-state members = N (M1 + M2 + M3)
                           = N (.0199 + .0139 + .0119)
                           = (.0457)(5288) = 242 members

Steady-state profit = (242)($50) = $12,100 per month

Therefore, if all 100 members take up the combined membership, the diet club loses $14,400 - 12,100 = $2,300. The profit lost per member is 2,300/100 = $23. So assuming all persons joining the combined option do so at the very beginning, the racket club should reimburse the diet club $23 for each member signed up for the combined plan.

SOLUTIONS FOR

OPTIMIZATION UNLIMITED

EXERCISES

CHAPTER 2 - ANSWERS

1. P{dry} = 67.9%
    P{wet} = 32.1%
    P{1} = 25.5%
    P{2} = 74.5%
    P{2|wet} = P{2,wet}/P{wet} = 66.1%
    P{2|dry} = 78.4%
    P{wet|1} = P{wet,1}/P{1} = 42.6%
    P{dry|1} = 57.4%

2. p = .745
    q = .255
    $(10!/8!2!)(.745)^8(.255)^2$ = 27.8%

3. $\bar{X}$ = 9967.5
    σ = 6978.35
    P{X > 20,000} = P{z > 1.4377} = .07493 = 7.5%
    Actual: 13/184 = 7.1%
    P{X < 5,000} = P{z < .7118} = .23885 = 23.9%
    Actual: 43/184 = 23.4%

CHAPTER 3 - ANSWERS

1. See CH3.WK1 for deseasonalized data.

    The seasonal indices are:

Month	Index
Jan	.991
Feb	1.164
Mar	.875
Apr	.678
May	1.021
Jun	.897
Jul	.949
Aug	.975
Sep	1.159
Oct	.982
Nov	1.049
Dec	1.259

2. See CH3.WK2 for smoothing data.

    Using an α of .3, the monthly forecast value is 2022.5.
    The warm-up MSE for α = .3 is 42,982.5.

3. Multiplying the forecast value by the seasonal indices, the
    forecasts for the next six months are:

Month	Sales
Oct	$1986
Nov	$2122
Dec	$2546
Jan	$2004
Feb	$2354
Mar	$1770

4. See CH3.WK3.

    Intercept = -2421.8
    Slope = 669.3

5. See CH3.WK3.

    α_1 = .9
    α_2 = .01

Warm-up MSE = 1,151,554.3
Week 52 value = 35,972.9 thousands of gallons

6. See CH3.WK4.

    ϕ = 1.01 (slightly exponential trend)
    Warm-up MSE = 1,141,021.9
    Week 52 value = 39,811.2 thousands of gallons

7. The cumulative quantity spilled shows a very slightly exponential trend, increasing at a rate of about 669,300 gallons a week.

CHAPTER 4 - ANSWERS

For Scenario 1 see CH4.WK1 (Conference), CH4.WK2 (Final Four) and CH4.WK3 (NCAA Champs).

For Scenario 2 see CH4.WK4 (Final Four) and CH4.WK5 (NCAA Champs).

For Scenario 3 see CH4.WK6 (NCAA Champs).

Scenario 1

Type of T-Shirt	(1) Number of Shirts	Expected Profit	(2) Expected Profit with Perfect Info	(3) Value of Perfect Info
Conference	6000	$14,306.25	$32,625	$9,318.75
Final Four	8000	$3,106.25	$22,837.50	$19,731.25
NCAA Champs	0	$0	$11,375	$11,375

Scenario 2

Type of T-Shirt	(1) Number of Shirts	Expected Profit	(2) Expected Profit with Perfect Info	(3) Value of Perfect Info
Conference		Same as Scenario 1		
Final Four	8000	$16,437.50	$32,625	$16,187.50
NCAA Champs	0	$0	$16,250	$16,250

Scenario 3

Type of T-Shirt	(1) Number of Shirts	Expected Profit	(2) Expected Profit with Perfect Info	(3) Value of Perfect Info
Conference		Same as Scenario 1		
Final Four		Same as Scenario 2		
NCAA Champs	10000	$6,250	$32,500	$26,250

1. With burn program, expected losses = $40,806,250.
   Without burn program, expected losses = $87,000,000.

2. The prescribed burning program is the most cost-effective
   option until the losses are assessed at between two and
   three times their direct costs. Then the optimal decision
   changes and the prescribed burning policy has greater
   expected losses.

3. With burn program, expected losses = $49,896,250.
   Without burn program, expected losses = $109,200,000.

4. a. The optimal solution is to mobilize and, if marginal
      weather conditions persist, burn anyway.

   b. The optimal solution is to mobilize and, if marginal
      weather conditions persist, don't burn.

5. a. The optimal solution is to mobilize and, if marginal
      weather persists, burn anyway.

   b. The optimal solution is to not mobilize.

CHAPTER 6 - ANSWERS

1. CHWs in Esmereldas should order from a mission pharmacy
    (44.78 orders per year). CHWs in Imbabura should order
    from a mission pharmacy (45.23 orders per year). CHWs in
    Guayas should order from a mission pharmacy (39.63 orders
    per year). CHWs in Bolivar should order from a mission
    pharmacy (45.17) orders per year). CHWs in Napo should
    order from a hospital pharmacy (40.92 orders a year).

    For details, see the appropriate worksheets:

Province	Government	Mission	Hospital
Esmereldas	CH6.WK1	CH6.WK2	CH6.WK3
Imbabura	CH6.WK4	CH6.WK5	CH6.WK6
Guayas	CH6.WK7	CH6.WK8	CH6.WK9
Bolivar	CH6.WKA	CH6.WKB	CH6.WKC
Napo	CH6.WKD	CH6.WKE	CH6.WKF

2. If CHWs in Esmereldas can order individual items from
    different sources, the optimal sources and number of orders
    per year are as follows. See worksheets CH6.WKG through
    CH6.WKP for details.

Item	Source	Orders/Year
Aspirin	Mission	.22
Alcohol	Mission	.06
Hydrogen peroxide	Mission	.05
Sterile gauze	Mission	.08
Adhesive tape	Hospital	.18
Anti-spasmodic	Hospital	.14
Merthiolate	Mission	.07
Anti-scabies lotion	Mission	.08
Cotton	Mission	.09
Eye ointment	Hospital	.08

3. Because each item in the inventory actually reflects a bulk
    quantity, the yearly usage rates for each item are
    relatively low. In addition, the ordering costs are
    significant, causing the EOQ model to calculate an
    extremely low number of orders per year for each item. It
    is clear that in this situation, it does not make sense to
    consider a separate ordering policy for each item as the
    standard EOQ model does. The CHWs would most likely

replenish inventory levels of all their items at one time,
only incurring an "ordering cost" once or twice a year.
Each "order" would then reflect a restocking of all items
to some recommended level. Consequently, a more
appropriate model would be able to link together the demand
for the various items into a combined inventory policy,
recommending an optimal restocking level for each item from
any depleted state.

CHAPTER 7 - ANSWERS

1. See CH7.WKA through CH7.WKY for additional data on each SKU.

Supplier	Product Name	Nᴜ	B

Packs

Camp Gear	Half Pint	37.08	28.32
Outdoor Equipment	Kidpack Scooter	36.48 25.06	28.78 20.95
Sportstuff	Shenandoah	44.80	30.47
Trails End	Packer Jr.	36.86	28.48

Child Carriers

| Sportstuff | Colt
Bronco
Stallion | 44.60
38.21
34.46 | 37.67
32.97
30.47 |
| Trails End | Kid Karrier | 28.45 | 25.83 |

Boots

Hi-Tek	Sierra Jr. Scout	38.23 29.65	27.46 24.79
Camp Gear	Kid Klimbers	40.62	31.02
Mtn. Footwear	Baby Packer Child Packer	35.63 36.83	23.57 25.66
South Face	Teddy Panda	36.86 40.38	28.48 31.20

Supplier	Product Name	Nᵤ	B

Sleeping Bags

Supplier	Product Name	Nᵤ	B
Sportstuff	Little Dipper Sprite	42.56 32.09	32.07 26.17
Outdoor Equipment	Littlefoot Bigfoot	26.74 21.62	23.56 19.42
Camp Gear	Sidekick Fledgling	35.26 24.22	29.78 21.67
South Face	Baby Bunting Kindling Red Fox	36.16 31.70 34.88	29.04 26.50 30.10

2. Total annual cost of the inventory system with backorders is $6,944.60.

3. Without backorders, the total annual cost is $16,439.89. Annual savings are $9,495.29.

4. For each boot, the backorder penalty that causes B to be 50% (or less) of EOQ is:

Hi-Tek Sierra Jr.	$25
Hi-Tek Scout	$50
Camp Gear Kid Klimbers	$35
Mtn. Footwear Baby Packer	$20
Mtn. Footwear Child Packer	$25
South Face Teddy	$35
South Face Panda	$35

1.   Let A1 be the number of hours worked by Adam on Monday, B2
     be the number of hours worked by Barbara on Tuesday, etc.
     Then the formulation is as follows:

     Minimize: 6.10(A1 + A2 + A3 + A4) + 6.30 (B2 + B4)
               + 5.80(C2 + C3 + C4 + C5) + 6.00(D1 + D2
               + D3 + D4 + D5) + 5.90(E1 + E5)
               + 6.75(F1 + F3 + F5)

     Subject to
      A1 + D1 + E1 + F1 ≥ 10
      A2 + B2 + C2 + D2 ≥ 10
      A3 + C3 + D3 + F3 ≥ 10
      A4 + B4 + C4 + D4 ≥ 10
      C5 + D5 + E5 + F5 ≥ 10
      A1 + A2 + A3 + A4 ≤ 20
      B2 + B4 ≤ 20
      C2 + C3 + C4 + C5 ≤ 20
      D1 + D2 + D3 + D4 + D5 ≤ 20
      E1 + E5 ≤ 20
      F1 + F3 + F5 ≤ 20
      A1 ≤ 4, A2 ≤ 8, A3 ≤ 4, A4 ≤ 8
      B2 ≤ 5, B4 ≤ 5
      C2 ≤ 6, C3 ≤ 4, C4 ≤ 6, C5 ≤ 4
      D1 ≤ 4, D2 ≤ 4, D3 ≤ 4, D4 ≤ 4, D5 ≤ 4
      E1 ≤ 8, E5 ≤ 8
      F1 ≤ 5,F3 ≤ 5, F5 ≤ 5
      All variables ≥ 0

     Note: one solution to the above LP is:
      A3 = 2, C2 = 6, C3 = 4, C4 = 6, C5 = 4, D1 = 2, D2 = 4,
      D3 = 4, D4 = 4, E1 = 8, E5 = 6, for a total cost of
      $294.80.

2.   The additional constraints are:

      A1 + A2 + A3 + A4 ≥ 8
      B2 + B4 ≥ 8
      C2 + C3 + C4 + C5 ≥ 8
      D1 + D2 + D3 + D4 + D5 ≥ 8
      E1 + E5 ≥ 8
      F1 + F3 + F5 ≥ 8

     Note: one optimal solution with these additional
     constraints is:
      A1 = 1, A3 = 4, A4 = 3, B2 = 5, B4 = 3, C2 = 5, C3 = 4,
      C5 = 1, D4 = 4, D5 = 4, E1 = 8, F1 = 1, F3 = 2, F5 = 5,
      for a total cost of $306.40.

3. Let B, W, and C represent thousands of acres of beans,
    wheat, and corn, respectively, planted by the Department of
    Agriculture. Then the constraint set is:

    B + W + C = 12,000
    8000B + 6500W + 7000C ≥ 50,000,000
    150B + 200W + 100C ≥ 1,500,000
    15B + 10W + 20C ≥ 300,000
    60,000B + 80,000W + 100,000C ≤ 1,000,000,000

4. Maximize: 8000B + 6500W + 7000C
    Maximize: 150B + 200W + 100C
    Maximize: 15B + 10W + 20C

5. Minimize: 60,000B + 80,000W + 100,000C

1. Ray would make 832.877 pounds of Peaceful Pasture, 698.630 pounds of Natural Beauty, 369.863 pounds of Country Meadow and 972.603 pounds of Field of Color. His total profit would be $4944.52.

   This solution would require the following amounts of the individual seeds:

Seed	Pounds
L	403.425
Y	350
O	407.534
J	384.932
C	263.699
V	300
H	250
W	350
S	164.384

2. If the selling price of Country Meadow dropped below $4.47 per pound (profit $1.39 per pound or less), Ray would mix fewer pounds of it. The new optimal solution, when Country Meadow profit equals $1.39, calls for 897.5 pounds of Peaceful Pasture, 637.5 pounds of Natural Beauty, only 300 pounds of Country Meadow and 1025 pounds of Field of Color, for a total profit of $4746.69.

3. Ray would pay up to $1.17 per pound for more Virginia Bluebell seed. At that price, he would buy 361.486 pounds, increasing his profit to $5367.91, before the solution changed. At that point, Peaceful Pasture enters the basis, indicating that the optimal solution involves making only the minimum 100 pounds of that mix. The amounts of Natural Beauty and Country Meadow increase to 1391.89 pounds and 1162.16 pounds, respectively, taking advantage of the large amounts of (inexpensive) Virginia Bluebell seed, and the amount of Field of Color is reduced to 378.38 pounds.

4. Ray would make 800 pounds of Peaceful Pasture, 642.857 pounds of Natural Beauty, 500 pounds of Country Meadow and 875 pounds of Field of Color. His profit would be $4856.25.

1. One optimal solution is to match the Tuesdays and Thursdays together in the following way. The total cost of this solution is $2150.

Tuesday	Thursday
1	2
2	1
3	4
4	3
5	6
6	5
7	8
8	7

2. The horses and riders are assigned to the classes as follows:

Class	Horse	Rank	Rider	Rank
Equitation	Bigfoot Saruk	1 3	Cindy Patti	2 1
Pleasure	Shadow Thunder	1 2	Karen Fred	2 3
Halter	Toby Patches	2 3	Roxane Joe	1 3
Trail	Buddy Lady	1 2	Marcy Ellen	1 2
Low Fences	Winston Red	2 1	Dawn Linda	1 3
Intermediate Fences	Ace Shasta	3 2	Tom Steve	3 6
Total		23		28

1. The early and late start schedules for the project are
    shown in the worksheet CH12.WK1. All tasks are on the
    critical path except 2, 3, 4, 8, 10, 13, 19, and 28. The
    schedule takes 505 days to complete.

CHAPTER 13 - ANSWERS

1. Let B, W, and C be the thousands of acres of beans, wheat, and corn planted, respectively. The goal programming problem can be formulated as follows:

    Minimize: UC + UF + UE + OW

    Subject to:
    8000B + 6500W + 7000C + 100UC - 100OC = 50,000,000
    150B + 200W + 100C + UF - OF = 1,500,000
    15B + 10W + 20C + 10UE - 100OE = 300,000
    60,000B + 80,000W + 100,000C + 1000UW - 1000OW = 1,000,000,000
    B + W + C = 12,000
    All variables ≥ 0

    An optimal solution to this problem is B = 6000, W = 0, and C = 6000. In this case, OC = 400,000, UE = 9000, and UW = 40,000. All other variables equal 0. The objective function value is 9000.

    In words, this solution means that 6 million acres each of beans and corn will be planted, but no acres of wheat. The foreign capital goal is exceeded by 40 million dollars; the number of citizens fed is exactly equal to the goal of 1,500,000; the number of citizens employed is short by 90,000; and 40 million gallons of water remain unused.

2. The stores will be located in tracts 1 and 3. The store in tract 1 will serve tracts 1, 2, and 5. The store in tract 3 will serve tracts 3 and 4. The maximum delivery time is 15 minutes.

CHAPTER 14 - ANSWERS

1. See CH14.WK1. P_w = .473, L_q + .769, W_s = .309

2. See CH14.WK2. P_w = .619, L_q = 1.006, W_s = .500

3. The single line, two server (guard) option is preferable.

4. See CH14.WK3. The results are shown in the following table.

Waiting Spaces	Total Capacity	P_m
0	1	.375
1	2	.184
2	3	.099
3	4	.056
4	5	.033
5	6	.019
6	7	.011

Mr. Reber should plan to have four waiting spaces.

1. One possible flow chart for the simulation described is
    shown in the following figure. Note that the race
    completion times (that is, the times of the arrivals at the
    finish line) must all be computed first and placed on the
    event calendar. Then the event list is processed,
    beginning with the first arrival (at the finish line) and
    ending with the final departure (from the finish line).

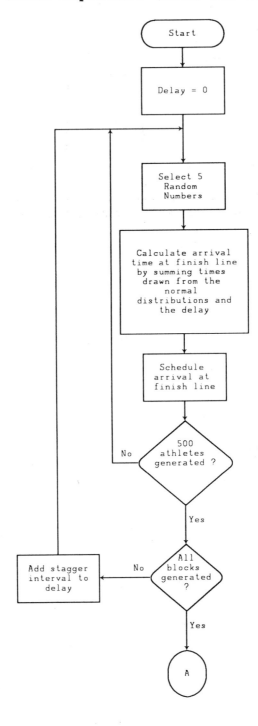

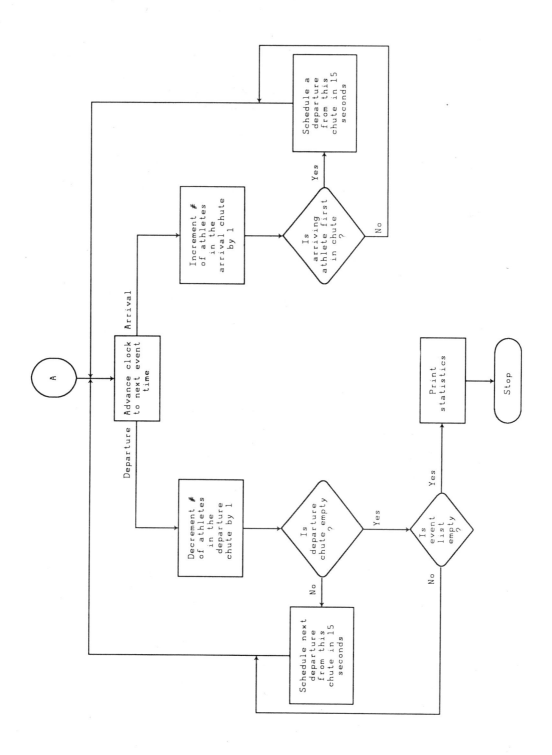

419

CHAPTER 16 - ANSWERS

1. See CH16.WK1. Long term distribution:
        F = .455
        C = .315
        U = .231

2. See CH16.WK2. In two generations, the percentage of farmers will have fallen below 50%. The percentages begin as follows:

Generation	Farmers	Craftsmen	Unskilled
0	.60	.25	.15
1	.52	.28	.20
2	.48	.30	.22
.			
.			
.			

3. a. See CH16.WK3. The long-term distribution is:
        F = .494
        C = .292
        U = .214

    b. See CH16.WK4. The long-term distribution is:
        F = .506
        C = .285
        U = .209

    c. See CH16.WK5. The long-term distribution is:
        F = .556
        C = .256
        U = .188

Scenario (c.) is the only one which meets all the stated requirements.

NOTES

NOTES